INSTRUCTION AND ASSESSMENT
FOR STRUGGLING WRITERS

CHALLENGES IN LANGUAGE AND LITERACY
Elaine R. Silliman and C. Addison Stone, *Series Editors*

Frame Work in Language and Literacy: How Theory Informs Practice
Judith Felson Duchan

Phonological Awareness: From Research to Practice
Gail T. Gillon

Handbook of Language and Literacy: Development and Disorders
*C. Addison Stone, Elaine R. Silliman,
Barbara J. Ehren, and Kenn Apel, Editors*

Language and Literacy Learning in Schools
Elaine R. Silliman and Louise C. Wilkinson, Editors

Children's Comprehension Problems in Oral and Written Language:
A Cognitive Perspective
Kate Cain and Jane Oakhill, Editors

Brain, Behavior, and Learning in Language and Reading Disorders
Maria Mody and Elaine R. Silliman, Editors

Instruction and Assessment for Struggling Writers:
Evidence-Based Practices
Gary A. Troia, Editor

Instruction and Assessment for Struggling Writers

Evidence-Based Practices

Edited by
GARY A. TROIA

THE GUILFORD PRESS
NEW YORK   LONDON

© 2009 The Guilford Press
A Division of Guilford Publications, Inc.
72 Spring Street, New York, NY 10012
www.guilford.com

Printed in the United States of America

This book is printed on acid-free paper.

Last digit is print number: 9 8 7 6 5 4 3 2 1

Library of Congress Cataloging-in-Publication Data

Instruction and assessment for struggling writers : evidence-based practices /
edited by Gary A. Troia.
     p. cm. — (Challenges in language and literacy)
   Includes bibliographical references and index.
   ISBN 978-1-59385-992-3 (hardcover : alk. paper)
   1. English language—Composition and exercises—Study and teaching.
   2. Language arts—Remedial teaching.   3. Basic writing (Remedial education)
   I. Troia, Gary A.
   LB1576.I654   2009
   808'.042071—dc22

                                                                    2008026778

About the Editor

Gary A. Troia, PhD, CCC-SLP, is Associate Professor of Special Education at Michigan State University, where he is also a Principal Investigator with the Literacy Achievement Research Center. He was a faculty member at the University of Washington in Seattle before assuming his current position at Michigan State. Prior to receiving his doctorate from the University of Maryland in 2000, he worked for 10 years in the public schools as a special educator and speech–language pathologist, and for 6 years as a university clinical supervisor. Dr. Troia is a consulting editor for several journals, including *Exceptional Children, Journal of Learning Disabilities*, and *Learning Disability Quarterly*, and is an associate editor of *Language, Speech, and Hearing Services in Schools*. He has written over two dozen research papers and book chapters and has given numerous presentations about his work in the areas of phonological processing, writing assessment and instruction, and teacher professional development in literacy.

Contributors

Robert D. Abbott, PhD, College of Education, University of Washington at Seattle, Seattle, Washington

Betty J. Benson, PhD, Disability Services, University of Minnesota at Minneapolis, Minneapolis, Minnesota

Virginia W. Berninger, PhD, College of Education, University of Washington at Seattle, Seattle, Washington

Heather M. Campbell, PhD, Department of Education, St. Olaf College, Northfield, Minnesota

Steven Cohen, MEd, Seattle Public Schools, Seattle, Washington

Carol Sue Englert, PhD, Department of Counseling, Educational Psychology, and Special Education, Michigan State University, East Lansing, Michigan

Noelia P. Garcia, PhD, College of Education, University of Washington at Seattle, Seattle, Washington

Maryl Gearhart, PhD, Graduate School of Education, University of California at Berkeley, Berkeley, California

Steve Graham, EdD, Department of Special Education, Peabody College of Education and Human Development, Vanderbilt University, Nashville, Tennessee

Anne W. Graves, PhD, Department of Special Education, San Diego State University, San Diego, California

Karen R. Harris, EdD, Department of Special Education, Peabody College of Education and Human Development, Vanderbilt University, Nashville, Tennessee

Robert M. Klassen, PhD, Department of Educational Psychology, University of Alberta, Edmonton, Alberta, Canada

Shin-ju C. Lin, MEd, College of Education, University of Washington at Seattle, Seattle, Washington

Pauline B. Low, MA, Department of Educational and Counselling Psychology, and Special Education, University of British Columbia, Vancouver, British Columbia, Canada

Charles A. MacArthur, PhD, School of Education, University of Delaware, Newark, Delaware

Troy V. Mariage, PhD, Department of Counseling, Educational Psychology, and Special Education, Michigan State University, East Lansing, Michigan

Louisa C. Moats, EdD, Sopris West Educational Services, Frederick, Colorado

Brandon W. Monroe, PhD, Department of Education, Eastern Connecticut State University, Willimantic, Connecticut

Nickola W. Nelson, PhD, Department of Speech Pathology and Audiology, Western Michigan University, Kalamazoo, Michigan

Cynthia M. Okolo, PhD, Department of Counseling, Educational Psychology, and Special Education, Michigan State University, East Lansing, Michigan

Natalie G. Olinghouse, PhD, Department of Educational Psychology, Neag School of Education, University of Connecticut, Storrs, Connecticut

Froma P. Roth, PhD, Department of Hearing and Speech Sciences, University of Maryland, College Park, Maryland

Robert Rueda, PhD, Rossier School of Education, University of Southern California, Los Angeles, California

Cheryl M. Scott, PhD, Department of Communication Disorders and Sciences, Rush University Medical Center, Chicago, Illinois

Timothy Shanahan, PhD, Department of Curriculum and Instruction, University of Illinois at Chicago, Chicago, Illinois

Linda S. Siegel, PhD, Department of Educational and Counselling Psychology, and Special Education, University of British Columbia, Vancouver, British Columbia, Canada

Gary A. Troia, PhD, Department of Counseling, Educational Psychology, and Special Education, Michigan State University, East Lansing, Michigan

Adelia M. Van Meter, PhD, College of Health and Human Services, Western Michigan University, Kalamazoo, Michigan

Christine Welton, MEd, (deceased), Department of Educational Psychology, University of Alberta, Edmonton, Alberta, Canada

Contents

Introduction   1
Gary A. Troia

PART I. THEORETICAL GROUNDING: THE NATURE OF WRITING PROBLEMS IN STRUGGLING WRITERS

CHAPTER 1   Multiple Processes That Matter in Writing   15
            Instruction and Assessment
            Virginia W. Berninger, Noelia P. Garcia,
            and Robert D. Abbott

CHAPTER 2   Self-Efficacy and Procrastination in the Writing   51
            of Students with Learning Disabilities
            Robert M. Klassen and Christine Welton

PART II. CONTEMPORARY CLASSROOM WRITING INSTRUCTION AND STRUGGLING WRITERS

CHAPTER 3   The Effects of Writing Workshop Instruction   77
            on the Performance and Motivation of Good
            and Poor Writers
            Gary A. Troia, Shin-ju C. Lin, Brandon W. Monroe,
            and Steven Cohen

CHAPTER 4   Connecting Reading and Writing Instruction   113
            for Struggling Learners
            Timothy Shanahan

CHAPTER 5   Informational Writing across the Curriculum   132
             Carol Sue Englert, Cynthia M. Okolo, and Troy V. Mariage

                   **PART III. TEACHING COMPOSING
                      TO STRUGGLING WRITERS**

CHAPTER 6   Teaching Composing to Students   165
             with Learning Disabilities: Scientifically Supported
             Recommendations
             Steve Graham, Natalie G. Olinghouse, and Karen R. Harris

CHAPTER 7   Written Composition Instruction and Intervention   187
             for Students with Language Impairment
             Nickola W. Nelson, Froma P. Roth, and Adelia M. Van Meter

CHAPTER 8   Teaching Written Expression to Culturally   213
             and Linguistically Diverse Learners
             Anne W. Graves and Robert Rueda

CHAPTER 9   Using Technology to Teach Composing   243
             to Struggling Writers
             Charles A. MacArthur

                   **PART IV. TEACHING SPELLING
                      TO STRUGGLING WRITERS**

CHAPTER 10   Teaching Spelling to Students with Language   269
             and Learning Disabilities
             Louisa C. Moats

CHAPTER 11   Spelling and English Language Learning   290
             Pauline B. Low and Linda S. Siegel

                   **PART V. ASSESSMENT OF WRITING
                      BY STRUGGLING WRITERS**

CHAPTER 12   Classroom Portfolio Assessment for Writing   311
             Maryl Gearhart

CHAPTER 13   Assessment of Student Writing   337
             with Curriculum-Based Measurement
             Betty J. Benson and Heather M. Campbell

CHAPTER 14   Language-Based Assessment of Written Expression   358
             Cheryl M. Scott

             Index   387

INSTRUCTION AND ASSESSMENT
FOR STRUGGLING WRITERS

Introduction

GARY A. TROIA

Writing is an essential part of schooling in all subject matter areas, as it gives students the opportunity to synthesize information from multiple sources and perspectives, to decide what information is relevant and important to share, and to judge how best to organize and present this information, all of which help students clarify, deepen, and expand their thoughts and feelings about a topic (Bruer, 1999; Lindemann, 1995). The importance of writing proficiency in education extends far and wide. For instance, writing competence helps determine eligibility for graduation and is pivotal in reaching decisions regarding grade retention and promotion in some states (e.g., Conley, 2005). Writing also is a significant predictor of performance on statewide *reading* assessments (e.g., Jenkins, Johnson, & Hileman, 2004) used to monitor adequate yearly progress under No Child Left Behind. According to Reeves (2000), a common characteristic of high-poverty schools in which an overwhelming majority of students pass high-stakes assessments in content-area subjects is a strong emphasis on writing. In postsecondary settings, proficient writing serves as a gateway to employment and promotion, especially in salaried positions, and is expected for matriculation into and completion of college degree programs (National Commission on Writing for America's Families, Schools, and Colleges, 2003, 2004, 2005; Smith, 2000).

Although writing competence is essential for success in and out of school, writing is and has been the most neglected of the three "Rs" (National Commission on Writing for America's Families, Schools, and Colleges, 2003). Not only has writing received short shrift in education reform efforts, but it has also received far less attention than reading from

1

researchers and sponsors of funded research (see Juzwik et al., 2006). This inadequate attention to writing has contributed to lackluster performance among America's school-age population; according to published National Assessment of Educational Progress (NAEP) data, only 28% of 4th graders, 31% of 8th graders, and 24% of 12th graders achieved at or above a proficient level (solid mastery needed to perform challenging academic tasks) in writing performance in 2002 (Persky, Daane, & Jin, 2003). Widespread limited proficiency in writing also has been noted by employers and college faculty, about three-fourths of whom rate students' writing as poor or at best only fair (Public Agenda, 2002). Consequently, businesses invest approximately $3.1 billion annually in remedial writing programs for their employees (National Commission on Writing for America's Families, Schools, and Colleges, 2004), and higher education institutions are forced to provide noncredit remedial courses in written composition (enrollment in which may increase dropout rates and time to degree completion, delay entry into the workforce, and add substantially to the cost of postsecondary education; see Adelman, 1998; Reder, 2000).

Fortunately, writing instruction and research on writing recently have taken center stage with the formation of the National Commission on Writing for America's Families, Schools, and Colleges, the release of *Writing Next: Effective Strategies to Improve Writing of Adolescents in Middle and High Schools* (Graham & Perin, 2007), and the publication of several essential volumes on writing such as *Best Practices in Writing Instruction* (Graham, MacArthur, & Fitzgerald, 2007), *Handbook of Research on Writing: History, Society, School, Individual, Text* (Bazerman, 2007), *Handbook of Writing Research* (MacArthur, Graham, & Fitzgerald, 2006), *Perspectives on Writing: Research, Theory, and Practice* (Indrisano & Squire, 2000), and, of course, this volume. This book is unique in that it places special emphasis on writing instruction and assessment for students who often find writing challenging—students with learning disabilities, language impairments, and those who are English language learners. It also is unique because there is a recurring theme in many of the sections and chapters: that writing instruction and assessment can and should attend to multiple levels of language knowledge and use—word, sentence, and discourse—and effectively integrate these to achieve maximum benefits for struggling writers. Finally, the volume is distinctive in that each author has made an effort to identify recommended practices that make use of the best available research evidence, which renders this not only an eminently practical book for K–12 educators but also an informative synthesis of research for scholars, teacher educators, and college students. It is my hope that because of these unique characteristics, this book will serve as a beneficial complement to the other excellent published manuscripts on writing.

The reader will note that, unlike many texts that address both assessment and instruction, the chapters on writing assessment are at the end rather than the beginning of this book. This was an intentional departure from the ordinary in consideration of two factors. First, in the domain of writing, instructional content and processes must take center stage and guide what is assessed. This is true in part because writing occurs within an ill-defined problem space (i.e., the final product can be shaped in so many ways and by so many factors) and in part because we simply do not have very good ways of determining how well a student is or is not writing in comparison with peers or standards (though we are making strides on this front, as one will see in the corresponding assessment chapters). Second, I wanted to set a positive tone for the book—writing assessments, especially those used for accountability purposes, are often viewed apprehensively by educators because they tend to focus on a limited set of genres (e.g., poetry is typically not assessed, but it can provide a gateway to writing enthusiasm and development when taught well) and frequently minimize authentic writing purposes and processes (e.g., state assessments may encourage students to use the writing process, but typically do not offer the time or material support for students to do so). Of course, assessment and instruction should form a symbiotic relationship—each informing and supporting the other. However, we know much more about effective writing instruction than about meaningful formative and summative writing assessment.

The first section of the book is intended to provide the reader with a broad overview of the theoretical perspectives on writing instruction that are prevalent today. Specifically, the cognitive, developmental, social, and motivational forces that influence the development of writing are presented. In the opening chapter of the book, Berninger, Garcia, and Abbott discuss paradigm shifts of the past 30 years in writing theory and practice; their review provides an excellent "bird's-eye view" of the topics featured throughout the remainder of the volume. They discuss the importance of exploiting varied genres of writing and of linking writing with reading, listening, and speaking and the relative advantages conferred by using different written output modalities (e.g., producing text through handwriting vs. through keyboarding). They explain how effective writing instruction depends on teacher knowledge, on attending to multiple levels of language, on appropriate timing, on leveraging processes that mediate response to writing instruction, and on evidence-based instructional strategies. Then the authors present their triple-word-form theory of spelling development, in which phonology, orthography, and morphology are believed to contribute in mutually facilitative but developmentally balanced ways to the acquisition of spelling skills. After identifying specific writing disabilities that may affect writing development, the authors posit that a not-so-simple view of writing may account for the interactive complexity of writing processes.

In Chapter 2, Klassen and Welton review the research on two opposed aspects of writing motivation—self-efficacy and procrastination (though the latter probably reflects behavior patterns more than internal motivational beliefs). Specifically, the authors define and compare these terms and describe how they change over time and are related to writing performance; they offer research-based suggestions about how to enhance self-efficacy and reduce procrastination in writing. They then attend to the unique motivational characteristics of students with poor writing skills, such as those with learning disabilities (LD). They note that self-efficacy beliefs among these students tend to be inflated in relation to their actual task performance—perhaps because they are unaware of their true capabilities and the demands of particular writing tasks— and that consequently these poor writers do not marshal strategic effort to approach writing activities. They report two studies that more closely examine the miscalibration of writing self-efficacy beliefs among students with LD and another study examining the procrastination behaviors (not specific to writing) of these students. In the third study, they find that students with LD report greater procrastination and that this behavior is predicted by some measures of self-efficacy. They wrap up their chapter by making instructional recommendations drawn from the research literature they review and by offering some suggestions for future investigations.

The second section of the book focuses on contemporary approaches to classroom writing instruction for all students, including those who struggle. Strong writing instruction in the general education setting serves to prevent or at least ameliorate writing problems in children at risk for or identified with disabilities. Given this, those professionals who work with struggling writers must be well versed in the characteristics of evidence-based writing instruction to effectively collaborate with classroom teachers to help them develop, implement, and sustain quality writing programs. Likewise, classroom teachers must appreciate the needs of struggling writers and understand how to adapt their instruction accordingly. Consequently, this section illuminates the characteristics and impact of contemporary writing programs, helps readers appreciate the complexity of classroom writing instruction, and identifies issues teachers face when attempting to implement evidence-based writing instruction. In Chapter 3, Troia, Lin, Monroe, and Cohen report a descriptive study in which they examined how writing workshop instruction, implemented within the context of extensive professional training and support, influenced the writing performance and motivation of good and poor elementary school writers. At the beginning and end of the school year, good and poor writers from six classrooms in one urban, high-poverty school were administered norm-referenced tests of writing skills, experimental narrative and persuasive composing tasks, and experimental writing motivation scales. Neither good nor poor writers benefited appreciably from writing workshop instruction in terms of their writing performance when entering literacy skills were held constant. However, based on writing portfolio samples collected throughout the school year and scored by students' classroom teachers, good writers demonstrated notable growth in the quality of their writing, though poor writers did not. Mastery goal pursuit, one aspect of writing motivation, improved regardless of writing competence. Their findings suggest that writing workshop instruction may not be powerful enough to help impoverished children attain substantial gains in their writing because this approach typically neglects explicit instruction in self-regulation and writing conventions.

In Chapter 4, Shanahan persuasively argues that reading instruction is vital to the development of writing competence (and vice versa) in students who do and do not struggle with writing. He first outlines how researchers have approached examining the interdependence of reading and writing, noting that policy has played an influential role in how the science has been conducted. He then provides examples of ways in which reading and writing instruction can be effectively taught in combination, though the effects of one on the other may occur for different reasons. Shanahan next explains how reading and writing, in fact, are different in a number of ways, and how their unique and shared attributes are altered through the course of development. He also gives concrete illustrations of the interplay of these factors and how teachers might take advantage of them in teaching a diverse group of students.

In Chapter 5, Englert, Okolo, and Mariage focus on informational text writing in varied content areas, which serves as a reminder that we must attend to other genres of text beyond the narrative to permit students to function in disciplinary contexts. The authors discuss the importance of text structure knowledge and point out that informational texts rarely adhere to one particular organizational scheme, which presents challenges in teaching and learning. They go on to describe the importance of graphic organizers, writing strategies, cognitive apprenticeship, and audience awareness in helping students improve their expository writing. Next, Englert and colleagues present an in-depth look at a multicomponent instructional model with all these elements to help students use writing to learn subject matter information. Finally, they describe inquiry learning activities in social studies and science classrooms that incorporate writing. Although the primary goal of inquiry activities is to increase disciplinary content knowledge, writing performance also can be enhanced.

In the third section, each chapter deals either with teaching composing to a different group of students who tend to struggle with writing or using technology to support struggling writers. The authors describe the specific needs of their target group of struggling writers (or, in the case of technology, specific difficulties that can be addressed with the technology), discuss evidence-based instructional methods, activities, and materials tailored for teaching writing to (or using technology with) that population of students, and explain the advantages and limitations of these methods, activities, and materials. In Chapter 6, Graham, Olinghouse, and Harris summarize research-validated and promising instructional practices for students with learning disabilities (LD) based on experimental, quasi-experimental, and single-case experimental design studies, as well as qualitative studies of highly effective teachers of writing. They situate their recommendations within a multi-tiered prevention and remediation framework, focusing specifically on the first (core writing instruction in general education classrooms) and second (supplementary interventions provided either in the classroom or in another setting) tiers. Recommendations for the first tier are drawn from studies in which an instructional practice helped all students improve their writing quality, whereas recommendations for the second tier were drawn from studies in which positive effects were observed specifically for students with LD and may have been associated with more discrete aspects of writing, such as composition length or text structure. The authors are careful to point out that their recommendations do not constitute a comprehensive writing program, most notably because many techniques, procedures, and materials have not been subjected to scientific inquiry and are derived primarily from informed professional judgment.

Nelson, Roth, and Van Meter help identify the similarities and differences between students with LD and those with language impairments in Chapter 7 and posit that instruction and intervention must involve (1) scaffolding at the word, sentence, and discourse levels of language, (2) collaboration between teachers, specialists, and clinicians, and (3) culturally and linguistically responsive pedagogical practices. Then the authors give examples, based on their work with struggling writers with language disorders, of how to improve these students' effective use of rhetorical structures, in particular the production of narrative and expository texts, through graphic organizers and text frames that cue genre structure. They go on to identify strategies for helping students increase their use of correct and more sophisticated morphological and syntactic patterns in their written language, such as sentence combining. Finally, the authors describe how an integrated focus on orthography and morphology can help poor writers with spoken language problems increase both their spelling proficiency and their use of a larger variety of words.

Next, in Chapter 8, Graves and Rueda discuss teaching composition to non-native English writers. They apply a sociocultural lens in their examination of the characteristics of learners, social relationships, and cultural institutions that affect teaching and learning in culturally and linguistically diverse contexts. Following this, the authors identify and describe writing intervention approaches that address intrapersonal needs, such as cognitive strategy instruction and process writing instruction, and illustrate how to adapt these for English learners to address their differences in background knowledge and motivation. Then they discuss procedures aimed at facilitating positive interpersonal interactions, such as flexible grouping practices, building a sense of autonomy and peer affiliation, and using dialogue. Finally, they highlight ways in which the institutions of families, schools, and communities can be leveraged to help promote better writing outcomes and even serve as buffers against negative influences on students' attainment of those outcomes.

Computer technology for assisting struggling writers is discussed by MacArthur in Chapter 9. Because the research in this area has not reached maturity, he draws on studies with typical learners and presents promising practices with little empirical validation. MacArthur gives a comprehensive summary of the research evidence associated with (1) word processing; (2) tools for compensating for transcription difficulties, such as speech recognition, speech synthesis, and word prediction; and (3) tools for aiding planning and revising activities, such as procedural prompting, interactive graphic organizers, and automated scoring. He also discusses how computers and the Internet offer novel ways and opportunities for children and youths to compose texts. The author reminds us that computer technology alone is insufficient to ensure writing success—high-quality instruction into which technology is carefully and thoughtfully woven (and in which the use of technology is explicitly modeled and practiced) is essential because the technology itself may not be particularly beneficial for all students under all circumstances.

Spelling is addressed in the fourth section of the book and is separate from composing instruction because (1) it often is one of the most vexing aspects of writing for students and (2) many teachers have difficulty teaching it in an explicit, systematic, and comprehensive manner. In response, the authors identify the specific spelling problems of students who struggle with writing and provide information regarding evidence-based instructional practices for improving their spelling skills. In Chapter 10, Moats opens with a description of reasons why students with language and learning disabilities may struggle with spelling, noting that accomplished spelling requires the coordination and integration of multiple levels of language with motor skills, attention, and self-regulation. She attends closely to how instructional content maps onto these aspects of spelling performance and provides many concrete suggestions for using multisensory teaching techniques and instructional adaptations to assist struggling spellers. Moats directly counters the commonly held notion that English spelling is inconsistent and somewhat arbitrary by explaining how the historical origins of words are embedded in the English orthography and that this information serves as an opportunity to help students examine multiple levels of language.

In Chapter 11, Low and Siegel review evidence associated with two competing views of literacy learning and transfer in English language learners—the linguistic-interdependence hypothesis and the script-dependent hypothesis. They then test which view appears to best explain the spelling performance of native English (a deep alphabetic orthography), Persian (a shallow alphabetic orthography), and Chinese (a nonalphabetic orthography) speakers in the third grade attempting to spell real and nonsense words in English. They report that students who speak Chinese as their first language are equally proficient as the others at spelling real words but produce less phonetically plausible spellings for pseudowords. Low and Siegel suggest that Chinese speakers may transfer their skills in visual analysis, acquired during the acquisition of Chinese literacy, to support their spelling performance on real words but that the script differences between Chinese and English make reliance on visual word form less efficient when spelling orthographically novel words. Thus both the linguistic-interdependence and script-dependent hypotheses appear to be valid.

The fifth and last section of the book deals with writing assessment issues, which are myriad and complicated. Simply put, the research in this area is quite limited, and one is left with many more questions than answers, in part as a result of the multifaceted nature of writing. Nevertheless, the authors of the chapters in this section do justice to the vast landscape of writing assessment. In Chapter 12, Gearhart gives a historical and conceptual overview of the varied uses of writing portfolios and describes different models of portfolio assessment and how they can be used with students with special needs and English language learners. She notes that portfolios can be used as a tool for assessment of learning or as a mechanism to promote learning; either way, portfolios can serve as means of reviewing, reflecting, and evaluating the processes and products of writing instruction over time. Gearhart points out that, although there are compelling arguments for using portfolios to inform instruction and to assist students in their acquisition of a critical stance toward their writing, to date no experimental or quasi-experimental studies have provided evidence of the relative value of portfolios as a component of effective writing instruction, as a reliable and valid indicator of writing performance, or as an assessment method that discriminates accomplished writers and less capable writers. As Gearhart explains, establishing the relevance and utility of portfolios is particularly challenging not only because portfolios may be constructed in a variety of ways using a range of evaluative criteria but also because it is often difficult to determine whether the contents of portfolios represent independent and representative samples of students' actual writing performance. She posits that portfolios may be best conceptualized as a supplement to other forms of assessment in order to triangulate data sources.

Benson and Campbell, in Chapter 13, describe various types of curriculum-based measures (CBM) for written products and summarize the research associated with them. CBM differs from other forms of written language measurement in that it uses brief and easily administered writing probes to collect general outcome data that mark growth in writing and that support informed instructional decision making through ongoing progress monitoring. Generally, their review of the extant research suggests that more complex measures of writing samples collected through CBM are required to yield reliable and valid findings, especially when examining writing samples from older students. Such measures include correct spelling sequences and correct word sequences, in which adjacent letters or words are judged as acceptable combinations, and correct-minus-incorrect word sequences. All of these measures demonstrate sufficient sensitivity to growth over the span of a school year and longer periods of time. Benson and Campbell note that, under some circumstances, the kind of writing prompt used to elicit a writing sample may be important to consider. They report that little is known about the utility of writing CBM for progress monitoring on a more frequent basis that could help educators adapt their pedagogical practices, which is at the heart of the CBM assessment paradigm.

In Chapter 14, the closing chapter of the book, Scott describes and critiques linguistic measures of written text at the lexical, sentential, and discourse levels. To help illustrate her points, she uses representative expository writing samples from a group of preadolescent and adolescent students, some of whom have language and learning disabilities. She notes that lexical measures such as corrected type–token ratio do not appear to be sufficiently sensitive to developmental changes across a wide age range or to ability differences between students with and without learning and language disorders. Likewise, measures of clausal density and morphosyntactic error rate seem to be inadequate for marking developmental changes and distinguishing between typical and atypical learners, whereas the specific characteristics of written subordinate clauses may help to accomplish these functions. For discourse-level measures, text length appears to be an adequate, albeit blunt, measure. Scott reminds us that, for some measures, performance differences are associated with different writing genres. Scott notes finally that very little work has been devoted to examining the nature of the relationships between measures or to exploring the responsiveness of these measures to the effects of instruction and intervention.

REFERENCES

Adelman, C. (1998). The kiss of death? An alternative view of college remediation. *National CrossTalk*, 6(3), 11. San Jose, CA: National Center for Public Policy and Higher Education. Retrieved February 1, 2008, from *www.highereducation.org/crosstalk/ct0798/voices0798-adelman.shtml*.

Bazerman, C. (2007). *Handbook of research on writing: History, society, school, individual, text*. Philadelphia: Erlbaum.

Bruer, J. (1999). *Schools for thought*. Boston: MIT Press.

Conley, M. W. (2005). *Connecting standards and assessment through literacy*. Boston: Pearson.

Graham, S., MacArthur, C. A., & Fitzgerald, J. (Eds.). (2007). *Best practices in writing instruction*. New York: Guilford Press.

Graham, S., & Perin, D. (2007). *Writing next: Effective strategies to improve writing of adolescents in middle and high schools—A report to Carnegie Corporation of New York*. Washington, DC: Alliance for Excellent Education.

Indrisano, R., & Squire, J. R. (Eds.). (2000). *Perspectives on writing: Research, theory, and practice*. Newark, DE: International Reading Association.

Jenkins, J. R., Johnson, E., & Hileman, J. (2004). When is reading also writing: Sources of individual differences on the new reading performance assessments. *Scientific Studies of Reading*, 8, 125–151.

Juzwik, M. M., Curcic, S., Wolbers, K., Moxley, K. D., Dimling, L. M., & Shankland, R. K. (2006). Writing into the 21st century: An overview of research on writing, 1999 to 2004. *Written Communication*, 23, 451–476.

Lindemann, E. (1995). *A rhetoric for writing teachers*. Oxford, UK: Oxford University Press.

MacArthur, C. A., Graham, S., & Fitzgerald, J. (Eds.). (2006). *Handbook of writing research*. New York: Guilford Press.

National Commission on Writing for America's Families, Schools, and Colleges. (2003, April). *The neglected R: The need for a writing revolution*. New York: College Entrance Examination Board. Retrieved February 1, 2008, from *www.writingcommission.org/prod_downloads/writingcom/neglectedr.pdf*.

National Commission on Writing for America's Families, Schools, and Colleges. (2004, September). *Writing: A ticket to work ... or a ticket out. A survey of business leaders*. New York: College Entrance Examination Board. Retrieved

February 1, 2008, from *www.writingcommission.org/prod_downloads/writingcom/writing-ticket-to-work.pdf*.

National Commission on Writing for America's Families, Schools, and Colleges. (2005, July). *Writing: A powerful message from state government*. New York: College Entrance Examination Board. Retrieved February 1, 2008, from *www.writingcommission.org/prod_downloads/writingcom/powerful-message-from-state.pdf*.

Persky, H. R., Daane, M. C., & Jin, Y. (2003). *The nation's report card: Writing 2002*. Washington, DC: U.S. Department of Education, Institute of Education Sciences, National Center for Education Statistics.

Public Agenda. (2002, March). *Reality check 2002: Finding five*. Retrieved June 5, 2008, from *www.publicagenda.org/specials/rcheck2002/reality1.htm*.

Reder, S. (2000). Adult literacy and postsecondary education students: Overlapping populations and learning trajectories. In J. P. Comings, B. Garner, & C. Smith (Eds.), *The annual review of adult learning and literacy* (Vol. 1, pp. 111–157). San Francisco: Jossey-Bass.

Reeves, D. (2000). *Accountability in action*. Denver, CO: Advanced Learning Press.

Smith, M. C. (2000). What will be the demands of literacy in the workplace in the next millennium? *Reading Research Quarterly, 35*, 378–379.

Part I

THEORETICAL GROUNDING

*The Nature of Writing Problems
in Struggling Writers*

CHAPTER 1

Multiple Processes That Matter in Writing Instruction and Assessment

VIRGINIA W. BERNINGER
NOELIA P. GARCIA
ROBERT D. ABBOTT

This chapter begins with an overview of the paradigm shifts at the end of the 20th century in writing instruction and assessment—from product to process to process plus product. We also discuss emerging themes that may influence writing paradigms during the 21st century. In the following section we contrast self-directed and other-directed writing and explain how each separately and jointly may contribute to different kinds of writing. We also emphasize the importance of linking writing with other language systems—reading, listening, and speaking. We discuss writing via word processor and the web and writing for daily living and work. Following a brief overview of writing development, we discuss Klein's (1999) distinction between learning to write and writing to learn. Because writing develops with instruction, we next consider how effective writing instruction depends on teacher knowledge of levels of language, on timing issues in instruction, on processes that mediate response to writing instruction, and on evidence-based instructional strategies. Following this discussion of instructional issues, we propose an evidence-based resolution to the debated issue of whether phonology, orthography, and morphology (1) contribute differentially to spelling development in distinct sequential stages or (2) contribute in mutually cooperative, developmentally sensitive ways throughout spelling development. Then we describe and differentiate three specific writing disabilities that may affect writing development. Because the writing processes in math learning have been neglected, new data on the comorbidity of written calculation and writing problems are reported. To integrate across sections, we end by comparing a simple model and a not-so-simple model of the writing process. Like the simple view of reading, a simple model may capture the most essential features of writing. However, a not-so-simple model may better account for multiple processes in writing, especially as it develops toward greater levels of proficiency.

WRITING: BOTH PROCESS AND PRODUCT

Paradigm Shifts at the End of the 20th Century

Writing instruction and assessment focused on the written product for generations of students prior to the 1980s. Teachers designed writing assignments and graded students' written products. Writing was conceptualized as a three-part sequential process, beginning with prewriting activities, followed by writing activities, then followed by editing before handing in the final product. Rarely did students revise those submitted products. Following Emig's (1971) groundbreaking study of the composing processes of 12th graders, Hayes and Flower (1980) further stimulated a paradigm shift in how writing was conceptualized and taught. They asked college students to think aloud while they composed and studied the think-aloud protocols. They discovered that planning, translating ideas into writing, and revising were processes that interacted recursively throughout the composing process rather than stages of writing that phased in sequentially. This model represents skilled writing as a nonlinear problem-solving process.

Shortly before Hayes and Flowers formulated their model of the cognitive processes in writing, Britton (1978) had elaborated perspectives on the social purpose of writing and the communication acts it performs. This perspective provided a needed correction for the previous overemphasis on the academic purposes of writing. Likewise, at a time when the prevailing view was that writing belonged in middle school, high school, and college classrooms (see Hillocks, 1984, 1986), Graves (1983) argued that writing instruction and writing activities also belong in the elementary grades, a time at which children have a natural desire to communicate in writing, as well as in speech. No longer should educators believe that they first teach reading in the elementary school years and then writing in the middle and high school grades. Moreover, Clay

(1982) pointed out that reading and writing instruction should be integrated in the elementary classroom.

Together, the insights of Emig (1971), Hayes and Flower (1980), Britton (1978), Graves (1983), and Clay (1982) led to innovation in educational practices in writing. Building on the concept of writing as a process, educators likened early and developing writers to professional writers who produce many writing products throughout the process, from first draft to revised drafts to final product. Building on the social communication purpose of writing, educators began to emphasize the authentic nature of writing in which writing is shared with others and is not a solitary activity. Rather, writing is produced for others who read the writing and provide feedback (e.g., when a student sits in the "author's chair" during a writers' workshop lesson), and sometimes writing is published for a wider audience (e.g., in a class anthology at the end of the school year). In addition, writing was not conceptualized as a separate activity from reading (Clay, 1982). Instead, children wrote about stories and other texts they first read with their teachers, peers, and family, read their written work to these significant others to receive informative feedback (Gere & Abbott, 1985), and reread their papers as they revised them for content and form.

However, this paradigm shift to the recognition that writing is both process and product did not generate a unified paradigm for writing instruction. One approach to writing instruction emphasizes engaging children in authentic, meaningful composing activities using the writing process (e.g., Applebee, 2000; Calkins, 1986; Clay, 1982), for example, through a writers' workshop. The other approach to writing instruction teaches the cognitive processes of writing explicitly through teachers' modeling, explanation, feedback, and other forms of scaffolding to support students' appropriation of writing strategies (e.g., Alley & Deshler, 1979; De La Paz & Graham, 1997; De La Paz, Swanson, & Graham, 1998; Englert, Raphael, Anderson, Anthony, & Stevens, 1991; Graham, MacArthur, & Schwartz, 1995; Harris & Graham, 1996; MacArthur, Schwartz, & Graham, 1991; Troia & Graham, 2002; Troia, Graham, & Harris, 1999; Wong, Butler, Ficzere, & Kuperis, 1996, 1997). A recent meta-analysis of research on writing instruction for grades 4 and above showed that the second approach—explicit strategy instruction in the writing process—was overall more effective than merely engaging students in the writing process during writers' workshop (Graham & Perrin, 2007). A review of effective writing instruction in grades 1–3 for at-risk writers points to the same conclusion: Explicit writing instruction grounded in the cognitive processes of writing is effective in preventing severe writing problems in at-risk beginning writers (Berninger, 2008a).

However, this explicit, process-oriented writing instruction can be implemented within a writers' workshop framework that encourages the social nature of writing (Berninger et al., 2007; Wong, Wong, Darlington, & Jones, 1991; Wong, Butler, Ficzere, Kuperis, & Corden, 1994; Wong et al., 1996, 1997). The influential Hayes and Flowers process writing model, which has been revised for both skilled adult writers (e.g., Hayes, 1996, 2000) and school-age writers (e.g., Berninger & Swanson, 1994; Berninger & Winn, 2006), generated a wealth of research on the cognitive processes of writing and moved writing research into mainstream cognitive psychology (e.g., Alamargot & Chanquoy, 2001; Butterfield, 1994; Hayes, Flower, Schriver, Stratman, & Carey, 1987; McCutchen, 1986; Scardamalia & Bereiter, 1989).

Paradigm Shifts in the 21st Century

A recent volume of writing research (MacArthur, Graham, & Fitzgerald, 2006) illustrates the diversity of approaches to writing instruction and assessment in the first decade of the 21st century. Only time will tell which paradigms will be most influential and will survive at the end of this new century. The growing body of research on writing (e.g., MacArthur et al., 2006) and syntheses of this research (e.g., Graham & Perrin, 2007) should help to overcome the *reading-centric view of literacy* that still dominates educational policy at the federal level and, to a large extent, educational practices at the state and local levels in the United States. Additionally, high-stakes tests that assess writing proficiency and require students to write explanations of how they arrive at answers in math and other domains (e.g., Jenkins, Johnson, & Hileman, 2004) should lead to greater understanding that *both* writing and reading contribute to literacy development and academic content knowledge.

Writing is not the mirror image of reading (Read, 1981); one cannot assume that a good reader is necessarily a good writer or that teaching reading alone will transfer to adequate writing proficiency. On the contrary, evidence suggests that there is reciprocity in the developmental trajectories of reading and writing competence and that writing instruction can help foster the acquisition of reading skills and vice versa (Berninger, Rutberg, et al., 2006). Moreover, the current wave of writing research emphasizes writing–reading connections (e.g., Altemeier, Jones, Abbott, & Berninger, 2006; Calfee & Patrick, 1995; Fitzgerald & Shanahan, 2000; MacArthur et al., 2006) and even their connections to listening and speaking (e.g., Berninger, Abbott, Jones, et al., 2006). The ability to integrate reading and writing is necessary to complete many academic written assignments beginning in the primary grades (e.g., Altemeier et al., 2006) and to meet graduation requirements for high school and college.

A current trend in assessment of writing achievement is the exclusive use of direct assessments of writing at one point in time in response to relatively neutral prompts. For example, most states have adopted high-stakes tests that include assessments of writing proficiency, administered in the second half of the school year, that involve one writing session in which there is little opportunity to apply the writing process in an authentic manner. The assessment results are usually not available to students' current teachers so that they can alter their writing instruction if necessary. Likewise, the National Assessment of Educational Progress (NAEP) assesses writing in a single session at one point in time (e.g., Greenwald, Persky, Campbell, & Mazzeo, 2006). Nevertheless, these one-session assessments of writing do provide valuable information about the relative level of writing achievement in reference to age or grade peers (norm-referenced assessment) or to criteria for writing performance (criterion-referenced assessment).

Fortunately, supplementary forms of writing assessment are also being considered that provide a *process approach* to assessing writing achievement. These include portfolio assessment (e.g., Valencia, 1998) and growth curve analyses (e.g., Berninger et al., 1997; Berninger et al., 1998). Given that writing is a process that benefits from multiple drafts and revisions, assessment of writing should be repeated across the academic year to evaluate change or growth in specific aspects of writing. The advantage of repeated assessment during a grade, whether teacher-, district-, or state-designed, is that teachers can use the assessment results to modify instruction if students are not making adequate progress in specific aspects of writing. Even good writers can benefit from this kind of feedback, and students in general like seeing visible evidence of their progress in writing. Thus there are advantages to combining traditional "one-shot" assessments of writing achievement with a process approach to writing assessment that takes into account students' ability to improve their writing across multiple drafts and time points in the school year.

An emerging trend extends research on writing development downward from the early school-age years to the preschool years. Earlier work on the emergence of invented spelling (Chomsky, 1979; Treiman, 1993) has given way to investigation of how very young children learn the conventions of writing letters and spelling words (e.g., Molfese, Beswick, Molnar, & Jacobi-Vessels, 2006), beginning with their names (e.g., Treiman & Broderick, 1998) and moving to the fast mapping of spoken and written words from one or a few exposures to establish phonological and orthographic representations in long-term memory (e.g., Apel, Wolter, & Masterson, 2006). Also, interest in the role of conventional spelling in vocabulary development (Wilkinson, Bahr, Silliman, & Berninger, 2007) has reemerged and is consistent with Ehri's (1978) amalgamation theory, according to which specific words are represented in long-term memory in such a way that their spelling, meaning, and pronunciation are inter-related.

Another cultural transformation—the widespread use of computers for word processing and web-based communication—will undoubtedly influence future writing research. Technology has spawned research on the use of computer keyboards as alternatives to handwriting (e.g., Mac-Arthur & Graham, 1987). Development of the mouse as an alternative to the keyboard has resulted in children as young as 2 years of age inter-acting with written language in a computer environment (Berninger & Winn, 2006). This trend has stimulated research on early emergence of keyboarding ability and its relationship to writing by hand (e.g., see the longitudinal study by Berninger, Abbott, Jones, et al., 2006, in which automaticity, fluency, and transcription speed are assessed for both key-boarding and handwriting).

The sociocultural perspective on writing (e.g., Englert, 1992; Wong et al., 1994), which to date has influenced much of the research and educational practice for process writing, is likely to continue to exert a strong influence. This line of research is likely to be supplemented with a renewed interest, fueled by high-stakes testing, in the role of writing in learning specific academic subjects. Writing requirements vary across the domain-specific-content subjects in the curriculum (Applebee, 1981). Each content area has its own unique vocabulary, domain-specific knowledge, and conceptual frameworks for integrating and writing about that knowledge. For example, writing to explain possible solu-tions to a math problem, writing to summarize the steps and findings of a science experiment, and writing to compare and contrast natives and immigrants in a specific culture require different constellations of writing skills.

Likewise, writing represents thinking and may facilitate thinking. A new line of research approaches writing as a window for conscious access to the unconscious thinking processes of the writer. This perspec-tive was given impetus by the work of Hayes and Flower (1980), who claimed that, in the process of writing one's thoughts on paper, one often discovers what one is thinking. These thoughts may remain in the vast unconscious internal mind unless they emerge in the conscious mind dur-ing the discipline of transforming one's thoughts into external written language. By making thought visible, *writing externalizes cognition* and allows writers access to thought processes that might otherwise remain inaccessible (Berninger & Winn, 2006). Just as oral language is both egocentric and sociocentric (e.g., Vygotksy, 1978), writing too may be directed either toward the self to regulate thinking processes or toward others to perform communicative acts. Self-directed writing may play an important role in learning to learn and thus in the learning of domain-specific-content subjects of the school curriculum. For example, writing notes during class lectures, writing notes while reading content-area source documents, writing content-specific reports, and writing answers to subject-area exam questions may lead to learning content-area vocabulary, information, and organizing schemata, as well as improving overall writing competence.

THE MOSAIC OF DIFFERENT KINDS OF WRITING PROCESSES

Self- and Other-Directed Writing

Egocentric and sociocentric writing contribute in unique ways to different writing genres. For instance, although storytelling is typically directed to others and journal writing is typically directed to oneself, this generalization may sometimes need qualification (Graesser & Clark, 1985). Following are some considerations of how both purposes for writing may be achieved across varied genres.

Storytelling and the Narrative Genre

The narrative is a vehicle for communicating personal, fictional, or semifictional historical events to others. Typically, children are exposed to written stories during the preschool years, when adults at home and/or school read storybooks to them and they view the written text as the adult reads aloud. From this other-oriented discourse that links spoken and written words, young children learn the schema of the narrative—a speaker or writer telling a story with characters, setting, and plot (a causally related series of events, actions, and outcomes). Thus the first genre young writers typically use is the narrative, and personal narrative (e.g., memoir), the most prevalent form in the primary grades, is typically other-directed. However, some teachers give writing assignments that treat narrative as a genre for exercising the imagination—creating what does not exist. Students are given permission to set reality aside and create imaginary worlds, characters, scenarios, and so forth. This kind of creative writing is self-directed in that it draws on one's ability to imagine and create, but it is other-directed in that it has the potential to entertain or enlighten an audience. This particular kind of narrative genre often is not related to the types of writing that are rewarded during the school years, but for those who perfect it, it may lead to vocational success (e.g., as scriptwriters for the entertainment industry or authors of novels for the general public).

Journal Writing

One of the consequences for educational practice of extending writing activities to the early elementary grades was the introduction of journal writing in many classrooms. Beginning in first grade or even kindergarten, young writers are encouraged to write in a personal journal, which may be their first experience in using writing to express their own ideas. Journal writing is typically self-directed writing that expresses one's own ideas without the goal of adapting the writing to the needs or desires of others. Despite the freedom of not having to write for an audience, some young writers do not write much in their journals, for various reasons. The notion that writing, rather than talking, is a way to express ideas may be novel to them. Or they may have never been encouraged to have their own ideas, let alone to express them in a private way. Or they may lack the transcription skills necessary for using written words to communicate their inner thoughts. Journal writing can also be used for other purposes that are not as personal. For example, during our Sequoyah Writing–Readers Workshop, participants wrote summaries in their journals of chapters they had read in a book to develop reading comprehension skills. Subsequently, they added to the summaries in their journals their critique or personal perspective—what they liked and what they did not like about what they read. Finally, they were taught a strategy for writing a book report based on the summaries and critiques in their journals, which had an additional requirement of taking a position as to whether or not they recommended the book to others and then using journal entries to substantiate the recommendation.

Poetry

Unlike other writing genres, poetry is not constrained by the syntax of language or conventions of writing for an audience. It is uniquely designed for self-expression of not only thoughts but also emotions. Moreover, it is a channel for expressing nonverbal thinking that references perceptual imagery. Although poetry may communicate with others and typically is shared with others, self-expression alone is a legitimate goal of writing poetry.

Expository Writing

Not all other-directed writing is based on the story grammar of oral discourse. Young writers are also likely to be exposed to books that are written to inform, and later in their literacy development they are likely to be exposed to other-directed writing that has as its goal persuasion to adopt a particular opinion or point of view (see Wong, 1997, for further discussion of the distinction between informational and persuasive expository writing). Although students may take longer to master expository writing genres than the genre of narrative, even young children can learn expository writing if teachers model and teach explicit strategies for generating such texts (e.g., Englert, Raphael, Fear, & Anderson, 1988; Englert, Stewart, & Hiebart, 1988). Although primary grade students may write longer narrative than expository texts, they can write both beginning in the first grade (Berninger et al., 1992). Most important, although expository writing is other-directed in its final version, the process the writer goes through in generating and revising drafts also serves as self-directed writing to refine thinking about a topic. Again, individuals who perfect this kind of writing may earn their living during adulthood as writers—journalists, technical writers in science or industry, or authors of textbooks. Those who become experts at reviewing, editing, and revising may work as copy editors for the publishing industry.

Integrating Writing with Other Language Systems

Writing cannot be defined solely on the basis of the genre of the product, as discussed in the previous section. Writing may also be defined on the basis of the integration of writing with other language processes, such as reading, listening, and/or speaking. Language is not a unitary construct; separate but interacting functional systems develop for language by ear (listening), language by mouth (talking), language by eye (reading), and language by hand (writing; Berninger, Abbott, Jones, et al., 2006).

Integrating Reading and Writing

Many of the activities in formal schooling require students to read source materials and to take written notes, which are subsequently transformed into a written report. The student must first read text generated by others and then must express in writing the main ideas and supporting details in this text that are relevant to the topic of the assigned report. These notes do not have to reflect the full discourse structure of well-honed prose but do need to be sufficiently precise to create such text at a later time. The reading of source material is other-directed in that the writer must extract the intended message of the writer of the source material. The writing of notes is self-directed in that the writer must link the source material with the knowledge in his or her own mind to create the notes and eventually the written report. That report will probably have to be revised several times so that the final product is other-directed; that is, it is easily understood by a reader.

Integrating Listening and Writing

Writing plays an important role in learning to learn from lectures in formal schooling. Lecture learning requires integration of listening comprehension and note taking. In a line of programmatic research on lecture note taking by Peverly and colleagues (Peverly, 2006; Peverly, Brobst, Graham, & Shaw, 2003; Peverly, Ramaswamy, Brown, Sumowski, Alidoost, & Garner, 2007), they showed that automaticity in letter writing contributes uniquely to note taking, which in turn contributes to grades that evaluate quality of knowledge expressed on written tests. Thus a form of writing for oneself that records a teacher's oral language may play a role in learning academic content material. At a later time, when the student studies for a test, the lecture notes may be integrated with other written notes from reading assignments and with prior topic knowledge. This integration of knowledge from multiple sources will influence the ability of the student to answer in writing questions posed by the teacher on a test. Once again, the writer ultimately integrates writing directed to the self with writing directed to others. Presumably, executive functions play a role in this kind of integration, but further research is required.

Executive Functions

Integrating oral (listening and speaking in oral discussions) and written (reading and writing) language activities in learning from text in content-area curricula has been shown to be effective in developing the writing skills of students with dyslexia (e.g., Berninger, Abbott, Abbott, Graham, & Richards, 2002). Such integration of writing with another language system draws on the executive functions of the brain (Altemeier et al., 2006). In fact, growth in executive functions (inhibition, rapid automatic switching, and inhibition/switching) across the primary grades is related to all literacy outcomes at fourth grade, but these low-level executive functions explain more variance in word-level reading and writing processes than in text-level reading comprehension and written composition (Altemeier, 2006; Altemeier, Abbott, & Berninger, 2008), which may be better explained by high-level executive functions such as planning (Altemeier et al., 2006). More research is needed on the role of executive functions in text processing and integrating across language systems (e.g., reading and writing or listening and writing).

Technology-Supported Writing

In the 21st century, most writers are bilingual in two output modes for language by hand—handwriting by pen or pencil and keyboarding.

Handwriting draws on the unique process of letter production, whereas keyboarding draws on the process of letter recognition, selection, and keystroking. Both common and unique neuropsychological processes (e.g., orthographic, phonological, and executive functions such as inhibition and inhibition/switching) contribute to these two writing modes in elementary school students, but executive functions contributed uniquely to manuscript writing in the third grade and to cursive writing in the fifth grade, though not to keyboarding (see Berninger, Abbott, Jones, et al., 2006), which may not place as great a demand on executive functions.

Word Processing

Computerized word processing tools—systems with external keyboards for input and monitors for output—have become widespread tools that support integrated writing and reading in generating and editing written text and graphics. Considerable research has studied the effectiveness of word processors for a variety of purposes, including teaching writing and planning, generating, reviewing, and revising writing (see Bridwell, Nancarrow, & Ross, 1983; MacArthur, 2006). Meta-analyses yield mixed results, but in general word processing had moderate beneficial effects on planning, revising, and the length and quality of texts; however, the effect sizes are greater for struggling than for average writers and for combining word processing with instruction in using it (MacArthur, 2006).

Web Authoring

Web authoring is a relatively recent kind of writing. Anecdotal observations suggest that web-based writing, when compared with conventional text writing, may be briefer, produced more quickly, less likely to be self-monitored for edits, and more likely to be forwarded in e-mail without the prior context for which it was a response; it may also have a higher ratio of interspersed visual displays (photographs and graphics). On the other hand, the increased use of visual displays along with linguistic text is likely to have beneficial effects on cognitive processes, as well as some kinds of writing processes (MacArthur, 2006). Although chat rooms foster a sharing of ideas, a body of replicated, converging research evidence is lacking on whether chat rooms lead to better quality writing than do (1) sharing of conventional texts, (2) face-to-face oral discussion, or (3) a combination of conventional and web-based communication. Also, as more citizens obtain their news of world events from websites or television comedy shows such as *The Daily Show* or *The Colbert Report* than from newspapers, evidence is needed on whether newspapers or web-based formats are more effective in keeping citizens informed in a global society. Further research is needed on all these issues.

Writing for Daily Living

Writing is often conceptualized only in reference to the formal require-ments of schooling. However, writing serves many useful pragmatic func-tions in daily living. These range from making lists and preparing forms to writing business or personal letters or brief e-mails. Insufficient research attention has been directed to whether formal schooling is adequately preparing students for these self- and other-oriented writing functions that are important to the management of daily living.

Little is known about whether and how the kinds of writing taught at school transfer to the ways in which writing is used in many occupations. For example, Whitaker (1994) (as cited in Berninger, Fuller, & Whitaker, 1996) studied the way in which trainees in a school psychology program, all of whom were skilled writers for academic purposes, learned a new genre of writing that was specific to the profession of psychology for which they were preparing—namely, the psychological report. She used the same think-aloud technique that Hayes and Flower (1980) had used and discovered how difficult it was for many skilled adult writers to learn a new genre of writing that drew on disciplinary knowledge but needed to be tailored to the child, family, and school at hand—multiple authentic audiences. Even when graduate students appeared to be mastering the new genre based on the products, the think-alouds revealed how hard they had to work to master it and in some cases the emotional toil of doing so. In an era in which schools are expected to be accountable in preparing students for the workplace, more research attention should be given to the development of occupation-specific writing skills, including those occupations that do not require a college education. Little research exists on the specific kinds of writing that members of specific occupa-tions engage in or that is required for success in specific vocations. Like-wise, little is known about how schools could better prepare students for the kinds of writing required for success on the job. It is possible that the kinds of writing assessed in high-stakes tests (e.g., writing a persuasive essay) may not be the kinds of writing required in many employment settings.

PROCESSES OF WRITING
DEVELOPMENT AND INSTRUCTION

Writing development begins when infants first learn that they can leave an external trace on the world with a writing implement and continues through the preschool years (Molfese et al., 2006), the early school years (Berninger, Abbott, Jones, et al., 2006), and middle childhood, adolescence, and adulthood (Berninger & Richards, 2002). However, what is developing is not only writing skills (e.g., see Berninger, Abbott, Jones, et al., 2006: for handwriting, Figure 5; for spelling, Figure 6; and for composing, Figure 7) but also the ability to use writing to learn academic content subjects (Klein, 1999; Newell, 2006). Analogous to Chall's (1979) distinction between first learning to read and later reading to learn, writing development may also proceed from an initial learning-to-write stage in the early grades to a subsequent writing-to-learn stage in the upper grades (Klein, 1999; Newell, 2006).

However, children who easily learn the transcription, executive function, and text generation skills of basic writing, as depicted in Figure 1.1, may use writing as a supportive tool for learning content knowledge beginning in the early grades. Children who struggle with learning the core skills in the simple view of writing (Figure 1.1) may not engage in writing and may avoid writing altogether, making it more difficult to master writing skills and to learn to use writing to learn either in the early grades or beyond. More research is needed on developmental trajectories and individual differences in learning to write and in using writing to learn.

Teacher knowledge (McCutchen & Berninger, 1999; Mather, Bos, & Babur, 2001) and teacher attitudes (Schuessler, Gere, & Abbott, 1981; Gere, Schuessler, & Abbott, 1983) also influence effective writing instruction; merely purchasing a set of instructional materials for teaching writing or a published curriculum of writing is woefully insuf-

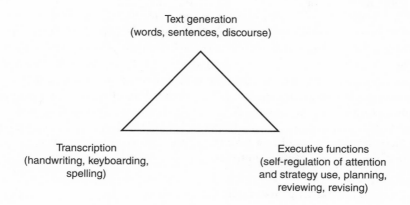

FIGURE 1.1. Simple view of a functional writing system. From Berninger and Amtmann (2003; based on Berninger, Vaughn, et al., 2002). Copyright 2003 by The Guilford Press. Reprinted by permission.

ficient for supporting, nurturing, and explicitly teaching young writers. Especially critical is teachers' knowledge of (1) levels of language; (2) organization of instructional time within lessons, days, and weeks; (3) processes in the learner's mind that may mediate response to instruction; and (4) evidence-based instructional strategies for preventing severe writing problems and treating persisting ones.

Levels of Language

Language can be analyzed and produced at different units of analysis, or grain size, ranging from subword to word to sentence to text or discourse levels. At different times in the history of writing instruction, one unit of analysis or set of units was emphasized at the expense of others. For example, historically in the elementary grades the quality of subword penmanship and the accuracy of word spellings in isolation (e.g., as in spelling bees) were overemphasized, but self-directed and other-directed composing were underemphasized. At another time, in the junior and senior high school grades, writing at the sentence level was overemphasized, and students were taught how to diagram sentences and asked to remember the rules of grammar usage but were not taught discourse schemas for generating expository or persuasive texts. At present, the emphasis in many classrooms is on engagement in meaningful writing at the discourse level rather than on systematic, explicit instruction in handwriting, spelling, or sentence-level syntax and grammar. A review of instructional research with at-risk writers in grades 1–4 indicates that, across studies, balanced instructional programs with explicit instruction at the subword, word, sentence, and text levels were more effective than control treatments (Berninger, in press). The need for balanced writing instruction should be emphasized in preservice and inservice professional development for teachers. Truly whole language draws on all the levels of language. Many of the controversies in education could be avoided if teachers had better knowledge of all the levels of language and the importance of directing instruction to all of them in teaching writing, as well as reading. Abbott and Berninger (1993) showed that handwriting, spelling, and composition are separable skills, all of which contribute to writing. Children may have relative strengths or weaknesses in one or more of these skills that should be taken into account in instructional planning, teaching, and progress monitoring.

Organizing Writing Instruction in Time

Within the Lesson

Much of the debate over which instructional components are necessary or most important has focused on instructional components in isolation, without consideration of how the components are organized within a lesson. Randomized, controlled instructional studies on writing validate an approach to organizing these components by teaching all levels of language close in time (Berninger, in press). One explanation for the effectiveness of this approach is that it helps children orchestrate the various processes in the functional writing system in time and thus overcome inefficiencies in working memory (see Figure 1.2).

Across the Day

Another consideration in planning the instructional program in writing is how writing instruction is organized across the day (Wong & Berninger, 2004). For instance, students who are pulled out of the general education program during part of the day for supplementary or special education

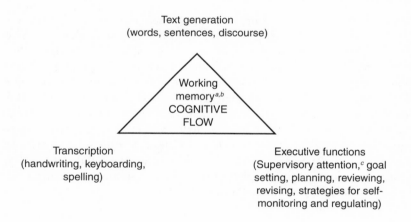

Text generation
(words, sentences, discourse)

Working
memory[a,b]
COGNITIVE
FLOW

Transcription
(handwriting, keyboarding,
spelling)

Executive functions
(Supervisory attention,[c] goal
setting, planning, reviewing,
revising, strategies for self-
monitoring and regulating)

FIGURE 1.2. Not-so-simple view of a functional writing system. [a]Activates long-term memory during planning, composing, reviewing, and revising and short-term memory during reviewing and revising output. [b]Components include (1) orthographic, phonological, and morphological storage units for verbal information; (2) a phonological loop for learning spoken words, pronouncing written words, and maintaining verbal information actively in working memory; (3) an orthographic loop for learning to spell words; and (4) executive supports that link verbal working memory with the general executive system (a distributed network of many executive functions) and with nonverbal working memory (which stores information in a visual–spatial sketchpad). [c]A complex system that regulates focused attention–selecting what is relevant and inhibiting what is not relevant, switching attention between mental sets, attention maintenance (staying on task), conscious attention (metalinguistic and metacognitive awareness), cognitive presence, and cognitive engagement. From Berninger and Winn (2006). Copyright 2006 by The Guilford Press. Reprinted by permission.

services benefit from coordination of writing instruction and assessment between the general education classroom and the pullout program. For example, if the supplemental instruction focuses on skills and the general education program focuses on authentic writing, children with special needs may not transfer skills to authentic writing without instruction explicitly designed to teach for this kind of transfer. Likewise, children may not transfer writing skills across the content subjects of the curriculum without explicit instruction and scaffolding related to disciplinary writing. For example, creative writing in language arts does not necessarily transfer to writing social studies reports, keeping a science lab journal for experiments, or writing explanations of how math problems are solved, all of which are written assignments often made by teachers in the upper grades.

Long-Term Assignments across Weeks

Many students have difficulty organizing their time for long-term writing assignments in which a week or several weeks may elapse between the assignment and the due date. All students, and particularly those who struggle with writing, may benefit from *explicit strategy instruction in time management related to written work completion* (Wong & Berninger, 2004). Because of their own limited educational experiences, many parents do not know how to supervise written homework assignments. Or, because of their work schedules, they may not have time to supervise writing assignments at home. One way some schools are dealing with these issues is to create supervised homework clubs after school to assist students with completion of written assignments during supervised after-school programs. Future research might address the effectiveness of these homework clubs.

Processes That Mediate Response to Writing Instruction

Some researchers and practitioners believe that only observable behaviors, and not the internal processes that produce the behaviors, can be assessed or studied. This persisting belief is often related to a behavioral orientation and an unwillingness to embrace the paradigm shifts to cognitive psychology and cognitive neuroscience in mainstream psychology. When the behavior at hand is literacy, such individuals often quote an earlier research literature on aptitude–treatment interactions as evidence that processes are invalid. However, those earlier studies are irrelevant. For example, earlier studies were based on processes such as visual perception that have not been shown to be uniquely related to writing or reading instead of processes such as phonology and orthography that have been shown to be uniquely related to both writing and reading (Berninger, Yates, & Lester, 1991; Berninger et al., 1992; Berninger, Cartwright, Yates, Swanson, & Abbott, 1994). Also, experimental designs often naively tested for single aptitude–single treatment interactions. In reality, both aptitudes and treatments are multidimensional. Research has shown that many component processes contribute to writing and that effective writing instruction teaches all the relevant component processes. If a student has a deficit or weakness in a particular process, that student may need supplementary instruction to develop that process, but effective writing instruction should still be directed to all the necessary instructional components for a functional writing system.

Motor Processes

The brain regulates two fine motor systems—one that outputs through the mouth and one that outputs through the hand—and two gross motor systems—one that outputs through the arms and one that outputs through the legs. Three graphomotor processes underlie output by hand: execution, control, and planning. If the brain structures underlying graphomotor execution are impaired by injury, disease, or neurogenetic disorder, the individual will not be able to write by hand and will require alternative modes of written communication, such as specially adapted keyboards. In some cases severely motorically impaired individuals can still develop written communication (Berninger, 1986). Graphomotor control processes can be developed through specialized training involving activities to strengthen muscles and regulate muscle use, such as tracing forms, drawing internal lines without touching boundary lines in outlined forms, connecting dots, and imitating sequenced strokes (Berninger, Rutberg, et al., 2006). Time required for graphomotor planning of successive finger movements uniquely predicts letter form production (Berninger et al., 1992). Other graphomotor planning processes influence letter alignment in space on paper (if using pen or pencil) or on a monitor (if using a mouse), spacing of letters within and between words, and letter sizing (absolute height and consistency; see Graham, Struck, Richardson, & Berninger, 2006).

Lexical and Sublexical Processes

Learning to spell written words is a process of learning how the letters of the alphabet represent the speech sounds in spoken words (Venezky, 1970, 1999). The genetic basis of spelling problems in developmental dyslexia involves impairment in the phonological processing of speech sounds in spoken words (Wijsman et al., 2000). Learning to spell involves creating precise phonological representations in memory of the words to be spelled and then translating that spoken word into a specific written word that has a precise spelling that corresponds to a specific meaning, typically signaled by context.

A process that contributes to the formation of word-specific written spelling is receptive orthographic coding of written words into short-term memory and processing of all the letters in specific word positions in working memory. A cross-sectional study (Berninger et al., 1991) showed that receptive coding undergoes considerable growth from first to third grade, when it levels off; and a longitudinal study (Garcia, 2006; Garcia, Abbott, & Berninger, 2008) replicated this finding. Expressive coding (i.e., integration of stored orthographic representations with output through the hand), in contrast, shows continued growth during the intermediate grades (Garcia, 2006; Garcia et al., 2008). Teaching children a strategy for learning written words was effective in improving orthographic coding and related spelling skill in at-risk second graders (Berninger & Traweek, 1991). First, children were prompted to look carefully at all the letters from left to right in a written word, which was then covered. Next, they were asked to image the written word in their mind's eye and recall orally and/or in writing (1) all the letters in the word; (2) designated single letters—for example, the first, last, or third letter; and (3) designated letter groups—for example, the first two, the last two, or the third and fourth. These designated letter positions can be selected to draw their attention to and memory for silent letters or letters with alternative spellings for the same sound.

Finally, morphology, the structure of the meaning-related word parts, including bases, roots, and affixes, influences spelling throughout the elementary grades (e.g., Carlisle, 1994; Nagy, Berninger, Abbott, Vaughan, & Vermeulen, 2003; Nagy, Berninger, & Abbott, 2006). English spelling is morphophonemic (Venezky, 1970, 1999), and morphological spelling rules for adding suffixes to bases and other affixed suffixes are needed to spell many multisyllabic, morphologically complex words (e.g., Dixon & Englemann, 2001).

Syntactic Processes

Accumulating words in English sentence units are organized by a complex syntactic coding system that includes, but is not restricted to, word order, word endings, structure or function words (prepositions, conjunctions, articles, pronouns), subject–predicate relationships (including subject–verb agreement), and identifying words as parts of speech with specific functions in sentence units. While spelling during composing, writers must attend to morphological constructions that fit particular syntactic contexts.

Attention, Executive Function, and Working Memory Processes

Processing of written words is influenced by factors such as attention and goal setting (Thomson et al., 2005). Attention affects processing of written words not only at the input stage of reading but also at the output stage of writing. For instance, pretreatment attention training has been shown to facilitate response to composition instruction (Chenault, Thomson, Abbott, & Berninger, 2006). Moreover, many aspects of the writing process are under the control of executive functions, including handwriting (Berninger, Nielsen, Abbott, Wijsman, & Raskind, 2008), spelling (Hooper, Swartz, de Kruif, & Montgomery, 2002), and text generation (Graham & Harris, 2005). Individual differences in working memory influence writing development and writing function (McCutchen, 1996; Swanson & Berninger, 1996): the phonological loop plays an important role in vocabulary acquisition and reading (Gathercole & Baddeley, 1993), whereas the orthographic loop (connection between written words in long-term or working memory and motor processes) plays an important role in writing (Berninger, Rutberg, et al., 2006). Likewise, automatic letter naming (Amtmann, Abbott, & Berninger, 2008a) and automatic letter writing influence writing development, in terms of both spelling and composing (Berninger et al., 1991; Berninger et al., 1992; Berninger, Cartwright, et al., 1994).

Automatic and Controlled Processing and Fluency

Both automatic and controlled processing (Schneider & Shiffrin, 1977) contribute to learning, processing, and producing written language. Controlled processing includes explicit application of strategies. Some strategies are *procedural*—explicit plans for performing an act, such as numbered arrow cues for letter formation (e.g., Berninger et al., 1997). Other strategies involve use of *declarative knowledge* cues (e.g., Graham & Harris, 2005), such as prompts for the genre elements of a narrative. Further research is needed on the relative effectiveness of different kinds of procedural and declarative knowledge cues in developing specific writing skills. Time or rate is often assumed to be an index of automaticity, though other dimensions also may affect automatic processing (Berninger, Abbott, Billingsley, & Nagy, 2001). Additionally, controlled, strategic processing may vary in the speed in which it is executed—it may be slow during initial learning but become faster with practice, though not necessarily fully automatic, that is, functioning completely outside conscious awareness. Much remains to be learned about the role of time in both automatic and controlled processing of written language. At the present time, automatic and fluent processing of written language may be overemphasized to the exclusion of nonautomatic, thought-driven, flexible processes that contribute to writing (and reading), such as reflection and metacognition (Berninger & Nagy, 2008).

Cognitive Flow and Linking Language with Cognition

Kellogg (1994) introduced the construct of cognitive flow in the writing process (see Figure 1.2). This nonlanguage process is often likened to a river with a moving current that is not constrained by language conventions. When flow is obstructed, the writer is said to have a writer's block. Flow may also be likened to free fall in outer space, which is unconstrained by gravity. Flow may reflect thinking unconstrained by consciousness, which has limited space and time resources in the human mind. Flow may be the source of idea generation, imagination (envisioning what does not yet exist), and creativity (e.g., seeing new relationships among existing concepts and knowledge in long-term memory). For further discussion of flow and writing, see Berninger and Winn (2006).

Differentiated Instruction

Although our knowledge of evidence-based instructional strategies for writing is growing (for review, see Berninger, 2008a), we know less about how writing instruction might be adapted for students with deficits in the specific kinds of processes just discussed. Teachers often request assistance in *differentiated writing instruction* within their classroom to meet the needs of individual students. Future research might be designed to study how individual differences in writing-related processes that mediate response to instruction might be accommodated within a writing program for the whole class.

RECONCILING STAGES OF SPELLING DEVELOPMENT WITH TRIPLE-WORD-FORM THEORY

Although spelling is often regarded as a mechanical skill, it is, to the contrary, a complex linguistic process without which writers could not generate written language. A debate continues regarding whether spelling development is best characterized by a set of sequential stages proceeding from phonology to orthography to morphology (e.g., Templeton & Bear, 1992) or by triple-word-form theory, according to which all three language processes contribute throughout spelling development. Recent findings in our longitudinal study of typical writing development are consistent with triple-word-form theory. For example, one of us (NPG)'s dissertation research showed that good, average, and poor spellers differ significantly in mean level of phonological, orthographic, and morphological skill from first through seventh grade (Garcia, 2007). Subsequent growth curve analyses demonstrated maximal growth in these spelling-related processes in the early elementary grades (phonology and orthography from grades 1–3 and morphology from grades 1–4, with some aspects of morphology continuing to grow beyond grade 4).

Table 1.1 offers a model that might reconcile the two views about spelling development. In the first column the three word-level language processes are listed in their developmental order according to stage theory. The second column reports our instructional research findings that illustrate what children are learning about the interrelationships among the three word forms at each of these stages. The nature of cross-word-form mapping (how phonology, orthography, and morphology become interrelated) may change across spelling development, but not in a way that can be described as purely phonological in the beginning, then purely orthographic, and then purely morphological. During the phonological stage, children learn flexible mappings at different units or grain size across word forms; this mapping requires conscious attention and effort. During the orthographic stage, children create an autonomous orthographic lexicon in which specific written words can be accessed directly without conscious attention and effort; the word-specific representations are based on the cross-word-form maps created earlier in spelling development. During the morphological stage, morphological awareness continues to be refined as children increasingly encounter longer, more complex words in school texts and learn the morphological spelling rules about dropping or adding letters at the end of base words when suffixes are added, all of which require coordination among phonology, morphology, and orthography. However, development is better characterized by cascading progression with overlaps, ebbs, and flows and discontinuities rather than discrete stages.

As summarized in the second column of Table 1.1, during the first stage, children learn multiple, flexible mappings of the three word forms and their parts at different units or grain size. At-risk second graders and third graders (Berninger, Rutberg, et al., 2006) and students with dyslexia in grades 4–6 (Berninger et al., 2003) benefited from mapping sounds and spellings and reflecting about morphological word forms and their parts. At-risk second-grade spellers benefited from mapping onset–rime and whole lexical units (which resulted in best transfer of taught spellings across word contexts) and mapping phonemes and graphemes (which resulted in best spelling during independent compos-

TABLE 1.1. Relationship between Three Stages of Spelling Development and Interrelationships of Phonological, Orthographic, and Morphological Word Forms

Stages	Interrelating phonological, orthographic, and morphological word forms
Phonological	Encoding spoken words into written words at different unit or grain size (Berninger et al., 1998; Berninger et al., 2000; Berninger et al., 2001): 1. Mapping phonemes onto letters (single letters or letter clusters in one- and two-syllable Anglo-Saxon words). 2. Mapping onset–rime units in spoken words onto onset–rime units in written words. 3. Mapping pronunciation of whole word (segmental and suprasegmental intonation contours) onto the complete spelling of a word. 4. Mapping phonemes onto spelling units that correspond to morphological units, such as verb tense markers (e.g., -*ing* as in *singing* and -*ed* as in *painted*, *jumped*, *hugged*) and plural markers (i.e., -*s* or -*es* as in *cats*, *dogs*, *buses*).
Orthographic	Creating an autonomous orthographic lexicon in long-term memory (Richards et al., 2005; Richards, Aylward, Berninger, et al., 2006; Richards, Aylward, Raskind, et al., 2006): 1. Memory contains all the letters in the spelling of a specific word and links to the pronunciation and morphological structure for that word's spelling. 2. Memory can be accessed automatically without going through the encoding process of the phonological stage.
Morphological	Learning and applying the morphophonemic spelling rules and transformation processes of English (Carlisle, 1994; Dixon & Englemann, 2001; Henry, 2003): 1. Spelling morphologically complex words, especially of Latin and Greek word origin (e.g., *nationality*, in which *al* is added to *nation* and *it* is inserted when adding *y* to *national*). 2. Mastering the transformation process whereby morphologically complex words are derived or generated from morphologically simple words or morphologically complex words are analyzed into their constituent parts.

ing tasks; Berninger et al., 1998). At-risk third-grade spellers benefited from classifying syllable types based on vowel and consonant patterns and high-frequency morphemes (Berninger et al., 2000). During the next stage (see Table 1.1), children create the word-specific autonomous orthographic lexicon. Following instruction in orthographic strategies that facilitate word-specific learning, the brain normalized during an fMRI task that requires access to the autonomous orthographic lexicon (Richards et al., 2005; Richards, Aylward, Berninger, et al., 2006). During the next stage (see Table 1.1), children continue to refine their morphological knowledge. Older students in grades 7–9 were more likely than those in grades 4–6 to respond to morphological instruction (Berninger et al., 2007).

DEVELOPMENTAL DISORDERS IN WRITING PROCESSES

Dysgraphia

Some students have unusual difficulty despite otherwise normal development in learning to (1) write letters legibly and automatically and/or (2) spell but not read. Whether handwriting only or handwriting and spelling are affected, these individuals, who have dysgraphia, struggle with learning to write compositions (e.g., Berninger, 2004). Their writing problems may be related to an impaired *orthographic loop* in working memory that integrates internal orthographic representations, such as letter forms and written words, with output through the hand (e.g., Berninger, 2007; Berninger, Rutberg, et al., 2006).

Dyslexia

Core deficits in developmental dyslexia include the phonological processes in each working memory component: (1) *phonological*, orthographic, and morphological storage of word forms for processing, (2) the *phonological* loop, and (3) executive functions such as inhibition, switching mental set, and verbal fluency for *phonology* and related processes (Berninger, Abbott, Thomson, et al., 2006). Dyslexia is both a reading and a writing disorder (Berninger et al., 2008) and represents impaired word-level processing that affects both reading and written spelling. In addition, some, but not all, students with dyslexia also have dysgraphia that affects their handwriting.

Oral and Written Language Learning Disability

Children with delays in learning oral language during the preschool years often have persistent problems with oral language and literacy during the school-age years (Botting, 2007). Children with these long-term oral language problems are sometimes said to have specific language impairment (SLI) or language learning disability (LLD), but we prefer a diagnostic label that draws attention to both the oral and written language learning disabilities—OWL LD—so that both are addressed in educational programming and teaching. The spelling errors of students with language-based LD reflect individual differences in processing phonological, orthographic, and morphological information in written words (Silliman, Bahr, & Peters, 2006). Students with language-based LD tend to use simpler and qualitatively different sentence syntax in their writing (Scott, 2002). Additionally, executive functions tend to be impaired in students with language-based reading and writing disorders (Singer & Bashir, 1999).

Differentiating Dysgraphia, Dyslexia, and OWL LD

Although impaired working memory is found in individuals with any of the three specific disorders affecting written language, the nature of the word form storage impairment within working memory may affect how the problems manifest (Berninger, 2008b). Children with only orthographic deficits tend to have dysgraphia, whereas those with orthographic and phonological deficits tend to have dyslexia and those with orthographic, phonological, and morphological problems tend to have OWL LD (Berninger, 2007, 2008b). Children with all three tend to have spelling problems that need to be assessed and treated, probably because orthographic, phonological, and/or morphological word-level processes are impaired and interfere with learning to spell words.

Written Math Calculation and Written Language Comorbidities

Although writing is usually taught and studied in relationship to language learning, writing also plays a major role in learning math. Children write numerals and solutions to calculation problems. A preliminary analysis of children in a phenotyping study during the first 4 years of a family genetics study (recruitment and inclusion criteria described in Berninger, Abbott, Thomson, & Raskind, 2001) showed that rapid automatic naming (RAN) of letters or numerals, which was slow in children with disabilities compared with their grade-level peers, was significantly faster in those who had only a reading disability than in those who had both a reading disability and a math disability (Busse, Thomson, Abbott, & Berninger, 1999). Children who had only phonological deficits exhibited problems just with reading, but those who also had a double deficit in RAN and phonological skills had more generalized learning disabilities that affected literacy and numeracy (Busse et al., 1999).

In this chapter we report a follow-up study, based on the first 5 years of the same study just mentioned. We identified children called probands, who qualified their families for participation. Some probands had only a written language disability ($n53$ probands) but other probands had both a written language disability and a math disability (n41 probands, 38 of whom met criteria for calculation disability and 3 of whom met criteria for math problem-solving disability). The same criteria were used for math disability as for written language disability (i.e., scores on norm-referenced measures were below the population mean and at least one standard deviation below prorated Verbal IQ). The written language disability only (WLang) and the comorbid written language and math disability (WLang + Math) groups did not differ in Verbal IQ (M110 for both groups), but there was a reliable difference in age (months), which was therefore used as a covariate in analyses of covariance (ANCOVA) that yielded the following findings.

The two groups differed significantly on all measures involving oral reading (recognition accuracy and rate of words and pseudowords presented in lists or in text), copying, and composition (writing quality and fluency) and on both math measures—written calculation and applied problems. On all measures the comorbid WLang + Math disabled group scored lower. Their writing problems were generalized across written language and written math calculation.

The research question at hand was which processes might account for the more severe and generalized impairments of the WLang + Math group compared with the WLang only group, despite their comparable Verbal IQs. These groups differed significantly on orthographic coding (letter clusters in written words), $F(1, 88) = 8.10, p. = 006$; RAN for letters, $F(1, 91) = 7.66, p = .007$; RAN for numerals, $F(1, 91) = 4.08, p = .046$; and rapid automatic switching (RAS) for letters and numerals, $F(1, 89) = 10.02, p = .002$, which were consistently lower in the WLang + Math group. The two groups did not differ in any measure of phonological processing (memory on a pseudoword repetition task or phonological awareness on sound deletion tasks), visual perception, or ratings for four attention/hyperactivity factors (Thomson et al., 2005).

The processes that differentiated those who were impaired in both written language and math and those who were impaired only in written language were: (1) the ability to code orthographic units in working memory; (2) RAN (which may assess the phonological loop of working memory; see Amtmann, Abbott, & Berninger, 2008b); and (3) RAS, which measures an executive function for switching between mental sets (Berninger, Abbott, Thomson, et al., 2006). Thus students who have writing problems should also be assessed for the writing aspects of math, orthographic coding, and RAN. Also, RAN may point to a more generalized problem in automatizing alphanumeric symbols that affects writing and math, as well as reading achievement. Moreover, most math curricula have a writing component that needs to be investigated, assessed, and treated, if impaired, with specialized instruction.

SIMPLE VERSUS NOT-SO-SIMPLE VIEWS OF WRITING

Figure 1.1 depicts the simple view of writing, which captures the essential skills in learning and teaching beginning writing. Transcription (lower left corner) contributes to translation, that is, text generation (top of triangle; Berninger et al., 1992), on which children show intraindividual variation in three levels of language—word, sentence, and text (Berninger, Mizokawa, Bragg, Cartwright, & Yates, 1994). Planning (goal setting), reviewing (self-monitoring), and revising (self-correcting) processes in the Hayes and Flower (1980) model are executive functions (lower right corner) that self-regulate writing. Supervisory attention in working memory is also an executive function that helps to self-regulate writing (Swanson & Berninger, 1996). In sum, the simple view of writing, with transcription and executive functioning driving text generation at the word, sentence, and text levels, accounts well for the development of writing in beginners. Moreover, training transcription skills during this period prevents severe writing problems (Berninger & Amtmann, 2003).

However, as the writing requirements of the curriculum become more complex, the simple view of writing may not be adequate to account for the multiple processes of writing. Working memory at the level of storing and processing multiword constructions, especially sentences, becomes increasingly important in writing (Berninger, Cartwright, et al., 1994; Berninger & Swanson, 1994), and executive functions required for managing the writing and writing–reading processes increase beyond higher level planning, reviewing, and revising to include lower level executive functions such as inhibition and switching attention (Altemeier, 2006; Altemeier et al., 2006; Altemeier et al., 2008). Cognitive flow (Kellogg, 1994) that links mind with language may also be evolving in the way it influences the writing process. In sum, as writing, which is complex and draws on multiple processes, develops, a not-so-simple view of writing may better account for the writing process (see Figure 1.2, especially the notes that explain the details of how this model differs from the simple model of writing in Figure 1.1).

CONCLUSIONS

As with good writing, conceptual models of the nature and purposes of writing, its normal development, and effective ways to teach it have been revised over the past three decades. Increasingly, both educators and scholars are grasping that writing is a multifaceted, complex process that takes on many forms and functions. Attempts to define the various kinds of writing may result in oversimplifications. Although a growing body of research has increased knowledge of how specific writing skills and related processes develop, less is known about how writing is used as a tool for learning. More research has focused on writing instruction than on the role of teacher knowledge in implementing evidence-based instructional strategies in writing. Spelling has received less research attention than word reading and decoding, but it plays a crucial role in learning to compose both by pen or pencil and keyboard (Berninger, Abbott, Jones, et al., 2006) and is impaired in many students with specific learning disabilities affecting written language. More research is needed to resolve the issue of whether one or more word-level (lexical and sublexical) language processes drive the spelling acquisition process in key stages of writing development. Also, more research is needed on the comorbidity of writing and written math problems. In all, a simple model of writing, consisting of transcription, text generation, and high-level executive functions for planning and reviewing and revising, accounts well for beginning writing (Figure 1.1), but a not-so-simple model may better capture the complexities and multiple processes of developing skilled writing (Figure 1.2).

ACKNOWLEDGMENTS

Preparation of this chapter was supported by Grant Nos. HD25858 and P5033812 from the National Institute of Child Health and Human Development.

REFERENCES

Abbott, R., & Berninger, V. (1993). Structural equation modeling of relationships among developmental skills and writing skills in primary and intermediate grade writers. *Journal of Educational Psychology, 85*, 478–508.

Alamargot, D., & Chanquoy, L. (2001). *Through the models of writing*. Dordrecht, Netherlands: Kluwer Academic.

Alley, G., & Deshler, D. (1979). *Teaching the learning-disabled adolescent: Strategies and methods*. Denver, CO: Love.

Altemeier, L. (2006, November). *The contribution of executive functions to reading and writing outcomes in typically developing readers and writers and in children and adults with dyslexia*. Unpublished doctoral dissertation, University of Washington, Seattle.

Altemeier, L., Abbott, R., & Berninger, V. (2008). Contribution of executive functions to reading and writing in typical literacy development and dyslexia. *Journal of Experimental and Clinical Neuropsychology, 30*, 588–606.

Altemeier, L., Jones, J., Abbott, R., & Berninger, V. (2006). Executive factors in becoming writing-readers and reading-writers: Note-taking and report writing in third and fifth graders. *Developmental Neuropsychology, 29,* 161–173.

Amtmann, D., Abbott, R., & Berninger, V. (2007). Mixture growth models for RAN and RAS row by row: Insight into the reading system at work over time. *Reading and Writing: An Interdisciplinary Journal, 20,* 785–813.

Amtmann, D., Abbott, R., & Berninger, V. (2008). Identifying and predicting classes of response to explicit, phonological spelling instruction during independent composing. *Journal of Learning Disabilities, 41,* 218–234.

Apel, K., Wolter, J., & Masterson, J. (2006). Effects of phonotactic and orthotactic probabilities during fast mapping on 5-year-olds' learning to spell. *Developmental Neuropsychology, 29,* 21–42.

Applebee, A. N. (1981). *Writing in the secondary school: English and the content areas.* Urbana, IL: National Council of Teachers of English.

Applebee, A. N. (2000). Alternate models of writing development. In R. Indrisano & J. R. Squire (Eds.), *Perspectives on writing* (pp. 90–111). Newark, DE: International Reading Association.

Berninger, V. (1986). Comparison of two microcomputer-assisted methods of teaching word decoding and encoding to non-vocal, non-writing, and learning disabled students. *Programmed Learning and Educational Technology, 23,* 124–129.

Berninger, V. (2004). Understanding the graphia in dysgraphia. In D. Dewey & D. Tupper (Eds.), *Developmental motor disorders: A neuropsychological perspective* (pp. 328–350). New York: Guilford Press.

Berninger, V. (2007). *PAL II User Guide.* San Antonio, TX: Psychological Corporation.

Berninger, V. (2008a). Evidence-based written language instruction during early and middle childhood. In R. Morris & N. Mather (Eds.), *Evidence-based interventions for students with learning and behavioral challenges* (pp. 215–235). Mahwah, NJ: Erlbaum.

Berninger, V. (2008b). Defining and differentiating dyslexia, dysgraphia, and language learning disability within a working memory model. In M. Mody & E. R. Silliman (Eds.), *Brain, behavior, and learning in language and reading disorders.* New York: Guilford Press.

Berninger, V., Abbott, R., Abbott, S., Graham, S., & Richards, T. (2002). Writing and reading: Connections between language by hand and language by eye. *Journal of Learning Disabilities, 35,* 39–56.

Berninger, V., Abbott, R., Billingsley, F., & Nagy, W. (2001). Processes underlying timing and fluency of reading: Efficiency, automaticity, coordination, and morphological awareness. In M. Wolf (Ed.), *Dyslexia, fluency, and the brain* (pp. 383–414). Baltimore: York Press.

Berninger, V., Abbott, R., Jones, J., Wolf, B., Gould, L., Anderson-Youngstrom, M., et al. (2006). Early development of language by hand: Composing-, reading-, listening-, and speaking-connections, three letter writing modes, and fast mapping in spelling. *Developmental Neuropsychology, 29,* 61–92.

Berninger, V., Abbott, R., Thomson, J., & Raskind, W. (2001). Language pheno-type for reading and writing disability: A family approach. *Scientific Studies in Reading, 5,* 59–105.

Berninger, V., Abbott, R., Thomson, J., Wagner, R., Swanson, H. L., Wijsman, E., et al. (2006). Modeling developmental phonological core deficits within a working-memory architecture in children and adults with developmental dyslexia. *Scientific Studies in Reading, 10,* 165–198.

Berninger, V., & Amtmann, D. (2003). Preventing written expression disabilities through early and continuing assessment and intervention for handwriting and/or spelling problems: Research into practice. In H. L. Swanson, K. R. Harris, & S. Graham (Eds.), *Handbook of research on learning disabilities* (pp. 345–363). New York: Guilford Press.

Berninger, V., Cartwright, A., Yates, C., Swanson, H. L., & Abbott, R. (1994). Developmental skills related to writing and reading acquisition in the inter-mediate grades: Shared and unique variance. *Reading and Writing: An Interdisciplinary Journal, 6,* 161–196.

Berninger, V., Fuller, F., & Whitaker, D. (1996). A process approach to writing development across the life span. *Educational Psychology Review, 8,* 193–218.

Berninger, V., Mizokawa, D., Bragg, R., Cartwright, A., & Yates, C. (1994). Intraindividual differences in levels of written language. *Reading and Writing Quarterly, 10,* 259–275.

Berninger, V., & Nagy, W. (2008). Flexibility in word reading: Multiple levels of representations, complex mappings, partial similarities, and cross-modality connections. In K. Cartwright (Ed.), *Flexibility in literacy processes and instructional practice: Implications of developing representational ability for literacy teaching and learning.* New York: Guilford Press.

Berninger, V., Nagy, W., Carlisle, J., Thomson, J., Hoffer, D., Abbott, S., et al. (2003). Effective treatment for dyslexics in grades 4 to 6. In B. Foorman (Ed.), *Preventing and remediating reading difficulties: Bringing science to scale* (pp. 382–417). Timonium, MD: York Press.

Berninger, V., Nielsen, K., Abbott, R., Wijsman, E., & Raskind, W. (2008). Writing problems in developmental dyslexia: Under-recognized and under-treated. *Journal of School Psychology, 46,* 1–21.

Berninger, V., & Richards, T. (2002). *Brain literacy for educators and psycholo-gists.* New York: Academic Press.

Berninger, V., Rutberg, J., Abbott, R., Garcia, N., Anderson-Youngstrom, M., Brooks, A., et al. (2006). Tier 1 and Tier 2 early intervention for handwrit-ing and composing. *Journal of School Psychology, 44,* 3–30.

Berninger, V., & Swanson, H. L. (1994). Modifying Hayes and Flower's model of skilled writing to explain beginning and developing writing. In E. Butterfield (Ed.), *Children's writing: Toward a process theory of development of skilled writing* (pp. 57–81). Greenwich, CT: JAI Press.

Berninger, V., & Traweek, D. (1991). Effects of two-phase reading intervention on three orthographic–phonological code connections. *Learning and Indi-vidual Differences, 3,* 323–338.

Berninger, V., Vaughan, K., Abbott, R., Abbott, S., Brooks, A., Rogan, L., et al. (1997). Treatment of handwriting fluency problems in beginning writing: Transfer from handwriting to composition. *Journal of Educational Psychology, 89,* 652–666.

Berninger, V., Vaughan, K., Abbott, R., Begay, K., Byrd, K., Curtin, G., et al. (2002). Teaching spelling and composition alone and together: Implications for the simple view of writing. *Journal of Educational Psychology, 94,* 291–304.

Berninger, V., Vaughan, K., Abbott, R., Brooks, A., Abbott, S., Reed, E., et al. (1998). Early intervention for spelling problems: Teaching spelling units of varying size within a multiple connections framework. *Journal of Educational Psychology, 90,* 587–605.

Berninger, V., Vaughan, K., Abbott, R., Brooks, A., Begay, K., Curtin, G., et al. (2000). Language-based spelling instruction: Teaching children to make multiple connections between spoken and written words. *Learning Disability Quarterly, 23,* 117–135.

Berninger, V., & Winn, W. (2006). Implications of advancements in brain research and technology for writing development, writing instruction, and educational evolution. In C. MacArthur, S. Graham, & J. Fitzgerald (Eds.), *Handbook of writing research* (pp. 96–114). New York: Guilford Press.

Berninger, V., Winn, W., Stock, P., Abbott, R., Eschen, K., Lin, C., et al. (2008). Tier 3 specialized writing instruction for students with dyslexia. *Reading and Writing: An Interdisciplinary Journal, 21,* 95–129.

Berninger, V., Yates, C., Cartwright, A., Rutberg, J., Remy, E., & Abbott, R. (1992). Lower-level developmental skills in beginning writing. *Reading and Writing: An Interdisciplinary Journal, 4,* 257–280.

Berninger, V., Yates, C., & Lester, K. (1991). Multiple orthographic codes in acquisition of reading and writing skills. *Reading and Writing: An Interdisciplinary Journal, 3,* 115–149.

Botting, N. (2007). Comprehension difficulties in children with specific language impairment and pragmatic language impairment. In K. Cain & J. Oakhill (Eds.), *Children's comprehension problems in oral and written language: A cognitive perspective* (pp. 81–103). New York: Guilford Press.

Bridwell, L. S., Nancarrow, P. R., & Ross, D. (1983). The writing process and the writing machine: Current research on word processors relevant to the teaching of composition. In R. Beach & L. S. Bridwell (Eds.), *New directions in composition research* (pp. 381–398). New York: Guilford Press.

Britton, J. (1978). The composing processes and the functions of writing. In C. Cooper & D. Odell (Eds.), *Research on composing: Points of departure* (pp. 13–28). Urbana, IL: National Council of Teachers of English.

Busse, J., Thomson, J., Abbott, R., & Berninger, V. (1999, August). *Cognitive processes related to dual disability in reading and calculation.* Paper presented at the annual meeting of the American Psychological Association, Boston.

Butterfield, E. (Ed.). (1994). *Children's writing: Toward a process theory of development of skilled writing* (pp. 57–81). Greenwich, CT: JAI Press.

Calfee, R., & Patrick, C. (1995). *Teach our children well: Bringing K–12 education into the 21st century.* Stanford, CA: Stanford Alumni Association.

Calkins, L. (1986). *The art of teaching writing.* Portsmouth, NH: Heinemann.

Carlisle, J. (1994). Morphological awareness, spelling, and story writing: Possible relationships for elementary-age children with and without learning disabilities. In N. Jordan & J. Goldsmith-Phillips (Eds.), *Learning disabilities: New directions for assessment and intervention* (pp. 123–145). Boston: Allyn & Bacon.

Chall, J. (1979). The great debate: Ten years later with a modest proposal for reading stages. In L. Resnick & P. Weaver (Eds.), *Theory and practice of early reading* (Vol. 1, pp. 22–25). Hillsdale, NJ: Erlbaum.

Chenault, B., Thomson, J., Abbott, R., & Berninger, V. (2006). Effects of prior attention training on child dyslexics' response to composition instruction. *Developmental Neuropsychology, 29,* 243–260.

Chomsky, C. (1979). Reading, writing, and phonology. *Harvard Educational Review, 40,* 287–309.

Clay, M. (1982). Learning and teaching writing: A developmental perspective. *Language Arts, 59,* 65–70.

De La Paz, S., & Graham, S. (1997). Effects of dictation and advanced planning instruction on the composing of students with writing and learning problems. *Journal of Educational Psychology, 89,* 203–222.

De La Paz, S., Swanson, P., & Graham, S. (1998). The contribution of executive control to the revising by students with writing and learning difficulties. *Journal of Educational Psychology, 90,* 448–460.

Dixon, R., & Englemann, S. (2001). *Spelling through morphographs.* DeSoto, TX: SRA/McGraw-Hill.

Ehri, L. (1978). Beginning reading from a psycholinguistic perspective: Amalgamation of word identities. In F. B. Murray (Ed.), *The development of the reading process* (Monograph No. 3, pp. 1–33). Newark, DE: International Reading Association.

Emig, J. (1971). *The composing processes of twelfth graders.* Urbana, IL: National Council of Teachers of English.

Englert, C. (1992). Writing instruction from a sociocultural perspective: The holistic, dialogue, and social enterprise of writing. *Journal of Learning Disabilities, 25,* 153–172.

Englert, C., Raphael, T., Anderson, L., Anthony, H., & Stevens, D. (1991). Making strategies and self-talk visible: Writing instruction in regular and special education classrooms. *American Educational Research Journal, 28,* 337–372.

Englert, C., Raphael, T., Fear, K., & Anderson, L. (1988). Students' metacognitive knowledge about how to write informational texts. *Learning Disability Quarterly, 11,* 18–46.

Englert, C., Stewart, S., & Hiebart, E. (1988). Young writers' use of text structure in expository text generation. *Journal of Educational Psychology, 8,* 143–151.

Fitzgerald, J., & Shanahan, T. (2000). Reading and writing relations and their development. *Educational Psychologist, 35,* 39–50.

Garcia, N. (2006, October). *Understanding the developmental trajectory and predictors of orthographic coding: A longitudinal study*. Poster presented at Washington State School Psychology annual meeting, Spokane.

Garcia, N. (2007, December). *Comparing the contribution of phonological, orthographic, and morphological processes to the longitudinal spelling development of good, average, and poor spellers*. Unpublished doctoral dissertation, University of Washington.

Garcia, N., Abbott, R., & Berninger, V. (2008). *Longitudinal growth of receptive and expressive orthographic coding and finger succession and predictors of this growth*. Manuscript submitted for publication.

Gathercole, S. E., & Baddeley, A. D. (1993). *Working memory and language*. Hove, UK: Erlbaum.

Gere, A. R., & Abbott, R. D. (1985). Talking about writing: The language of writing groups. *Research in the Teaching of English, 19*, 362–385.

Gere, A. R., Schuessler, B., & Abbott, R. D. (1983). Measuring teachers' attitudes toward writing instruction. In R. Beach & L. S. Bridwell (Eds.), *New directions in composition research* (pp. 348–361). New York: Guilford Press.

Graesser, A. C., & Clark, L. (1985). *Structures and procedures of implicit knowledge*. Norwood, NJ: Ablex.

Graham, S. (1997). Executive control in the revising of students with learning and writing difficulties. *Journal of Educational Psychology, 89*, 223–234.

Graham, S., & Harris, K. R. (2005). *Writing better: Effective strategies for teaching students with learning difficulties*. Baltimore: Brookes.

Graham, S., MacArthur, C. A., & Schwartz, S. (1995). Effects of goal setting and procedural facilitation on the revising behavior and writing performances of students with writing and learning problems. *Journal of Educational Psychology, 87*, 230–240.

Graham, S., & Perrin, D. (2007). *Writing next: Effective strategies to improve writing of adolescents in middle and high schools: A report to the Carnegie Corporation of New York*. New York: Alliance for Excellence in Education.

Graham, S., Struck, M., Richardson, J., & Berninger, V. (2006). Dimensions of good and poor handwriting legibility in first and second graders: Motor programs, visual–spatial arrangement, and letter formation parameter setting. *Developmental Neuropsychology, 29*, 43–60.

Graves, D. (1983). *Writing: Teachers and children at work*. Exeter, NH: Heinemann.

Greenwald, E., Persky, H., Campbell, J., & Mazzeo, J. (2006). NAEP 1998 writing report card for the nation and states. *Educational Statistics Quarterly—Elementary and Secondary, 1*(4), 3–14.

Harris, K. R., & Graham, S. (1996). *Making the writing process work: Strategies for composition and self-regulation*. Cambridge, MA: Brookline.

Hayes, J. R. (1996). A new framework for understanding cognition and affect in writing. In C. M. Levy & S. Randall (Eds.), *The science of writing: Theories, methods, individual differences, and applications* (pp. 1–27). Mahwah, NJ: Erlbaum.

Hayes, J. R. (2000). A new framework for understanding cognition and affect in writing. In R. Indrisano & J. R. Squire (Eds.), *Perspectives on writing* (pp. 6–44). Newark, DE: International Reading Association.

Hayes, J. R., & Flower, L. S. (1980). Identifying the organization of writing processes. In L. W. Gregg & E. R. Steinberg (Eds.), *Cognitive processes in writing* (pp. 3–30). Hillsdale, NJ: Erlbaum.

Hayes, J. R., Flower, L. S., Schriver, K. A., Stratman, J., & Carey, L. (1987). Cognitive processes in revision. In S. Rosenberg (Ed.), *Advances in applied psycholinguistics: Vol. 2. Reading, writing, and language processes* (pp. 176–240). New York: Cambridge University Press.

Henry, M. (2003). *Unlocking literacy: Effective decoding and spelling instruction*. Baltimore: Brookes.

Hillocks, G. (1984). What works in teaching composition: A meta-analysis of experimental treatment studies. *American Journal of Education, 93*, 133–170.

Hillocks, G. (1986). *Research on written composition: New directions for teaching*. Urbana, IL: National Conference on Research in English.

Hooper, S., Swartz, C., Wakely, M., de Kruif, R., & Montgomery, J. (2002). Executive functions in elementary school children with and without problems in written expression. *Journal of Learning Disabilities, 35*, 37–68.

Jenkins, J. R., Johnson, E., & Hileman, J. (2004). When is reading also writing: Sources of individual differences on the new reading performance assessments. *Scientific Studies in Reading, 8*, 125–151.

Kellogg, R. (1994). *The psychology of writing*. New York: Oxford University Press.

Klein, P. (1999). Reopening inquiry into cognitive processes in writing-to-learn. *Educational Psychology Review, 11*, 203–270.

MacArthur, C. (2006). The effects of new technologies on writing and writing processes. In C. MacArthur, S. Graham, & J. Fitzgerald (Eds.), *Handbook of writing research* (pp. 248–262). New York: Guilford Press.

MacArthur, C. A., & Graham, S. (1987). Learning disabled students' composing with three methods: Handwriting, dictation, and word processing. *Journal of Special Education, 21*, 2–42.

MacArthur, C. A., Graham, S., & Fitzgerald, J. (Eds.). (2006). *Handbook of writing research*. New York: Guilford Press.

MacArthur, C. A., Schwartz, S., & Graham, S. (1991). Effects of a reciprocal peer revision strategy in special education classrooms. *Learning Disabilities Research and Practice, 6*, 201–210.

Mather, N., Bos, C., & Babur, N. (2001). Perceptions and knowledge of preservice and inservice teachers about early literacy instruction. *Journal of Learning Disabilities, 4*, 471–482.

McCutchen, D. (1986). Domain knowledge and linguistic knowledge in the development of writing ability. *Journal of Memory and Language, 25*, 431–444.

McCutchen, D. (1996). A capacity theory of writing: Working memory in composition. *Educational Psychology Review, 8*, 299–325.

McCutchen, D., & Berninger, V. (1999). Those who know, teach well. *Learning Disabilities Research and Practice, 14*, 215–226.

Molfese, V., Beswick, J., Molnar, A., & Jacobi-Vessels, J. (2006). Alphabet skills in preschools: A preliminary study of letter naming and letter writing. *Developmental Neuropsychology, 29,* 5–19.

Nagy, W., Berninger, V., & Abbott, R. (2006). Contributions of morphology beyond phonology to literacy outcomes of upper elementary and middle school students. *Journal of Educational Psychology, 98,* 134–147.

Nagy, W., Berninger, V., Abbott, R., Vaughan, K., & Vermeulen, K. (2003). Relationship of morphology and other language skills to literacy skills in at-risk second graders and at-risk fourth-grade writers. *Journal of Educational Psychology, 95,* 730–742.

Newell, G. (2006). Writing to learn: How alternative theories of school writing account for school performance. In C. MacArthur, S. Graham, & J. Fitzgerald (Eds.), *Handbook of writing research* (pp. 235–262). New York: Guilford Press.

Peverly, S., Ramaswamy, V., Brown, C., Sumowski, J., Alidoost, M., & Garner, J. (2007). Skill in lecture note-taking: What predicts? *Journal of Educational Psychology, 99,* 167–180.

Peverly, S. T. (2006). The importance of handwriting speed in adult writing. *Developmental Neuropsychology, 29,* 197–216.

Peverly, S. T., Brobst, K., Graham, M., & Shaw, R. (2003). College adults are not good at self-regulation: A study on the relationship of self-regulation, note-taking, and test-taking. *Journal of Educational Psychology, 95,* 335–346.

Read, C. (1981). Writing is not the inverse of reading for young children. In C. Frederickson & J. Domminick (Eds.), *Writing: The nature, development, and teaching of written communication* (Vol. 2, pp. 105–117). Hillsdale, NJ: Erlbaum.

Richards, T., Aylward, E., Berninger, V., Field, K., Parsons, A., Richards, A., et al. (2006). Individual fMRI activation in orthographic mapping and morpheme mapping after orthographic or morphological spelling treatment in child dyslexics. *Journal of Neurolinguistics, 19,* 56–86.

Richards, T., Aylward, E., Raskind, W., Abbott, R., Field, K., Parsons, A., et al. (2006). Converging evidence for triple word form theory in children with dyslexia. *Developmental Neuropsychology, 30,* 547–589.

Richards, T., Berninger, V., Nagy, W., Parsons, A., Field, K., & Richards, A. (2005). Brain activation during language task contrasts in children with and without dyslexia: Inferring mapping processes and assessing response to spelling instruction. *Educational and Child Psychology, 22*(2), 62–80.

Scardamalia, M., & Bereiter, C. (1989). Knowledge telling and knowledge transforming in written composition. In S. Rosenberg (Ed.), *Advances in applied psycholinguistics: Vol. 2. Reading, writing, and language learning* (pp. 142–175). Cambridge, UK: Cambridge University Press.

Schneider, W., & Shiffrin, R. (1977). Controlled and automatic human information processing: Detection, search, and attention. *Psychological Review, 84,* 1–66.

Schuessler, B., Gere, A. R., & Abbott, R. D. (1981). The development of four scales measuring teacher attitudes toward written composition: A preliminary investigation. *Research in the Teaching of English, 15,* 55–63.

Scott, C. (2002). A fork in the road less traveled: Writing intervention based on language profile. In K. Butler & E. Silliman (Eds.), *Speaking, reading, and writing in children with language learning disabilities* (pp. 219–237). Mahwah, NJ: Erlbaum.

Silliman, E., Bahr, R., & Peters, M. (2006). Spelling patterns in preadolescents with atypical language skills: Phonological, morphological, and orthographic factors. *Developmental Neuropsychology, 29,* 93–123.

Singer, B., & Bashir, A. (1999). What are executive functions and self-regulation and what do they have to do with language-learning disorders? *Language, Speech, and Hearing Services in Schools, 30,* 265–273.

Swanson, H. L., & Berninger, V. (1996). Individual differences in children's working memory and writing skills. *Journal of Experimental Child Psychology, 63,* 358–385.

Templeton, S., & Bear, D. (1992). *Development of orthographic knowledge and the foundations of literacy: A memorial Feltschrift for Edmund Henderson.* Mahwah, NJ: Erlbaum.

Thomson, J., Chennault, B., Abbott, R., Raskind, W., Richards, T., Aylward, E., et al. (2005). Converging evidence for attentional influences on the orthographic word form in child dyslexics. *Journal of Neurolinguistics, 18,* 93–126.

Treiman, R. (1993). *Beginning to spell.* Cambridge, UK: Cambridge University Press.

Treiman, R., & Broderick, V. (1998). What's in a name? Children's knowledge about the letters in their own names. *Journal of Experimental Child Psychology, 70,* 97–116.

Troia, G. A., & Graham, S. (2002). The effectiveness of a highly explicit, teacher-directed strategy instruction routine: Changing the writing performance of students with learning disabilities. *Journal of Learning Disabilities, 35,* 290–305.

Troia, G. A., Graham, S., & Harris, K. (1999). Teaching students with learning disabilities to mindfully plan when writing. *Exceptional Children, 65,* 235–252.

Valencia, S. (1998). *Literacy portfolios in action.* Fort Worth, TX: Harcourt Brace.

Venezky, R. (1970). *The structure of English orthography.* The Hague, Netherlands: Mouton.

Venezky, R. (1999). *The American way of spelling.* New York: Guilford Press.

Vygotsky, L. (1978). *Mind and society.* Cambridge, MA: Harvard University Press.

Whitaker, J. K. (1994, October). *How school psychology trainees learn to communicate through the psychological report.* Unpublished doctoral dissertation, University of Washington, Seattle.

Wijsman, E., Peterson, D., Leutenegger, A., Thomson, J., Goddard, K., Hsu, L., et al. (2000). Segregation analysis of phenotypic components of learning disabilities: I. Nonword memory and digit span. *American Journal of Human Genetics, 67,* 631–646.

Wilkinson, C., Bahr, R., Silliman, E., & Berninger, V. (2007, August). *Spelling patterns from grades 1–9: Implications for vocabulary development*. Paper presented at the European Conference on Reading, Berlin, Germany.

Wong, B. Y. L. (1997). Research on genre-specific strategies for enhancing writing in adolescents with learning disabilities. *Learning Disability Quarterly*, *20*, 140–159.

Wong, B. Y. L., & Berninger, V. (2004). Cognitive processes of teachers in implementing composition research in elementary, middle, and high school classrooms. In B. Shulman, K. Apel, B. Ehren, E. Silliman, & A. Stone (Eds.), *Handbook of language and literacy: Development and disorders* (pp. 600–624). New York: Guilford Press.

Wong, B. Y. L., Butler, D. L., Ficzere, S. A., & Kuperis, S. (1996). Teaching low achievers and students with learning disabilities to plan, write, and revise opinion essays. *Journal of Learning Disabilities*, *29*, 197–212.

Wong, B. Y. L., Butler, D. L., Ficzere, S. A., & Kuperis, S. (1997). Teaching adolescents with learning disabilities and low achievers to plan, write, and revise compare-and-contrast essays. *Learning Disabilities Research and Practice*, *12*, 2–15.

Wong, B. Y. L., Butler, D. L., Ficzere, S. A., Kuperis, S., & Corden, M. (1994). Teaching problem learners revision skills and sensitivity to audience through two instructional modes: Student–teacher versus student–student interactive dialogues. *Learning Disabilities Research and Practice*, *9*, 78–90.

Wong, B. Y. L., Wong, R., Darlington, D., & Jones, W. (1991). Interactive teaching: An effective way to teach revision skills to adolescents with learning disabilities. *Learning Disabilities Research and Practice*, *6*, 117–127.

CHAPTER 2

Self-Efficacy and Procrastination in the Writing of Students with Learning Disabilities

Robert M. Klassen
Christine Welton

Perhaps no academic task is as susceptible to the influences of motivation—and procrastination—as writing. Writing is an essential skill in and outside of school settings, and although computers and word processing software may supplant pencil and paper as the tools of choice for many people, writing continues to demand effort, knowledge of relevant strategies, and specific skills. For students, important academic paths are determined by writing facility, and success at planning, scribing, and revising plays a key role in determining the opportunities that become available as a student progresses through school. Writing requires not only thoughtful planning and skillful execution but also the motivation or will to expend effort, to persist, and to make the choices necessary to ensure successful completion of a complex and demanding undertaking. In light of the heavy cognitive load necessary to support writing (Torrance & Galbraith, 2006), it is not surprising that one essential key to successful writing is a strong sense of self-efficacy, or a belief in the capability to

This chapter is dedicated to the memory of Christine Welton, who died unexpectedly during its preparation. Christine is greatly missed by her family and by those of us who had the great pleasure to work with her during her graduate student career at the University of Alberta.

carry out the courses of action required to attain a specified goal (Bandura, 1997). Equally, it is not surprising that writing is especially prone to procrastination, or delay in the starting or completing of a desired task within an expected time frame (Ferrari, O'Callaghan, & Newbegin, 2005). For students with typical learning abilities, writing is a challenging task; for students with learning problems,[1] writing can present itself as the type of overwhelming task that is subject to delay and avoidance.

In this chapter we address motivation beliefs that influence the writing performance of individuals with learning disabilities (LD). In particular, we focus on two opposing motivation constructs—self-efficacy and procrastination—that have been shown to be critical factors influencing the academic and, in particular, writing success of students with and without learning problems, including those with LD. We begin by reviewing the literature that explores the academic self-efficacy beliefs of children and adolescents with LD, with a particular focus on how self-efficacy influences writing. Next, we look at two recent studies that use quantitative and qualitative approaches to examine the self-efficacy of adolescents with LD. Following this, we review how procrastination adversely affects writing and general academic functioning in typical and atypical students and then present selected results from a recent study that examines the procrastination patterns of individuals with LD. To conclude, we examine the implications arising from the research reports we have discussed and present a case for the next steps in the quest to understand the motivation beliefs of individuals with LD and other learning problems.

MOTIVATION AND STRUGGLING WRITERS WITH LD

Self-Efficacy and Procrastination

In Bandura's social-cognitive theory, self-efficacy is defined as beliefs in one's abilities to carry out a desired course of action. These self-beliefs are formed from four sources: mastery experience (performance on previous similar tasks); vicarious experience (modeling, or the observation of others' performance on similar tasks); verbal persuasion (feedback from significant others); and physiological and emotional reactions (e.g., anxiety) to specific tasks. Although the informal term *confidence* is sometimes used as a synonym for self-efficacy, it fails to capture the specificity and theoretical base of the construct of self-efficacy (Bandura, 1997). According to self-efficacy theory, high self-efficacy beliefs facilitate task choice, task engagement, effort, and performance; low self-efficacy beliefs weaken resolve and hinder performance (Pajares, 1996). Self-efficacy beliefs are related to self-concept beliefs, but there are some critical differences that distinguish the two motivation constructs. Whereas self-concept is defined as a reflection on one's competence ("I'm pretty good at writing"), self-efficacy captures one's perceived capabilities within a specific context ("I'm confident that I can do a good job writing this paragraph"). In contrast to self-efficacy measurement, most self-concept definitions include a greater emphasis on comparison with others, evaluation of affect, and past versus future orientation (Bong & Skaalvik, 2003). Self-efficacy research has been conducted in a wide range of academic and nonacademic domains, and it has been shown to be negatively related to dysfunctional motivation beliefs, such as procrastination (e.g., Wolters, 2003).

In stark contrast to motivation beliefs such as self-efficacy, procrastination reflects the absence of a motivated, planned approach to academic tasks such as writing and studying. A few recent studies have elaborated on the links between procrastination and self-efficacy (e.g., Haycock, McCarthy, & Skay, 1998; Howell, Watson, Powell, & Buro, 2006; Wolters, 2003), with results showing that procrastination is inversely related to the strength of individuals' beliefs in their capabilities to carry out a desired task (i.e., self-efficacy) and to the levels of cognitive and metacognitive skills shown by motivated and self-regulated learners. Academic procrastination is remarkably common, with estimations of incidence ranging up to 70% (Ellis & Knaus, 1977). It is likely that all students postpone completing tasks at some point in their schooling, and even children as young as 9 years old report feelings of anxiety that are related to their procrastination behaviors (Scher & Osterman, 2002). However, research to this point has included only individuals with assumed typical learning profiles and has not addressed how individuals with diverse learning needs, such as LD, experience procrastination in relation to other motivation variables. Just as students with LD may display different motivation patterns from those of individuals without learning disabilities, students with LD may also experience procrastination differently from those without LD.

Self-Efficacy and Writing

Parents and teachers frequently bemoan the lack of motivation seen in children and adolescents, especially for writing tasks. The self-efficacy component of social-cognitive theory describes how self-perceptions of the capability to perform specific tasks strongly influence one's engagement in and successful completion of a task. This is especially true for writing, in which the demands of the task are many—spelling, punctuation, grammar, word choice, ideas, and organization—and the need for belief in one's own capabilities to address and monitor these demands, often simultaneously, is correspondingly high. Learning to write can be viewed as a transition from conversation to composition that begins at school entry and develops through formal schooling and beyond (Bereiter & Scardamalia, 1987). Motivation beliefs also change and develop through the school years, with perceptions of ability typically optimistic in the early school years and declining thereafter (Anderman & Maehr, 1994). Children begin to accurately differentiate between performance, effort, and ability around the age of 10 (Stipek, 1998), and children who doubt their competence begin to show less perseverance for difficult tasks around the same age (Licht, 1992). At the same time, writing tasks begin to assume greater importance, especially as children entering middle school are faced with the challenge of demonstrating their knowledge and creativity largely through writing (Hooper et al., 1993). Difficulties with writing increase in early adolescence: Hooper et al. (1993) found that more than half of their middle school participants experienced significant difficulties with writing. Learning to write is a daunting task for many children and youths, and a lack of confidence inhibits academic success.

Bandura (1997) suggests that students may perform poorly because of a lack of skill but also because of a lack of perceived efficacy in making use of their skills. Writing self-efficacy is influenced by the acquisition of writing skills, but it is not merely a reflection of existing skills and previous performance—students with similar skills in writing perform at very different levels depending on the strength of their beliefs in their abilities to use these skills on specific writing tasks. Researchers and educators understand students' writing challenges more clearly when they consider how motivation factors interact with the writing process. Bruning and Horn (2000) suggest that writing motivation is enhanced when teachers: (1) nurture functional beliefs about writing; (2) foster student engagement through authentic writing goals and contexts; (3) provide a supportive context for writing; and (4) create a positive emotional environment for writing. It is in this last sphere that many students experience difficulties, because anxiety about writing tasks is common (Bruning & Horn, 2000) and the physiological reactions of stress interfere with the confidence to complete academic tasks involving writing. Students with low self-efficacy are especially vulnerable to anxiety about writing, and this anxiety is not necessarily baseless—the stakes for students, especially as they enter adolescence, are high, and important opportunities and career paths are opened up through writing success. Bandura notes that social pressure for academic success is beginning earlier and earlier and that, for many children, "there is a lot to be anxious about in scholastic life" (1997, p. 235). For children with LD, these social pressures and academic anxieties may be even more pronounced.

Recent reviews of the self-efficacy and writing literature (Klassen, 2002b; Pajares, 2003; Pajares & Valiante, 2006) have produced some constructive ideas about how students' self-beliefs about their capabilities influence their writing performance and suggestions for how teachers and parents can support students in their writing. Pajares (2003), echoing William James (1892/2001), suggests that beliefs of personal competence about writing develop into "habits of thinking that are developed like habits of conduct" (2003, p. 153) and that teachers play an important role in helping students develop the self-belief habits that aid success. Teachers also play a role in monitoring levels of their students' self-efficacy beliefs and need to watch out for unwarranted low-confidence levels. Students with low writing self-efficacy beliefs are prone to feelings of anxiety about writing and to give up easily when faced with a challenging writing task, which perpetuates further failure and continuing low self-efficacy. Pajares and Valiante (2006) suggest that although self-beliefs, in themselves, are no guarantee of writing success, teachers and parents can maintain a joint focus on the development of strong writing skills and appropriate self-beliefs that are needed to ensure writing success. For example, teachers and parents can draw attention to the *sources* of writing self-efficacy in discussion with student writers by reminding them of previous successes with writing, by modeling and demonstrating appropriate writing practices, by providing feedback about their use of writing strategies and linking use with improved writing performance, and by acknowledging and discussing anxieties arising from writing tasks.

Klassen (2002b) explored the literature related to the writing self-efficacy beliefs of early adolescents by critically examining 16 articles that included a writing task, a measure of self-efficacy, and participants between the 6th and 10th grades. Results of the critical review showed self-efficacy to be the strongest or among the strongest predictors of writing competence in the studies reviewed, establishing adolescent writing self-efficacy beliefs as a powerful force influencing writing success. Several methodological weaknesses were found to plague the studies in the review, with several of the studies including self-efficacy measures that were conceptually unclear and other studies failing to establish clear correspondence between the self-efficacy measure and the criterion task. Another of the key findings of the review was that students with LD appeared in many cases to possess unusually high self-efficacy beliefs, in spite of relatively poor performance. Klassen commented that the apparent self-efficacy overestimates may have been due to students' difficulties in understanding the measurement tasks employed or to the hypothesized faulty self-knowledge of adolescents with LD. Importantly, the review concluded that motivation beliefs may operate very differently for individuals with LD than for individuals without LD.

Motivation and Students with LD

Mounting evidence suggests that individuals with LD experience more social, emotional, and motivational difficulties than those without LD (e.g., Chapman, 1988; Sridhar & Vaughn, 2001). Students with LD experience the same physical, educational, and social transitions as their peers, but they experience the added challenge of significant learning deficits in specific domains. In school, students with LD have writing difficulties (Troia, 2006) coupled with lower academic self-concept (Gans, Kenny, & Ghany, 2003; Tabassam & Grainger, 2003) and lower self-perceptions and self-esteem (e.g., Grolnick & Ryan, 1990; Rosenthal, 1973). According to motivation researchers, failure and poor performance lead to doubts about general intellectual abilities, which in turn lead to reduced effort, further failure, and poor academic outcomes (Licht & Kirstner, 1986). It is not surprising that children and adolescents with LD possess lower academic self-concept, a tendency toward learned helplessness, and low expectations of future academic success. However, the lower self-concept of students with LD may be limited to the school context. Gans et al. (2003) found that early adolescents with LD scored lower than their peers without LD on intellectual and school status self-concept but not on more generalized self-concept measures. Moreover, relatively lower self-concept beliefs do not necessarily mean *low* self-concept beliefs in absolute terms. Meltzer, Roditi, Houser, and Perlman (1998) found students with LD to express lower academic self-concept than their typically developing peers but still within the "average" to "above-average" range. These comparatively lower self-beliefs are considered to reflect the academic difficulties inherent in an LD profile and to reciprocally contribute to continuing failure in which poor academic performance reinforces already negative feelings about school (Chapman, 1988).

Although researchers have explored the self-concept and self-esteem of individuals with LD, less attention has been paid to self-efficacy beliefs and procrastination, even though self-efficacy is considered "an essential motive to learn" (Zimmerman, 2000, p. 82) and academic procrastination is an almost universal experience (Ferrari, Johnson, & McCown, 1995). Only a small number of studies have examined the writing self-efficacy beliefs of children and adolescents with LD, and little attention has been paid to the procrastination patterns of individuals with LD. In the remainder of this chapter, we first explore the self-efficacy beliefs of students with LD and then switch our attention to the procrastination patterns of students with LD.

Academic Self-Efficacy and LD

For most students, possessing optimistic self-efficacy beliefs is a positive attribute, because it means that they believe they can achieve what they set out to do and can accomplish challenging tasks with the requisite effort and persistence. Bandura (1997) recounts the example of students with higher-than-warranted self-efficacy beliefs who set higher goals for themselves, were more strategic problem solvers, and performed at a higher level than students with equivalent cognitive abilities but lower self-efficacy. But high academic self-efficacy beliefs may not operate in the same way for students with LD. Klassen (2002a) recently reviewed 22 articles that explored the self-efficacy beliefs of students with LD. More than half of the studies exploring writing self-efficacy concluded that students with LD were markedly overoptimistic about their writing abilities, even though the students had specific difficulties with writing. In other words, the students with LD felt very confident about their writing skills even in the face of daily evidence that they were poor writers. Thus high degrees of self-efficacy may be functional for some students and dysfunctional for others. Students with LD may possess high self-efficacy about writing, but their overoptimism may result in failure to adequately prepare to carry out demanding tasks such as writing. The inflated self-efficacy beliefs may be related to overall deficits in metacognitive awareness and may be seen in inadequate preparation, ineffective self-advocacy, and a lack of awareness of one's strengths and weaknesses.

Motivational beliefs such as self-efficacy influence task approaches and affect the development of metacognitive skills. Well-developed skills in metacognition—awareness of one's cognitive processes, cognitive strengths and weaknesses, and self-regulation (Flavell, 1976)—are necessary for successful academic functioning, but it is thought that students with LD experience difficulties analyzing task requirements, selecting and implementing strategies, and monitoring and adjusting performance (Butler, 1998). With writing tasks, individuals with LD have been found to focus on lower order processes, such as spelling or grammar, while ignoring higher order demands such as writing to an audience or organizing ideas (Wong, Butler, Ficzere, & Kuperis, 1996). When compared with their normally achieving peers, students with LD are, in general, less metacognitively aware, and they experience difficulty in evaluating and predicting future performance (Butler, 1998). The forming of self-efficacy beliefs is a metacognitive activity that demands a conscious awareness of self and task. It is worth considering in what ways lower metacognitive awareness might influence writing self-efficacy and predictions of writing performance. We next turn to two studies that explore how self-efficacy operates in academic tasks for adolescents with LD.

SOME RECENT RESEARCH ON MOTIVATION IN STRUGGLING WRITERS WITH LD

Study 1: Spelling and Writing Self-Efficacy of Adolescents with LD

In this section, we present the results from a recent study that explores the spelling, writing, self-efficacy for self-regulation, and general self-efficacy (confidence for problem solving) of adolescents with LD (Klassen, 2007). This study used adolescents' direct predictions of their performance as a way of gauging calibration between self-efficacy and performance. Students' predictions of their performance can be seen as an indication of their confidence in completing a task or, equally, as an indicator of their metacognitive self-appraisal; that is, judgments about personal cognitive abilities (Paris & Winograd, 1990). Predictions can be viewed as a proxy for self-efficacy; they are task-specific performance expectations (Zimmerman, 2000) that reflect one's beliefs about one's capabilities to complete a task. Comparisons were made between predictions and performance and between performance and postdictions (post hoc self-evaluations) for groups with and without LD in spelling and writing. Finally, in order to provide further clues about the self-efficacy and metacognitive beliefs of early adolescents, the participants also rated their self-efficacy for self-regulation (Zimmerman, Bandura, & Martinez-Pons, 1992) and their general self-efficacy (Scholz, Doña, Sud, & Schwarzer, 2002; Schwarzer & Born, 1997).

Participants were 133 (68 with LD [46 males, 22 females] and 65 without LD [30 males, 35 females]) grade 8 and 9 students. Participants completed a grade-level spelling test and a writing task in which the participants were asked to write short, syntactically correct sentences using three stimulus words (e.g., "table, lunch, ate") within a 4-minute time limit. We used conventional self-efficacy measures (e.g., "Rate your degree of confidence of getting 10 [12, 14, etc.] correct on this spelling test") and prediction scores (e.g., "I believe I can correctly complete _____ items in 4 minutes"). Participants also completed measures assessing levels of self-efficacy for self-regulation (e.g., "How well can you study when there are other interesting things to do?") and for general self-efficacy (e.g., "I am confident I can deal with unexpected events").

Participants with LD displayed lower self-efficacy than the group without LD, but they were more optimistic (relative to their performance) in both domains assessed. The students with LD overestimated their performance by 52% on the spelling task and by 19% on the writing task and continued to hold overoptimistic beliefs about their performance in spelling even after they had completed the task. The ratings of the students with LD of their efficacy for self-regulation were significantly lower than the ratings in the group without LD (mean item score of about 6 out of 10 for group with LD compared with about 7 out of 10 for group without LD), suggesting moderate difficulties for self-regulatory tasks such as planning and organizing schoolwork and participating in class discussions. An examination of individual items on the self-regulation scale showed that the students with LD lagged behind their peers without LD (i.e., effect sizes were largest) in finishing homework by deadlines, in concentrating on school subjects, in planning schoolwork, and in motivation to complete schoolwork. The students with LD rated themselves lower in general self-efficacy than the group without LD, but the mean item ratings of students with LD (6.8 out of 10, in the "moderately true" range, compared with 7.5 for the group without LD) suggests a moderately optimistic perspective on problem solving and general coping skills.

Why do individuals with LD, who very likely have a history of negative feedback (e.g., failed tests or poor grades) about their performance in their domains of greatest weakness, persist in overestimating their skills in spelling and writing? Kruger and Dunning (1999) argue that the skills required to succeed in a domain are the very same skills required to evaluate competence in that domain. They suggest that people who lack skill and understanding in a domain suffer from a "dual burden"; they are unskilled but also unaware—they lack the metacognitive ability to recognize their own lack of skill. To paraphrase Miyake and Norman (1978), to solve a problem, one must know enough to know what is not known. From this point of view, the writing overconfidence of students with LD might be expected, because these students not only lack skills in literacy but may also be relatively unaware of their lack of skills. The overly optimistic self-efficacy beliefs seen in students with LD reflect this lack of self-awareness and may arguably result in inferior academic functioning.

For teachers, the implications are clear: Adolescents with LD might be confident about their writing but oblivious to their poor performance. This study confirms that adolescents with LD may lack not only the skills to complete writing tasks but also the "reflective awareness about knowledge" (Butler, 1998, p. 282) that defines metacognition. Because of this overconfidence, adolescents with LD may write less than their peers without LD and may spend less time revising written work; the students who need to spend the most time on a writing task may end up doing the least work because they fail to recognize their academic deficits. Although we researchers have measured the optimistic self-efficacy of adolescents with LD, little has been heard from the students themselves about *why* they might overestimate their capabilities in academic areas. To add depth to our findings of adolescent overconfidence, we next designed a qualitative study to explore the self-efficacy of students with LD from an insider's perspective.

Study 2: Students' and Teachers' Perspectives on Self-Efficacy and LD

Whereas quantitative methods offer the advantages of statistical reliability, comparability of findings, and the potential to include large numbers of participants in a single study, qualitative inquiries offer the advantage of an insider's perspective, more depth, and a rich and authentic context. We next report selected results from a recent qualitative study (Klassen & Lynch, 2007) that investigates the academic self-efficacy of adolescents with LD from the perspective of the students and their special education teachers.

We conducted focus group interviews with 28 early adolescents diagnosed with severe LD (based on provincial Ministry of Education criteria) and individual interviews with 7 special education teachers who teach students with LD. Our research questions were:

- How are self-efficacy beliefs understood by adolescents with LD and by their teachers?
- What do students with LD and their teachers say about the miscalibration of efficacy and performance?
- What are ways to overcome the motivation deficits of students with learning disabilities?

Although the study did not focus exclusively on motivation for writing, we included scenarios that focused on writing, and students and teachers often made references to writing motivation. For the focus groups, sample scenarios/questions included, "Imagine you've been assigned an in-class assignment in English that involves reading a chapter and then writing an essay about it in a one-hour class. Tell me about your confidence to complete this task once the teacher has finished explaining it." For the individual teacher interviews, questions included "What can you tell me about the confidence levels of students with LD? Can you give me an example?" (In order to ensure understanding, we used the colloquial term *confidence* as a substitute for *self-efficacy* for all focus groups and individual interviews.) Five major themes emerged from the sequential analysis of our 34 codes: self-efficacy, calibration of efficacy and performance, students' self-awareness, attributions for failure, and motivation-related problems and solutions. For the sake of brevity, we discuss only the first two of these themes in this chapter. Participants' quotes were used to provide voice to the participants and concrete evidence to support the themes (Creswell, 1998).

Students and teachers alike discussed self-efficacy (stated as confidence) as a major factor contributing to academic performance: "Yeah, it's like a mental thing. If your brain says, like, 'I can do this,' then you do way better" (G14, i.e., a 14-year-old girl), and "Well, say in math, or something, if I can multiply and somebody else can multiply just the same, if I have confidence going into the test, and they're like 'Oh, I'm going to do badly,' and they look on the down side of things, they will probably do worse than me" (B13). Students noted the effects of low self-efficacy beliefs: "Well, if you have no confidence, you're not going to be able to do anything at all" (B13), and "Somebody with low confidence levels might just think, 'Oh, I can't do it' and then not do it at all or just half-(hearted)ly" (B14). Teachers noted the importance, but also the fragility, of the academic efficacy beliefs of their students: "I worked incredibly hard not to let him lose the self-confidence that he had—he knew he had the skills, but he also had tremendous frustration" (Hedda, 8 years of experience), and "We've got to be really careful that we don't kick the confidence out of them" (Marie, 28 years of experience). Teachers and students in all focus groups and individual interviews agreed that academic confidence beliefs contribute to academic achievement and that low confidence hampers performance.

Students with LD characterized themselves as being either accurate or underconfident in calibrating their self-efficacy with performance: "Yeah, I guess sometimes I haven't studied that much, but on some tests I do better than I expect, so I underestimate myself, but I know I should have studied more" (B13), and "I never really try to guess, but it's always a surprise when [an assignment] comes back—usually they're pretty high compared to what I expected, so I guess I underestimate" (G14). When directly asked about the accuracy of their confidence beliefs on an essay-writing task, 25 of 28 students characterized their academic predictions as generally accurate. In contrast to the students' perspective, but congruent with the research findings that students with LD are overly optimistic about their performance, teachers were most likely to characterize students as overconfident about academic tasks. Sherry suggested, "If they're an extremely damaged student, they will tell you they are going to do wonderfully.... They are constantly surprised at what they get (marks)." Hedda commented, "I think they're way too overconfident for tests and exams; they tend to think they know more than they do." Three of the teachers reported that students seemed to become more accurate in their efficacy–performance calibrations as they moved through high school (seven comments): "Grade 8s and 9s seem to be the ones who are too confident, and the grade 10s and 11s are more realistic—they seem to be aware of where their strengths and weaknesses lie" (Fraser). No teachers suggested that students with LD were generally accurate in their calibration of confidence and performance.

We asked students, "Do you think students with LD have less or more confidence about completing academic tasks than their peers?" Almost all students with LD responded that they had less confidence: "Students with LD? Less confident, definitely" (B14), and "They're [students with LD] less confident—it's because they have to work way harder just to keep up" (B13). Students expressed higher levels of confidence about certain subjects, with most students suggesting that they are more confident in subjects that they found appealing. Interest and enjoyment were noted by eight of the students: "I think that you have more confidence in something you like" (G13), and "Well, if you're good at it, then you will always be much more confident" (B13). Several students noted specific subject areas in which they were most confident: "If you're really good at what you do, then you feel pretty confident—I'm confident in metalwork, but not confident in English" (B14). "I'm confident in my electives, but I don't have very much confidence to do that (a writing task); I basically think, 'Oh well, even if I try my hardest, there's no way I'm going to get very good in this,' so I just don't try" (B13).

Self-efficacy beliefs were seen as a potent influence on writing and other academic functioning by both teachers and students, but the level of self-efficacy varied according to domain. Students with LD expressed stronger confidence for nonacademic tasks but rated their own confidence as "definitely lower" than that of their peers for academic tasks. The results from this study suggest that adolescents with LD believe themselves to be accurate in predicting their performance, but objective evidence (e.g., Klassen, 2007) suggests otherwise. Improving individuals' metacognitive awareness, according to Kruger and Dunning (1999), improves the accuracy of self-appraisals and consequently allows individuals to more accurately determine areas of weakness that need attention. A lack of metacognitive self-knowledge is a serious obstacle that impedes current and future performance (Butler, 1998) and adversely influences students' engagement with writing tasks.

The results from this qualitative study suggest that the confidence beliefs of adolescents with LD are more complex than initially believed and may be influenced by subject area and student developmental level. Teachers noted a developmental difference in levels of confidence and in accuracy of calibration; students discussed differences in confidence based on domain and sex (boys were considered to possess higher levels of confidence regardless of level of performance). Furthermore, the idea of "overconfidence" is understood differently by participants and observers: teachers agreed that students with LD display overly optimistic efficacy beliefs, whereas the students were apparently unaware of their miscalibration. For some theorists, the students' persistent optimism might be considered unexpected, in light of their history of academic difficulty. Academic beliefs are developed in school settings, and the students in this study had all experienced some degree of poor academic performance, yet they maintained generally optimistic beliefs (according to their teachers) about their academic performances and expressed the belief that with a little effort they would achieve as well as their peers. This persistent hopefulness might also be present in part because of the strong support and encouragement provided by teachers to students in LD programs in this study—low-achieving students who cannot access similar levels of support might experience very different motivation patterns. For adolescents with LD, overly optimistic self-beliefs and a conviction that their academic performance is fully within their control might be an adaptive and functional response to a difficult reality.

Miscalibrated self-efficacy beliefs mean that students with LD may need significant help from their teachers in writing but may not be aware of the level of their need. Teachers in our study were very aware of the degree to which students with LD miscalibrate their self-efficacy and performance and suggested that, with time, students became better able to gauge the fit between task demands and academic skills. Teachers were also sensitive to the vulnerability of the self-efficacy of their students with LD and advised that those working with students with learning difficulties be vigilant to protect the fragile self-beliefs of their charges. In summary, teachers face a difficult balancing act: They must recognize that their students with LD may possess inflated self-beliefs about writing, and so must strive to increase students' awareness of task demands and the effort needed to successfully complete writing tasks. At the same time, teachers need to ensure that students maintain the necessary level of confidence so that they attempt new and challenging writing tasks and maintain the self-belief that they are able to succeed at writing through effort, persistence, and use of appropriate strategies. In the next section we discuss another serious obstacle—procrastination—that influences the writing performance of students with LD.

Study 3: Procrastination and Writing of Students with LD

Writers of all kinds—academics, novelists, and ninth-grade students—know from first-hand experience that writing is more prone to procrastination than other tasks. Research backs this up; Solomon and Rothblum (1984) found that college students procrastinated more with writing than with any other academic activity. More than 45% of students procrastinated in writing tasks, compared with 30% in reading, 28% in studying for exams, 11% in administrative tasks, and 10% in school activities in general. In addition to the higher incidence of procrastination in writing, Solomon and Rothblum (1984) also found that procrastination in writing was more severe than in other domains, with nearly one-quarter of students characterizing their writing avoidance as "nearly always" or "always" a problem. Procrastination is also a problem for graduate students, with 42% reporting regular procrastination in writing assignments (Onwuegbuzie & Collins, 2001). That writing procrastination leads to undesirable physical and psychological states has been recognized by psychologists for nearly 100 years. William James wrote to fellow psychologist Carl Stumpf about the emotional cost of procrastinating: "Nothing is so fatiguing as the eternal hanging on of an uncompleted task" (James & James, 1920/2003, p. 263). More recently, a study completed by Fritzsche, Young, and Hickson (2003) found that writing procrastination resulted in high levels of academic and general anxiety in undergraduates and negatively influenced the likelihood of college success. The authors suggested that feedback from instructors was associated with better writing outcomes for high procrastinators, but high procrastinators were less likely than other students to seek this feedback.

For students who struggle with learning, and especially for those with weak literacy skills, writing in all its guises—note taking, essay exams, or term-paper writing—can be the *bête noire* of school life. Students with LD produce writing that is shorter, more poorly organized, more error prone, and weaker in overall quality than students without LD (Troia, 2006). Faced with such daunting obstacles, one might expect that avoidance and delay of writing tasks would be a common response for students with LD. Surprisingly, apart from anecdotal reports, little is known about the procrastination practices of students with LD. Our recent review of the procrastination research found no studies that have explored the procrastination practices of individuals with LD (Klassen, Krawchuk, Lynch, & Rajani, 2008). As we have argued in this chapter, motivation variables operate in different ways for students with LD, with spelling and writing self-efficacy, for example, being overstated by adolescents with learning disabilities. Procrastination, too, may operate differently for individuals with LD. In this section, we define procrastination and present some initial findings from an exploration of the patterns of academic procrastination and academic motivation of undergraduates with and without LD.

Procrastination is defined as the delay of completion of a relevant task within an expected or desired time frame that often results in unsatisfactory performance on the task (Ferrari et al., 2005). Definitions of procrastination variously include aspects of delay, substandard performance, irrationality, and emotional upset (Ferrari et al., 1995; Milgram, 1991), and it can be measured in everyday settings (e.g., delaying completion of income tax paperwork) or academic settings (e.g., delaying completion of an assigned essay). Procrastination may be responsible for late written assignments, cramming, test and social anxiety, use of self-handicapping strategies, and fear of failure, and it often results in poorer performance than the person is capable of attaining (Ferrari & Scher, 2000; Lee, 2005). Among all of the variables that have been investigated in relationship to academic procrastination, self-efficacy and self-regulation have perhaps received the most attention (e.g., Wolters, 2003), with most studies showing significant inverse relationships with procrastination.

We recently explored the procrastination patterns of 208 undergraduate students with and without LD (Klassen et al., 2008). Our study investigated the procrastination, general academic self-efficacy, metacognitive self-regulation, self-efficacy for self-regulation, and help-seeking behaviors of 101 undergraduates with LD and 107 undergraduates without LD. We wondered whether students with LD would experience higher levels of academic procrastination than students without LD, and we wondered about the relationship of procrastination and other motivation variables for undergraduate students with LD.

In order to answer our questions, we administered questionnaires to undergraduates with and without LD in three universities and colleges in Western Canada. The participants with LD were recruited from disabilities services centers; they were 65% female, with a mean age of 24.6 and a reported grade-point average (GPA) of 2.96 on a 4-point scale. The participants without LD were recruited from undergraduate classrooms and were 74% female, with an average age of 22.8 years, and reported a GPA of 3.04. Individuals with LD self-reported their disability status in response to the question, "Do you have a diagnosed learning disability?"

To measure procrastination, we used Tuckman's 16-item procrastination measure, which provides a measure of time wasting, delay, and putting off of desired tasks (Tuckman, 1991). We used components of the Motivated Strategies for Learning Questionnaire (MSLQ) to assess participants' general academic self-efficacy, metacognitive self-regulation, and help seeking. The MSLQ is a widely used tool for measuring motivational orientations and strategy use (Pintrich, Smith, Garcia, & McKeachie, 1993). Self-efficacy for self-regulation was measured using the scale from the academic motivation study conducted by Zimmerman et al. (1992). We began by comparing levels of GPA and motivation across the two groups, with sex and LD status as independent variables. Next, bivariate correlations were calculated to explore the interrelationships among the variables for each of the two groups, and multiple regression analysis was used to explore prediction of procrastination.

We did not find any significant sex-related differences within or between groups, but when we compared the groups with and without LD, we found that individuals with LD reported higher levels of academic procrastination and lower metacognitive self-regulation and self-efficacy for self-regulation than the group without LD. There were no significant differences (after adjusting the significance level for the number of comparisons) between the two groups for GPA, general academic self-efficacy, or help-seeking behaviors. Effect sizes, using Cohen's d, were in the medium range (0.40–0.56), suggesting that the differences were not only statistically significant but of a meaningful magnitude. Undergraduates with LD displayed a different learning profile than undergraduates without LD—they reported greater procrastination, were less metacognitively aware, and possessed less confidence in controlling their learning (i.e., self-efficacy for self-regulation).

Procrastination showed the strongest bivariate relationship with self-efficacy for self-regulation in both groups ($r = -.64$ and $-.66$ for the groups with and without LD, respectively). General academic self-efficacy was not significantly related to procrastination for the group with LD ($r = .06$) and was modestly inversely related to procrastination for the group without LD ($r = -.25$). Significant negative correlations with procrastination were also seen in both groups for metacognitive self-regulation and help-seeking behavior. The results of standard multiple regression showed that, for the group with LD, the three motivation variables of self-efficacy for self-regulation, metacognitive self-regulation, and help-seeking significantly predicted procrastination, $R^2 = .44$, $F(3, 100) = 25.52$, $p < .001$. Self-efficacy for self-regulation was the strongest predictor of procrastination for the group with LD ($\beta = .616$), and help seeking also inversely predicted procrastination ($\beta = -.177$). For the group without LD, the three motivation variables as a group significantly predicted procrastination, $R^2 = .46$, $F(3, 106) = 29.07$, $p < .001$. Self-efficacy for self-regulation was again the strongest predictor of procrastination ($\beta = -.515$), but for the group without LD, metacognitive self-regulation was a significant predictor ($\beta = -.236$), and help-seeking did not significantly predict procrastination.

To summarize, in the absence of any previous procrastination research involving individuals with LD, we wondered whether procrastination operates the same way for students who have LD as for those without LD in a college or university setting. Although not specifically designed to address procrastination in writing, based on previous research that highlights writing as being especially prone to procrastination (e.g., Solomon & Rothblum, 1984), we believe our results are relevant to writing research. There are two important findings from this study. First, individuals with LD reported higher levels of procrastination and lower metacognitive self-regulation and self-efficacy for self-regulation than participants without LD. Second, the strongest predictor of procrastination behaviors for both groups was self-efficacy for self-regulation, and for the group without LD, high levels of help seeking significantly decreased procrastination.

Possessing strong self-efficacy beliefs is hypothesized to increase effort, persistence, and resilience, but in this study, general academic self-efficacy was not related to procrastination for the group with LD, although self-efficacy for self-regulation was a strong (inverse) predictor of procrastination. The explanation for this finding might be found in the studies presented in the first part of this chapter in which individuals with LD were shown to display "too much confidence," wherein the miscalibrations or overconfidence of individuals with LD led to *lower* academic performance and a certain unawareness of task demands. In the procrastination study, undergraduates with LD who reported high levels of general academic self-efficacy—to "understand the most difficult material," "do an excellent job on the assignments and tests," and "master the skills being taught"—did not report lower levels of procrastination. For these students, possessing too much general academic confidence might be a warning sign that they are at risk for dysfunctional self-regulation strategies and for delaying and avoiding task completion. This same overconfidence effect did not hold true with the self-efficacy for self-regulation variable, with its specific examples of self-regulation (e.g., "How well can you ... study when there are other interesting things to do/take notes during class/arrange a place to study without distractions?"). For students with LD, a strong sense of self-efficacy for self-regulation, coupled with a willingness to seek help from others, acted as a preventative against academic procrastination.

IMPLICATIONS AND FUTURE RESEARCH

In this chapter we have examined how the motivation beliefs of students with LD might influence writing performance. We reviewed the literature examining self-efficacy, writing, and LD and summarized the results of three studies that explored the academic motivation of adolescents with LD. The review of the literature found students with LD to be prone to overconfidence and found that beliefs about writing were more likely to be inflated in comparison with beliefs in other academic areas. In the first study reported, adolescents with LD overestimated their spelling ability by 52% and their writing ability by 19%, and they continued to hold optimistic beliefs about spelling even after they had completed the task. We also reported results from a qualitative study in which we interviewed adolescents with LD and their teachers and found that adolescents with LD believed that they accurately calibrated their self-efficacy and performance, whereas their teachers perceived them to be "way too overconfident," for many academic tasks. In addition, teachers believed that calibration accuracy increased as students with LD progressed through high school. Results from the third study found that students with LD reported higher levels of procrastination than students without LD and that, although general academic self-efficacy was not correlated with procrastination for students with LD, self-efficacy for self-regulation was associated with lower levels of procrastination for all students. A theme running through this chapter is that students with LD display a motivational pattern that operates differently from that of students without LD.

The results from the procrastination study suggest that individuals with LD may procrastinate more on academic tasks such as writing than do their peers without LD, perhaps due to a false sense of confidence in general academic abilities but also, paradoxically, because of a lack of confidence in regulating their own learning. Students with LD may express confidence that they are capable of carrying out a general academic task, but at the same time they possess less confidence that they can carry out specific actions to ensure optimal learning. It is important to note that the participants in our study—students with LD who are studying in a college or university setting—may possess a unique pattern of achievement and motivation not found in lower educational levels such as elementary or secondary schools. The high levels of general academic self-efficacy reported by our undergraduate participants may act as a preventative that allows them to overcome the obstacles of their learning difficulties.

Four Suggestions for Practitioners

Our motivation research suggests four key points that teachers and parents need to be aware of in their quest to understand and improve the writing of students with LD. First, poor writers may display unexpectedly high confidence about their writing abilities, and this "naïve optimism" may mask real problems in awareness of the complex demands of most writing tasks. Teachers and parents need to be aware that for students with learning problems such as LD, high levels of confidence might not signal healthy confidence about capabilities but might instead cover up poor task analysis, limited self-awareness, and critical skills deficits and also might serve an important self-protective role. Pajares (1996) suggests, and we concur, that teachers should focus on improving their students' calibration through improved task understanding, rather than focusing on lowering students' efficacy beliefs.

Second, because writing achievement is strongly related to confidence in self-regulating, teachers need to directly instruct students with and without LD in how to manage the demands of writing. Students with LD need to learn how to judge how long the various steps of a writing task might take, they need to know how to structure a writing task, and they need to be aware of how to work around any specific areas of writing weakness. When students learn to develop self-regulatory strategies, they become better writers (Pajares, 2003) and more motivated and successful students (Pintrich & De Groot, 1990). But direct teaching of self-regulatory strategies is not enough. Our third suggestion is that teachers need to monitor the self-regulatory confidence of students with LD. For students with LD, expressions of general academic confidence may conceal a lack of confidence in specific self-regulatory skills. The confidence to implement self-regulation comes from successful past experiences, verbal persuasion from teachers and parents, observation of successful implementation of self-regulation strategies by others, and interpretation of emotional and physiological responses to academic success.

Finally, our research suggests that encouraging students to seek help will minimize procrastination and improve writing quality. Students with LD need to develop independent learning skills, but they also need access to learning support that—especially in adolescence—is offered in a considerate and careful manner (see Klassen & Lynch, 2007).

Future Research

Because the goal of motivation research is ultimately to improve students' performance, future research needs to examine the educational implications of overly optimistic self-efficacy beliefs. Is naïve self-efficacy a problem that needs solving, or does it serve a useful purpose for some people in some settings? The answer is probably both, with educators needing to be aware of the problems that inappropriately high confidence beliefs are likely masking but also to be sensitive to the protective role played by these beliefs. The students with LD in the studies described in this chapter were perhaps naïvely optimistic, but they were experiencing a degree of academic success, so their optimism may have played an important role in building resilience. Future studies investigating the motivation beliefs of students with LD should focus on whether or not developing task analysis skills, strategy use, and metacognitive awareness results in more accurate self-efficacy beliefs and improved writing. In many studies, students with LD display comparatively low self-efficacy for self-regulation, and this lower level of confidence in managing learning may prove to be an important key in designing writing remediation for students with LD. Poor writers need more than just instruction in *how* to write; they need explicit instruction in self-regulation and strategy use. It is these metacognitive self-regulation skills that will increase confidence in and motivation for writing and ultimately increase the quality of writing (Pressley & Harris, 2006).

In the area of procrastination research, we propose that the next stage involve an attempt to ascertain whether the patterns seen in the undergraduate population hold true with younger students.

We also believe a qualitative exploration of the ways in which academic procrastination and academic motivation interact and are experienced by students with LD would provide additional depth and insight into this phenomenon. In-depth qualitative research with students with LD can help researchers and practitioners better understand the emotional and academic consequences of motivational dysfunction and encourage the discovery of ways to build healthy motivation beliefs that foster optimal learning.

NOTE

1. For the purposes of this chapter we focus on students with learning disabilities (LD), but we also discuss the writing of students with other learning difficulties. We use the term *LD* to refer to disorders that affect the acquisition, organization, retention, and understanding of information (Learning Disabilities Association of Canada, 2002). Individuals with LD have specific learning difficulties that cannot be attributed to inadequate instruction, environmental factors, or other handicapping disorders. Most of the research we review in this chapter involves individuals who have LD who are diagnosed by psychologists using conventional definitions, usually based on IQ–achievement discrepancy. Much debate has ensued over definitional issues, and we applaud ongoing changes to traditional LD definitions, but in this chapter we do not address root causes of learning problems, and we take the stance that although etiologies of learning difficulties may differ, the interventions for and solutions to many learning problems share more similarities than differences. Many of the findings emerging from motivation research involving participants with LD also apply to individuals with more generalized learning problems, that is, those who struggle with writing for reasons other than LD.

REFERENCES

Anderman, E. M., & Maehr, M. L. (1994). Motivation and schooling in the middle grades. *Review of Educational Research, 64,* 287–309.

Bandura, A. (1997). *Self-efficacy: The exercise of control.* New York: Freeman.

Bereiter, C., & Scardamalia, M. (1987). *The psychology of written composition.* Hillsdale, NJ: Erlbaum.

Bong, M., & Skaalvik, E. M. (2003). Academic self-concept and self-efficacy: How different are they really? *Educational Psychology Review, 15,* 1–40.

Bruning, R., & Horn, C. (2000). Developing motivation to write. *Educational Psychologist, 35,* 25–37.

Butler, D. L. (1998). Metacognition and learning disabilities. In B. Y. L. Wong (Ed.), *Learning about learning disabilities* (2nd ed., pp. 277–307). New York: Academic Press.

Chapman, J. W. (1988). Cognitive-motivational characteristics and academic achievement of learning disabled children: A longitudinal study. *Journal of Educational Psychology, 80,* 357–365.

Creswell, J. W. (1998). *Qualitative inquiry and research design: Choosing among five traditions.* Thousand Oaks, CA: Sage.

Ellis, A., & Knaus, W. J. (1977). *Overcoming procrastination.* New York: New American Library.

Ferrari, J. R., Johnson, J. L., & McCown, W. G. (1995). *Procrastination and task avoidance: Theory, research, and treatment.* New York: Plenum Press.

Ferrari, J. R., O'Callaghan, J., & Newbegin, I. (2005). Prevalence of procrastination in the United States, United Kingdom, and Australia: Arousal and avoidance delays among adults. *North American Journal of Psychology, 7,* 1–6.

Ferrari, J. R., & Scher, S. J. (2000). Toward an understanding of academic and nonacademic tasks procrastinated by students: The use of daily logs. *Psychology in the Schools, 37,* 359–366.

Flavell, J. H. (1976). Metacognitive aspects of problem solving. In L. B. Resnick (Ed.), *The nature of intelligence* (pp. 231–235). Hillsdale, NJ: Erlbaum.

Fritzsche, B. A., Young, B. R., & Hickson, K. C. (2003). Individual differences in academic procrastination tendency and writing success. *Personality and Individual Differences, 35,* 1549–1557.

Gans, A. M., Kenny, M. C., & Ghany, D. L. (2003). Comparing the self-concept of students with and without learning disabilities. *Journal of Learning Disabilities, 36,* 287–295.

Grolnick, W. S., & Ryan, R. M. (1990). Self-perceptions, motivation, and adjustment in children with learning disabilities: A multiple group comparison study. *Journal of Learning Disabilities, 23,* 177–184.

Haycock, L. A., McCarthy, P., & Skay, C. L. (1998). Procrastination in college students: The role of self-efficacy and anxiety. *Journal of Counseling and Development, 76,* 317–324.

Hooper, S. R., Swartz, C. W., Montgomery, J. W., Reed, M. S., Brown, T. T., Wasileski, T. J., et al. (1993). Prevalence of writing problems across three middle school samples. *School Psychology Review, 22,* 610–622.

Howell, A. J., Watson, D. C., Powell, R. A., & Buro, K. (2006). Academic procrastination: The pattern and correlates of behavioral postponement. *Personality and Individual Differences*, 40, 1519–1530.

James, W. (2001). *Psychology: The briefer course.* Toronto, Ontario, Canada: General. (Original work published 1892)

James, W., & James, H. (2003). *Letters of William James.* Kila, MT: Kessinger. (Original work published 1920)

Klassen, R. M. (2002a). A question of calibration: A review of the self-efficacy beliefs of students with learning disabilities. *Learning Disability Quarterly*, 25, 88–103.

Klassen, R. M. (2002b). Writing in early adolescence: A review of the role of self-efficacy beliefs. *Educational Psychology Review*, 14, 173–203.

Klassen, R. M. (2007). Using predictions to learn about the self-efficacy of early adolescents with and without learning disabilities. *Contemporary Educational Psychology*, 32, 173–187.

Klassen, R. M., & Lynch, S. L. (2007). Self-efficacy from the perspective of adolescents with learning disabilities and their specialist teachers. *Journal of Learning Disabilities*, 40, 494–507.

Klassen, R. M., Krawchuk, L. L., Lynch, S. L., & Rajani, S. (2008). Procrastination, motivation, and individuals with learning disabilities. *Learning Disabilities Research and Practice*, 23, 137–147.

Kruger, J., & Dunning, D. (1999). Unskilled and unaware of it: How difficulties in recognizing one's own incompetence lead to inflated self-assessments. *Journal of Personality and Social Psychology*, 77, 1121–1134.

Learning Disabilities Association of Canada. (2002). Official definition of learning disabilities. Retrieved September 15, 2006, from *ldac-taac.ca/Defined/defined_new-e.asp*.

Lee, E. (2005). The relationship of motivation and flow experience to academic procrastination in university students. *Journal of Genetic Psychology*, 166, 5–14.

Licht, B. G. (1992). The achievement-related perceptions of children with learning problems: A developmental analysis. In D. H. Schunk & J. L. Meece (Eds.), *Student perceptions in the classroom* (pp. 247–264). Hillsdale, NJ: Erlbaum.

Licht, B. G., & Kirstner, J. A. (1986). Motivational problems of learning-disabled children: Individual differences and their implications for treatment. In J. K. Torgesen & B. Y. L. Wong (Eds.), *Psychological and educational perspectives on learning disabilities* (pp. 225–255). New York: Harcourt Brace Jovanovich.

Meltzer, L., Roditi, B., Houser, R. F., Jr., & Perlman, M. (1998). Perceptions of academic strategies and competence in students with learning disabilities. *Journal of Learning Disabilities*, 31, 437–451.

Milgram, N. (1991). Procrastination. In R. Dulbecco (Ed.), *Encyclopedia of human biology* (Vol. 6, pp. 149–155). New York: Academic Press.

Miyake, N., & Norman, D. (1978). To ask a question, one must know enough to know what is not known. *Journal of Verbal Learning and Verbal Behavior*, 18, 357–364.

Onwuegbuzie, A. J., & Collins, K. M. T. (2001). Writing apprehension and academic procrastination among graduate students. *Perceptual and Motor Skills, 92,* 560–562.

Pajares, F. (1996). Self-efficacy beliefs in academic settings. *Review of Educational Research, 66,* 543–578.

Pajares, F. (2003). Self-efficacy beliefs, motivation, and achievement in writing: A review of the literature. *Reading and Writing Quarterly: Overcoming Learning Difficulties, 19,* 139–158.

Pajares, F., & Valiante, G. (2006). Self-efficacy beliefs and motivation in writing development. In C. A. MacArthur, S. Graham, & J. Fitzgerald (Eds.), *Handbook of writing research* (pp. 158–170). New York: Guilford Press.

Paris, S. G., & Winograd, P. (1990). How metacognition can promote academic learning and instruction. In B. F. Jones & L. Idol (Eds.), *Dimensions of thinking and cognitive instruction* (pp. 15–51). Hillsdale, NJ: Erlbaum.

Pintrich, P. R., & De Groot, E. V. (1990). Motivational and self-regulated learning components of classroom academic performance. *Journal of Educational Psychology, 82,* 33–40.

Pintrich, P. R., Smith D. A. F., Garcia, T., & McKeachie, W. J. (1993). Reliability and predictive validity of the Motivated Strategies for Learning Questionnaire (MSLQ). *Educational and Psychological Measurement, 53,* 801–813.

Pressley, M., & Harris, K. R. (2006). Cognitive strategies instruction: From basic research to classroom instruction. In C. A. MacArthur, S. Graham, & J. Fitzgerald (Eds.), *Handbook of writing research* (pp. 265–286). New York: Guilford Press.

Rosenthal, J. (1973). Self-esteem in dyslexic children. *Academic Therapy, 9,* 27–33.

Scher, S. J., & Osterman, N. M. (2002). Procrastination, conscientiousness, anxiety, and goals: Exploring the measurement and correlates of procrastination among school-aged children. *Psychology in the Schools, 39,* 385–398.

Scholz, U., Doña, B. G., Sud, S., & Schwarzer, R. (2002). Is general self-efficacy a universal construct? *European Journal of Psychological Assessment, 18,* 242–251.

Schwarzer, R., & Born, A. (1997). Optimistic self-beliefs: Assessment of general perceived self-efficacy in thirteen cultures. *World Psychology, 3,* 177–190.

Solomon, L. J., & Rothblum, E. D. (1984). Academic procrastination: Frequency and cognitive behavioral correlates. *Journal of Counseling Psychology, 31,* 503–509.

Sridhar, D., & Vaughn, S. (2001). Social functioning of students with learning disabilities. In D. P. Hallahan & B. K. Keogh (Eds.), *Research and global perspectives in learning disabilities* (pp. 65–92). Mahwah, NJ: Erlbaum.

Stipek, D. J. (1998). *Motivation to learn: From theory to practice.* Needham Heights, MA: Allyn & Bacon.

Tabassam, W., & Grainger, J. (2002). Self-concept, attributional style and self-efficacy beliefs of students with learning disabilities with and without attention deficit hyperactivity disorder. *Learning Disability Quarterly, 25,* 141–151.

Torrance, M., & Galbraith, D. (2006). The processing demands of writing. In C. A. MacArthur, S. Graham, & J. Fitzgerald (Eds.), *Handbook of writing research* (pp. 67–80). New York: Guilford Press.

Troia, G. A. (2006). Writing instruction for students with learning disabilities. In C. A. MacArthur, S. Graham, & J. Fitzgerald (Eds.), *Handbook of writing research* (pp. 324–336). New York: Guilford Press.

Tuckman, B. W. (1991). The development and concurrent validity of the procrastination scale. *Educational and Psychological Measurement, 51,* 473–480.

Wolters, C. A. (2003). Understanding procrastination from a self-regulated learning perspective. *Journal of Educational Psychology, 95,* 179–187.

Wong, B. Y. L., Butler, D. L., Ficzere, S. A., & Kuperis, S. (1996). Teaching low achievers and students with learning disabilities to plan, write, and revise opinion essays. *Journal of Learning Disabilities, 29,* 197–212.

Zimmerman, B. J. (2000). Self-efficacy: An essential motive to learn. *Contemporary Educational Psychology, 25,* 82–91.

Zimmerman, B. J., Bandura, A., & Martinez-Pons, M. (1992). Self-motivation for academic attainment: The role of self-efficacy beliefs and personal goal-setting. *American Educational Research Journal, 29,* 663–676.

Part II

CONTEMPORARY CLASSROOM WRITING INSTRUCTION AND STRUGGLING WRITERS

The Effects of Writing Workshop Instruction on the Performance and Motivation of Good and Poor Writers

GARY A. TROIA
SHIN-JU C. LIN
BRANDON W. MONROE
STEVEN COHEN

Nearly 25 years ago, a paradigm shift occurred in writing instruction in America's schools. Prior to that time, traditional approaches to teaching writing were characterized by teacher-directed lessons on discrete skills using contrived writing assignments, infrequent requests to compose texts longer than a few paragraphs, and a focus on the attributes (especially the conventions) of a finished product over the processes used to generate texts (e.g., Pollington, Wilcox, & Morrison, 2001; Tidwell & Steele, 1995). The seminal work of such individuals as Donald Graves (1983), Lucy Calkins (1986), and Nancy Atwell (1987), coupled with the cognitive model of writing developed by Hayes and Flower (1980), paved the way for the widespread adoption of process-oriented writing instruction and, in particular, writing workshop in elementary classrooms in the mid-1980s. Writing workshop varies in how it is instantiated, but the key elements include (1) minilessons on workshop procedures, writing skills (e.g., spelling patterns, punctuation rules), composition strategies (e.g., timelines for planning biographies, editing checklists), and craft elements (e.g., writing quality traits, effective leads for exposition); (2) sustained time (about 20–30 minutes) for personally meaningful writing nearly every day to help students become comfortable with the writing process (i.e., planning, drafting, revising, editing, and publishing) and with varied writing tasks with different purposes; (3) teacher- and student-led conferences about writing plans and written products to help students appropriate habits of mind associated with good writers and make the most of their writing; and (4) frequent opportunities for sharing with others, sometimes through formal publishing activities, to enhance the authenticity of writing activities and cultivate a sense of community. Contemporary approaches to writing instruction that emphasize the writing process generally appear to be associated with better writing outcomes, at least in terms of written products, than traditional approaches (e.g., Bruno, 1983; Graham & Perin, 2007; Hamilton, 1992; Hillocks, 1984; Honeycutt & Pritchard, 2005; Monteith, 1991; Scannella, 1982; Varble, 1990), though the number and quality of studies that have examined this issue are limited. However, a process-oriented approach does not necessarily yield a more positive motivational stance toward writing (cf. Bottomley, Truscott, Marinak, Henk, & Melnick, 1999; Honeycutt & Pritchard, 2005; Monteith, 1991; Pollington et al., 2001; Scannella, 1982).

Teachers today typically employ some form of process writing instruction such as writing workshop in their classrooms (e.g., Bridge, Compton-Hall, & Cantrell, 1997; Patthey-Chavez, Matsumura, & Valdes, 2004; Wray, Medwell, Fox, & Poulson, 2000). According to data collected through the National Assessment of Educational Progress (NAEP), nearly 7 out of 10 teachers reported using process-oriented instruction to teach written composition. Yet no more than a third of those same teachers said they spend 90 minutes or more per week teaching writing. Additionally, many of the teachers surveyed reported that they infrequently ask their students to produce multiple drafts or revise and edit their work (National Center for Education Statistics, 1999). Clare, Valdez, and Patthey-Chavez (2000) found that nearly 60% of teachers' comments on narrative and expository papers written by students in third- and seventh-grade classes in which process instruction was used were directed at microstructural concerns about correct usage of writing conventions rather than macrostructural elements such as content, organization, and style. Thus there is some question about just how teachers define and implement process writing instruction in their classrooms.

Recent evidence suggests that teachers do indeed display quite a bit of variability in how they enact process-oriented instruction and that this variability is influenced by their epistemologies, their experiences as teachers and writers, and their teaching context (Graham, Harris, Fink, & MacArthur, 2001; Graham, Harris, MacArthur, & Fink, 2002; Lipson,

Mosenthal, Daniels, & Woodside-Jiron, 2000; Pritchard & Honeycutt, 2006; Tschannen-Moran, Woolfolk-Hoy, & Hoy, 1998). For example, Lipson et al. (2000) observed that 11 fifth-grade teachers who reported using process writing instruction differed in how much control they exerted over students' writing, in their treatment of the writing process as a flexible tool versus an object of study, and in how central peer- and teacher-led conferences were to explicit writing instruction. Moreover, these differences in teaching practices were linked to one of four different theoretical orientations regarding writing instruction. Agate and Graham (in press) found that about three-quarters of a national sample of primary grade teachers reported using a combination of process-oriented instruction and skill-based instruction, whereas the rest used one or the other, and that 65% of teachers reported that they did not use a commercial program (which potentially could help standardize writing instruction) to teach writing. They also found that teachers varied considerably in their use of specific instructional practices and in how much instructional time they allotted for composing texts of a paragraph or longer in length (median of about 20 minutes per day). Such variability helps explain the lackluster performance of America's children and youths on the NAEP writing assessment (Persky, Daane, & Jin, 2003). The NAEP for writing is administered approximately every 4 years to a representative sample of students in grades 4, 8, and 12. Each student responds to two 25-minute narrative, informative, or persuasive prompts accompanied by a brochure with guidelines for planning and revising the compositions. Each paper is rated on a 6-point rubric, and this score is converted to a scale score (ranging from 0–300). The scale score corresponds to one of four levels of performance—below basic, basic (partial mastery of fundamental knowledge and skills), proficient (solid mastery needed to perform challenging academic tasks), or advanced (superior mastery). According to published NAEP data, only 28% of 4th graders, 31% of 8th graders, and 24% of 12th graders achieved at or above a proficient level of writing performance in 2002. Furthermore, the writing performance of students from culturally diverse households is substantially inferior to that of middle-class Caucasian students.

Struggling writers, who may come from marginalized families or live in impoverished neighborhoods, typically write papers that are shorter, more poorly organized, and weaker in overall quality than those written by their peers (e.g., Graham & Harris, 1991; Thomas, Englert, & Gregg, 1987). In addition, these students' compositions typically contain more irrelevant information and more mechanical and grammatical errors that render their texts less readable (Fulk & Stormont-Spurgin, 1995; Graham & Harris, 1991; Thomas et al., 1987). The problems experienced by struggling writers are attributable, in part, to their difficulties with executing and regulating the processes underlying proficient composing, especially planning and revising (e.g., Englert, Raphael, Fear, & Anderson, 1988; Graham & Harris, 1997; Graham, Harris, & Troia, 1998). Motivational factors such as negative self-efficacy beliefs also are causally related to struggling writers' diminished performance (e.g., Pajares, 2003; Troia, Shankland, & Wolbers, in press). Although NAEP data suggest that writing instruction in today's classrooms is not adequate to meet the needs of these students, it is not clear exactly how weak writers respond to writing workshop instruction in comparison with their more accomplished peers and how variability in enacting process-oriented instruction might influence student writing performance and motivation. The study we report here was designed to answer these questions, particularly how writing workshop affects growth in writing for good and poor writers. This study was part of a larger investigation that examined school, teacher, and student characteristics that influence teachers' capacity for adopting innovative writing instruction practices and how the interplay of these characteristics and practices affects student performance.

INVESTIGATIVE METHODS

We conducted our investigation during the 2002–2003 school year in an urban school, Cascadia Elementary (a pseudonym), located in the Seattle metropolitan area. Cascadia Elementary in many ways represents a typical urban school (see Table 3.1). Three-quarters of the students receive free or reduced-price meals, and thus the school qualifies for Title I funding. The student population is racially, ethnically, and linguistically diverse—only about 7% are Caucasian, and almost 20% are classified as English language learners. Yet this school appears to be "bucking the odds," because nearly 6 out of every 10 students in the fourth grade, even those from low-income families, have met or exceeded standards on the Washington Assessment of Student Learning (WASL; see Table 3.1), the state's key accountability measure, in reading (WASL-R) and writing (WASL-W).

The year before our investigation, staff at Cascadia had agreed that a focus on high-quality literacy teaching and learning was a priority. This focus was meaningfully aligned with prior professional development activities at the school, including those provided by a local nonprofit agency (see later in the chapter). As a result, all staff participated in sustained literacy instruction training aimed at increasing their use of evidence-based strategies for reading and writing, including word study (e.g., structural analysis, vocabulary in context), varied approaches to reading instruction (sustained silent reading, guided reading, teacher

TABLE 3.1. Cascadia Elementary School Demographics and WASL Performance Data

Student characteristic	Percent enrollment (*n* = 418)	Number of fourth graders tested	% met/ exceeded WASL-R standard	% met/ exceeded WASL-W standard	% met/ exceeded WASL-M standard
Gender					
Male	54.8	33	54.5	51.5	45.5
Female	45.2	33	60.6	63.6	45.5
Race/ethnicity					
Black	46.2	25	64.0	60.0	40.0
Asian	31.6	24	58.3	62.5	54.2
Hispanic	13.4	12	50.0	41.7	33.3
White	7.2	4	N/A	N/A	N/A
Native American	1.7	1	N/A	N/A	N/A
All students		66	56.7	56.7	44.8
Free/reduced meals	74.8		57.6	57.6	45.5
Title I reading	—		56.3	59.4	45.3
ESL	18.5		21.4	35.7	14.3
Special education	11.1		—	—	—

Note. All enrolled fourth graders were tested in all three domains. WASL performance data for white and Native American students were not available from the state because fewer than 10 students in each category were tested.

read-aloud, partner reading), writing-to-learn activities (e.g., academic journals, reading response logs, mini-lessons, collaborative writing), student self-assessment, and leveled books to accommodate diverse reading abilities in the classroom.

Participants

Six teachers volunteered to participate in our larger research project, and each was asked to nominate 6 children from his or her classroom to serve as participants in our examination of the impact of writing workshop instruction on children's writing motivation and writing performance. The teachers were instructed to identify 2 strong writers, 2 average writers, and 2 weak writers based on the students' classroom writing performance. Ten strong writers, 11 average writers, and 10 weak writers were included in the study. Two students moved before the completion of the study, one (a 5th grader) was expelled, and replacements could not be found for another 2 students whose parents did not grant permission for inclusion. Of the 31 participants, 6 were 2nd graders, 14 were 3rd graders, 6 were 4th graders, and 5 were 5th graders. Two students received special education services for learning disabilities, and both were identified as weak writers by their teachers. Three other students were designated English language learners and were identified as average writers by their teachers. Nearly 50% of the sample were African American, about 25% were European American, about 22% were Asian American, and one student (3%) was of undetermined ethnicity. Approximately 30% of the sample came from homes in which the caregiver(s) held occupations coded as 5 or lower (out of 9) on the Hollingshead Occupational Scale (1975).

Norm-Referenced Measures

In October, we administered a battery of standardized norm-referenced assessment tasks to children to verify the teachers' nominations of strong, average, and weak writers. Specifically, we assessed students' reading abilities and writing skills, which were significantly correlated (rs ranged from .61 to .91). All tasks were administered individually (or, in the case of most of the writing tasks, in a small group of 3–4 students) in a quiet room at the school. The writing measures were administered again in May to help determine how much progress students made in their writing.

Reading Abilities

Four tasks from Form A of the Woodcock–Johnson–III Tests of Achievement (WJ-III; Woodcock, McGrew, & Mather, 2001) were administered to evaluate each student's reading abilities: the Letter–Word Identification, Word Attack, Reading Fluency, and Passage Comprehension subtests. The Letter–Word Identification subtest requires students to read aloud upper- and lower-case letters and real words. For the Word Attack subtest, children pronounce phonologically and orthographically regular pseudowords. For the Reading Fluency subtest, students are given 3 minutes to respond to as many printed statements as possible by indicating whether the sentences are true or false. Finally, the Passage Comprehension subtest requires students to read short passages and identify the missing word in each passage that makes sense given the passage context. For all but the Reading Fluency subtest, testing proceeds until a ceiling of six consecutive incorrect responses is reached. The median internal-consistency reliability coefficients for the Letter–Word Identification, Word Attack, Reading Fluency, and Passage Comprehension subtests are .91, .87, .90, and .83, respectively, for students between 5 and 19 years old. The test–retest correlations (1-year interval) for these subtests range from .70 (Reading Fluency) to .86 (Passage Comprehension).

Writing Skills

Five tasks from Form A of the WJ-III Tests of Achievement (Woodcock et al., 2001) were administered to evaluate each student's writing skills: the Writing Fluency, Writing Samples, Spelling, Punctuation/Capitalization, and Editing subtests. The Writing Fluency subtest is a timed measure in which students are provided with a picture stimulus and three related words for each test item and asked to write a complete sentence using the words. Students finish as many items as possible in 7 minutes. Errors in writing mechanics are not penalized. For the Writing Samples subtest, children are asked to write relevant sentences in response to pictures, topic prompts, and incomplete paragraphs, sometimes using specified vocabulary. Errors in writing mechanics are generally not penalized. The Spelling subtest uses a common dictated spelling word format—the word is read by the examiner, read in sentence context, and then read again in isolation and the student is expected to write the target word. The Punctuation/Capitalization subtest also uses a dictation format—children are read words and phrases to write that require the application of various rules for punctuation and capitalization. For the Editing subtest, students must verbally identify and correct errors in capitalization, punctuation, spelling, and grammar in written sentences and paragraphs. For all but the Writing Fluency and Writing Samples subtests, testing proceeds until a ceiling of six consecutive incorrect responses is obtained. The median internal-consistency reliability coefficients for the Writing Fluency, Writing Samples, Spelling, Punctuation/Capitalization, and Editing subtests are .86, .84, .89, .77, and .91, respectively, for students between 5 and 19 years old. The test–retest correlations (1-year interval) for these subtests range from .63 (Editing) to .88 (Spelling).

Experimental Measures

Writing Skills

We administered in October and again in May experimental writing tasks to evaluate students' growth in narrative and persuasive writing. Students were provided with a choice of two prompts and asked to write either a creative, novel story or a persuasive opinion essay in response to one of the prompts. The prompt choices for stories were from a set of four pictures (a boy riding a bike jumps off a ramp while other children watch in amazement, a giant toddler walks across the landscape of a town, a group of men in a sailboat try to avoid being capsized by a storm at sea, and an astronaut working on the surface of a colonized planet watches several spaceships leave orbit). The prompt choices for opinion essays were from a set of four topics ("Do you think children should be allowed to choose the TV shows they watch?" "Should children be allowed to choose their own bedtimes?" "Do you think your parents should decide who your friends are?" and "Do you think children should have to go to school during the summer?"). The prompt choices were counterbalanced across participants and testing time to avoid order effects. Prompts for the stories and essays were administered on separate days within 1 week and were not timed. Spelling assistance was provided if necessary; otherwise, students were not given help or feedback.

Two multidimensional product measures were used to evaluate students' stories and opinion essays: *quality traits* and *structural elements*. *Quality traits* included content (i.e., the degree to which the ideas presented in text are clear, focused, and interesting), organization (i.e., the degree to which the order and structure of the text enhances its meaning), sentence fluency (i.e., the degree to which the sentences are well crafted and varied to increase the flow and rhythm of the piece), word choice (i.e., the degree to which the vocabulary is clear, precise, and vivid), and conventions (i.e., the degree of control over the mechanics of writing, including spelling, capitalization, and punctuation). These traits were derived from the six-traits assessment and feedback framework developed by Spandel (2001). Each trait was scored separately and sequentially (in the order listed) on a 6-point scale (see Appendix 3.1). A trained undergraduate student who did not administer the experimental writing tasks scored the writing samples (these were typed before scoring to increase legibility, though errors in writing conventions were not corrected). A second trained graduate student scored 20% of the writing samples (all the papers generated by 6 of the participants selected at random) to determine the reliability of the quality traits scale. The interjudge reliability coefficients were .87 for content, .77 for organization, .76 for sentence fluency, .79 for word choice, .89 for conventions, and .83 for all traits combined.

Structural elements for narratives and persuasive papers were different due to the unique characteristics of each genre. The elements for stories included the three categories of setting (description of the main character, locale, and time), plot (the initiating event, character goals, attempts to resolve the problem, outcome, and emotional reactions of the main character), and other (title and dialogue). A scale (for previous versions, see Graham & Harris, 1989; Troia, Graham, & Harris, 1999) to evaluate the presence and degree of development of these elements was used to score each narrative paper (see Appendix 3.2). For each element, a score of 0 was awarded if the element was not present, a score of 1 was awarded if the element was present, and a score of 2 was awarded if the element was highly developed. An additional point was awarded if the main character had more than one clearly articulated goal (this never occurred). Likewise, an additional point was awarded if more than one story grammar episode (i.e., a unique plotline including an initiating event, attempt, and direct consequence) was evident (this never occurred). Based on this scoring scheme, we calculated the average for each element category (coincidentally, the maximum average score for each category was 2). A trained graduate student scored the typed writing samples, and a second trained graduate student scored one-fourth of the papers, selected at random, to determine the reliability of the narrative structural elements scale. The interjudge reliability coefficients were .68 for setting, .84 for plot, .89 for other, and .88 for all elements combined. Due to this range in reliability across coding categories, all subsequent analyses were based on the total story structure elements.

The elements for opinion essays included functional components identified by Scardamalia, Bereiter, and Goelman (1982)—premise, reasons, elaborations, and conclusion. A premise is a statement specifying the authors' position on a topic. Reasons are explanations to support or refute the position, another reason, or an elaboration. Elaborations are units of text that qualify or clarify another unit of text. Finally, a conclusion is defined as a summary statement that reiterates the author's position. The guidelines for parsing essays into elements are given in Appendix 3.2. One point was awarded for each functional element, and the total served as the score for each essay. A trained graduate student scored the typed writing samples, and a second trained graduate student scored one-half of the papers, selected at random, to determine the reliability of the persuasive structural elements scoring method. The interjudge reliability coefficients were .87 for premise, .58 for reasons, .66 for elaborations, .88 for conclusion, and .97 for all elements combined. The reliability estimates for reasons and elaborations were depressed because, in some instances, reasons were incorrectly coded as elaborations or vice versa. Due to this range in reliability across coding categories, all subsequent analyses were based on the total essay structure elements.

Motivational Attributes

We administered two experimental motivation scales in October and May—one to assess students' attitudes and self-efficacy beliefs with regard to writing (the Attitudes and Self-Efficacy Rating Scale, or ASERS) and another to assess students' writing-related goal orientations (the Writing Goals Scale, or WGS). Both used a 6-point scale, with 1 representing strong disagreement with a statement and 6 representing strong agreement. The ASERS, adapted from an instrument developed by Graham, Schwartz, and MacArthur (1993), included 14 items and evaluated how much students like to write (e.g., "I do writing of my own outside of school") and the degree to which they view writing as a worthwhile endeavor (e.g., "Writing is a waste of time"), as well as their perceived competence in varied writing tasks (e.g., "When my class is asked to write a story, mine is one of the best"). The WGS, adapted from an instrument developed by Nolen and Valencia (2000), included 18 items and evaluated the degree to which students endorsed three types of goals—task goals (with a focus on learning how to write better; e.g., "In writing, I feel most successful if I see that my writing has really improved"), ego goals (with a focus on displaying one's writing abilities; e.g., "In writing, I feel most successful if I get one of the highest grades on a writing assignment"), and avoidance goals (with a focus on doing as little writing as possible; e.g., "In writing, I feel most successful if I don't have to revise my work"). Evidence of reliability is not available for either of these scales, and our small sample size precluded determining reliability estimates.

Portfolios

We asked each of the six teachers who nominated participants for our study to collect five samples of their target students' writing during the academic year, one approximately every 2 months. We informed teachers that the samples, which were required to represent narrative, expository, and at least one other genre (e.g., persuasive or poetic), would be used to: (1) help document growth in writing, (2) celebrate students' efforts and teachers' instructional success, and (3) facilitate students' critical reading of their own texts. The writing samples also were required to be products of classroom work rather than assignments completed at home. Each writing sample was accompanied by two entry slips—one completed by the teacher that focused on the teacher's instructional goals, methods, evaluation, and future plans and one completed by the student that focused on the student's evaluation and helpful writing strategies (we do not describe the entry slips in more detail here because they were not included in the data analyses for this study). Additionally, each writing sample was accompanied by a quality trait rating scale (described earlier) completed by the teacher—the scores assigned by the teachers were used in our analyses. Two trained students also independently scored 20% of the portfolio samples to determine reliability. The independent raters achieved an interjudge reliability coefficient of .77 for all traits combined. The reliability estimate for teachers' combined scores and those assigned by one of the independent raters was at least .61. Generally, the teachers assigned higher scores than did the independent raters.

Writing Workshop Instruction

The teachers who nominated participants for our study and all the other first- through fifth-grade teachers at Cascadia Elementary were participating in a comprehensive schoolwide program to support their use of writing workshop. The program, developed and managed by a community nonprofit agency serving several low-income schools in the area, included six core components: (1) ongoing professional development opportunities through bimonthly workshops and weekly individual coaching sessions to assist teachers in implementing daily writing instruction; (2) weekly classroom demonstrations to support the orchestrated use of exemplary children's literature, the writing process, and instructed composing knowledge, skills, and strategies; (3) weekly curriculum planning meetings and debriefings in grade-level teams; (4) trained volunteers to help students plan, draft, revise, and publish their work, primarily in the context of individual and small-group conferences; (5) placement of resident authors who shared craft lessons and their love of writing with students and teachers; and (6) publishing opportunities, including book-binding support and public readings. Although the year we conducted our investigation was the first in which the majority of teachers at the school participated in the program, a small group of teachers, including three in our research project, had worked with staff developers from the nonprofit agency for several years.

Much of the instructional content of the professional development program was derived from the work of Donald Graves (1983), Nancy Atwell (1998), Lucy Calkins (1986, 1998), and Ralph Fletcher (Fletcher & Portalupi, 1998, 2001), influential leaders in the dissemination of the writing workshop model. The essential features of this model are listed in Table 3.2 and include authentic and self-guided student work that is typically shared or published, an instructional approach that employs mini-lessons, regular teacher modeling, feedback, and follow-up instruction, and routines for daily workshops, conferring, and collaboration. The teachers devoted 4–5 days per week, 45 minutes per day, to writing workshop instruction. The writing curriculum was rooted in genre study, with each genre cycle lasting about 9 weeks. Thus teachers covered four different genres—personal narrative, expository, poetry, and fictional narrative—during the academic year.

Within each genre cycle, several phases of instruction were employed. First, students experienced immersion, in which they were introduced to the structural elements of the genre, read and listened to touchstone texts that exemplified these elements, and generated "seed" ideas for their papers (e.g., favorite memories, area of expertise). Next, they engaged in planning, in which they selected one of their ideas for further develop-

TABLE 3.2. Essential Features of Writing Workshop Instructional Model

Student work
- Students work on a wide range of composing tasks for multiple authentic audiences and purposes.
- Students often select their own writing topics within a given genre.
- Students work through the writing process at their own pace over a sustained period of time.
- Students present works in progress, as well as completed papers, to other students in and out of the classroom to receive praise and feedback.
- Students' written work is prominently displayed in the classroom and throughout the school.

Instructional approach
- Teacher-directed mini-lessons are designed to help students master workshop procedures (e.g., using writing notebooks, working on multiple compositions simultaneously), craft elements (e.g., text structure, character development), writing skills (e.g., punctuation, capitalization), and process strategies (e.g., planning and revising tactics).
- Teachers overtly model the writing process, writing strategies and skills, and positive attitudes toward writing.
- A common language is used to communicate shared expectations and to give students feedback (e.g., traits).
- Follow-up instruction is provided to facilitate acquisition of target knowledge, skills, and strategies.

Routines
- A typical workshop entails a mini-lesson (10–15 minutes), then an individual progress check (5 minutes), followed by independent writing and conferencing (20–25 minutes), and finally group sharing (5–10 minutes).
- Regular student–teacher conferences are scheduled to discuss progress, establish writing goals, and provide individualized feedback, all in the context of high expectations.
- Collaborative arrangements are established by which students help one another plan, draft, revise, edit, and publish their written work.

---

ment, collected additional information (e.g., discussed their idea with a partner to gauge potential audience interest, researched facts about their topic using primary and secondary sources), learned how to incorporate unique text features (e.g., dialogue, key vocabulary and phrases, captions), and organized all the information they had gathered (e.g., completed a timeline or planning sheet). Then students drafted their compositions, receiving substantial teacher and peer support through conferences. In these conferences, students shared their work, discussed how they were using what had been taught, and received extensive feedback. Following drafting, students revised their papers, reading and sharing their texts multiple times. During this phase of instruction, the bulk of assistance was provided through conferencing, though mini-lessons were devised to help students improve their writing through adding supporting details, zooming in on pivotal moments, and deleting trivial information. Then students edited their work with an editing checklist, both independently and with a peer. Finally, they published their work.

The observations we conducted throughout the school year in each classroom indicated that each teacher generally adhered to the writing workshop model, which was anticipated given the level of support provided by the professional development staff. Specifically, the teachers displayed use of between 70 and 85% of 27 critical workshop features we identified (these closely aligned with those listed in Table 3.2). However, teachers differed with respect to the specific management procedures (e.g., external reinforcement, physical arrangements), student engagement tactics (e.g., checking in, degree of autonomy), and instructional supports (e.g., materials, communicative transactions) they used. Because of space constraints, we do not discuss these variations here but report them elsewhere (see Troia, Lin, Cohen, & Monroe, in preparation).

EMPIRICAL FINDINGS

Group Differences at Pretest

We first compared the performances of the strong, average, and weak writers on the norm-referenced measures of reading achievement (means and standard deviations are given in Table 3.3) with multivariate analysis of variance (MANOVA) and associated post hoc pairwise multiple comparisons. There was a significant multivariate effect, $F(8, 50) = 3.93$, $p < .01$, and subsequent univariate tests showed group effects for all four WJ-III reading measures: Letter–Word Identification, $F(2, 28) = 20.34$, $p < .01$, $MSE = 104.95$; Word Attack, $F(2, 28) = 14.23$, $p < .01$, $MSE = 103.67$; Reading Fluency, $F(2, 28) = 8.03$, $p < .01$, $MSE = 180.88$; and Passage Comprehension, $F(2, 28) = 11.41$, $p < .01$, $MSE = 118.95$. On each reading subtest, strong and average writers performed similarly to each other and outperformed the weak writers.

We then conducted MANOVA with the WJ-III writing subtests administered at pretest (see Table 3.3 for means and standard deviations) as criterion measures in order to confirm the teachers' nominations of three distinct groups of writers. There was a significant multivariate effect, $F(10, 48) = 3.29$, $p < .01$, and subsequent univariate tests showed group effects for all five measures: Writing Fluency, $F(2, 28) = 12.53$, $p < .01$, $MSE = 367.81$; Writing Samples, $F(2, 28) = 13.18$, $p < .01$, $MSE = 117.50$; Spelling, $F(2, 28) = 14.95$, $p < .01$, $MSE = 134.89$; Punctuation/ Capitalization, $F(2, 28) = 7.15$, $p < .01$, $MSE = 183.70$; and Editing $F(2, 28) = 5.58$, $p < .01$, $MSE = 389.50$. On all but two of these subtests, strong writers performed better than weak writers, and average writers performed better than weak writers, though strong and average

TABLE 3.3. Literacy Achievement at the Beginning of the School Year for Teacher-Nominated Strong, Average, and Weak Writers

Test	Weak ($n = 10$)	Average ($n = 11$)	Strong ($n = 10$)
WJ-II Reading			
Letter–Word	85.90 (9.41)	105.25 (11.58)	114.80 (9.85)
Word Attack	87.30 (12.88)	103.33 (7.55)	111.20 (9.47)
RFluency	85.10 (15.93)	102.92 (11.43)	108.30 (12.53)
Passage Comp	83.90 (11.95)	99.17 (8.76)	106.90 (11.80)
WJ-III Writing			
WFluency	79.60 (31.78)	111.64 (6.15)	120.20 (9.59)
WSamples	92.00 (14.51)	111.00 (9.42)	115.30 (7.51)
Spelling	83.60 (14.29)	103.82 (10.42)	110.90 (9.73)
Punct/Cap	86.00 (12.50)	94.40 (17.94)	108.90 (6.10)
Editing	84.00 (29.85)	102.90 (10.05)	112.40 (13.23)

writers performed similarly. On the Punctuation/Capitalization and Editing subtests, however, strong writers obtained significantly higher scores than weak writers, but average writers did not differ from either of these groups.

Given the results of these post hoc comparisons, which failed to verify the teachers' nominations, we conducted pairwise MANOVAs for strong versus average writers, average versus weak writers, and strong versus weak writers. There was not a significant multivariate effect for group when comparing strong and average writers, $F(5, 15) = 1.97$, $p > .14$, but there was when comparing average and weak writers, $F(5, 15) = 2.98$, $p < .05$, and strong and weak writers, $F(5, 14) = 5.61$, $p < .01$. These findings, in conjunction with those from the analyses of students' entering reading achievement, suggested that there were only two distinct groups of writers in our sample—good and poor writers. Consequently, we combined the strong and average writers into a single group for all subsequent data analyses. The descriptive statistics for good and poor writers are presented in Table 3.4.

We compared the good and poor writers on the pretest writing measures using MANOVA and obtained a significant multivariate effect, $F(5, 25) = 7.01$, $p < .01$. Subsequent univariate tests showed significant group differences favoring the good writers for all five writing subtests: Writing Fluency, $F(1, 29) = 23.99$, $p < .01$, $MSE = 368.37$; Writing Samples, $F(1, 29) = 25.70$, $p < .01$, $MSE = 116.79$; Spelling, $F(1, 29) = 27.06$, $p < .01$, $MSE = 139.30$; Punctuation/Capitalization, $F(1, 29) = 8.92$, $p < .01$, $MSE = 204.94$; and Editing, $F(1, 29) = 10.46$, $p < .01$, $MSE = 386.45$. We also

TABLE 3.4. Student Achievement and Motivation Performance at the Beginning and End of the School Year

	Performance level			
	Poor writers (n = 10)		Good writers (n = 21)	
Measure	October	May	October	May
WJ-III Reading				
Letter–Word	85.90 (9.41)		109.14 (11.73)	
Word Attack	87.30 (12.88)		106.86 (9.41)	
RFluency	85.10 (15.93)		105.10 (12.20)	
Passage Comp	83.90 (11.95)		102.52 (10.98)	
WJ-III Writing				
WFluency	79.60 (31.78)	80.56 (14.81)	115.71 (8.92)	115.62 (11.80)
WSamples	92.00 (14.51)	92.67 (19.05)	113.05 (8.64)	110.67 (12.14)
Spelling	83.60 (14.29)	82.67 (14.34)	107.19 (10.49)	107.24 (10.47)
Punct/Cap	86.00 (12.50)	76.89 (18.84)	102.43 (15.06)	103.05 (15.57)
Editing	84.00 (29.85)	88.67 (15.52)	108.43 (12.63)	110.25 (11.77)
Narrative Writing Probes				
Content	1.70 (0.82)	1.80 (0.79)	3.14 (1.11)	2.71 (0.96)
Organization	2.10 (0.88)	1.90 (0.74)	3.24 (0.83)	2.90 (1.00)
Sent. Fluency	1.60 (0.70)	1.60 (0.70)	2.81 (1.25)	2.76 (0.89)
Word Choice	1.90 (0.88)	1.80 (0.63)	2.90 (1.00)	2.76 (0.83)
Conventions	1.90 (0.88)	2.20 (0.92)	3.14 (1.11)	3.19 (0.93)
Total Quality	1.84 (0.59)	1.86 (0.60)	3.05 (0.86)	2.87 (0.72)
Total Elements	0.30 (0.17)	0.37 (0.22)	0.62 (0.24)	0.58 (0.20)
Essay Writing Probes				
Content	1.70 (0.67)	1.60 (0.52)	2.38 (1.07)	2.43 (0.93)
Organization	1.90 (0.57)	1.80 (0.63)	2.52 (0.68)	2.62 (0.92)
Sent. Fluency	2.10 (0.88)	2.20 (0.92)	2.14 (0.79)	2.38 (0.86)
Word Choice	2.10 (0.88)	2.00 (0.82)	2.38 (0.80)	2.38 (0.80)
Conventions	2.60 (0.70)	2.60 (0.70)	3.33 (0.86)	3.10 (0.83)
Total Quality	2.08 (0.54)	2.04 (0.55)	2.55 (0.63)	2.58 (0.63)
Total Elements	0.48 (0.32)	0.55 (0.44)	1.26 (0.94)	1.23 (0.75)
ASERS				
Attitudes	3.24 (0.51)	3.70 (0.60)	3.99 (0.50)	3.89 (0.67)
Self-Efficacy	3.13 (0.74)	3.29 (0.62)	3.63 (0.51)	3.80 (0.63)
WGS				
Task Goals	4.21 (0.49)	4.53 (0.50)	4.39 (0.52)	4.41 (0.43)
Ego Goals	4.28 (0.59)	4.28 (0.54)	4.27 (0.61)	4.21 (0.72)
Avoid Goals	2.87 (1.02)	2.97 (1.53)	2.32 (0.99)	2.26 (1.10)

compared the performances of the good and poor writers on the pretest experimental narrative and persuasive writing probes with respect to total structural elements and quality traits. There was a significant multivariate effect for group, $F(12, 18) = 3.24$, $p < .05$. Subsequent univariate tests revealed significant group differences favoring the good writers for total narrative elements, $F(1, 29) = 14.53$, $p < .01$, $MSE = .05$, and total essay elements, $F(1, 29) = 6.54$, $p < .05$, $MSE = 0.64$. For narrative quality, there were significant group differences favoring good writers for each trait and total quality: content, $F(1, 29) = 13.33$, $p < .01$, $MSE = 1.06$; organization, $F(1, 29) = 12.29$, $p < .01$, $MSE = 0.71$; sentence fluency, $F(1, 29) = 8.06$, $p < .01$, $MSE = 1.23$; word choice, $F(1, 29) = 7.43$, $p < .05$, $MSE = 0.92$; conventions, $F(1, 29) = 9.64$, $p < .01$, $MSE = 1.09$; total quality, $F(1, 29) = 15.87$, $p < .01$, $MSE = .62$. For essay quality, there were significant group differences favoring good writers for organization, $F(1, 29) = 6.30$, $p < .05$, $MSE = 0.42$; conventions, $F(1, 29) = 5.54$, $p < .05$, $MSE = 0.66$; and total quality, $F(1, 29) = 4.21$, $p < .05$, $MSE = 0.36$; but not for content, sentence fluency, or word choice, $F(1, 29) = 3.37$, $F(1, 29) = 0.02$, and $F(1, 29) = 0.78$ (all $ps > .07$), respectively. Finally, we compared the performances of the groups on the pretest measures of motivational attributes. The multivariate effect for group was significant, $F(5, 24) = 3.44$, $p < .05$. Subsequent univariate tests showed significant group differences favoring good writers for attitudes, $F(1, 28) = 13.69$, $p < .01$, $MSE = 0.25$, and self-efficacy, $F(1, 28) = 4.27$, $p < .05$, $MSE = 0.34$, but not for task goals, ego goals, or avoidance goals, $F(1, 28) = 0.53$, $F(1, 28) = 0.00$, and $F(1, 28) = 1.73$ (all $ps > .15$), respectively.

Growth in Writing Performance and Motivational Attributes

Because there were pretest differences between groups on most of the dependent measures, variance in posttest scores attributable to pretest scores needed to be statistically controlled. Additionally, variance in writing performance attributable to reading achievement (recall that scores on the reading subtests were strongly correlated with pretest scores on the writing subtests) also needed to be statistically controlled. A composite reading achievement score was derived for each student by averaging the standard scores obtained on the four WJ-III reading subtests we administered, which were significantly intercorrelated (rs ranged from .77 to .93). Consequently, a series of repeated-measures multivariate analyses of covariance (MANCOVAs) was conducted, in which time of testing (October and May) served as the within-subjects repeated measure, group (good writers and poor writers) served as the between-subjects factor, and reading achievement and grade level served as covariates when appropriate. The use of MANCOVAs corrected for the experiment-wise error rate associated with multiple hypothesis testing using univariate tests. Separate MANCOVAs were used for the WJ-III writing subtests, the experimental writing probes, and the writing motivation scales, respectively. If the assumptions of homogeneity of covariance matrices and error variances for the dependent variables were not met (this occurred infrequently), appropriate statistical alternatives were used. Given our small sample size and the corresponding likelihood of committing a Type II error, we adopted a critical alpha level of 0.10 (approximate alpha levels are reported).

The first MANCOVA included the WJ-III subtest scores as criterion measures. There was no significant multivariate main effect attributable to time of testing, $F(5, 22) = 1.15$, $p > .36$, but the multivariate main effect attributable to group was significant, $F(5, 22) = 3.15$, $p < .03$. The interaction of time and group was not significant, $F(5, 22) = 1.21$, $p > .33$. Subsequent univariate tests showed significant group differences for Writing Fluency, $F(1, 26) = 11.00$, $p < .01$, $MSE = 180.54$, and Spelling, $F(1, 26) = 3.27$, $p < .09$, $MSE = 83.14$, but not Writing Samples, Punctuation/Capitalization, or Editing, $F(1, 26) = 1.38$, $F(1, 26) = 0.37$, and $F(1, 26) = 0.03$ (all $ps > .25$), respectively. Specifically, good writers performed better than poor writers on Writing Fluency (adjusted $M = 110.34$ and adjusted $M = 93.62$, respectively) and Spelling (adjusted $M = 101.46$ and adjusted $M = 95.27$, respectively).

The second MANCOVA, in which genre (narrative and persuasive) served as an additional within-subjects variable and grade served as the sole covariate (the reading composite was not a significant covariate for the experimental writing measures), included total elements, total quality, and the five separate quality traits as dependent measures. There were no significant multivariate main effects attributable to time of testing, $F(6, 23) = 1.78$, $p > .14$, or genre, $F(6, 23) = 1.02$, $p > .43$, but there was a significant main effect for group, $F(6, 23) = 4.36$, $p < .01$. The interactions of time and group, $F(6, 23) = 0.55$, $p > .76$, time and genre, $F(6, 23) = 0.59$, $p > .73$, and time, genre, and group, $F(6, 23) = 0.55$, $p > .76$, were not significant. However, the interaction of genre and group was significant, $F(6, 23) = 3.26$, $p < .02$. Subsequent univariate tests showed significant group differences that varied with genre for sentence fluency, $F(1, 28) = 14.60$, $p < .01$, $MSE = 8.20$; word choice, $F(1, 28) = 5.73$, $p < .03$, $MSE = 2.95$; conventions, $F(1, 28) = 3.12$, $p < .09$, $MSE = 1.69$; total quality, $F(1, 28) = 8.29$, $p < .01$, $MSE = 2.53$; and total elements, $F(1, 28) = 4.82$, $p < .04$, $MSE = 1.64$. Good writers wrote significantly better stories than poor writers in terms of sentence fluency (adjusted $Ms = 2.79$ and 1.59, respectively), word choice (adjusted $Ms = 2.84$ and 1.84, respectively), and conventions (adjusted $Ms = 3.16$ and 2.06, respectively), but the two groups performed simi-

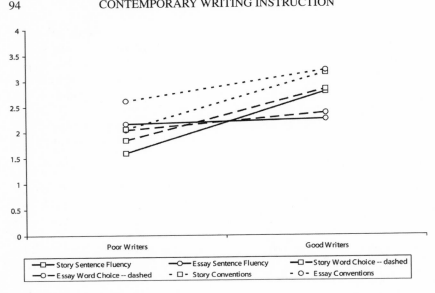

FIGURE 3.1. Adjusted means for sentence fluency, word choice, and conventions for each group on the experimental writing measures.

larly on these traits when writing persuasive essays (see Figure 3.1). As is evident in Figure 3.2, good writers wrote significantly better narratives than poor writers in terms of total quality (adjusted Ms = 2.96 and 1.85, respectively), but the groups' essays did not differ on this dimension. Conversely, good writers wrote better essays than poor writers in terms of total elements (adjusted Ms = 1.25 and 0.49, respectively), but their stories were similar in this respect.

The third MANCOVA, in which a composite measure of writing achievement derived from averaging pretest WJ-III writing subtest scores (rs between subtests ranged from .56 to .86) served as a covariate (grade was not a significant covariate for the writing motivation measures), included the ASERS and WGS dependent measures. There was a significant main effect attributable to time of testing, $F(5, 21) = 3.61$, $p < .02$, but the multivariate main effect due to group was not significant, $F(5, 21) = 1.03$, $p > .42$. Moreover, the interaction of time and group was not significant, $F(5, 21) = 1.16$, $p > .36$. Subsequent univariate tests showed a significant pretest (adjusted $M = 4.35$) to posttest (adjusted $M = 4.46$) increase for task goals, $F(1, 25) = 10.09$, $p < .01$, $MSE = 0.27$, a significant pretest (adjusted $M = 4.34$) to posttest (adjusted $M = 4.18$) decrease for ego goals, $F(1, 25) = 4.35$, $p < .05$, $MSE = 0.24$, and a significant pretest (adjusted $M = 2.60$) to posttest

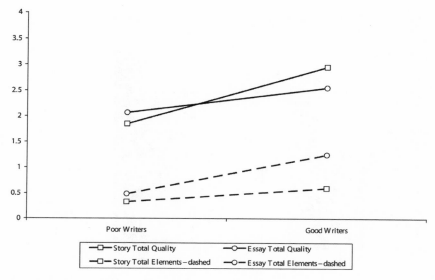

FIGURE 3.2. Adjusted means for total quality and total elements for each group on the experimental writing measures.

(adjusted $M = 2.48$) decrease for avoidance goals, $F(1, 25) = 4.56$, $p < .05$, $MSE = 0.10$.

Portfolios

Finally, we examined the writing samples collected by teachers over the school year for student portfolios. The writing samples were collected approximately every 2 months and represented the four genre study cycles of the writing curriculum—personal narratives were collected in November, expository feature articles were collected in January, poems were collected in March, and fictional narratives were collected in June. The first writing sample, a descriptive essay, was collected in September and was part of the school district's assessment program. We used paired-samples t-tests to identify significant changes over time in combined quality trait scores (see Figure 3.3) for the good and poor writers. Because some teachers were less diligent than others in collecting and scoring writing samples (i.e., some portfolios only contained three or four samples rather than all five), and because the scores for poems appeared to be inflated (see Figure 3.3), we compared only samples collected in September, January, and June. Significant differences in the quality of good writers' papers emerged when we compared writing samples from September and January, $M_{T3-T1} = 0.46$, $SD = 0.84$, $t(18) = -2.39$,

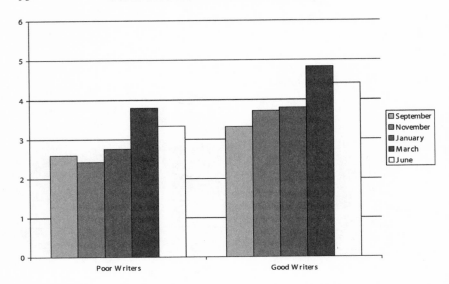

FIGURE 3.3. Combined quality trait scores for portfolio samples for each group.

$p < .03$; January and June, $M_{T5-T3} = 0.58$, $SD = 0.96$, $t(16) = -2.47$, $p < .03$; and September and June, $M_{T5-T1} = 1.11$, $SD = 1.02$, $t(16) = -4.49$, $p < .01$. Poor writers did not show this pattern of growth: $M_{T3-T1} = 0.38$, $SD = 1.46$, $t(7) = -0.73$, $p > .48$; $M_{T5-T3} = 0.49$, $SD = 0.73$, $t(6) = -1.76$, $p > .12$; and $M_{T5-T1} = 0.69$, $SD = 1.25$, $t(6) = -1.45$, $p > .19$, respectively.

DISCUSSION AND IMPLICATIONS

Since the pioneering work of such scholars and practitioners as Donald Graves (1983) in the early 1980s, writing workshop has become the zeitgeist for apprenticing young authors. Yet only a handful of studies have attempted to establish the effectiveness or efficacy of this instructional model, and none have determined what differential effects, if any, are present for writers with different levels of proficiency. We thus set out to examine how writing workshop instruction, implemented within the context of extensive professional training and support, influences writing-related outcomes for elementary school students who vary in their writing abilities. There are three important findings relevant to this research question. First, based on two sources of data—norm-referenced tests of writing achievement and experimental written composition probes—we found that good and poor writers did not benefit appreciably from writing workshop instruction in terms of their writing performance when entering literacy skills were held constant. Rather, a number of initial differences between groups that favored good writers were also observed at the end of the school year, which means that the writing achievement gap between these students was not closed. Second, we found that good writers demonstrated significant growth (a 32.8% score increase) in the quality of their writing portfolio samples, scored by their classroom teachers, from September to June. In contrast, though poor writers made a 28.5% improvement in the quality of their portfolio samples, this gain was not significant. Third, children's motivational stance toward writing improved regardless of writing competence—there was a small but significant increase in task goals (2.5%) and small but significant decreases in ego goals (3.7%) and avoidance goals (4.6%).

Three issues must be considered when interpreting these findings. First is how much students' progress was affected by variability in the writing workshop instruction they experienced. For instance, although we did not perform statistical analyses to compare students' growth between the six classrooms, an inspection of average portfolio scores suggests that students placed in classrooms with teachers who had the most teaching experience and who had worked previously with the non-profit professional development staff made the largest gains ($M = 1.4$, range = 1.2 to 1.8), whereas students placed with teachers who had the least amount of experience with teaching in general and with writing workshop instruction in particular made the smallest gains ($M = 0.4$, range = −0.4 to 1.0). This difference is particularly interesting given that the quality scores for the portfolio samples were assigned by the students' classroom teachers.

Prior research has documented writing workshop implementation variability (e.g., Agate & Graham, in press; Lipson et al., 2000), and we too found that, although the essential components of writing workshop (e.g., daily workshop time, student-centered assignments, teacher modeling and feedback, and guiding routines) were evident in each classroom, teachers differed with respect to how they managed the workshop environment and the specific teaching strategies they employed. It may be that students made less progress in classrooms with teachers who used less effective management, engagement, and instructional tactics, perhaps largely due to the teachers' inexperience. We did observe that the three teachers whose students made the smallest gains in writing performance engaged in less diverse communicative transactions with their students and made fewer adaptations for struggling writers. Furthermore, two of the three teachers employed more punitive consequences and provided fewer opportunities for students to collaborate on writing projects and manage their own or others' writing behaviors. These findings foreground the importance of exploring links between teacher attributes, quality of writing instruction, and student writing outcomes.

The second issue is the reliability of the portfolio writing quality scores, which were assigned by teachers and found to have somewhat low correspondence with scores assigned by independent raters and to be generally higher by comparison. It may be that teachers were biased in their assessment of their students' writing performance because of the investments they each had made to writing workshop instruction. Understandably, teachers would expect their students to show growth in their writing during the school year, and these expectations might be reflected in their scoring. Gearhart's research (Gearhart & Herman, 1998; Gearhart & Wolf, 1997) has demonstrated how difficult it is to isolate and control the influence of differentiated teacher support across writing samples and across students when using classroom portfolios to evaluate students' writing performance, raising the question, "Whose work is it?" In essence, she suggests that portfolio entries are suspect as reliable and valid indicators of student's writing skills because the extent and type of assistance provided during the planning, drafting, revising, and publishing of papers can be expected to vary in the context of different classroom writing assignments and of a diverse group of students. It is not simply that reliable scoring is critical—the papers that are scored may not represent independent observations of writing performance in the first place.

The third issue is related to our research design: because we did not use an experimental or pseudo-experimental control group design, we cannot draw conclusions regarding the causality of changes (or lack thereof) in students' writing performance and motivational attributes. We simply do not know whether writing workshop instruction and/or support from the nonprofit agency led to the outcomes we observed or whether there are more suitable explanations. For instance, though our sample did not display notable progress in their writing performance on independently scored measures, it is entirely possible that they may have actually lost ground in their writing had they been in classrooms in which writing workshop was not implemented or in which teachers did not have the same degree of professional development and instructional support. In fact, Glasswell (1999) reported that Matthew effects are evident in writing just as they are in reading—there is a widening gap between writers over time that is exacerbated by poor instruction and limited individualized assistance and adaptation.

Why did these students fail to make substantive gains in their writing performance? We surmise that, aside from variability in the quality of teaching, the writing workshop instruction implemented in these students' classrooms did not include two critical agents of successful outcomes, especially for struggling writers—systematic and integrated teaching of transcription skills and a focus on self-regulation in writing through goal setting, progress monitoring, and self-evaluation (De La Paz, 2007; Gersten & Baker, 2001; Gleason & Isaacson, 2001; Graham, 1999; Troia & Graham, 2003). Handwriting and spelling instruction rarely receive more than a passing nod from those who advocate writing workshop, as was the case in our investigation, but research has found that transcription skills account for two-thirds of the variance in writing fluency and one-fourth of the variance in writing quality for children in the primary grades and about 40% of the variance in written output for students in the intermediate grades (e.g., Graham, Berninger, Abbott, Abbott, & Whitaker, 1997). If children have difficulty with handwriting and spelling and, consequently, must devote substantial effort to transcribing their ideas, they will have fewer cognitive resources left available to engage in effective planning and revising behaviors and to focus on writing content, organization, and style (Graham, 1990; Graham & Harris, 1997; McCutchen, 1996). Without adequate instruction to help students become more accurate and fluent in text transcription, growth in writing will be limited.

Likewise, self-regulation is essential for writing success because it can: (1) help students attain greater awareness of their writing strengths and limitations and consequently be more strategic in their attempts to accomplish writing tasks; (2) enable them to reflect on their writing capabilities; (3) adequately manage paralyzing thoughts, feelings, and behaviors; and (4) empower them to make adaptations to composing strategies when necessary (see Harris & Graham, 1992; Troia, 2006). Although the writing workshop approach used by teachers in our study did promote self-management via student-selected topics, individualized pacing, and self-evaluation during conferencing and while using procedural facilitators (e.g., checklists), there was little emphasis on establishing concrete process- and product-related goals or using data to monitor progress in writing; the professional development program privileged celebrating the accomplishments of students (i.e., completing a genre cycle) over critical feedback about their writing. Inexperienced writers need explicit instruction in goal setting, progress monitoring, and self-evaluation because they typically fail to do these things on their own and because good writing places a heavy premium on these components of self-regulation (e.g., Graham, MacArthur, Schwartz, & Page-Voth, 1992; Harris, Graham, Reid, McElroy, & Hamby, 1994; Schunk & Swartz, 1993).

Writing workshop, when implemented well, can serve as a strong foundation for improving the writing performance of students. However, our research suggests that young writers do not necessarily benefit from this approach. Moreover, such an approach does not appear to be adequate for narrowing the achievement gap between good and poor writers. Even after accounting for initial score differences, good writers in our study outperformed poor writers in writing fluency by 1.1 *SD* and in spelling by 0.4 *SD*; they also displayed about a 1-point advantage in story writing quality on the 6-point scale we used, though the groups were relatively equal in the quality of their argumentative essays (although good writers did use over 2.5 times the average number of essay elements used by poor writers). To bolster the effectiveness of process writing instruction, teachers should address basic writing skills such as handwriting and spelling, which are still being developed in elementary school students, and consider how to incorporate into their writing programs the critical elements of writing strategy instruction that positively affect struggling writers' knowledge, skills, and dispositions (see Honeycutt & Pritchard, 2005, for concrete examples). Moreover, teachers should be mindful of the specific needs of struggling writers and plan and implement instructional adaptations (e.g., use computer technology to support writing, reteach specific skills and strategies, confer more often) accordingly. In a national survey of primary grade teachers conducted by Graham, Harris, Fink-Chorzempa, and MacArthur (2003), nearly 75% of all reported adaptations for struggling writers were made by just 29% of the respondents, and no single adaptation was made by more than 40% of the teachers. Nearly 20% of the teachers reported making no adaptations for poor writers, whereas another fourth of the sample reported making only one or two adaptations. We also observed rather limited application of adaptations among our small group of teachers. Apparently, instructional adaptations in writing are not widely used, and this does not bode well for the many students in our schools who struggle with writing.

ACKNOWLEDGMENT

This research was supported, in part, by a grant to the first author from the Royalty Research Fund at the University of Washington, Seattle.

REFERENCES

Agate, L., & Graham, S. (in press). Primary grade writing instruction: A national survey. *Journal of Educational Psychology*.

Atwell, N. (1987). *In the middle: Writing, reading, and learning with adolescents*. Portsmouth, NH: Boynton/Cook.

Atwell, N. (1998). *In the middle: New understanding about writing, reading, and learning*. Portsmouth, NH: Heinemann.

Bottomley, D. M., Truscott, D. M., Marinak, B. A., Henk, W. A., & Melnick, S. A. (1999). An affective comparison of whole-language, literature-based, and basal literacy instruction. *Reading Research and Instruction, 38,* 115–129.

Bridge, C. A., Compton-Hall, M., & Cantrell, S. C. (1997). Classroom writing practices revisited: The effects of statewide reform on writing instruction. *Elementary School Journal, 98,* 151–170.

Bruno, D. D. (1983). The writing process method versus the traditional textbook–worksheet method in the teaching of composition skills to third, fourth, and fifth grade students. *Dissertation Abstracts International, 44* (09A), 2663. (UMI No. AA18400878)

Calkins, L. M. (1986). *The art of teaching writing* (1st ed.). Portsmouth, NH: Heinemann.

Calkins, L. M. (1998). *The art of teaching writing* (2nd ed.). Portsmouth, NH: Heinemann.

Clare, L., Valdes, R., & Patthey-Chavez, G. G. (2000). *Learning to write in urban elementary and middle schools: An investigation of teachers' written feedback on student compositions* (Center for the Study of Evaluation Technical Report No. 526). Los Angeles: National Center for Research on Evaluation, Standards, and Student Testing.

De La Paz, S. (2007). Managing cognitive demands for writing: Comparing the effects of instructional components in strategy instruction. *Reading and Writing Quarterly: Overcoming Learning Difficulties, 23,* 249–266.

Englert, C. S., Raphael, T. E., Fear, K., & Anderson, L. M. (1988). Students' metacognitive knowledge about how to write informational texts. *Learning Disability Quarterly, 11,* 18–46.

Fletcher, R., & Portalupi, J. (1998). *Craft lessons: Teaching writing K–8.* Portland, ME: Stenhouse.

Fletcher, R., & Portalupi, J. (2001). *Writing workshop: The essential guide.* Portsmouth, NH: Heinemann.

Fulk, B. M., & Stormont-Spurgin, M. (1995). Spelling interventions for students with disabilities: A review. *Journal of Special Education, 28,* 488–513.

Gearhart, M., & Herman, J. L. (1998). Portfolio assessment: Whose work is it? Issues in the use of classroom assignments for accountability. *Educational Assessment, 5,* 41–56.

Gearhart, M., & Wolf, S. A. (1997). Issues in portfolio assessment: Assessing writing processes from their products. *Educational Assessment, 4,* 265–296.

Gersten, R., & Baker, S. (2001). Teaching expressive writing to students with learning disabilities: A meta-analysis. *Elementary School Journal, 101,* 251–272.

Glasswell, K. (1999). *The patterning of difference: Teachers and children constructing development in writing.* Unpublished doctoral dissertation, University of Auckland, New Zealand.

Gleason, M. M., & Isaacson, S. (2001). Using the new basals to teach the writing process: Modifications for students with learning problems. *Reading and Writing Quarterly, 17,* 75–92.

Graham, S. (1990). The role of production factors in learning disabled students' compositions. *Journal of Educational Psychology, 82,* 781–791.

Graham, S. (1999). Handwriting and spelling instruction for students with learning disabilities: A review. *Learning Disability Quarterly, 22,* 78–98.

Graham, S., Berninger, V. W., Abbott, R. D., Abbott, S. P., & Whitaker, D. (1997). The role of mechanics in composing of elementary school students: A new methodological approach. *Journal of Educational Psychology, 89,* 170–182.

Graham, S., & Harris, K. R. (1989). A components analysis of cognitive strategy instruction: Effects on learning disabled students' compositions and self-efficacy. *Journal of Educational Psychology, 81,* 353–361.

Graham, S., & Harris, K. R. (1991). Self-instructional strategy development: Programmatic research in writing. In B. Y. L. Wong (Ed.), *Contemporary intervention research in learning disabilities: An international perspective* (pp. 47–64). New York: Springer-Verlag.

Graham, S., & Harris, K. R. (1997). It can be taught, but it does not develop naturally: Myths and realities in writing instruction. *School Psychology Review, 26,* 414–424.

Graham, S., Harris, K. R., Fink, B., & MacArthur, C. A. (2001). Teacher efficacy in writing: A construct validation with primary grade teachers. *Scientific Studies of Reading, 5,* 177–202.

Graham, S., Harris, K. R., Fink-Chorzempa, B., & MacArthur, C. A. (2003). Primary grade teachers' instructional adaptations for struggling writers: A national survey. *Journal of Educational Psychology, 95,* 279–292.

Graham, S., Harris, K. R., MacArthur, C. A., & Fink, B. (2002). Primary grade teachers' theoretical orientations concerning writing instruction: Construct validation and a nationwide survey. *Contemporary Educational Psychology, 27,* 147–166.

Graham, S., Harris, K. R., & Troia, G. A. (1998). Writing and self-regulation: Cases from the self-regulated strategy development model. In D. H. Schunk & B. J. Zimmerman (Eds.), *Developing self-regulated learners: From teaching to self-reflective practice* (pp. 20–41). New York: Guilford Press.

Graham, S., MacArthur, C. A., Schwartz, S. S., & Page-Voth, V. (1992). Improving the compositions of students with learning disabilities using a strategy involving product and process goal setting. *Exceptional Children, 58,* 322–334.

Graham, S., & Perin, D. (2007). *Writing next: Effective strategies to improve writing of adolescents in middle and high schools—A report to Carnegie Corporation of New York.* Washington, DC: Alliance for Excellent Education.

Graham, S., Schwartz, S., & MacArthur, C. A. (1993). Knowledge of writing and the composing process, attitude toward writing, and self-efficacy for students with and without learning disabilities. *Journal of Learning Disabilities, 26,* 237–249.

Graves, D. H. (1983). *Writing: Teachers and children at work.* Portsmouth, NH: Heinemann.

Hamilton, A. C. (1992). Performance assessment of personal correspondence on the development of written language use and functions in traditional and process writing second-grade classrooms. *Dissertation Abstracts International, 53* (07A), 2235. (UMI No. AA19234729)

Harris, K. R., & Graham, S. (1992). Self-regulated strategy development: A part of the writing process. In M. Pressley, K. R. Harris, & J. Guthrie (Eds.),

Promoting academic competence and literacy in school (pp. 277–309). New York: Academic Press.

Harris, K. R., Graham, S., Reid, R., McElroy, K., & Hamby, R. (1994). Self-monitoring of attention versus self-monitoring of performance: Replication and cross-task comparison studies. *Learning Disability Quarterly, 17,* 121–139.

Hayes, J. R., & Flower, L. S. (1980). Identifying the organization of writing processes. In L. W. Gregg & E. R. Steinberg (Eds.), *Cognitive processes in writing* (pp. 3–30). Hillsdale, NJ: Erlbaum.

Hillocks, G. (1984). What works in teaching composition: A meta-analysis of experimental treatment studies. *American Journal of Education, 93,* 133–170.

Hollingshead, A. B. (1975). *Four factor index of social class.* New Haven, CT: Yale University.

Honeycutt, R. L., & Pritchard, R. J. (2005). Using a structured writing workshop to help good readers who are poor writers. In G. Rijlaarrsdan, H. van den Bergh, & M. Couzijin (Eds.), *Studies in writing: Vol. 14. Effective teaching and learning of writing* (2nd ed., pp. 141–150). Amsterdam: Kluwer.

Lipson, M. Y., Mosenthal, J., Daniels, P., & Woodside-Jiron, H. (2000). Process writing in the classrooms of eleven fifth-grade teachers with different orientations to teaching and learning. *Elementary School Journal, 101,* 209–231.

McCutchen, D. (1996). A capacity theory of writing: Working memory in composition. *Educational Psychology Review, 8,* 299–325.

Monteith, S. K. (1991, November). *Writing process versus traditional writing classrooms: Writing ability and attitudes of second grade students.* Paper presented at the annual meeting of the Mid-South Educational Research Association, Lexington, KY. (ERIC Document Reproduction Service No. ED340024)

National Center for Education Statistics. (1999). *National assessment of educational progress (NAEP).* Washington, DC: U.S. Department of Education.

Nolen, S. B., & Valencia, S. W. (2000). *The writing goals scale.* Unpublished manuscript.

Pajares, F. (2003). Self-efficacy beliefs, motivation, and achievement in writing: A review of the literature. *Reading and Writing Quarterly, 19,* 139–158.

Patthey-Chavez, G. G., Matsumura, L. C., & Valdes, R. (2004). Investigating the process approach to writing instruction in urban middle schools. *Journal of Adolescent and Adult Literacy, 47,* 462–477.

Persky, H. R., Daane, M. C., & Jin, Y. (2003). *The nation's report card: Writing 2002.* Washington, DC: U.S. Department of Education, National Center for Education Statistics.

Pollington, M. F., Wilcox, B., & Morrison, T. G. (2001). Self-perception in writing: The effects of writing workshop and traditional instruction on intermediate grade students. *Reading Psychology, 22,* 249–265.

Pritchard, R. J., & Honeycutt, R. L. (2006). The process approach to writing instruction: Examining its effectiveness. In C. A. MacArthur, S. Graham,

& J. Fitzgerald (Eds.), *Handbook of writing research* (pp. 275–290). New York: Guilford Press.

Scannella, A. M. (1982). A writing-as-process model as a means of improving composition and attitudes towards composition in high school. *Dissertation Abstracts International, 43* (08A), 2582. (UMI No. AA18301605)

Scardamalia, M., Bereiter, C., & Goelman, H. (1982). The role of production factors in writing ability. In M. Nystrand (Ed.), *What writers know: The language, process, and structure of written discourse* (pp. 173–210). New York: Academic Press.

Schunk, D. H., & Swartz, C. W. (1993). Goals and progress feedback: Effects on self-efficacy and writing achievement. *Contemporary Educational Psychology, 18*, 337–354.

Spandel, V. (2001). *Creating writers through 6-trait writing assessment and instruction* (3rd ed.). New York: Addison Wesley Longman.

Thomas, C. C., Englert, C. S., & Gregg, S. (1987). An analysis of errors and strategies in the expository writing of learning disabled students. *Remedial and Special Education, 8*, 21–30.

Tidwell, D. L., & Steele, J. L. (1995, December). *I teach what I know: An examination of teachers' beliefs about whole language.* Paper presented at the annual meeting of the National Reading Conference, San Antonio, TX. (ERIC Document Reproduction Service No. ED374391)

Troia, G. A. (2006). Writing instruction for students with learning disabilities. In C. A. MacArthur, S. Graham, & J. Fitzgerald (Eds.), *Handbook of writing research* (pp. 324–336). New York: Guilford Press.

Troia, G. A., & Graham, S. (2003). Effective writing instruction across the grades: What every educational consultant should know. *Journal of Educational and Psychological Consultation, 14*, 75–89.

Troia, G. A., Graham, S., & Harris, K. R. (1999). Teaching students with learning disabilities to mindfully plan when writing. *Exceptional Children, 65*, 235–252.

Troia, G. A., Lin, S. C., Cohen, S., & Monroe, B. W. (in preparation). *A year in the writing workshop: Effects of professional development on teachers' writing instruction.*

Troia, G. A., Shankland, R. K., & Wolbers, K. A. (in press). Motivation research in writing: Theoretical and empirical considerations. *Reading and Writing Quarterly: Overcoming Learning Difficulties.*

Tschannen-Moran, M., Woolfolk-Hoy, A., & Hoy, W. (1998). Teacher efficacy: Its meaning and measure. *Review of Educational Research, 68*, 202–248.

Varble, M. E. (1990). Analysis of writing samples of students taught by teachers using whole language and traditional approaches. *Journal of Educational Research, 83*, 245–251.

Woodcock, R. W., McGrew, K. S., & Mather, N. (2001). *Woodcock–Johnson–III Tests of Achievement.* Itasca, IL: Riverside.

Wray, D., Medwell, J., Fox, R., & Poulson, L. (2000). The teaching practices of effective teachers of literacy. *Educational Review, 52*, 75–84.

APPENDIX 3.1. Quality Traits Scale

IDEAS/CONTENT

6   Exceptionally clear, focused, and interesting. Writing holds the reader's attention throughout. Main ideas stand out and are developed by strong support and rich details suitable to the audience.

5   Clear, focused, and interesting. Writing holds the reader's attention. Main ideas stand out and are developed by supporting details suitable to the audience.

4   Clear and focused. Reader can easily understand the main ideas. Support is present, although it may be limited or rather general.

3   Reader can understand main ideas, although they may be overly broad or simplistic. Detail is often limited, insubstantial, overly general, or occasionally off topic.

2   Main ideas and purpose are somewhat unclear or development is attempted but minimal.

1   Writing lacks a central idea or purpose. Paper is too short to develop ideas.

ORGANIZATION

6   Organization enhances the central idea and its development. Order and structure are compelling and move the reader through the text easily.

5   Organization enhances the central idea and its development. Order and structure move the reader through the text.

4   Organization is clear and coherent. Order and structure are present but formulaic.

3   Attempt made to organize writing; however, the overall structure is inconsistent or skeletal.

2   Lacks structure. An occasional organizational device is discernible; however, the writing is either difficult to follow or the piece is simply too short to demonstrate organizational skills.

1 Writing lacks coherence. An organization device is not discernible, so the story seems haphazard and disjointed. Reader is confused.

SENTENCE FLUENCY

6 Writing has an effective flow and rhythm. Sentences show a high degree of craftsmanship, with consistently strong and varied structure that makes expressive oral reading easy and enjoyable.

5 Writing has an easy flow and rhythm. Sentences are carefully crafted, with strong and varied structure that makes expressive oral reading easy and enjoyable.

4 Writing flows; however, connections between phrases or sentences may be less than fluid. Sentence patterns are somewhat varied, contributing to ease in oral reading.

3 Writing is mechanical rather than fluid. Occasional awkward constructions may force rereading.

2 Writing tends to be either choppy or rambling. Awkward constructions often force rereading.

1 Writing is difficult to follow. Sentences tend to be incomplete, rambling, or very awkward.

WORD CHOICE

6 Word choice is very well suited for the piece. The vocabulary is exceptionally clear and precise. Lively and memorable words paint a strong image in the reader's mind.

5 Word choice is well suited for the piece. The vocabulary is clear and precise. Some lively and memorable words help paint a strong image in the reader's mind.

4 Word choice is adequate for the piece. The vocabulary is mostly clear and concise, but economy of expression could be improved. Some well-chosen words help the reader paint a mental image.

3 Word choice lacks precision, although it is generally acceptable. Economy of expression could be greatly improved. The reader must struggle to create a mental image because so many words lack vividness.

2 Word choice is generally poor. Many words lack explicitness or are used incorrectly. Some redundancy is evident. A mental image is almost impossible to create given the vagueness of the chosen vocabulary.

1 Word choice is very poor and may be indicative of a limited vocabulary. The chosen words are vague or are used incorrectly. Much redundancy is evident. The reader is confused and unable to paint a mental image.

CONVENTIONS

6 Writing demonstrates exceptionally strong control of standard writing conventions (i.e., spelling, capitalization, and punctuation) and uses them effectively to enhance communication. Paper is free from errors or they are very minor.

5 Writing demonstrates strong control of standard writing conventions and uses them effectively to enhance communication. Errors are few and noticeable only if reader searches for them.

4 Writing demonstrates control of standard writing conventions. Minor errors, although perhaps noticeable, do not impede readability.

3 Writing demonstrates limited control of standard writing conventions. Errors impede readability.

2 Writing demonstrates little control of standard writing conventions. Frequent, significant errors impede readability.

1 Numerous errors in standard writing conventions make text very difficult to read. Severity and frequency of errors are overwhelming. Reader finds it difficult to focus on message and must reread.

APPENDIX 3.2. Structural Elements Scoring

STORY GRAMMAR ELEMENTS

Setting Elements

Main Character

0   No main character is established in the story.
1   A main character is established but very few descriptive details are given; the character may or may not have a name.
2   The main character is presented and described in great detail (e.g., personality traits and physical attributes).

Locale

0   No locale or place is mentioned.
1   A locale (e.g., "the woods," "Mt. Everest") is given, but little description is offered.
2   The locale given is described vividly or is unique (e.g., "the town of Atlanta, which sits between two rivers and covers over ten square miles"; "the newly colonized planet Mintaka").

Time

0   The time when the story took place is not provided.
1   The time is given but is traditional in reference (e.g., "a long time ago," "twenty years in the future"); note that "one day" is not an adequate time reference and should be scored a zero.
2   The time given is unusual or described in great detail (e.g., "during prehistoric times when man lived in caves and hunted for his food"; "March 31st at 3:00 A.M.").

Plot Elements

Initiating Event

0 The problem or event that causes the main character to take action is not presented.
1 The precipitating event is clearly evident; it can be a natural occurrence (e.g., "a landslide destroyed the village"), an internal response (e.g., "he felt lonely"), or an external event (e.g., "the gnome stole the king's crown").
2 The initiating event is well described, unusual, or complex (e.g., "a meteor hit the mountain, which started the landslide that destroyed the village and everything that the man owned").

Goals

0 A goal is not established.
1 A goal is presented but ill-defined (e.g., "Billy decided he would do something").
2 A goal is clearly articulated (e.g., "Billy decided he would rescue his friend").
* Add 1 additional point if two or more goals are clearly articulated.

Attempt

0 The actions which the main character initiates to solve the problem are not presented or could not possibly lead to a resolution.
1 The attempt of the main character to solve the problem is presented and would be expected to lead to a resolution.
2 The actions of the main character demonstrate ingenuity or originality (e.g., "Billy used an anti-proton beam to disable the containment field surrounding his friend").
* Add 1 additional point if more than one episode is present (i.e., an initiating event, attempt, and direct consequence).

Direct Consequence

0 The direct consequences of the main character's attempt to solve the problem and achieve the goal are not presented; the story does not come to a conclusion; the problem is not resolved.
1 The direct consequences of the main character's actions are presented (e.g., "the man built a new home far away from any mountains and he lived there happily ever after"; "Billy rescued his friend").
2 The direct consequences are presented, but the ending is unusual, humorous, or contains a moral (e.g., "it just goes to show that crime doesn't pay"; "this

is how he got the name Eagle Arrow"; "the boy's horse died just as it crossed the finish line in first place").

Reactions (Can Be Expressed Anywhere in the Story)

0   The emotional reactions of the main character are not presented.
1   Some feelings of the main character are presented, but they are cursory (e.g., "Billy was relieved"; "the boy felt sad").
2   The emotional reactions of the main character are expressed with depth (e.g., "the boy's heart sunk in his chest as he watched his horse, his friend, die").

Other Elements

Title

0   No title is given.
1   A title is given, but it is vague (e.g., "The Outlaw").
2   A title is given that is creative and well suited to the story (e.g., "The Gunfight at White Snake Bluff"; "A Valuable Lesson").

Dialogue

0   No dialogue is present in the story.
1   Dialogue is present in the story (e.g., " `Yes,' she said").
2   Dialogue is present and is integral to plot progression (e.g., " 'One day I'll have my cake and eat it, too,' she mumbled in protestation as she huffed her way out of the room").

FUNCTIONAL PERSUASIVE ELEMENTS

Premise (P)

The premise represents the author's stated point of view about the topic. It is important to note that a premise should be able to stand alone (i.e., you should be able to infer the topic without looking at the essay prompt). "Yes" and/or "no" without accompanying text to indicate what a *yes* or *no* means does not constitute a premise.

An essay can have more than one premise: an original premise (P) and a contrasting premise (cP). The original premise may be a statement that is: (1) affirmative ("I believe boys and girls should play sports together"), (2) negative ("Boys and girls should not play sports together" or "Boys and girls should play sports separately"), (3) combined ("I do and I don't believe that boys and girls should play sports together"), or (4) neither ("I don't believe that they should or they shouldn't be allowed to play sports together").

Reasons (R)

A reason is an explanation for a writer's believing a particular premise. Reasons can be stated to support both an original and a contrasting premise (cR). In addition, some reasons can refute (rR) a previously stated premise, reason, or elaboration.

> "Children should not eat junk food (P) because it is bad for their teeth (R)."
>
> "Children should not eat junk food (P) because it is fattening (R), messy (R), and will ruin their appetite (R). On the other hand, I think children should eat junk food (cP) because you need to have some comfort food (cR). Also, junk food is not really all that bad (cR), but you can't eat it all the time (rR)."

Elaborations (E)

An elaboration is a conditional statement that modifies a premise (EP), reason (ER), another elaboration (EE), or conclusion (EC). Repetitions that serve a rhetorical purpose are also coded as elaborations. Elaborations of nonfunctional text are also considered to be nonfunctional and are not counted.

> "I think boys and girls should play sports together (P) as long as they are friendly towards each other (EP)."
>
> "Girls and boys should not play sports together (P) because boys are better at sports (R). They are better at bowling, tennis, and football (ER)."
>
> "Boys and girls should play sports together (P). It is good to play games together (R). If boys want to play soccer (ER), then girls should also be able to play (ER). Boys and girls shouldn't play sports together all the time (EP) because girls might play with dolls (EE)."
>
> "They should definitely play sports together (C), then they'd be friends (EC)."

Conclusion (C)

A conclusion closes the essay ("That is why I feel boys and girls should play sports together"). "The End" does not count as a conclusion.

Nonfunctional Units (NF)

Nonfunctional elements include repetitions that do not serve rhetorical purposes
(NF/R) and other information that does not appear to be relevant to the topic or
that cannot be coded as some type of functional element (NF/O). Thus any unit
of text that does not directly support or clarify an argument or counterargument
is a nonfunctional text unit. Poor quality (i.e., weakness) of a reason or elaboration is not grounds for scoring it as nonfunctional.

> "Children should have brothers and sisters (P). They should have sisters and
> brothers (NF/R)."
> "It's better to be the only child (P). You can get a lot of toys (R) and a lot of
> shoes for Christmas (R). You can get a lot of shoes (NF/R)."
> "I think boys and girls should play sports together (P). Here's how I would
> divide them into teams (NF/O)."
> "It's good to be the only child (P). You don't have anybody telling you no
> all the time (R). I can play with my cousins (NF/O). So I can get more
> clothes (R) and shoes (R) and toys (R)."

CHAPTER 4

Connecting Reading and Writing Instruction for Struggling Learners

Timothy Shanahan

It is widely recognized that reading is important, and, consequently, reading is heavily stressed in both federal and state educational reforms. For instance, in the No Child Left Behind legislation, the federal government authorized $5 billion to improve primary grade reading achievement. Reading improvement has been the subject of extensive research (e.g., National Institute of Child Health and Human Development [NICHD], 2000), and reading attainment is monitored biennially—more often than any other subject area—by the National Assessment of Educational Progress (NAEP). There is little wonder as to why preeminence has been accorded reading in K–12 education, as research clearly shows reading to be implicated in aspects of academic achievement such as high school completion and college success (American College Testing, 2006), financial accomplishments (Arc, Phillips, & McKenzie, 2000; Barton & Jenkins, 1995), social and civic participation (Kirsch, Jungeblut, & Jenkins, 1993), one's ability to avoid entry into the criminal justice system (Beck & Harrison, 2001), and capacity to take care of one's health (Berkman et al., 2004).

Substantially less attention has been devoted to writing achievement—in research and instruction—though the idea of redressing this imbalance is beginning to gain attention (National Commission on Writing, 2003). Writing, too, is important for economic success (National Commission on Writing, 2004), and it has a role to play in many other academic and social endeavors, though its value is definitely more circumscribed than that of reading. Moreover, writing ability depends on reading proficiency to some extent (e.g., Fitzgerald & Shanahan, 2000), so attention to writing may seem premature in a society in which children cannot read well enough. Nevertheless, writing has value, it can be taught effectively (e.g., Graham & Perin, 2007; Hillocks, 1986), and many students do not write well (Persky, Daane, & Jin, 2003).

Over the years much research attention has been accorded to the idea that reading and writing are connected. In learning to read, one masters particular knowledge and skills that facilitate writing development, and the opposite can happen as well; that is, what is learned in writing can be applied to reading. Research shows that reading and writing are connected in various ways, that the nature of these connections changes over time, and that, indeed, teachers can exploit the relationships between reading and writing in order to improve achievement, increase efficiency, or introduce aspects of reading and writing that might otherwise be neglected (Tierney & Shanahan, 1991).

The purpose of this chapter is to explore what research says about the role that reading plays in the writing development of students with learning problems and how reading instruction can better support these students as they learn how to write. Past reviews of reading–writing relationships, even those emphasizing such relationships for students with learning problems (Gleason & Isaacson, 2001), have not been able to identify differentiated instructional effects because of the way the original research was conducted. That is to say, although studies of reading–writing relationships have revealed how reading and writing are connected and the effectiveness of particular instructional approaches that combine reading and writing activities, they rarely have separated out the relationships or treatment effects for different achievement groups (and, in the rare instances in which they have done this, few differences have emerged). Consequently, this chapter must be somewhat speculative in its approach. What can be done instructionally to take advantage of reading–writing relationships with struggling learners is much the same approach that would be recommended for all students. This review considers the roles that reading development and reading instruction play in writing, especially for students with learning problems. But even when the basic instructional approaches work equally well for struggling students and their more successful peers, it should be expected that poor readers and writers will require much more explicit teaching and greater scaffolding and that the emphasis of instruction will be on a somewhat different set of skills and abilities than would be the case for normally achieving same-age students.

For the purposes of this chapter, reading is defined as the ability to comprehend, interpret, and use written information. Writing is analogously defined as the ability to compose texts that can successfully convey an author's ideas. These definitions of reading and writing entail a plethora of underlying purposes, knowledge, skills, and strategies. Decoding skills, for example, are part of reading and are requisite for successful reading to take place (Adams, 1990), although these skills are not explicitly mentioned in my definition. Similarly, handwriting is a component of composing (Berninger, 2000), though it may not be essential to writing in the same way that decoding is to reading, because handwriting can be replaced by dictation or the use of a word processor. Nevertheless, handwriting is often a part of writing, and it has been implicated in writing quality and student progress (e.g., Smits-Engelsman & Van Galen, 1997). Reading and writing, in this chapter, are used to refer both to the overall domain of achievement and to the various component skills or processes that reading and writing entail.

READING–WRITING RELATIONS

Reading and writing are closely related. The connections among reading and writing are conceptually obvious even to naïve observers, because reading and writing both involve language and communication and depend on the same alphabetic coding system, vocabulary, real-world knowledge, rhetorical traditions, and so on. Empirical research bears out these obvious connections, providing extensive evidence of significant correlations among particular components of reading and writing (Abbott & Berninger, 1993; Berninger, 2000; Berninger, Abbott, Abbott, Graham, & Richards, 2002; Berninger, Cartwright, Yates, Swanson, & Abbott, 1994; Shanahan, 1984; Shanahan & Lomax, 1986, 1988), as well as among the cognitive processes, such as metacognition, that are used in reading and writing (Langer, 1986). These correlations simply mean that students who are good at particular reading skills tend to be good at particular writing skills, and vice versa. Correlational studies, although valuable and provocative—they identify specific relationships and the strengths of these relations—typically cannot determine two important aspects of the relationships: order or sequence (i.e., does reading affect writing or does writing affect reading?) and the causal nature of the connections (e.g., would instruction in some aspect of reading improve writing?).

To illustrate this point, in a study of 64 elementary children with a history of language impairment (Dockrell, Geoff, Connelly, & Mackie, 2007), it was found that these students, at the age of 10, tended to write short texts with poor sentence structure, weak idea development, and limited organization. The problems found in these students' writing were closely connected via strong correlations to their poor reading skills and limited receptive vocabularies, suggesting that both oral language and reading limitations are implicated in students' writing struggles. Although it is possible from these data to hypothesize that limitations in reading are blocking the writing development of these students, it would be just as valid to hypothesize that the problems being uncovered in the students' writing explain the problems evident in their reading. For instance, it could be that these students with language deficits struggle so much with decoding that their spelling is labored, and consequently they write very little. One instructional implication of this conclusion is that increased teaching of decoding skills will improve both their writing (via spelling improvement) and their reading. However, it also could be that students who have trouble using text organization—as revealed by poorly organized written products—have greater difficulty thinking along with an author during reading; these students would struggle to understand. One instructional implication of this conclusion is that increasing students' knowledge of textual schemata, perhaps through writing instruction, will improve both reading and writing. The instructional implications drawn in both cases are causal in nature; that is, they assume that instruction that exploits these correlations will indeed improve both reading and writing. However, experimental study of the relationships is needed to determine whether such implications are actually justified.

To identify sequence and causality of relationship, other types of research are needed. For instance, more complex correlational studies can be used to help tease out issues of what comes first. In such a study conducted with 83 Finnish children in grade 1 (Lerkkanen, Rasku-Puttonen, Aunola, & Nurmi, 2004), the children's reading and writing skills were tested four times during the school year, and these data were entered into a complex statistical model. Early in the year, children's reading and spelling skills were reciprocally connected, with reading and spelling evidently contributing to each other's growth. However, in contrast to other research findings (Foorman et al., 2006), early writing skills contributed to later reading development, but early reading skills did not predict later writing development.

Written language works because it is based on a socially agreed-on system of conventions. The conventions of written English include letters, punctuation, capitalization, spelling, word meaning, grammar, discourse structure, and so on, and they are both arbitrary and necessary for communication to take place. Readers can interpret meaning from squiggles marked on paper only because we have agreed on how those squiggles can be used to convey meaning. By definition, students must learn to interpret these shared conventions before they can use them productively in writing. For this reason, writing development is assumed to follow reading development (one would need to be already aware of these conventions in order to even use their nascent forms to produce writing). Typically, knowledge, skills, and strategies that appear later in the developmental arc cannot influence the development of knowledge, skills, and strategies that appear earlier. However, with regard to reading and writing, this is not the case, because both entail the development of many types of knowledge, varied skills, and multiple strategies over an extended period of time. Given this, it is possible for writing—the later-developing ability—to support aspects of reading development that have not yet been fully established. For example, in a study aimed at testing the efficacy of a spelling emphasis in early decoding instruction, kinder-garten children considered to be at risk of failure because of their limited knowledge of letters and weak phonological awareness were assigned to one of three instructional conditions (Santoro, Coyne, & Simmons, 2006). One group was taught phonological awareness (oral segmenting and blending) and letter names and sounds; a second group was taught these same skills, but with a spelling emphasis; and a third group received vocabulary and comprehension instruction. The two groups who were taught decoding skills outperformed the third group in decoding devel-opment, and the instruction that had a spelling emphasis did best (even though the amount of instruction and instructional content were the same). Writing had a positive impact on these struggling students' early decoding development, probably because the writing activity itself made the instruction more explicit and intensified the practice by giving stu-dents clearer feedback. Similar results were evident in combinations of spelling and decoding instruction in grades 1 and 2 reported by other researchers (Foorman et al., 2006).

Counterintuitively, most scientific explorations of the reading–writing relationship have aimed at identifying how writing might be used to improve reading achievement (Tierney & Shanahan, 1991). This is surprising because writing is generally harder to do well than is read-ing, it lags behind reading developmentally in the learning sequence, and because reading itself can be thought of as a subpart of writing, as read-ing is used during writing (such as when someone rereads what they have written for revision). The reason scholars have placed more emphasis on the impact of writing on reading is mainly the relative places that read-ing and writing hold in the U.S. curriculum (Clifford, 1989): Reading has been accorded considerable attention, whereas writing instruction has not. Researchers often have pursued the reading–writing relationship in order to encourage a redress of this imbalance, the idea being that writing would more likely be taught if it was known to enhance reading achievement.

Theoretically, there are several good reasons to begin to rebalance reading and writing. First, writing has gained social importance, and there is now a need to help larger numbers and proportions of students to become good writers. Second, there is good reason to believe that writing can be taught earlier in children's development than was once believed, and this earlier introduction will require more explicit attention to how reading and writing influence each other. Finally, writing instruction allows or demands a greater amount of explicitness on the part of the teacher and the learner; for example, it tends to be easier to observe a student's difficulties in writing than in reading because of the written record that is left. Similarly, students usually need more explicit guidance in writing to produce a text than is required to get students started with reading (in reading the student only has to react to the information provided by the author). Research suggests that more explicit teaching is needed for struggling learners (NICHD, 2000; Oxaal, 2005), so literacy teaching that relies on writing activities can be expected to be generally more effective for students who have learning difficulties.

BEST PRACTICES IN TEACHING READING–WRITING RELATIONS

Reading and Writing Need to Be Taught Simultaneously

There is a strong awareness of the importance of instructional time in reading. Various instructional approaches and programs, such as Success for All and Reading First, make sure that children receive substantial amounts of reading instruction by establishing a specific number of minutes to be devoted to reading instruction. Reading First, for example, has increased the amount of primary grade reading instruction by about 1 hour per week (Moss, Jacob, Boulay, Horst, & Poulos, 2006). This is particularly important with low achievers, because they typically do not have adequate opportunity to develop their reading skills away from school (Entwisle, Alexander, & Olson, 1997; Heyns, 1978). Unfortunately, writing is often neglected in U.S. education, and it is doubtful that writing achievement will improve much without a more specific and intentional commitment of time and resources for writing instruction; students make the greatest gains in writing when sufficient amounts of time are made available for writing instruction and practice (Coker, 2006; Duin & Graves, 1987). Studies show that the amount of writing instruction is variable across classrooms and that the amounts provided are insufficient for students who struggle with learning (Christenson, Thurlow, Ysseldyke, & McVicar, 1989). The high correlations between reading and writing suggest that the children who are poor at reading (e.g., children living in poverty, minority children, English language learners, those with learning disabilities) also struggle with writing, and these students are not likely to develop these skills on their own.

Of course, the fact that these children tend to be low in reading can become an excuse for reducing the amount of writing instruction that they receive, as school personnel may conclude that the best thing that can be done to eventually stimulate these students' writing development is to build up their reading skills (even at the cost of neglecting writing for the time being). However, research suggests that in order to take full advantage of the benefits that can be derived from exploiting the relationships between components of reading and writing, both must be taught along the entire continuum of learning (Coker, 2006; Shanahan & Lomax, 1986, 1988). How can children benefit from the intensification that writing can provide to the development of reading skills if the teaching of writing is delayed to a time when those reading skills have already been fully learned? Historically, it was common in U.S. schools to provide students with reading instruction throughout the elementary school years and then eventually to offer some writing instruction to students who already had well-developed reading abilities ("senior composition"). However, this makes no sense if the goal is to teach reading and writing as powerfully and efficiently as possible. What is shared between reading and writing differs at different points in time, and if one or the other is slighted in its curricular coverage, then students lose the opportunity to capitalize on the shared resources between them and the unique contributions of each to the other.

Reading and Writing Instruction Can Be Combined Successfully

Benefits can be derived from combining reading and writing instruction (Tierney & Shanahan, 1991). Although it would be possible to have two separate reading and writing curricula running on parallel tracks, the explicit combination of reading and writing instruction can lead to more thorough attainment of particular knowledge, skills, and strategies. How reading and writing are combined has an impact on what is learned (McGinley & Tierney, 1989). The greatest benefit that reading holds for poor writers is that it provides vivid examples of text and discourse features that the writer needs to master.

For example, Dickson (1999) developed an instructional procedure aimed at teaching students to read and write compare–contrast texts in social studies. Students were taught to analyze texts that had particular comparison structures and then to develop their own paragraphs using the same structures and the same analytical frames that were employed in practice exercises for comprehending social studies passages. This instructional procedure was based on an earlier study in which similar expository text training had positive impacts on both reading and writing achievement (Raphael, Englert, & Kirschner, 1986). Other efforts to teach students the structural organization of what they read using exemplary text models (e.g., mentor or touchstone texts) and then how to use these structures in their own writing have been found to be effective with narrative and persuasive genres as well (Graham & Perin, 2007).

Some forms of reading and writing instruction are so completely combined that it can be difficult to sort out whether they are more about reading or writing. Studies of sentence combining, in which students are given kernel sentences to interpret and then to combine through recursion into more sophisticated grammatical patterns, have been found to improve both reading comprehension and writing quality (Fusaro, 1994; Graham & Perin, 2007). Another example of this is summarization instruction, in which students read texts and are taught how to condense these texts by writing cogent statements including only the most important textual information. As with sentence combining, written text summarization enhances both reading comprehension and writing quality (Graham & Perin, 2007).

These rather straightforward examples show that reading and writing can be combined effectively to improve both reading and writing achievement. However, consideration of these and other combinations of reading and writing instruction that appear in the research literature suggest that reading and writing tend to operate on each other in somewhat different ways and that these differences should be considered when designing combined instruction. For reading, writing activities tend to create a greater explicitness of experience, and these activities may be more demanding than what is actually required for successful reading. Writing seems to create a kind of hyperawareness of particular text features and leads to an overlearning of those features; for example, spelling tends to be harder than decoding, but if a student knows word structure well enough that he or she can spell words from memory, then decoding is virtually ensured (Frith, 1980). Conversely, for writing, reading provides an opportunity to examine clear, overt exemplars or models to which a writer can aspire through emulation. Reading alone may lead to increased understanding of key text features for some students (Cox, Shanahan, & Tinzman, 1991), but most successful efforts to use reading experiences to improve writing are accompanied by some kind of scaffolded deep analysis of the texts (Korat & Schiff, 2005). These mentor texts may be as limited and focused as a sound–symbol spelling–decoding pattern or may be as complex and extended as a rhetorical purpose (e.g., persuasiveness), craft element (e.g., a strong lead), or organizational pattern (e.g., a science experiment).

Efforts to combine reading and writing explicitly have been found to benefit students across a wide range of abilities (Tierney & Shanahan, 1991). Nevertheless, because they emphasize and make explicit particular aspects of reading and writing, it seems evident that the guidance provided by such combinations would be particularly beneficial for students who are more challenged.

Reading and Writing Can Operate Independently

Reading and writing can be combined, and their combination can be powerful. Although reading and writing have lots of similarities and rely on many similar funds of knowledge, skills, and strategies, it is evident that they are not identical. For example, research has been able to identify students who are good readers and poor writers, and vice versa (Stotsky, 1983). The correlational studies noted previously have found less than perfect correlations (generally speaking, about 65–85% of variance in one domain is explained by performance in the other in multivariate studies; Fitzgerald & Shanahan, 2000), and logical analysis shows that even when there are clear overlaps between reading and writing, the functional differences are significant. For example, both reading and writing rely on underlying world knowledge. This knowledge comes into play when readers confront an author's ideas—to help anticipate the author's message, to draw inferences, to disambiguate confusions, and to guide the storage of information in memory. The use of such knowledge is even more obvious in writing; the blank page ultimately is filled with knowledge that the author draws from his or her mind.

But while readers and writers both use their knowledge of the world in order to read and write successfully, their functional starting points are quite different (Fitzgerald & Shanahan, 2000). The reader receives input from the text that guides the instantiation and use of prior knowledge. The writer, on the other hand, has to be self-cueing, determining what knowledge to use without much external guidance. Also, the writer typically has to extract a more extensive representation of memory in order to compose a message. This difference helps explain why individuals perform better on multiple-choice test items than on open-ended ones.

Even in areas such as alphabetics (knowing the relationships between spelling and pronunciation), reading and writing are incommensurate. When the reader confronts a particular letter or letter combination, his or her job is to generate an appropriate approximation of the sounds that usually go with that letter. In English, there is usually more than one possibility, and this means that contextual information embedded in the letter combinations has to be interpreted. Nevertheless, decoding and spelling are not just mirror images of each other, either in how knowledge is put to use or in how the processes are carried out. The alternative routes from sound to spelling are markedly different from the choices from spelling to sound: to spell *gain*, a student has to consider several alternatives for spelling the "long a" vowel—*ain, ane, eign, ayn, aen*—some more likely than others; however, when presented with the word *gain* in text, there are only two real choices (the "long a" pronunciation or the "short a" pronunciation). Clearly reading and writing are not just the reverse of each other, and therefore it is not enough to expect students to simply transform their reading skills into writing achievement.

Another case in point has to do with the role of punctuation in reading and writing. Punctuation provides readers with partial clues to prosodic shaping that must be added to the written discourse to allow for its interpretation (Breznitz, 2006). However, punctuation is used so differently in reading and writing that it is not clear whether combined reading and writing instruction would be helpful in this regard. For example, commas mark pauses in text, but quite intentionally not all reading pauses are marked by commas or any other punctuation, and some commas need to be read through rather quickly in oral reading (such as commas in a series that are dividing a list of related items). There are no research studies that demonstrate that the ability to appropriately punctuate a text in writing is related to the ability to read a text orally in an appropriate manner or that proper reliance on punctuation during reading is an effective harbinger of appropriate punctuation in writing. Some aspects of reading and writing need to be taught separately if students are going to adequately learn these aspects of reading and writing; teachers and curriculum designers need to consider the functional differences in how various parts of reading and writing come into play to determine what needs separate attention.

Reading and Writing Change Developmentally, and Therefore Their Relationships Change

Often people refer to reading–writing relations as if they are one thing. In fact, there are many types of reading–writing relations, and they change with learning and development. Studies reveal, for instance, a close relationship between handwriting, letter name knowledge, spelling, and early decoding skills (e.g., phonemic awareness, phonics) for children up to about second grade (Abbott & Berninger, 1993; Shanahan, 1984; Shanahan & Lomax, 1986, 1988). Although spelling continues to play a role in later reading achievement, the other text production elements become less important, and the overlaps among other more sophisticated discourse features grow in value.

The same patterns are evident in reading and writing achievement themselves, of course. Children evidence developmental variation in particular literacy skills at particular points in time (Paris, 2005). Some skills have low ceilings of development, so there is no continued variation in their patterns. For example, young children need to learn to recognize letters and name them. Initially, there is a great deal of variation in letter name knowledge, with some children learning the letters quickly and others more slowly. However, because there are only 26 letters (or 52 with upper and lower case), this variation in learning attenuates, and just about everyone—even the slowest learners—eventually manage to master the letter names. Conversely, there are other skills that have much more gradual growth curves—vocabulary knowledge, for instance—and these continue to evidence variation across the entire developmental continuum. This explains why a writer might produce a text that is sufficiently long with all the words spelled correctly but without adequate content development or word choice to represent effective writing (Cragg & Nation, 2006).

Instruction designed to take advantage of the spelling–decoding relationship can be quite useful (Coker, 2006), but its value will likely dissipate as children progress in learning to read and write. The nature of this particular reading–writing relationship changes with student reading level, and the effectiveness of instructional approaches designed to exploit the relationship also needs to change as children advance (Shanahan, 1984). The most salient difference between struggling readers and writers and their classmates is that the struggling students have lower levels of attainment or achievement. What this means is that the kinds of instruction aimed at helping students to decode and spell are likely to be of value for a longer period of time with low achievers than with other students. A national survey of primary grade teachers (Graham, Harris, Fink, & MacArthur, 2003) shows that these teachers quite appropriately provide more instruction in handwriting and spelling to poor writers than to other students, though this was not true of all of the teachers surveyed. With faster-developing children, it might be sensible to shift attention to other aspects of literate discourse and to teach these for both reading and writing; but with struggling writers (who initially have trouble even producing text), it is incumbent on the teacher to teach the enabling skills sufficiently and to continue to take advantage of the combinations of these aspects of reading and writing.

Consider the Similarity of Reading and Writing Processes

Most of the examples used up to this point have emphasized similarities in text and discourse features. Clearly, reading and writing mutually depend on a variety of text and discourse features—letters, spelling pat-

terns, punctuation, grammar, organization, and style. Poor writers struggle with these aspects of writing (Troia, 2006), and reading can provide
valuable models of how these features work, which can help guide struggling writers to learn how to incorporate them more effectively in their
own texts. However, research also indicates that there are relationships
between the cognitive processes used in reading and writing (Langer,
1986), and it is possible that instruction could exploit these connections
as well. This is particularly important given that studies show that students with learning disabilities struggle with such cognitive processes as
planning, content generation, and revising (Troia, 2006).

In a fascinating study that compared the reasoning operations (e.g.,
questioning, hypothesizing, validating), strategies (e.g., generating ideas,
evaluating, revising), monitoring approaches, process or product focus,
use of knowledge sources, and timing of 8-, 11-, and 14-year-old readers
and writers, it was found that there were clear similarities and differences
in how readers and writers made meaning. For example, across both
reading and writing tasks, most students' comments focused on their
knowledge and how they were using this information to read or write,
but they did this somewhat more in reading than in writing, and their
comments were related to mechanics more often when they wrote.

> Though children's behavior while both reading and writing was domi-
> nated by the content of the text-worlds being created, the differing
> purposes underlying reading and writing led to different problems and
> emphases in the reasoning operations the children brought to bear
> upon the task. Reading, with the author's text to channel the reader's
> ideas, led to more focusing on specific content, and to validating of
> the text-world that was being developed. Writing, on the other hand,
> forces the writer to take more overt control of the process, leading to a
> greater focus on the strategies that could be used to create their mean-
> ings. (Langer, 1986, p. 94)

How can reading and writing instruction be linked so as to support
children's planning, revising, and other cognitive activities during writing? Providing this kind of reading–writing support through instruction
is much more complicated than simply guiding students to read a text
model thoughtfully and then to try to create a new version of the same
thing. A good example of this more complex approach is provided in a
study in which diverse middle school students were effectively taught to
incorporate historical reasoning in their social studies essays (De La Paz,
2005). During a period of about a month, students were taught to read
historical accounts with an eye to sourcing (to evaluate an author's purpose), textual inconsistency, and bias. They were given opportunities to

read a variety of historical accounts, including textbooks, and then were taught how to develop an essay by comparing one source against another. Writing models were provided, but the students also received specific guidance in how to plan their writing—guidance that was subtly linked to the historical reading experiences that were provided. Thus the emphasis was more on cognitive strategy than on replicating the models themselves. For example, students examined various argument structures, including claims, rebuttals, countered rebuttals, justifications, and warrants—but the focus was not so much on what these looked like in a text but more on how and when authors used them to influence their audience. Langer (1986) concluded that student writers, even by the age of 14, rarely paid attention to the potential impact of their writing on readers; but in this historical reasoning instruction, students were learning why authors used certain structures, and then they were guided to try to have the same kind of communicative impact by using them. The difference is one in which, instead of teaching students how to structurally create a five-paragraph essay, the teacher provides scaffolded experiences to help them understand why an author would want to communicate in a particular way and then steers the student writer into similar rhetorical situations so that a five-paragraph essay is a reasonable rhetorical choice.

De La Paz's (2005) approach to the teaching of historical thinking is interesting both in the specific procedures used to teach the reading and writing of history and in the degree to which it treats literacy as an intentional interaction between authors and readers. Modern reading instruction tends to obscure the role of the author, and author-oriented reading techniques are not widely used (Shanahan, 1992, 1998). However, when reading instruction highlights the author's intentions and provides planning mechanisms (as was done in the De La Paz study), writing tends to improve, even for struggling readers (Graham & Perrin, 2007; Monroe & Troia, 2006).

Paxton (2002), also in a study of history reading and writing, divided students into two groups: one read a passage from a history text that was written in third person with an anonymous author, and the other read a comparable passage from a history text written in the first person with a visible author. Students were asked to think aloud during their readings and to write an essay based on the article that they read (and some other historical documents). The students who read the visible author passage "tended to hold mental conversations with text authors, making judgments about those authors and thinking more about the history under discussion. The essays they wrote were longer and showed greater personal agency and awareness of audience" (Paxton, 2002, p. 197). Other studies of the visibility of authors have shown similar impacts on reading measures (Nolen, 1995; Paxton, 1997).

These studies highlight the idea that the planning required in writing can be especially difficult for poor readers because they often lack strategies for planning or much insight into the rhetorical intentions of authors. Enhanced reading instruction can increase author awareness (Shanahan, 1992, 1998), and struggling writers can be introduced to planning schemes that help them to remember the structural properties of particular kinds of texts (Graham & Perin, 2007; Monroe & Troia, 2006).

Revision poses its own problems, because revision is one aspect of writing that always has to have its basis in reading (the reading of one's own text). Successful revision means that an author has been able to improve the quality or clarity of what was originally drafted, and this involves both writing skills (being able to add appropriate and helpful new information, to delete what is unnecessary or confusing, and to clarify or improve on existing information) and reading skills (the ability to recognize these problems). Unfortunately, many students who have the writing skills to improve their initial drafts lack the ability to read their texts with a sufficiently critical eye (Beal, 1996). Children tend to see their ideas in a text and assume that others can see them, too, whether or not their words actually convey those ideas. Even when confronted by interpretations of their writing that conflict with their own ideas, they tend to have difficulty determining the source of the problem (Beal, 1996).

Personal experience tells me that these kinds of reading problems are best addressed by distance, that revision should not occur too quickly. Even professional writers recommend that drafts be laid aside in order to create some distance, making it easier to recognize what needs fixing. Furthermore, research shows that students can be taught to monitor their understanding of text to an extent that can improve their general reading comprehension (NICHD, 2000) and that this might transfer to an improved ability to look critically at their own efforts, an idea supported by research in which providing students with various kinds of checklists and teaching them self-questioning procedures appear to improve their writing quality (Beal, 1993; Monroe & Troia, 2006).

SUMMING UP

The research is clear that reading and writing are connected; that is, readers and writers depend on the same knowledge and skill base, the same text and discourse features, and the same rhetorical devices to make meaning. Despite these similarities, the functional demands of reading and writing require that these various features and elements be conjured up and used in somewhat different ways that are not always symmetrical—reading and writing are more than just two sides of the same coin.

Reading and writing are connected in some other ways, as well. Writers do more than create text objects, and readers do more than interpret text objects. Reading and writing are communication processes; they have rhetorical purposes that require consideration of intentions, bias, and perspective. Being a participant in communication provides insights that can be useful in improving communications: Readers come to understand how authors confuse them, and writers come to recognize when their messages do not convey the meanings intended. Furthermore, reading and writing can be combined together to accomplish other goals, such as learning.

Research on reading–writing relations suggests that some combinations of reading and writing in the classroom can provide greater power and efficiency, even for struggling students. Specifically, the research suggests that it is essential to teach both reading and writing explicitly and to ensure that students participate in sufficient amounts of reading and writing activity. There are times when it makes no sense to combine reading and writing because of functional differences in particular aspects, but it also can help to infuse reading into writing, particularly by providing students with appropriate text models of particular textual or discourse features and by guiding students to analyze and to try to reproduce such features in their own writing.

Reading and writing are developmental processes, meaning that they are learned over time, and the focus of learning at one point in time might be very different from the focus at another. The changing faces of reading and writing across the school grades alter the nature of reading and writing relationships, and this means that bringing reading into writing will be different at various points in time. Teachers need to vary the ways they try to combine reading and writing on the basis of the students' literacy level—focusing more on handwriting, spelling, and text format features when children are mastering their counterparts in the early grades and more on vocabulary, discourse structure, and text organization as they progress.

Most combinations of reading and writing instruction have used reading to provide students with models of appropriate writing. However, more complex combinations of reading and writing can be used to develop other abilities (such as historical reasoning). Making students aware of the rhetorical choices that authors make, the reasons for these choices, and how to execute them requires complex combinations of reading and writing—and these, too, are valuable for improving the reading and writing abilities of struggling learners.

REFERENCES

Abbott, R. D., & Berninger, V. W. (1993). Structural equation modeling of relationships among developmental skills and writing skills in primary and intermediate grade writers. *Journal of Educational Psychology, 85,* 478–508.

Adams, M. J. (1990). *Beginning to read: Thinking and learning about print.* Cambridge, MA: MIT Press.

American College Testing. (2006). *Reading between the lines: What the ACT reveals about college readiness in reading.* Iowa City, IA: ACT.

Arc, G., Phillips, K. R., & McKenzie, D. (2000). *On the bottom rung: A profile of Americans in low-income working families.* Washington, DC: Urban Institute.

Barton, P. E., & Jenkins, L. (1995). *Literacy and dependency: The literacy skills of welfare recipients in the United States.* Princeton, NJ: Educational Testing Service.

Beal, C. R. (1993). Contributions of developmental psychology to understanding revision: Implications for consultation with classroom teachers. *School Psychology Review, 22,* 643–655.

Beal, C. R. (1996). The role of comprehension monitoring in children's revision. *Educational Psychology Review, 8,* 219–238.

Beck, A. J., & Harrison, P. M. (2001). *Prisoners in 2000.* Washington, DC: U.S. Department of Justice, Bureau of Justice Statistics.

Berkman, N. D., DeWalt, D. A., Pignone, M. P., Sheridan, S. L., Lohr, K. N., Lux, L., et al. (2004). *Literacy and health outcomes* (Evidence Report/Technology Assessment No. 87). Rockville, MD: Agency for Healthcare Research and Quality.

Berninger, V. W. (2000). Development of language by hand and its connections with language by ear, mouth, and eye. *Topics in Language Disorders, 20*(4), 65–84.

Berninger, V. W., Abbott, R. D., Abbott, S. P., Graham, S., & Richards, T. (2002). Writing and reading: Connections between language by hand and language by eye. *Journal of Learning Disabilities, 35,* 39–56.

Berninger, V. W., Cartwright, A. C., Yates, C. M., Swanson, H. L., & Abbott, R. D. (1994). Developmental skills related to writing and reading acquisition in the intermediate grades. *Reading and Writing: An Interdisciplinary Journal, 6,* 161–196.

Breznitz, Z. (2006). *Fluency in reading: Synchronization of processes.* Mahwah, NJ: Lawrence Erlbaum Associates.

Christenson, S. L., Thurlow, M. L., Ysseldyke, J. E., & McVicar, R. (1989). Written language instruction for students with mild handicaps: Is there enough quantity to ensure quality? *Learning Disability Quarterly, 12,* 219–229.

Clifford, G. J. (1989). A Sisyphean task: Historical perspectives on writing and reading instruction. In A. H. Dyson (Ed.), *Collaboration through writing and reading* (pp. 25–83). Urbana, IL: National Council of Teachers of English.

Coker, D. (2006). Impact of first-grade factors on the growth and outcomes of urban schoolchildren's primary-grade writing. *Journal of Educational Psychology*, *98*, 471–488.

Cox, B. E., Shanahan, T., & Tinzman, M. (1991). Children's knowledge of organization, cohesion, and voice. *Research in the Teaching of English*, *25*, 179–218.

Cragg, L., & Nation, K. (2006). Exploring written narrative in children with poor reading comprehension. *Educational Psychology*, *26*, 55–72.

De La Paz, S. (2005). Effects of historical reasoning instruction and writing strategy mastery in culturally and academically diverse middle school classrooms. *Journal of Educational Psychology*, *97*, 139–156.

Dickson, S. (1999). Integrating reading and writing to teach compare–contrast text structure: A research-based methodology. *Reading and Writing Quarterly*, *14*, 49–79.

Dockrell, J. E., Geoff, L., Connelly, V., & Mackie, C. (2007). Constraints in the production of written text in children with specific language impairments. *Exceptional Children*, *73*, 147–164.

Duin, A. H., & Graves, M. F. (1987). Intensive vocabulary instruction as a prewriting technique. *Reading Research Quarterly*, *22*, 311–330.

Entwisle, D. R., Alexander, K. L., & Olson, L. S. (1997). *Children, schools, and inequality*. Boulder, CO: Westview Press.

Fitzgerald, J., & Shanahan, T. (2000). Reading and writing relations and their development. *Educational Psychologist*, *35*, 39–50.

Foorman, B. R., Schatschneider, C., Eakin, M. N., Fletcher, J. M., Moats, L. C., & Francis, D. J. (2006). The impact of instructional practices in grades 1 and 2 on reading and spelling achievement in high poverty schools. *Contemporary Educational Psychology*, *31*, 1–29.

Frith, U. (1980). Unexpected spelling problems. In U. Frith (Ed.), *Cognitive process in spelling* (pp. 495–515). London: Academic Press.

Fusaro, J. A. (1994). A meta-analysis of the effect of sentence-combining on reading comprehension. *Reading Improvement*, *20*, 228–231.

Gleason, M. M., & Isaacson, S. (2001). Using the new basals to teach the writing process: Modifications for students with learning problems. *Reading and Writing Quarterly*, *17*, 75–92.

Graham, S., Harris, K. R., Fink, B., & MacArthur, C. A. (2003). Primary grade teachers' instructional adaptations for struggling writers: A national survey. *Journal of Educational Psychology*, *95*, 279–292.

Graham, S., & Perin, D. (2007). A meta-analysis of writing instruction for adolescent students. *Journal of Educational Psychology*, *99*(2), 445–476.

Heyns, B. (1978). *Summer learning and the effects of schooling*. New York: Academic Press.

Hillocks, G. (1986). *Research on written composition*. Urbana, IL: National Conference on Research in English.

Kirsch, I. S., Jungeblut, A., & Jenkins, L. (1993). *Adult literacy in America: A first look at the results of the National Adult Literacy Survey*. Washington, DC: U.S. Department of Education, National Center for Education Statistics.

Korat, O., & Schiff, R. (2005). Do children who read more books know "what is good writing" better than children who read less? A comparison between grade levels and SES groups. *Journal of Literacy Research, 37,* 289–324.

Langer, J. A. (1986). *Children reading and writing: Structures and strategies.* Norwood, NJ: Ablex.

Lerkkanen, M. K., Rasku-Puttonen, H., Aunola, K., & Nurmi, J. E. (2004). The developmental dynamics of literacy skills during the first grade. *Educational Psychology, 24,* 793–810.

McGinley, W., & Tierney, R. J. (1989). Traversing the topical landscape: Reading and writing as ways of knowing. *Written Communication, 6,* 243–269.

Monroe, B. W., & Troia, G. A. (2006). Teaching writing strategies to middle school students with disabilities. *Journal of Educational Research, 100,* 21–33.

Moss, M., Jabob, R., Boulay, B., Horst, M., & Poulos, J. (2006). *Reading First implementation evaluation: Interim report.* Cambridge, MA: Abt.

National Commission on Writing. (2003). *The neglected "R": The need for a writing revolution.* New York: College Board.

National Commission on Writing. (2004). *Writing: A ticket to work ... or a ticket out.* New York: College Board.

National Institute of Child Health and Human Development. (2000). *Report of the National Reading Panel. Teaching children to read: An evidence-based assessment of the scientific research literature on reading and its implications for reading instruction: Reports of the subgroups.* Washington, DC: U.S. Government Printing Office.

Nolen, S. B. (1995). Effects of a visible author in statistical texts. *Journal of Educational Psychology, 87,* 47–65.

Oxaal, I. (2005). Accelerating student learning in kindergarten through grade 3: Five years of OSEP-sponsored intervention research. *Journal of Special Education, 39,* 2–5.

Paris, S. G. (2005). Reinterpreting the development of reading skills. *Reading Research Quarterly, 40,* 184–203.

Paxton, R. (2002). The influence of author visibility on high school students solving a historical problem. *Cognition and Instruction, 20,* 197–248.

Paxton, R. J. (1997). "Someone with like a life wrote it": The effects of a visible author on high school history students. *Journal of Educational Psychology, 89,* 235–250.

Persky, H. R., Daane, M. C., & Jin, Y. (2003). *The nation's report card: Writing 2002.* Washington DC: U.S. Department of Education, Institute of Education Sciences. National Center for Education Statistics.

Raphael, T. E., Englert, C. S., & Kirschner, B. W. (1986). *The impact of text structure instruction and social context on students' comprehension and production of expository text* (Research Series No. 177). East Lansing: Michigan State University, Institute for Research on Teaching.

Santoro, L. E., Coyne, M. D., & Simmons, D. C. (2006). The reading–spelling connection: Developing and evaluating a beginning spelling intervention for children at risk of reading disability. *Learning Disabilities Research and Practice, 21,* 122–133.

Shanahan, T. (1984). Nature of the reading-writing relation: An explanatory multivariate analysis. *Journal of Educational Psychology, 76,* 466–477.

Shanahan, T. (1992). Reading comprehension as a conversation with an author. In M. Pressley, K. R. Harris, & J. T. Guthrie (Eds.), *Promoting academic competence and literacy in school* (pp. 129–148). San Diego, CA: Harcourt Brace Jovanovich.

Shanahan, T. (1998). Readers' awareness of author. In N. Nelson & R. C. Calfee (Eds.), *The reading–writing connection* (Ninety-seventh yearbook of the National Society for the Study of Education, pp. 88–111). Chicago: University of Chicago Press.

Shanahan, T., & Lomax, R. G. (1986). An analysis and comparison of theoretical models of the reading–writing relationship. *Journal of Educational Psychology, 78,* 116–123.

Shanahan, T., & Lomax, R. G. (1988). A developmental comparison of three theoretical models of reading–writing relationship. *Research in the Teaching of English, 22,* 196–212.

Smits-Engelsman, B. C. M., & Van Galen, G. P. (1997). Dysgraphia in children: Lasting psychomotor deficiency or transient developmental delay? *Journal of Experimental Child Psychology, 67,* 164–184.

Stotsky, S. (1983). Research of reading/writing relationships: A synthesis and suggested directions. *Language Arts, 60,* 568–580.

Tierney, R. J., & Shanahan, T. (1991). Research on the reading–writing relationship: Interactions, transactions, and outcomes. In R. Barr, M. L. Kamil, P. Mosenthal, & P. D. Pearson (Eds.), *Handbook of reading research* (Vol. 2, pp. 246–280). Mahwah, NJ: Erlbaum.

Troia, G. A. (2006). Writing instruction for students with learning disabilities. In C. A. MacArthur, S. Graham, & J. Fitzgerald (Eds.), *Handbook of writing research* (pp. 324–336). New York: Guilford Press.

CHAPTER 5

Informational Writing across the Curriculum

CAROL SUE ENGLERT
CYNTHIA M. OKOLO
TROY V. MARIAGE

This chapter focuses on writing across the curriculum, with a specific focus on struggling writers. In the empirical literature, this work is described in various ways, including expository writing, writing-to-learn, and content area writing. A central concern among these various perspectives is the effective use of writing tools and strategies within a learning and communication process that supports the acquisition, comprehension, and expression of expository ideas.

As students progress through school, they must learn from textual materials that are increasingly complex, conceptually dense, and less well structured (Jetton & Alexander, 2004; Jetton & Dole, 2004). New abilities are required of students as they learn from these texts—they must be able to establish learning purposes, integrate new information with prior knowledge, resolve conflicting ideas, interpret multiple texts and perspectives, clarify ambiguities, and recognize or communicate the author's perspective (Biancarosa & Snow, 2004). Without a specific instructional focus on these abilities in content-area classrooms, many students will struggle to move beyond the more familiar narrative structures they are exposed to in the English language arts curriculum to the less familiar domains of content-area curricula. Unfortunately, the probability is high that teachers' provision of academic supports and explicit instruction in reading and writing strategies in the content areas declines (Alexander & Jetton, 2000) just as students reach the most rigorous and challenging aspects of the expository curriculum in the upper grades.

The combination of increased demands and limited instructional support has profound ramifications for today's readers and writers, many of whom are struggling. Generally, 27% of eighth graders demonstrate reading skills below a basic level, and nearly 73% of them demonstrate reading skills below a proficient level, according to the most recent National Assessment of Educational Progress (NAEP; National Center for Education Statistics [NCES], 2005). At the fourth-grade level, about one-third of students read proficiently, whereas one-third have only partial mastery, and 36% fail to reach even basic levels of performance (NCES, 2005). Furthermore, according to the results of the NAEP for writing, only 28% of fourth graders attained performance levels that were judged to be at or above proficient, and, conversely, 72% exhibited only partial mastery of the knowledge and skills that are considered fundamental for fourth-grade writing (Persky, Daane, & Jin, 2003). The picture darkens when informational literacy is considered. On the NAEP expository writing task, fewer than 17% of the fourth-grade students performed at the proficient level, as measured by students' production of texts that included main ideas and details and that displayed sensitivity to their target audience (Persky et al., 2003).

Even beyond high school, students' problems with informational literacy continue to threaten their academic progress. Among high school graduates, 53% must enroll in remedial courses in postsecondary education programs because they failed to acquire the necessary skills in secondary education (NCES, 2001). Among these individuals, more freshman entering degree-granting postsecondary institutions take remedial writing courses than take remedial reading courses (NCES, 2003b). In the workplace, writing proficiency affects hiring and promotion decisions (National Commission on Writing, 2004). Unless educators teach strategies for informational reading and writing, many students will struggle with academic tasks, fail to thrive in postsecondary institutions, and miss opportunities for career success (Biancarosa & Snow, 2004).

Addressing the problems students have with reading and writing expository texts requires an understanding of the skills, strategies, and processes that underlie writing-to-learn in the content areas. There are at least three fundamental abilities that must be addressed in the informational writing curriculum: knowledge of text structures, the use of writing-to-learn activities and tools in content-area learning, and disciplinary-related writing activities. These literacy functions are described in further detail in the following three sections.

KNOWLEDGE OF EXPOSITORY TEXT STRUCTURES

Informational texts in content-area curricula are challenging because of their structural unfamiliarity to students. However, they are organized in particular ways according to a formal academic register that specifies regularities in how information is arranged to reflect the author's purpose (Tower, 2003). These organizational patterns, known as text structures, enhance the predictability, comprehensibility, and compositionality of the texts for students who are cognizant of their importance. The types of expository text structures that are commonly found in content area textbooks include problem–solution, compare–contrast, classification, explanation, and persuasion (Meyer, 1975, 1977; Meyer, Brandt, & Bluth, 1980; Meyer & Freedle, 1984). Each of these text structures requires different types of information, and each employs different linguistic devices to signal the location of the requisite textual information to readers (Cope & Kalantzis, 1993).

Sensitivity to these types of text structures helps students read, understand, and compose informational texts. For example, history texts are often organized to provide answers to questions related to the problem–solution structure (e.g., What was the problem? What were the causes of the problem? What were the solutions? What were the outcomes of the solutions?). Linguistic devices that signal readers about the location of the relevant problem–solution information might include discourse markers such as *causes*, *problem*, *effects*, *solution*, and *outcome*. In biology, classification and description schemes that encompass taxonomies with classes and subclasses of concepts might dominate the textbook, whereas procedural explanations might govern the type of writing found in the science laboratory notebook. In social studies, on the other hand, texts are often organized according to different social classification schemes (e.g., culture, geography, economics, etc.), as well as varied text structures, such as problem–solution, compare–contrast, and chronological sequence. Linguistic devices to cue the location of important compare–contrast information might include discourse markers such as *similarly*, *in contrast*, *comparatively*, and *difference*; those to signal sequence might include transition words such as *first*, *then*, *next*, and *finally*.

Rarely do expository texts present a single uniform text structure; more typically, they contain a composite of various text structures that seamlessly thread back and forth to provide depth and breadth to the author's treatment of a topic. That is, a history chapter might present information that is organized according to one text structure for one or two paragraphs and then shift to another text structure for a brief section. As a reader, the student must be able to recognize and identify these text structures to support comprehension; as a writer, the student must be able to independently search, retrieve, and restructure the text information to address different writing purposes, such as to create and report a chronology or timeline of events, to compare and contrast two people or events within or across chapters, or to identify the problems, solutions, and outcomes associated with a particular event or time period. Knowledge of text structures helps students to select and apply the interpretative tools that they can use to reorganize the expository information to satisfy different questions and reader–writer purposes, as well as to flexibly identify, construct, comprehend, or compose meanings.

There is another level of organization that is used by readers and writers when they seek to interpret or construct texts. In addition to the more global macrostructures just discussed, expository texts are organized at the local level through topic sentences that introduce readers to the theme or purpose of a subsection of text and that stage the textual information that follows. These introductory statements foreshadow the supporting subtopics that, in turn, are embellished with relevant details that elaborate on the subtopics (Englert, Zhao, Dunsmore, Collings, & Wolbers, 2007). Expository text is hierarchically and recursively structured with introductory statements, elaborative details, and concluding or summary remarks that offer a wave-like movement through the text and that signal the prominence and connection among the various clusters of ideas (Halliday & Martin, 1993). Good readers and writers flexibly work on text at these multiple levels to build meaningful associations within and across the various sections of the text, or even across multiple texts or concepts.

Research suggests that sensitivity to expository text structures is developmentally acquired by students (Kamberelis, 1999). Younger and less successful students perform less well in remembering and constructing ideas that conform to the organizational patterns of expository texts than do older and more successful students. In contrast to mature readers, for example, young students show less sensitivity to the textual importance of ideas (Englert et al., 1991; McGee, 1982; Meyer et al., 1980; Richgels, McGee, Lomax, & Sheard, 1987; Spivey & King, 1989; Taylor & Samuels, 1983). Likewise, poor readers tend to approach texts as though the ideas of a passage are haphazardly organized rather than organized based on predictable patterns and hierarchical relationships (Taylor & Samuels, 1983). This affects their ability to identify the main ideas and related details of an informational text (Williams, 2003, 2005), as well as to recall the information in a manner that preserves the topical relationships, organizational patterns, and relational meanings of the referential material (Meyer et al., 1980).

In writing, similar differences have been reported for students at different grade or ability levels. Kamberelis and Bovino (1999) examined children's understanding and use of narrative and informational genres. They asked kindergarten, first-grade, and second-grade students to write stories and biology reports in an unscaffolded condition (students were simply asked to write a story or a factual report) and a scaffolded condition (students were asked to recall a fictional tale or an informative text and then write it from memory). The results indicated that although most children could compose narratives, fewer children could compose factual reports. The scaffolded condition resulted in more well-formed texts than the unscaffolded condition. Sensitivity to expository text structures also affects the writing performance of students with language and learning disabilities (LLD). Studies suggest that students with LLD persist in using an inefficient strategy known as knowledge telling, in which they retrieve and compose ideas from memory in whatever associative order comes to mind, without planning, organizing, or hierarchically arranging the ideas into organized or predictable relationships (Bereiter & Scardamalia, 1985). Even given a generative prompt or clue that is intended to trigger a particular topic and text structure (e.g., "There are many breeds of dogs"), students with LLD tend to generate information in an associative manner (e.g., "My neighbor has a dog") that touches on the topic in a tangential manner but that fails to satisfy the requirements of the prompted informational text structure (Englert, Hiebert, & Stewart, 1987; Englert, Raphael, Fear, & Anderson, 1988). This difficulty obviously affects writing performance in a number of ways, most notably when students are asked to plan, organize, generate, or monitor informational texts (Englert et al., 1991).

Despite the difficulties of many students in perceiving and using text structures appropriately, research suggests that explicit instruction has a powerful effect on students' ability to compose expository papers that conform to a given text structure (Graham, 2006). A number of text structures have been explicitly taught to students in intervention studies, including compare–contrast (Wong, Butler, Ficzere, & Kuperis, 1997), problem–solution, cause–effect (Ciardiello, 2002), enumeration (Englert et al., 1987), and opinion or persuasive essays (De La Paz, 2005; Troia & Graham, 2002; Wong, Butler, Ficzere, & Kuperis, 1996). The principal findings emanating from this research are that text structures can be reliably taught, that text structure instruction improves students' writing performance, and that the effects of such instruction are strong (Graham & Perin, 2007).

Four instructional features seem to typify effective expository writing programs (see Baker, Gersten, & Graham, 2003; Gersten & Baker, 2001; Graham, 2006; Vaughn, Gersten, & Chard, 2000), including (1) the incorporation of graphic organizers to represent the component elements of the expository text structures, (2) emphases on text structures and writing strategies within the writing process, (3) the creation of instructional apprenticeships that are designed to promote the writers' independence and self-regulation, and (4) the construction of writing contexts that focus students' attention on the importance of expository writing purposes and the perspectives of their audiences.

Graphic Organizers

Graphic organizers have been proven to be an essential teaching tool that makes visible the organizational features of a given text structure (Kamil, 2003; Kim, Vaughn, Wanzek, & Wei, 2004). Graphic organizers support writing performance by reminding students of the topically relevant information that must be generated and by visually diagramming the hierarchical patterns and associations among the component elements. In many studies, students have been taught to memorize the text structure elements and transition words, in addition to using graphic organizers to generate and compose topically relevant information (e.g., Harris, Graham, & Mason, 2003; Troia & Graham, 2002). Providing examples and nonexamples of papers that students can evaluate for the presence or absence of the essential text structure components and transition words is another practical method for deepening students' sensitivity to and analysis of the expository text structure features (Graham & Perin, 2007). Ultimately, students are expected to emulate the qualities of the well-formed texts they read, and they are taught to transfer the text structure components and evaluative criteria to construct and monitor their own expository texts.

Writing Strategies

Effective expository writing programs work best when teachers are explicit about the way written language is organized to construct various meanings and when teachers model how strategies can be used in the writing process (Cope & Kalantzis, 1993). In particular, students need to learn how to use text structures within a process of writing that involves planning, organizing, composing, and revising/editing strategies. For example, De La Paz (2005) guided students to use the PLAN and WRITE strategies. In PLAN, students were taught to (1) Pay attention to the prompt, (2) List main ideas, (3) Add supporting ideas, and (4) Number ideas. At the conclusion of this planning stage, students had generated main ideas and related details that could serve as a frame to organize their compositions. In WRITE, students were taught to: (1) Work from the plan to develop a thesis statement, (2) Remember goals, (3) Include transition words for each paragraph, (4) Try to use different kinds of sentences, and (5) use Exciting, interesting $100,000 words. The PLAN and WRITE mnemonics prompted students to plan the organizational pattern framed by the main ideas and details and then guided them in translating those plans into well-signaled and differentiated textual ideas in compositions. The results showed that students wrote longer and better organized papers.

In Cognitive Strategy Instruction in Writing (CSIW), a program developed by Englert and her colleagues (Englert et al., 1991; Englert & Mariage, 2003), students learn to use self-questions to guide them through the writing process. The CSIW acronym for the writing process is POWER, which included: *Plan* ("Who am I writing for? Why am I writing this? What do I know?"), *Organize* ("What ideas go together? What can I call those ideas? How can I label the order of the ideas?"), *Write* ("How can I best translate my plans into text?"), *Edit* ("Did I introduce the topic of my paper? Did I introduce each category with topic sentences? Did I include 3–5 categories of main ideas? Did I include 2–3 details for each main idea? Did I use transition words? Did I write a concluding sentence?"), and *Revise*. At one level, the CSIW strategies help students stage the text structure by reminding them to generate the introductory statements that prepare readers for the forthcoming text and by offering structural reminders that prompt students to provide supporting details and concluding sentences that fulfill the discourse-level expectations of their readers. At a second level, CSIW teachers model the role of text structure components and traits within the organizing and editing process through the use of graphic organizers and self-evaluation rubrics. Thus CSIW is designed to help students understand the requirements of a well-organized text and the strategic processes that help one integrate, organize, and compose ideas based on text structure during the writing process. CSIW instruction has resulted in significant improvements in students' abilities to employ expository text structures in their informational writing (Englert et al., 1991).

Another strategy instruction program, Self-Regulated Strategy Development (SRSD), developed by Harris and Graham (1996, 1999), articulates six steps to facilitate the development of writing proficiency: (1) develop background knowledge for the strategy, (2) discuss the purpose and benefits of the strategy, (3) model the strategy, (4) memorize it (i.e., have the students memorize the steps of the strategy and accompanying mnemonics), (5) support it (i.e., the teacher supports or scaffolds students' mastery of the strategy), and (6) provide independent practice. Their research efforts have shown that effective writing instruction should include the types of self-talk, instructional scaffolds, and strategic processes that align well with the goal of helping students to self-regulate and self-direct the writing process (e.g., Graham & Harris, 2003).

Apprenticeship Instructional Model

Effective instructional programs attend to the pedagogical processes that support a full learning apprenticeship (Biemiller & Meichenbaum, 1996; Collins, Brown, & Holum, 1991). Apprenticeship means that teachers give high support to students practicing new skills in the early phases of instruction and then slowly decrease that support to increase student ownership and self-sufficiency in the later phases of instruction (Biancarosa & Snow, 2004). Research suggests that effective teachers begin their instruction by *modeling* and *thinking aloud* as they demonstrate writing strategies and explain text structures within authentic writing activities in which teachers generate ideas and compose texts (Graham & Harris, 2003). To transfer control of the strategies and self-talk, teachers involve students in jointly composing papers while students think aloud as they employ the strategies, and the teacher stands by to step in to mediate performance when students falter or demonstrate difficulties. During *collaborative practice*, students work with a partner or small group to write a composition, drawing on procedural facilitators in the form of cue cards, rubrics, or think sheets that continue to prompt strategy use, text structures, and self-talk during the writing and editing process. For instance, De La Paz (2005; De La Paz & Graham, 2002) and Englert et al. (1991) used strategy cue cards and think sheets together with peer collaboration to prompt students to apply writing strategies that were appropriate for particular writing phases. Collaborative writing has a strong positive impact on quality when students are able to direct and support each other in the use of strategies and text structures during writing activities (Graham & Perin, 2007). Finally, students engage in *independent practice* as they employ the strategies to direct and regulate their own writing combined with the teachers' provision of feedback and dynamic assistance on the basis of students' performance. These instructional supports are effective in scaffolding performance until students become independent in regulating their use of strategies during the writing process (see Baker, Gersten, & Scanlon, 2002).

Writing Audience and Purpose

Effective instructional programs highlight the purpose of and audience for informational writing. Expository writing is intended to inform an audience, and the audience–author relationship is an essential aspect of making the social function, purpose, and requirements of informational writing apparent to the writer. To achieve this goal, teachers need to provide an audience who can respond with compelling questions and authentic comments. The patterns of interaction between the author and audience that are initially enacted on the interpersonal plane are expected to be internalized and transformed by the author to constitute an inner dialogue that is reenacted on the psychological or intrapersonal plane. As Bakhtin (1986) has suggested, every written utterance is shaped by these prior conversations, which lead speakers and writers to lay down their own answering words to the questions of an envisioned audience. Thus prior social relationships and interactions provide an important basis for authors to understand the knowledge and the perspectives of their readers. Without an audience, it is quite difficult for young authors to realize the role of expository text in the communication process and to understand their responsibilities as informants who must anticipate and satisfy the knowledge demands of a distant audience of readers.

To summarize, effective expository writing instruction includes instruction that promotes mastery of the text structure genres that are used by the members of particular disciplinary communities. To be effective, teachers must apprentice students in the writing tools, strategies, and text structures that underlie successful performance in the subject matter curriculum (Wells, 1999). Graphic organizers and procedural facilitators can be used by students to support their employment of the writing strategies in advance of independent performance. To the extent that students can deftly and independently employ the text structures and strategies in the composition process, they will be successful at expressing and monitoring their ideas.

INTEGRATING WRITING-TO-LEARN STRATEGIES IN CONTENT-AREA CURRICULA

Writing plays a vital role in the content-area curriculum. Writing about content is a fundamental way to engage students in learning and rehearsing expository information (Bangert-Drowns, Hurley, & Wilkinson, 2004). From this perspective, we view writing as a medium to heighten students' awareness of their own cognitive processes, as well as a mechanism by which students can acquire a better understanding of the meaning and importance of expository content. Writing promotes "thinking about thinking" and "thinking about texts" during a larger process of learning (Paris & Paris, 2001; Schraw, 1998). The activities in this writing-to-learn domain include a number of written responses that teachers might ask students to perform to enhance their surface- or deep-level processing of information (Fox & Alexander, 2004), such as that involved in note taking, summarizing, critiquing, and answering comprehension questions. Without explicit instruction, it is unlikely that such domain-specific tools will spontaneously develop, because reading and writing in response to content-area texts constitute a different set of skills than that needed to comprehend or write literature (Pearson & Duke, 2002).

Project ACCEL

Project ACCEL (Accelerating Expository Literacy) (Englert, Mariage, et al., 2007) is a program designed to integrate reading and writing strategies as literacy tools in the content areas. This program embeds literacy strategies in subject-matter domains through the explicit teaching and application of cognitive routines, which are used alone or in combination within a learning-to-learn process. The instructional program is premised on the assumption that readers and writers engage in a variety of activities to enhance their literacy performance. Prior to reading or writing, for example, skilled learners clarify their purpose, preview the text, activate their prior knowledge, and make a plan for how they might read or write (Neufeld, 2005). During or after reading or writing, accomplished learners ask questions of the text, relate information to prior knowledge, summarize key points, make notes, and clarify their understandings (Klinger, Vaughn, & Schumm, 1998; Neufeld, 2005; Palincsar & Brown, 1984). ACCEL attempts to incorporate component literacy strategies such as these in a process of learning to support students' flexible use of the strategies as tools in content-area subjects. Figure 5.1 displays the ACCEL process with its attendant cognitive strategies and text structures.

PLANS-It

PLANS-It is a preparatory stage for reading and writing in which students consider the topic, make plans, and brainstorm ideas. Because goal setting and activating background knowledge are challenges for struggling readers and writers (e.g., Graham & Harris, 2003; Troia & Graham, 2002; Troia, Graham, & Harris, 1999), this phase is designed to address deficiencies that affect students' ability to anticipate and predict information, as well as to apply their prior knowledge to engage in inferential reasoning. Meta-analyses show that prereading and prewriting activities that involve students in advance planning have a small to moderate positive impact on performance (Graham & Perin, 2007). Accordingly, ACCEL seeks to build on the initial ideas (knowledge and beliefs) of students in a planning stage.

During *PLANS-It*, teachers help students prepare to read, as they (1) consider their reading/writing **P**urpose, (2) **L**ist relevant topics, (3) **A**ctivate prior knowledge and form connections, (4) **N**ote their questions, and (5) anticipate the probable **S**tructure of the text (Ogle & Blachowicz, 2002). These activities prime students to examine the text and to

Phases	PLANNING	GATHERING	ORGANIZING	INTERPRETING	REPORTING
		Reads It			
ACCEL Framework	PLANS It	Highlight It / Mark It	Note It / Map It	Respond to It	Report It
Purpose	• Preview information • List topics • Apply prior knowledge • Note questions • Assess the structure of the information	• Highlight information • Markup and record questions, connections, interpretations • Identify main ideas • Summarize ideas • Self-question • Connect to self, text, and world	• Gather information • Integrate multiple sources • Take notes on key ideas • Use multiple representations • Organize information from multiple sources • Record information on graphic organizer	• Identify author credibility and bias • Query, critique, and interpret evidence • Identify multiple perspectives • Interpret and question using text structures • Connect to self, texts, world	• Generate a written report • Communicate findings • Use multiple representations • Discuss and collaborate • Share oral and written ideas
Disciplinary Tools: Strategies and Text Structures	**P**urpose **L**ist topics and preview **A**ctivate prior knowledge and connect to self, text, world **N**ote your questions **S**tructure: What text structure(s)? •Cause–Effect •Problem–Solution •Compare–Contrast •Time sequence •Classification •Explanation	• Highlight main ideas • Highlight key details • Mark-it with symbols: CL– clarify PK– prior knowledge Q– question P– predict S– summarize I– Imagery C– connect D– detail MI– main idea ***– key point ?– confusing part	**Note and Map It with Text Structure Tools:** • Cause–Effect • Problem–Solution • Compare–Contrast • Time sequence • Classification • Explanation **Apply Literacy Strategies** • Clarify unfamiliar vocabulary • Draw inferences • Self-question • Visualize • Summarize • Sequence • Make connections	**Take a Critical Stance** • Critique the author, text, and ideas • Examine the evidence • Consider multiple perspectives • Support opinions with claims and examine the validity of claims • Connect to text, self, and world **Respond to It with Text Structure Tools:** • Cause–Effect • Problem–Solution • Compare–Contrast • Time sequence • Classification • Explanation	• Oral sharing techniques • Writing genres • Using data to represent findings **Report It Using Text Structure Tools:** •Cause–Effect •Problem–Solution •Compare–Contrast •Time sequence •Classification •Explanation

FIGURE 5.1. ACCEL strategies and text structure.

anticipate how that textual information will be organized, as well as to consider the possible relationship of the expository information to their prior knowledge and reading and writing goals (Palincsar, 2006). Think sheets that correlate to these activities are used by teachers and students to prepare for the instructional units.

Reads-It

During *Reads-It*, students clarify vocabulary and summarize key ideas in expository texts. Many struggling readers tend to be passive during the reading process, and they have great difficulty identifying and summarizing the main ideas and details from informational texts (Block & Pressley, 2002; Pearson & Duke, 2002; Williams, 2003, 2005). Instructional research shows that students can be actively engaged in the learning process through strategy frameworks that involve students in summarizing, predicting, clarifying, and questioning the ideas in texts (Beck, McKeown, Hamilton, & Kucan, 1997; Palincsar & Brown, 1984; Pressley, 2002). Accordingly, ACCEL is designed to teach these learning-to-learn strategies in the content-area curriculum. Using the apprenticeship model for teaching and learning that was discussed previously, teachers model for students and guide them in five *Reads-It* strategies, including: (1) Summarize the main ideas and details, (2) Ask questions about the main ideas and details, or ask questions based on text structures, (3) Clarify confusing ideas or words (see Vaughn & Klingner, 1999), (4) Connect to self, text, and world, and (5) Predict what will be read next (Palincsar & Brown, 1984). Based on the reciprocal teaching framework (Palincsar & Brown, 1984), students apply the strategies to the comprehension of expository texts in discussion with partners or groups, supported by strategy cue cards that prompt strategy application.

In addition, there are four subcomponent phases of *Reads-It* that involve students in ever-deepening ways in developing and transferring the component strategies as learning tools in situated reading and writing contexts. In the first phase, *Highlight-It*, students receive guided practice in identifying the main ideas and details using a highlighting strategy. Teachers model highlighting as part of a summarization routine, helping students understand how to delete redundant or unimportant information, select and highlight a main idea or topic sentence if one is present, and invent a superordinate label or topic sentence that subsumes exemplars if the main idea is omitted from the text (Brown & Day, 1983; Day, 1986; Neufeld, 2005). Students then collaborate with partners and work independently to employ the highlighting strategies. In the process, students are sensitized to the identification of main ideas, detecting critical details, and inventing labels that describe essential meanings within a text comprehension process. Similar techniques have been used to teach summarization strategies to elementary (Williams, 2003, 2005) and junior college students (Brown & Day, 1983; Day, 1986). In Project ACCEL, the purpose and value of the highlighting strategy is explicitly taught to help students transfer the strategy when they study for tests or to identify and summarize the main ideas and details in other content-area materials (Knipper & Duggan, 2006).

In the second subcomponent phase, students elaborate on the author's meaning by using the *Marks-It* strategies to record their own questions, predictions, claims, conclusions, connections, and clarifications in the margins of the text. In *Marks-It*, the students go beyond the literal meanings of the text by holding conversations with the text and by making personal connections and asking questions, which are all strategic processes associated with making meaning (Block & Pressley, 2002; Palincsar & Brown, 1984). The *Marks-It* strategies are taught in combination with highlighting so that students think actively about the text and elaborate on the meanings through inner dialogues and personal reactions. To make visible these inner conversations, students record their thoughts and strategies in the margins of the text or on sticky notes that they affix to the pages of nonconsumable textual materials. Some of the strategies that are recorded by students are questions, clarifications, predictions, summaries, and text structures (e.g., cause–effect, problem–solution, compare–contrast, classification, explanation, multiple perspectives, and persuasion). To intensify their understanding of the repertoire of strategies that is being applied, students share not only their marked-up text with peers and teachers but also the strategies that they apply in the interpretation and meaning-making process.

In the third subcomponent phase, *Notes-It*, students learn to generate written notes about their ideas within a more in-depth rehearsal and study process. During *Notes-It*, students take notes about the ideas in the expository passage(s). Students use their highlighted text to capture the essence of an expository passage. They identify the topic of a passage and the relevant details and then record their written summaries of these critical ideas in two-column tables that match up to the main ideas and details, respectively. Some teachers add a third column so that students might record the *Marks-It* strategies that correspond to their interpretative activity. By recording expository ideas in the note-taking process, students learn to use writing as a tool for reflection and learning, as well as a repository for ideas that can be subsequently retrieved, shared, rehearsed, or disseminated. Note taking also serves as a representational form that reveals the underlying structure of texts and ideas, furthering students' knowledge of text structure and their facility in using writing-to-learn tools in the expository curriculum.

In some cases, graphic organizers are better suited as representational forms for note taking. Several graphic organizers that correspond to varied text structures are taught and made available to students during the reading, writing, and note-taking process. Graphic organizers are especially useful when a written product is the final learning outcome or when students need to synthesize information from multiple sources or multimedia formats (e.g., movies, websites, texts, trade books, and experiments). In these situations, teachers teach the text structure components and instruct students to map the text information corresponding to the components in the graphic organizer. When graphic organizers are used, the fourth subphase is called *Map-It*. The *Map-It* instruction is intended to prompt deeper processing than reading or summarizing alone and entails a type of graphical literacy that underlies reasoning about the structure and meaning of informational texts across multiple sections or chapters of the text or across multiple textual sources.

Respond-to-It

Respond-to-It is a set of strategies that are designed to further students' independence. This component incorporates the interpretive skills that are involved when readers/writers are asked to read, interpret, evaluate, and synthesize evidence—skills that do not develop without instruction (Palincsar, 2006). With the increasing emphasis on digital texts and multimedia websites in informational learning, it is especially important that students critically interpret and evaluate the credibility of textual resources.

Two response formats are utilized. In the *Respond-to-It with Text Structure*, students use text structures to frame their thoughts by identifying and constructing a responsive interpretation based on one or more common content-area text structures: cause–effect, sequence, problem–solution, chronological timeline, classification (categories and details), compare–contrast, or argumentation. Students, for example, might organize social studies information using a timeline, a compare–contrast chart, or a problem–solution diagram. Other students might reorganize the same textual information using a different text structure framework. We see the potential of this instruction for helping students become more metacognitive about interpretation, as well as more insightful about how ideas can be rearranged to create new meanings and relationships or to address different purposes (Spivey, 1997). This type of written response is a critical part of developing inferential reasoning and independent thinking.

The second response format, *Respond-to-It with Critical Literacy*, requires that students go beyond the facts by employing critical literacy skills, such as examining the credibility of information, recognizing points of view or multiple perspectives, making a personal response, and critiquing the text or author's position (Raphael, Kehus, & Damphousse, 2001). These skills are important in digital literacy contexts in which students must appraise the trustworthiness of textual sources and the presence of bias in them. Moreover, bearing in mind that research suggests that students with reading difficulties have difficulty explaining their ideas to peers and self-directing project work (Okolo & Ferretti, 1996), we encourage critical literacy by emphasizing a discursive framework based on Okolo and Ferretti (1996) to assist students in constructing strong arguments. Students must: (1) state their opinions or provide evidence, (2) give reasons for those opinions, (3) explain why the reasons are good reasons, and (4) give examples that illustrate their positions.

Report-It

Finally, during *Report-It*, students develop competence in expressing their ideas (oral and written), learn to write well-structured expository reports representing any number of different text structures, and develop their abilities to coordinate learning-to-learn and inquiry. As part of *Report-It*, students engage in an inquiry process to study an expository topic, and they apply the *Plans-It*, *Reads-It*, *Notes-It*, *Map-It*, and *Respond-to-It* strategies. The information that is gathered by students in the various phases is assembled in a notebook or report that is organized to reflect the writers' questions, purposes, and audience. The publication of reports and the dissemination of the information are important for enhancing students' motivation and their awareness of the authentic purposes of studying, interpreting, and creating expository texts.

Students' performance in the ACCEL program has been evaluated using literacy assessments that required students to highlight, take notes, organize information from multiple sources, summarize, and write expository reports (Englert et al., 2008). The results are generally positive, indicating that junior high students improved their baseline performances when participating in ACCEL instruction classrooms. Average scores on highlighting, note taking, mapping, retelling, and expository writing measures increased over time.

DISCIPLINARY-BASED STRATEGIES

The final key aspect of writing-to-learn involves the use of writing in content-area contexts as part of an inquiry-based approach to learning.

In these contexts, writing is cultivated by the disciplinary demands of the informational domain. We use examples from social studies and science to illustrate how teachers can deepen students' mastery of foundational reading and writing skills and strategies in the content areas, with a particular focus on the dispositions and inquiry skills that capture what it means to read and write like a historian or scientist (Shanahan, 2004; Stahl & Shanahan, 2004).

Social Studies

Experts and novices write about history and social studies in different ways. Academic historians are known for their abilities to construct interpretations of historical issues, whereas high school students have difficulty using rhetorical strategies to integrate historical information into well thought-out explanations or arguments (De La Paz, 2005; Wineburg, 1991). Because social studies textbooks often present a single unquestioned version of historical events, it is challenging for students to develop the ability to engage in historical understanding and to interpret historical events from multiple perspectives (De La Paz & MacArthur, 2003; Paxton, 1999). At the same time, the act of examining the historical record through primary source documents and written arguments about specific issues may be a particularly useful activity in helping students learn to interpret and organize information in new ways (Newman, 1990; De La Paz, 2005). However, because the primary record almost always contains gaps and inconsistencies among multiple perspectives, students must engage in interpretative processes to construct an understanding of historical figures and events that will stand up to the scrutiny of others (VanSledright, 2002).

De La Paz (2005) taught students a strategy that was designed to help them to engage in historical reasoning. The strategy guided students to: (1) judge the integrity and the rhetorical purpose of primary source documents as they analyzed the texts for inconsistencies and bias, (2) compare multiple sources as they looked for conflicting points of view, and (3) make notes on what seemed believable from each primary source. Then, based on their analysis, students learned to plan and compose argumentative essays. They were taught two strategies to aid them in their writing. The STOP strategy prompted students to consider both sides of an argument as they completed four steps: Suspend judgment, Take a side, Organize (select and number ideas), and Plan more as you write. A second mnemonic, DARE, prompted students to generate four major rhetorical argumentative elements in their essays: Develop a topic sentence, Add supporting ideas, Reject an argument for the other side, and End with a conclusion. Comparisons of experimental students, who learned the strategy in social studies and language arts classes, and control students revealed that experimental students wrote papers that were significantly longer. Furthermore, the experimental students' papers were rated significantly more persuasive than those written by students in the control condition, and they contained more arguments in support of their opinions. Finally, the papers written by students who received the strategy instruction were rated as demonstrating greater historical accuracy. The researcher concluded that many middle school students fail to realize that history is an interpretative process and that specific activities are required to engage students in a meaningful analysis of primary source documents. In this regard, writing was viewed as a critical tool to support the development of historical reasoning and interpretation.

Okolo and her colleagues undertook two programs of research in social studies: project-based (e.g., Ferretti & Okolo, 1996; Okolo & Ferretti, 1997) and strategy-supported project-based learning (e.g., Ferretti, MacArthur, & Okolo, 2001). The purpose of the instructional research was to develop students' historical understanding (i.e., understanding that goes beyond knowledge of historical facts) and historical reasoning (i.e., understanding of historical evidence and how it can be used to construct interpretations). In the project-based program, students were involved in inquiry and collaborative activities as they conducted research to address controversial social studies issues (Ferretti et al., 2001; MacArthur, Ferretti, & Okolo, 2002). Learning activities were designed to develop students' understanding of multiple perspectives in history and to enhance their ability to interpret history by taking a position on historical issues and supporting that position with evidence. To deepen their understanding of historical issues, students conducted research, interpreted the historical evidence, and compiled the results of their historical inquiry into a multimedia presentation that was designed to represent their perspectives on a given issue, as well as to present the evidence or data in support of their position. In one study, analyses of the pretest–posttest measures showed that students made significant gains in their knowledge of history topics (Okolo & Ferretti, 1997). In another study, students acquired a better understanding of the historical events and their causes and consequences (De La Paz & MacArthur, 2003).

In the strategy-supported project-based program, the researchers extended the instructional model to provide explicit strategies that could support the historical inquiry of students with disabilities (Ferretti et al., 2001; MacArthur et al., 2002). Students worked in collaborative groups to investigate human migration and westward expansion by reading primary and secondary sources. Teachers taught a compare–contrast strategy routine and a narrative text structure framework, and students then applied these as analytical tools to examine the lives of people who were affected by migration and to understand the resulting conflicts between different cultural groups. To further anchor their learning, students observed multimedia presentations (videos, slide shows) about westward migration and designed their own multimedia presentations to communicate their research question, historical inquiry, and findings to others. Throughout the teaching and learning process, several pedagogical practices were emphasized to enhance students' performance. First, emphasis was placed on substantive discussion to deepen students' understanding of the issues and to further their participation in a discourse community in which they expressed themselves, took positions on issues, and defended their points of view using historical evidence and reasoning. Second, a number of primary and secondary sources were made available in multimedia and text formats to anchor and support students' understanding and communication skills. Third, collaboration among students and between students and the teacher were critical factors in teaching and learning, inasmuch as they offered a developmentally responsive context to deepen students' historical knowledge and strategy use, as well as offering an interactive context in which teachers could assess and scaffold students' historical understanding, knowledge, and reasoning abilities.

Several studies were conducted in which the strategy-supported project-based program was implemented in upper elementary, ethically diverse inclusion classrooms. The findings revealed significant gains in the historical knowledge and reasoning of students with and without disabilities, although the gains were greatest among the group of students without disabilities. Importantly, the multimedia presentations anchored the learning of all students, and students frequently referred to the multimedia materials throughout the instructional units. The involvement of students in the design of their own multimedia presentations was a highly motivating learning activity that supported the development of historical knowledge. These presentations involved students in the creation of written texts and graphics to present historical evidence to an authentic audience of members of the classroom community. Finally, inspection of the field notes of observers revealed that teacher scaffolding and the assessment of group knowledge during discussion provided an important opportunity for teachers to correct misunderstandings (Ferretti et al., 2001; MacArthur et al., 2002; Okolo, Ferretti, & MacArthur, 2007).

By way of summary, history is a rich domain in which to promote thinking, problem solving, and literacy—areas of keen interest and primary importance to educators. Historical problems represent a type of ill-structured domain that does not yield to simple solutions and that challenges students to define goals, identify and analyze evidence that can be used to construct or evaluate plausible solutions, develop persuasive arguments in support of proposed solutions, and critically evaluate arguments (Ferretti & Okolo, 1996; Newman, 1990). Furthermore, as widely acknowledged by contemporary history educators and reflected in current reform efforts, historical understanding develops from "doing" history—that is, making use of the available historical record to construct an interpretation of history that is accurate, plausible, and representative. Because of these traits, the study of history invites students to apply literacy skills within a process of gathering information (or evidence) about a historical topic, reading and comparing multiple sources of evidence, asking questions of the evidence, formulating interpretations that are accurate and that take into account multiple perspectives, defending interpretations based on evidence, and creating written and multimedia texts that report the results of the investigative process. In the process of doing historical inquiry, opportunities abound not only to learn about history and the nature of historical inquiry but also to teach and put into practice literacy skills that involve reading for meaning, reasoning from evidence, vocabulary development, and persuasive writing.

Science

There are also prominent examples of the ways in which literacy and writing skills have been linked within a process of inquiry in the science domain. Scientific writing has a strong tradition in which scientists maintain records or notebooks that contain information pertaining to their research hypotheses, questions, data, and results. Importantly, too, within the science curriculum, students can employ a number of expository writing forms for legitimate purposes and functions. Students can write descriptions, explain their investigative procedures and experimental steps, generate timelines or cause–event sequences, write explanatory texts, and construct persuasive arguments (Gilbert & Kotelman, 2005). Within the science curriculum, opportunities abound for teachers to develop writing skills and strategies for legitimate scientific inquiry and communicative purposes.

Three school-based programs stand out for their intensive focus on the integration of literacy-related tools within the science curriculum. Guthrie et al. (1996, 2004) developed an instructional framework that combined motivational support and strategy instruction in the science domain in an approach known as Concept-Oriented Reading Instruction (CORI). The premise for the program was that students who have intrinsic goals and commitments to learning that involve literacy-related activities are more likely to understand the content.

In CORI, teachers and students engaged in four instructional phases using trade books that integrate science inquiry with reading. These four phases encompassed the following inquiry activities: (1) observing and personalizing concrete objects in the real world (e.g., observing objects and generating questions relevant to the topic of the text being read), (2) searching and retrieving (e.g., searching through resources, references, and pictures; categorizing the reference materials; identifying and extracting the essential details using note taking, paraphrasing, summarizing, and synthesizing strategies), (3) comprehending and integrating (e.g., determining the topic of a text selection, reading to identify critical details, summarizing the text, making comparisons between texts and synthesizing, critically reflecting on the organization of information and the author's point of view), and (4) communicating to others through texts (e.g., presenting findings in a written report, diorama, chart, information story, or class-authored book).

Throughout the CORI phases, teachers provided explicit instruction in the cognitive and metacognitive strategies that correlate with successful performance (Guthrie, 2004). Teachers also enhanced motivation by using interesting texts, emphasizing social collaboration during reading, promoting strategy use, offering students options for topics and texts, and providing hands-on science activities. Hands-on experimentation combined with textual inquiry were considered the motivational backbone of the program, and literacy activities were designed to spark students' engagement with topics through their own personal involvement in self-generated questions and research.

CORI was experimentally tested in a series of studies that were aimed at evaluating the effects of the instructional framework on elementary students' engagement and reading comprehension. The studies showed that CORI students increased their motivation and passage comprehension (Guthrie et al., 1996; Guthrie, Anderson, Alao, & Rinehart, 1999; Guthrie, Wigfield, & VonSecker, 2000; Guthrie et al., 2004). CORI students also improved in a composite measure of cognitive strategies related to their skills in activating background knowledge during reading, searching for information in books, and organizing information (Guthrie et al., 2004). Overall, literacy engagement using informational texts in science was highly associated with the CORI instruction.

Two other programs of research have yielded similar results. In Guided Inquiry Supporting Multiple Literacies (GIsML), teachers engaged middle-school students in firsthand and secondhand investigations (Magnusson, Palincsar, Hapgood, & Lomangino, 2004). Firsthand investigations entailed inquiry-based science instruction using hands-on experimentation and direct experience with real phenomena. Simultaneously, the firsthand investigations were modeled on the types of inquiry processes used by scientists, including the creation of a community in which students could engage, investigate, explain, and report in a process of scientific inquiry (Palincsar, Magnusson, Collins, & Cutter, 2001). In addition, secondhand investigations involved the introduction of notebook texts that were modeled on the notebooks of scientists, with entries that featured hypothetical scientists' written statements that pertained to the inquiry process and that modeled the ways in which scientists: (1) identify a problem to investigate, (2) model the problem for investigation, (3) represent the data collected to support their analysis, (4) write claims that can be made from the data, (5) respond to critical reactions of colleagues as they weigh the evidence of the claims, and (6) revise thinking in light of new data (Magnusson et al., 2004). Throughout the GIsML phases, students maintained their own writing notebooks as part of the investigative process, ensuring that they engaged in scientific reasoning, argumentation, and representations of their theories and data through their written journal entries (Palincsar & Magnusson, 2001; Palincsar, 2006).

Results showed that the GIsML process and notebook texts influenced the learning of scientific concepts (Palincsar & Magnusson, 2001). Students' inquiry conversations and interactions were enhanced when there were first- and secondhand investigations. Students drew heavily on the formatting and concepts in the scientist's notebook in framing their own written entries, with evidence that they appropriated the scientists' representational ideas, scientific language, and processes (Palincsar & Magnusson, 2001). Scientific texts provided models for students of the processes associated with investigation, interpretation, reasoning, argumentation, and representation of theories and evidentiary data (Palincsar, 2006; Palincsar & Magnusson, 2001). The researchers concluded that scientific reasoning was advanced through the use of notebook texts in inquiry-based science instruction, as a resource for both the learning and doing of science. For students, notebook writing served as an important tool for recording observations, generalizing, hypothesizing, reasoning, and problem solving (Baxter, Bass, & Glaser, 2001). In the process, students were apprenticed in the literacy practices that helped them to think, write, and communicate like scientists.

Finally, another project in which reading and writing were embedded in inquiry-based science is the Seeds of Science/Roots of Reading project (Cervetti, Pearson, Marco, Bravo, & Barber, 2005; Pearson, 2006). As in the GIsML project, the researchers on this project emphasized the importance of both firsthand and secondhand investigations. Texts were used to support inquiry science before, during, and after firsthand investigations. That is, secondhand texts were selected and used to present scientific concepts, as well as to model inquiry and literacy processes, to illustrate the nature of science and scientists, and to provide experience with data, conclusions, and claims. Embedded in the first- and secondhand investigations, teachers taught and modeled strategies that supported science and literacy activity, such as activating prior knowledge, establishing purpose and goals, making and reviewing predictions, drawing inferences and conclusions, and making connections and recognizing relationships. Throughout the investigations, teachers modeled an academic language that could inform students' oral and written discourse, with science being used as the social context in which students could participate in the established ways of talking, reading, doing, and writing science (Pearson, 2006).

In a large-scale study involving 73 Seeds of Science/Roots of Reading experimental classrooms and 45 comparison group classrooms, the researchers compared the relative performance of students on their science vocabulary knowledge, science concept attainment, and reading comprehension in science texts. The intervention clearly favored students in the experimental treatment condition. The researchers concluded that students learn more science and gain in literacy when literacy and science content are embedded and grounded in disciplinary activities (Pearson, 2006).

In summary, this body of work highlights the fact that writing lies at the heart of the method of academic scientists. The integration of reading and writing in content-area curricula has positive effects on both science and literacy performance. As Pearson (2006) suggests, literacy strategies are inquiry strategies, and both share cognitive functions related to processes associated with regulating metacognition, acquiring information, solving problems, drawing inferences, recognizing relationships, and making connections. To the extent that the strategies and language of science and social studies can be integrated in the oral and written discourse of the curriculum, then both the literacy and content-area performances of students can be enhanced.

CONCLUSIONS

The research literature on the role of informational writing and strategic processes within the content-area curricula points to the importance of explicit instruction in literacy strategies in the context of the disciplinary studies. Literacy strategies that are taught and acquired as part of the English language arts curriculum do not spontaneously generalize to expository contexts. This is particularly problematic for struggling readers and writers, because the content-area curriculum imposes a greater cognitive burden on learners in that it requires that they employ a variety of expository text structures and strategies in flexible ways in order to adequately respond to the shifting content of textbooks, primary source documents, and their own learning purposes.

An essential area of instruction involves the explicit teaching of expository text structures to support reading and writing in the content areas. Students need to learn to recognize these text structures as they read and to apply these structures to summarize, synthesize, and compose informational texts. The positive findings of researchers indicate that these expository text structures can be taught to improve the reading and writing performance of all students but especially that the benefit may be greatest for the struggling readers and writers who are not intuitive about the ways in which expository ideas are structured, organized, and signaled to create meanings.

In addition, there are domain-specific literacy strategies that are important to helping learners process, understand, and learn expository content. These literacy strategies are quite similar to the tools used by skilled learners in the subject matter disciplines. In brief, these strategic tools include a number of literacy practices that support deeper understanding, rehearsal, interpretation, and documentation such as a learner might use to understand or interpret documents (e.g., highlighting, note taking, and summarizing, to name but a few). Because of the difficulties of struggling readers and writers in employing these tools, it is essential that teachers provide the direct instruction and guided support to ensure that these strategies are mastered, employed, and monitored by learners to support their own learning and knowledge acquisition process. Hand in hand with cognitive activity, recording and reporting information play an essential role in heightening students' consciousness of the expository content within the content-area curricula and deepens their insights into their own strategic behaviors.

Finally, students require writing strategies that function as tools that can be applied within a discipline-specific process of inquiry. Students need to use these literacy tools and methods as part of an inquiry or investigative process in which they gather information, record their notes and observations, make interpretations (graphical or written), formulate hypotheses, express their findings and results to others, make arguments or counterarguments, and offer evidence to support their positions and conclusions. By accomplishing this goal, teachers will have not only succeeded in improving students' inquiry skills but will also have accomplished the more far-reaching goal of producing critical thinkers and independent learners.

Further research needs to explore how to build students' facility in using informational reading and writing tools as part of an inquiry process in the content areas. Equally important, literacy interventions that target students with LLD and other struggling readers and writers in the content areas remain a vital concern. The types of efficacious teaching methods and specific tools and strategies that improve these students' self-regulation during content-area comprehension and composition activities likely will benefit all students, not just those who struggle. Finally, investigations of the teaching methods and literacy practices that advance students' interpretative and reasoning skills in the disciplinary subjects are fundamental to our endeavors to develop critical readers, writers, and thinkers.

REFERENCES

Alexander, P. A., & Jetton, T. L. (2000). Learning from text: A multidimensional and developmental perspective. In M. L. Kamil, P. B. Mosenthal, P. D. Pearson, & R. Barr (Eds.), *Handbook of reading research* (Vol. III, pp. 285–310). Mahwah, NJ: Erlbaum.

Baker, S., Gersten, R., & Graham, S. (2003). Teaching expressive writing to students with learning disabilities: Research-based applications and examples. *Journal of Learning Disabilities, 36,* 109–123.

Baker, S., Gersten, R., & Scanlon, D. (2002). Procedural facilitators and cognitive strategies: Tools for unraveling the mysteries of comprehension and the writing process and for providing meaningful access to the general curriculum. *Learning Disabilities Research and Practice, 17,* 65–77.

Bakhtin, M. M. (1986). *Speech genres and other late essays* (Vern W. McGee, Trans.). Austin: University of Texas Press.

Bangert-Drowns, R. L., Hurley, M. M., & Wilkinson, B. (2004). The effects of school-based writing-to-learn interventions on academic achievement: A meta-analysis. *Review of Educational Research, 74,* 29–58.

Baxter, G. P., Bass, K. M., & Glaser, R. (2001). Notebook writing in three fifth-grade science classrooms. *Elementary School Journal, 102,* 123–140.

Beck, I., McKeown, M., Hamilton, R., & Kucan, L. (1997). *Questioning the author: An approach for enhancing student engagement with text.* Newark, DE: International Reading Association.

Bereiter, C., & Scardamalia, M. (1985). Cognitive coping strategies and the problem of "inert knowledge." In S. F. Chipman, J. W. Segal, & R. Glaser (Eds.), *Thinking and learning skills: Vol. 2. Research and open questions* (pp. 65–80). Hillsdale, NJ: Erlbaum.

Biancarosa, G., & Snow, C. E. (2004). *Reading next—A vision for action and research in middle and high school literacy: A report to the Carnegie Corporation of New York.* Washington, DC: Alliance for Excellent Education.

Biemiller, A., & Meichenbaum, D. (1996). The consequences of negative scaffolding for students who learn slowly. *Journal of Learning Disabilities, 31,* 365–369.

Block, C. C., & Pressley, M. (Eds.). (2002). *Comprehension instruction: Research-based best practices.* New York: Guilford Press.

Brown, A. L., & Day, J. D. (1983). Macro rules for summarizing texts: The development of expertise. *Journal of Verbal Learning and Verbal Behavior*, 22, 1–14.

Cervetti, G. N., Pearson, P. D., Marco, A., Bravo, M. A., & Barber, J. (2005). *Reading and writing in the service of inquiry-based science.* Unpublished manuscript, University of California Berkeley.

Chall, J. S., Jacobs, V. A., & Baldwin, L. E. (1990). *The reading crisis: Why poor children fall behind.* Cambridge, MA: Harvard University Press.

Ciardiello, A. V. (2002). Helping adolescents understand cause/effect text structures in social studies. *Social Studies*, 93, 31–37.

Collins, A., Brown, J. S., & Holum, A. (1991). Cognitive apprenticeship: Making thinking visible. *American Educator*, 15, 6–11.

Cope, B., & Kalantzis, M. (1993). The power of literacy and the literacy of power. In B. Cope & M. Kalantzis (Eds.), *The powers of literacy: A genre approach to teaching writing* (pp. 63–89). Pittsburgh, PA: University of Pittsburgh Press.

Day, J. (1986). Teaching summarization skills: Influences of student ability level and strategy difficulty. *Cognition and Instruction*, 3, 193–210.

De La Paz, S. (2005). Teaching historical reasoning and argumentative writing in culturally and academically diverse middle school classrooms. *Journal of Educational Psychology*, 97, 139–158.

De La Paz, S., & Graham, S. (2002). Explicitly teaching strategies, skills, and knowledge: Writing instruction in middle school classrooms. *Journal of Educational Psychology*, 94, 291–304.

De La Paz, S., & MacArthur, C. (2003). Knowing the how and why of history: Expectations for secondary students with and without learning disabilities. *Learning Disability Quarterly*, 26, 142–154.

Duffy, G. G. (2002). The case for direct explanation of strategies. In C. C. Block & M. Pressley (Eds.), *Comprehension instruction: Research-based best practices* (pp. 28–41). New York: Guilford Press.

Englert, C. S., Hiebert, E. H., & Stewart, S. R. (1987). Detecting and correcting inconsistencies in the monitoring of expository prose. *Journal of Educational Psychology*, 79, 221–227.

Englert, C. S., & Mariage, T. V. (2003). The sociocultural model in special education interventions: Apprenticing students in higher-order thinking. In H. L. Swanson, K. R. Harris, & S. Graham (Eds.), *Handbook of learning disabilities* (pp. 450–467). New York: Guilford Press.

Englert, C. S., Mariage, T. V., Okolo, C. M., Chen, H.-Y., Courtad, C. A., Moxley, K. D., & Shankland, R. K. (2008, March). *Content area literacy in inclusive middle grade classrooms: A two-year study of Project ACCEL.* Paper presented at the Annual Meeting of the American Educational Research Association, New York.

Englert, C. S., Mariage, T. V., Okolo, C. M., Courtad, C., Shankland, R. K., Moxley, K. D., et al. (2007). Accelerating expository literacy in the middle grades. In B. Taylor & J. Ysseldyke (Eds.), *Educational interventions for struggling readers* (pp. 138–172). New York: Teachers College Press.

Englert, C. S., Raphael, T. E., Anderson, L. M., Anthony, H. M., Stevens, D. D., & Fear, K. L. (1991). Making writing strategies and self-talk visible: Cognitive strategy instruction in writing in regular and special education classrooms. *American Educational Research Journal, 28,* 337–372.

Englert, C. S., Raphael, T. E., Fear, K. L., & Anderson, L. M. (1988). Students' metacognitive knowledge about how to write informational texts. *Learning Disability Quarterly, 11,* 18–46.

Englert, C. S., Zhao, Y., Dunsmore, K., Collings, N. Y., & Wolbers, K. (2007). Scaffolding the writing of students with disabilities through procedural facilitation: Using an Internet-based technology to improve performance. *Learning Disability Quarterly, 30,* 9–29.

Ferretti, R. P., MacArthur, C. A., & Okolo, C. M. (2001). Teaching for historical understanding in inclusive classrooms. *Learning Disability Quarterly, 24,* 59–71.

Ferretti, R. P., MacArthur, C. D., & Okolo, C. M. (2002). Teaching effectively about historical things. *Teaching Exceptional Children, 34*(6), 66–69.

Ferretti, R. P., & Okolo, C. M. (1996). Authenticity in learning: Multimedia design projects in social studies for students with disabilities. *Journal of Learning Disabilities, 29,* 450–460.

Fox, E., & Alexander, P. A. (2004, April). *Reading, interest, and the model of domain learning: A developmental model of interest, knowledge, and strategy use in text comprehension.* Paper presented at the annual meeting of the American Educational Research Association, San Diego, CA.

Gersten, R., & Baker, S. (2001). Teaching expressive writing to students with learning disabilities: A meta-analysis. *Elementary School Journal, 101,* 251–272.

Gilbert, J., & Kotelman, M. (2005). Five good reasons to use science notebooks. *Science and Children, 43*(3), 28–32.

Graham, S. (2006). Strategy instruction and the teaching of writing: A meta-analysis. In C. A. MacArthur, S. Graham, & J. Fitzgerald (Eds.), *Handbook of writing research* (pp. 187–207). New York: Guilford Press.

Graham, S., & Harris, K. R. (2003). Students with learning disabilities and the process of writing: A meta-analysis of SRSD studies. In H. L. Swanson, K. R. Harris, & S. Graham (Eds.), *The handbook of learning disabilities* (pp. 323–344). New York: Guilford Press.

Graham, S., & Perin, D. (2007). *Writing next—Effective strategies to improve writing of adolescents in middle and high schools: A report to Carnegie Corporation of New York.* Washington, DC: Alliance for Excellent Education.

Guthrie, J. T. (2004). Classroom contexts for engaged reading: An overview. In J. T. Guthrie, A. Wigfield, & K. C. Perencevich (Eds.), *Motivating reading comprehension: Concept-Oriented Reading Instruction* (pp. 1–24). Mahwah, NJ: Erlbaum.

Guthrie, J. T., Anderson, E., Alao, S., & Rinehart, J. (1999). Influences of concept-oriented reading instruction on strategy use and conceptual learning from text. *Elementary School Journal, 99,* 343–366.

Guthrie, J. T., Van Meter, P., McCann, A., Wigfield, A., Bennett, L., Poundstone,

C. C., et al. (1996). Growth of literacy engagement: Changes in motivations and strategies during concept-oriented reading instruction. *Reading Research Quarterly, 31*, 306–332.

Guthrie, J. T., Wigfield, A., Barbosa, P., Perencevich, K. C., Taboada, A., Davis, M. H., et al. (2004). Increasing reading comprehension and engagement through concept-oriented reading instruction. *Journal of Educational Psychology, 96*, 403–423.

Guthrie, J. T., Wigfield, A., & VonSecker, C. (2000). Effects of integrated instruction on motivation and strategy use in reading. *Journal of Educational Psychology, 92*, 331–341.

Halliday, M. A. K., & Martin, J. R. (Eds.). (1993). *Writing science: Literacy and discursive power.* Pittsburgh, PA: University of Pittsburgh Press.

Harris, K. R., & Graham, S. (1996). *Making the writing process work: Strategies for composition and self-regulation.* Cambridge, MA: Brookline.

Harris, K. R., & Graham, S. (1999). Programmatic intervention research: Illustrations from the evolution of self-regulated strategy development. *Learning Disability Quarterly, 22*, 251–262.

Harris, K. R., Graham, S., & Mason, L. H. (2003). Self-regulated strategy development in the classroom: Part of a balanced approach to writing instruction for students with disabilities. *Focus on Exceptional Children, 35*(7), 1–16.

Jetton, T. L., & Alexander, P. A. (2004). Domains, teaching, and literacy. In T. L. Jetton & J. A. Dole (Eds.), *Adolescent literacy research and practice* (pp. 15–39). New York: Guilford Press.

Jetton, T. L., & Dole, J. A. (Eds.). (2004). *Adolescent literacy research and practice.* New York: Guilford Press.

Kamberelis, G. (1999). Genre development: Children writing stories, science reports and poems. *Research in the Teaching of English, 33*, 403–460.

Kamberelis, G., & Bovino, T. D. (1999). Cultural artifacts as scaffolds for genre development. *Reading Research Quarterly, 34*, 138–170.

Kamil, M. L. (2003). *Adolescents and literacy: Reading for the 21st century.* Washington, DC: Alliance for Excellent Education.

Kim, A., Vaughn, S., Wanzek, J., & Wei, S. (2004). Graphic organizers and their effects on the reading comprehension of students with LD: A synthesis of research. *Journal of Learning Disabilities, 37*, 105–118.

Klinger, J. K., Vaughn, S., & Schumm, J. S. (1998). Collaborative strategic reading during social studies in heterogeneous fourth-grade classrooms. *Elementary School Journal, 99*, 3–22.

Knipper, K. J., & Duggan, T. J. (2006, February). Writing to learn across the curriculum: Tools for comprehension in content area classes. *Reading Teacher, 59*(5), 462–470.

Lemke, J. (1990). *Talking science: Language, learning, and values.* Norwood, NJ: Ablex.

Magnusson, S. J., Palincsar, A. S., Hapgood, S., & Lomangino, A. (2004). How should learning be structured in inquiry-based science instruction? Investigating the interplay of 1st- and 2nd-hand investigations. In Y. Kafai, W. Sandoval, N. Enyedy, A. Nixon, & F. Herrera (Eds.), *Proceedings of the Sixth International Conference of the Learning Sciences* (pp. 310–317). Mahwah, NJ: Erlbaum.

McGee, L. M. (1982). Awareness of text structure: Effects on children's recall of expository text. *Reading Research Quarterly, 17,* 581–590.

Meyer, B. J. F. (1975). *The organization of prose and its effects on memory.* Amsterdam: North-Holland.

Meyer, B. J. F. (1977). The structure of prose: Effects on learning and memory and implications for educational practice. In R. C. Anderson, R. J. Spiro, & W. E. Montague (Eds.), *Schooling and the acquisition of knowledge* (pp. 179–200). Hillsdale, NJ: Erlbaum.

Meyer, B. J. F., Brandt, D. M., & Bluth, G. J. (1980). Use of top-level structure in text: Key for reading comprehension of ninth-grade students. *Reading Research Quarterly, 16,* 72–103.

Meyer, B. J. F., & Freedle, R. O. (1984). Effects of discourse type on recall. *American Educational Research Journal, 21,* 121–143.

National Center for Education Statistics. (2001). *The condition of education, 2001* (Appendix 1, Table 29-3). Retrieved January 1, 2008, from *nces. ed.gov/pubsearch/pubsinfo.asp?pubid=2001072.*

National Center for Education Statistics. (2003a). *Nation's report card: Reading 2002.* Retrieved January 1, 2008, from *nces.ed.gov/pubsearch/pubsinfo. asp?pubid=2003521.*

National Center for Education Statistics. (2003b). *Remedial education at degree-granting postsecondary institutions in fall 2000.* Retrieved January 1, 2008, from *nces.ed.gov/pubsearch/pubsinfo.asp?pubid=2004010.*

National Center for Education Statistics. (2005). *Nation's report card: Reading 2005.* Washington, DC: U.S. Government Printing Office, Institute of Education Sciences.

National Commission on Writing in America's Schools and Colleges. (2003). *The neglected "R": The need for a writing revolution.* New York: College Entrance Examination Board.

National Commission on Writing for America's Families, Schools, and Colleges. (2004). *Writing: A ticket to work … or a ticket out. A survey of business leaders.* New York: College Entrance Examination Board.

Neufeld, P. (2005). Comprehension instruction in content area classes. *The Reading Teacher, 59,* 302–312.

Newman, F. (1990). Qualities of thoughtful social studies classes: An empirical profile. *Curriculum Studies, 22,* 253–275.

Ogle, D., & Blachowicz, C. L. Z. (2002). Beyond literature circles: Helping students comprehend informational texts. In C. C. Block & M. Pressley (Eds.), *Comprehension instruction: Research-based best practices* (pp. 259–274). New York: Guilford Press.

Okolo, C. M., & Ferretti, R. P. (1996). Knowledge acquisition and technology-supported projects in the social studies for students with learning disabilities. *Journal of Special Education Technology, 13*(2), 91–103.

Okolo, C. M., Ferretti, R. P., & MacArthur, C. D. (2007). Talking about history: Discussion in a middle-school inclusive classroom. *Journal of Learning Disabilities, 40,* 154–166.

Palincsar, A. S. (2006, March). *Reading in science: Why, what, and how.* Paper presented at the University of Michigan School of Education Adolescent Literacy Symposium, Ann Arbor, MI.

Palincsar, A. S., & Brown, A. L. (1984). Reciprocal teaching of comprehension-fostering and comprehension-monitoring activities. *Cognition and Instruction, 1,* 117–175.

Palincsar, A. S., & Magnusson, S. J. (1999, June). *The interplay of first-hand and text-based investigations to model and support the development of scientific knowledge and reasoning.* Paper presented at the Carnegie Symposium on Cognition, Pittsburgh, PA.

Palincsar, A. S., & Magnusson, S. J. (2001). The interplay of first-hand and text-based investigations to model and support the development of scientific knowledge and reasoning. In S. Carver & D. Klahr (Eds.), *Cognition and instruction: Twenty-five years of progress* (pp. 151–194). Mahwah, NJ: Erlbaum.

Palincsar, A. S., Magnusson, S. J., Collins, K. M., & Cutter, J. (2001). Making science accessible to all: Results of a design experiment in inclusive classrooms. *Learning Disability Quarterly, 24,* 15–32.

Paris, S. G., & Paris, A. H. (2001). Classroom applications of research on self-regulated learning. *Educational Psychologist, 36,* 89–101.

Paxton R. J. (1999). A deafening silence: Textbooks and the students who read them. *Review of Educational Research, 69,* 315–339.

Pearson, P. D. (2006, October). *Toward a model of science–literacy integration.* Paper presented at the meeting of the State of Washington Reading and Science Organizations, Spokane, WA.

Pearson, P. D., & Duke, N. K. (2002). Comprehension instruction in the primary grades. In C. C. Block & M. Pressley (Eds.), *Comprehension instruction: Research-based best practices* (pp. 247–258). New York: Guilford Press.

Persky, H. R., Daane, M. C., & Jin, Y. (2003). *The nation's report card: Writing 2002.* Washington, DC: National Center for Education Statistics.

Pressley, M. (2002). Comprehension strategies instruction: A turn-of-the-century status report. In C. C. Block & M. Pressley (Eds.), *Comprehension instruction: Research-based best practices* (pp. 11–27). New York: Guilford Press.

Raphael, T. E., Kehus, M., & Damphousse, K. (2001). *Book club for middle school.* Lawrence, MS: Small Planet Communications.

Richgels, D. J., McGee, L. M., Lomax, R. G., & Sheard, C. (1987). Awareness of four text structures: Effects on recall of expository text. *Reading Research Quarterly, 22,* 177–196.

Schraw, G. (1998). Promoting general metacognitive awareness. *Instructional Science, 26,* 113–125.

Shanahan, C. (2004). Teaching science through literacy. In T. L. Jetton & J. A. Dole (Eds.), *Adolescent literacy research and practice* (pp. 75–93). New York: Guilford Press.

Sinatra, G. M., Brown, K. J., & Reynolds, R. E. (2002). Implications of cognitive resource allocation for comprehension strategies instruction. In C. C. Block & M. Pressley (Eds.), *Comprehension instruction: Research-based best practices* (pp. 62–76). New York: Guilford Press.

Stahl, S. A., & Shanahan, C. (2004). Learning to think like a historian: Disciplinary knowledge through critical analysis of multiple documents. In T. L.

Jetton & J. A. Dole (Eds.), *Adolescent literacy research and practice* (pp. 94–118). New York: Guilford Press.

Spivey, N. N. (1997). *The constructivist metaphor: Reading, writing, and the making of meaning.* New York: Academic Press.

Spivey, N. N., & King, J. R. (1989). Readers as writers composing from sources. *Reading Research Quarterly, 24,* 7–26.

Taylor, B. M., & Samuels, S. J. (1983). Children's use of text structure in the recall of expository material. *American Educational Research Journal, 20,* 517–528.

Tower, C. (2003). Genre development and elementary students' informational writing: A review of the literature. *Reading Research and Instruction, 42,* 14–39.

Troia, G. A., & Graham, S. (2002). The effectiveness of a highly explicit, teacher-directed strategy instruction routine: Changing the writing performance of students with learning disabilities. *Journal of Learning Disabilities, 35,* 290–305.

Troia, G. A., Graham, S., & Harris, K. R. (1999). Teaching students to plan mindfully: Effects on the writing performance of students with learning disabilities. *Exceptional Children, 65,* 235–252.

VanSledright, B. (2002). Confronting history's interpretive paradox while teaching fifth graders to investigate the past. *American Educational Research Journal, 39,* 131–162.

Vaughn, S., Gersten, R., & Chard, D. J. (2000). The underlying message in LD intervention research: Findings from research syntheses. *Exceptional Children, 67,* 99–114.

Vaughn, S., & Klingner, J. K. (1999). Teaching reading comprehension through collaborative strategic reading. *Intervention in School and Clinic, 34,* 284–292.

Wells, G. (1999). *Dialogic inquiry: Toward a sociocultural practice and theory of education.* New York: Cambridge University Press.

Williams, J. P. (2003). Teaching text structure to improve reading comprehension. In H. L. Swanson, K. R. Harris, & S. Graham (Eds.), *Handbook of learning disabilities* (pp. 293–305). New York: Guilford Press.

Williams, J. P. (2005). Instruction in reading comprehension for primary-grade students: A focus on text structure. *Journal of Special Education, 39,* 6–18.

Wineburg, S. S. (1991). Historical problem solving: A study of cognitive processes used in the evaluation of documental and pictorial evidence. *Journal of Educational Psychology, 83,* 73–87.

Wong, B. Y. L., Butler, D. L., Ficzere, S. A., & Kuperis, S. (1996). Teaching low achievers and students with learning disabilities to plan, write, and revise opinion essays. *Journal of Learning Disabilities, 29,* 197–212.

Wong, B. Y. L., Butler, D. L., Ficzere, S. A., & Kuperis, S. (1997). Teaching adolescents with learning disabilities and low achievers to plan, write, and revise compare–contrast essays. *Learning Disabilities Research and Practice, 9,* 78–90.

Part III

TEACHING COMPOSING TO STRUGGLING WRITERS

CHAPTER 6

Teaching Composing to Students with Learning Disabilities

Scientifically Supported Recommendations

STEVE GRAHAM
NATALIE G. OLINGHOUSE
KAREN R. HARRIS

Learning how to write well is not an easy task. This fact was illustrated in the most recent national assessment of students' writing. Two out of every three students in grades 4, 8, and 12 did not write well enough to meet expected grade-level demands (Persky, Daane, & Jin, 2003). Difficulties in mastering writing are even more pronounced for students with learning disabilities (LD), as they experience problems with multiple aspects of the composing process, including setting goals for writing, generating and organizing ideas, transforming ideas into acceptable sentences, transcribing these sentences onto paper, revising and editing text, creating fully developed papers, and sustaining the writing process (Graham & Harris, 2003, 2005; Troia, 2006).

Students who do not learn to write well are at a considerable disadvantage. Their grades are likely to suffer, as many teachers use writing to assess students' progress in content subjects. They are also less likely to use writing to support and extend their learning of new material (Graham, 2006a). Their chances of attending college are reduced, as universities increasingly evaluate applicants' qualifications in terms of their writing. Participation in social and community life is likely to be restricted, as e-mail has progressively supplanted the telephone as the primary means for communicating with friends and others. Writing has progressively become a gateway to employment and promotion, especially in salaried positions (National Commission on Writing for America's Families, Schools, and Colleges, 2004, 2005). Employees in business, as well as government (local, state, and federal), are now expected to produce written documentation, visual presentations, memoranda, technical reports, and electronic messages.

As a result, it is critical that students with LD and other struggling writers be provided with the very best writing instruction available. The question of how to best teach writing to youngsters in general and to students with LD in particular has vexed both teachers and writing experts (Graham, in press). Two basic approaches to designing writing instruction are briefly presented here. We consider each before offering our own recommendations.

DESIGNING WRITING INSTRUCTION ON THE BASIS OF EXPERIENCE AND AUTHORITY

One approach to designing writing instruction is to base it on the experiences of teachers, the insights of writing experts, the advice of professional writers (e.g., Saltzman, 1993), or all of these. For example, many of the writing instructional procedures commonly used by teachers were directly derived from classroom practice. In some instances, teachers took the lead in identifying and sharing instructional procedures they judged to be effective (e.g., Atwell, 1987). In other instances, experts and researchers who observed teachers in action recommended specific practices they viewed as worthwhile (e.g., Graves, 1983).

Teachers, writing experts, and professional writers undoubtedly possess considerable and useful knowledge about the teaching of writing. Nevertheless, it is difficult to separate the wheat from the chaff, to use a colloquial expression. There is often no direct evidence that a procedure based on this approach actually produces the desired effects. When evidence is provided, it frequently takes the form of testimonials or the presentation of selected students' writing, making it impossible to determine whether the evidence is atypical or representative. Rarely is such evidence based on the writing of students with LD (the focus of this chapter). In some instances, the supporting evidence is based on the experiences of just a single teacher, expert, or professional writer. As a result, there is no way to predict whether the practice will be effective for other teachers. Therefore, developing a writing program solely on the basis of experience or authority is a risky proposition, as the reliability, validity, and generalizability of the instructional procedures are typically unknown.

DESIGNING WRITING INSTRUCTION
ON THE BASIS OF SCIENTIFIC EVIDENCE

Another approach to designing writing instruction is to base it on instructional procedures validated through empirical studies (these procedures can be and often are ones initially developed by teachers). This provides a more trustworthy approach than experience and authority to identifying effective teaching practices, as these studies provide evidence as to whether the instructional procedure has the desired impact. They also allow the researcher to determine whether the observed effects are representative and how much confidence can be placed in them. Because the observed effect of an intervention is quantified in these studies, the findings from individual studies can be converted into a common metric (i.e., effect size), making it possible to determine the strength of an intervention's impact across investigations.

Three types of studies that are especially useful in examining the effectiveness of an instructional procedure are true experimental designs, quasi-experimental designs, and single-subject designs. With true experimental and quasi-experimental designs, the performance of a group that receives the treatment is compared with that of a control group that receives an alternative treatment or no treatment. The primary difference between the two designs is that students are randomly assigned to conditions in the former but not in the latter. An experimental design is preferable to a quasi-experimental design, as the use of random assignment better controls for alternative explanations (i.e., threats to internal validity), such as a student improving on a given skill due to maturation rather than to the intervention (Cambell & Stanley, 1963). For both types of designs, findings are based on the average performance of students in each condition (treatment and control).

In contrast to true experiments and quasi-experimental research, single-subject design studies evaluate the effectiveness of a treatment at the individual level. These studies involve repeatedly measuring a student's writing performance before as well as during and/or after instruction to establish a stable baseline and treatment effect (assuming that treatment has a positive impact). The researcher also controls the times at which the treatment is presented to a student or across students to rule out rival explanations, such as improvement in performance because of something that happened outside of the treatment setting. With a multiple-baseline design, for instance, the researcher provides instruction to one student and repeatedly measures the impact of this instruction, while simultaneously assessing the writing performance of other study participants who have not yet received the treatment. If the instructed students demonstrate a reliable improvement on the target writing variable, whereas uninstructed students demonstrate a reliable lack of improvement, there is evidence that the treatment caused the positive change in writing performance. If this pattern is repeated successively across multiple students, the claim for treatment effectiveness is strengthened (Horner et al., 2005).

In this chapter, we provide specific recommendations for teaching writing to students with LD. These recommendations are based on the findings from true experimental, quasi-experimental, and single-subject design intervention studies. We present them within the context of a two-tiered model. At the first tier (primary instruction) are recommendations for teaching writing to all students in the general education classroom. Providing consistent quality writing instruction to all students is advantageous for three reasons (Graham & Harris, 2002). One, it should maximize the writing development of children in general. Two, it should minimize the number of children who experience writing problems due to ineffective instruction and who are subsequently classified as LD. Three, it should ameliorate the severity of writing difficulties experienced by students with LD, as much of their writing instruction occurs in the regular classroom.

The Tier I recommendations are drawn from a recent meta-analysis, *Writing Next: Effective Strategies to Improve Writing of Adolescents in Middle and High School* (Graham & Perin, 2007), of true experimental and quasi-experimental writing intervention research conducted with students in grades 4 through 12. Each recommendation was based on the findings from at least four studies (providing evidence that the findings could be reasonably replicated across situations). In addition, this analysis included only studies that assessed whether the target treatment improved the overall quality of students' writing, measured via reliable means. Interventions that improve the overall quality of students' writing should have a more pronounced effect than ones that enhance a more discrete writing trait, such as spelling, vocabulary, sentence structure, and so forth. Consequently, we think that it is particularly important that these recommendations are incorporated into regular or Tier I writing programs.

It is important to acknowledge that the recommendations derived from *Writing Next* (Graham & Perin, 2007a) are not comprehensive enough to develop a complete general education writing program. Simply put, there are many aspects of writing instruction that have not been subjected to scientific scrutiny. Similarly, some instructional procedures have been studied, but there is no additional verification (through replication) that the findings are reliable (see Graham & Perin, 2007b). Thus the development of Tier I writing programs must, for the present time, rely on more than scientifically supported practices.

We think that an excellent source from which to derive additional recommendations for Tier I writing programs can be examining the instructional practices of teachers and schools that produce exceptional writing and literacy achievement. Although such examination of these practices cannot establish that a particular instructional procedure is directly associated with students' writing performance, it is reasonable to assume that teaching practices evident in the majority of available descriptive studies are potentially more important than ones used by a single teacher or school. Following this logic, Graham and Perin (2007c) identified 10 writing practices that were used in the majority of studies examining exceptional teachers and schools. Our recommendations for Tier I primary instruction include these practices. Of course, these particular recommendations must be treated more cautiously, as the evidence supporting them is more tenuous than the evidence used to establish the *Writing Next* (Graham & Perin, 2007a) recommendations.

We also provide recommendations for a second tier of writing instruction (secondary interventions). Tier II recommendations are aimed specifically at students with LD, with the assumption that one or more of these would be provided to these youngsters who were not writing well enough to meet classroom demands. These Tier II interventions could be implemented in the general education classroom (by the classroom teacher or a specialist) or outside the classroom in a resource room or other setting. Of course, Tier II writing instruction does not have to be limited to students with LD; it could also be provided to other youngsters who struggle with writing.

The Tier II recommendations presented here are based on interventions that had a positive impact on the writing performance of students with LD. This was determined through evidence collected via true experimental, quasi-experimental, and/or single-subject design studies. These studies were reviewed in meta-analyses conducted by Graham and his colleagues (Graham, 2006b, in press; Graham & Harris, 2003; Graham & Perin, 2007a, 2007b, 2007c; Rogers & Graham, in press). Whereas Tier I recommendations are limited to instructional practices that improved the overall quality of students' writing, Tier II recommendations include those that improved more specific areas of writing, such as the amount of written text generated or the number of important ideas included in a report.

We did not have the luxury of requiring that all Tier II recommendations, in contrast to Tier I recommendations, be based on the findings from at least four studies. Only a few instructional practices, such as the teaching of writing strategies (see Graham, 2006b), have been repeatedly investigated with students with LD. As a result, we made a decision to make the best of the available evidence, indicating when a recommendation must be viewed more cautiously. In addition, some recommendations are based on studies conducted with struggling writers who were not classified as having LD. The practices described in these recommendations must be viewed as promising. For all Tier II recommendations, we present one or more examples of each practice.

Finally, there is considerable overlap between Tier I and Tier II recommendations. We do not see this as a problem for two reasons. First, there is no guarantee that teachers will implement Tier I recommendations. Thus the presumed overlap may simply not exist in some schools. Second, even when teachers implement a specific Tier I instructional practice, such as teaching writing strategies for planning or revising to all students, some students with LD will need additional Tier II intervention to master the strategies. This might include teaching the strategies using the same basic approach but providing these youngsters with more individual attention during instruction (e.g., small-group instruction) or with additional guided practice in applying the strategies. Tier II instruction could also involve a different approach to teaching writing strategies.

WRITING INSTRUCTION FOR ALL STUDENTS: TIER I RECOMMENDATIONS

Table 6.1 includes 21 recommendations for teaching writing to all youngsters (Tier I primary writing instruction). The first 11 recommendations are drawn from *Writing Next* (Graham & Perin, 2007a) and are based on findings from true experimental and quasi-experimental studies. These 11 recommendations are ordered so that practices that produced the strongest positive impact on the quality of students' writing are presented first, followed by those that produced a moderate positive effect, a small positive effect, and a small negative effect (for additional details, see *www. all4ed.org/publications/WritingNext/index.html*). An effect size for a true experiment or a quasi-experimental study was calculated by subtracting the mean posttest performance of the control group from the mean posttest performance of the treatment group and dividing the difference by the pooled standard deviation for both groups' posttest scores. A widely used rule of thumb for interpreting effect sizes is that 0.20 is small, 0.50 is moderate, and 0.80 is strong. The next 10 recommendations in Table 6.1 are taken from the analysis done by Graham and Perin (2007c) and are based on investigations of exceptional teachers and schools. As noted

TABLE 6.1. Recommendations for Teaching Writing to All Students (Tier I)

From *Writing Next* (Graham & Perin, 2007)

1. Explicitly teach students strategies for planning, revising, and editing their compositions (strong positive impact; ES = 0.82). Such instruction involves the teacher's modeling ways to use the target strategies and providing students with assistance in applying them until they can use them independently. Strategies can range from general procedures such as brainstorming to strategies designed for specific types of writing, such as writing an explanation or writing a story.

2. Explicitly teach students strategies and procedures for summarizing reading material, as this improves their ability to concisely and accurately present this information in writing (strong positive impact; ES = 0.82). Summarization instruction ranges from explicitly teaching strategies for summarizing written materials to teaching summarization by providing students with models of a good summary and progressively fading the models as they practice writing summaries.

3. Develop instructional arrangements by which students work together to plan, draft, revise, and edit their compositions (moderate to strong positive impact; ES = 0.75). This includes developing a structure for students' collaborative efforts.

4. Set clear and specific goals for what students are to accomplish in their writing (moderate to strong positive impact; ES = 0.70). This includes identifying the purpose of the assignment, as well as the characteristics of the final product.

5. Use word processing as a tool for writing, as it has a positive influence on what students write (moderate positive impact; ES = 0.55). The effective use of word processing ranges from students using personal laptop computers to teaching them how to use word processing and related software under teacher guidance.

6. Explicitly teach students how to write increasingly complex sentences. Instruction in combining simpler sentences into more sophisticated ones enhances the quality of their writing (moderate positive impact; ES = 0.50). Sentence combining typically involves the teacher modeling how to combine two or more sentences into a more complex one. Students practice combining similar sentences to produce the same type of sentence the teacher did. Students then apply the sentence combining skill they are learning while revising one or more of their papers.

7. Implement a process writing approach (small positive impact; ES = 0.32). This approach involves extended opportunities for writing; writing for real audiences; engaging in cycles of planning, translating, and reviewing; personal responsibility and ownership of writing projects; high levels of student interactions; creation of a supportive writing environment; self-reflection and evaluation; and personalized individual assistance and instruction.

8. Involve students in writing activities designed to sharpen their skills in inquiry (small positive impact; ES = 0.32). Effective inquiry activities in writing are characterized by a clearly specified goal (describing the actions of people), analysis of concrete and immediate data (observing one or more peers during specific activities), use of specific strategies to conduct the analysis (retroactively asking the person being observed the reason for his or her action), and applying what was learned (writing a paper in which the insights from the inquiry are incorporated into the composition).

(continued)

TABLE 6.1. (*continued*)

From *Writing Next* (Graham & Perin, 2007)

9. Engage students in activities that help them gather and organize ideas for their composition before they write a first draft (small positive impact; ES = 0.32). This includes activities such as gathering possible information for a paper through reading or developing a visual representation of ideas before writing.

10. Provide students with good models for each type of writing that is the focus of instruction (small positive impact; ES = 0.25). These examples should be analyzed by students, and students should be encouraged to imitate the critical elements embodied in the models.

11. Avoid the teaching of grammar using formal methods, such as the study of parts of speech, sentence diagramming activities, and so forth (small negative impact; ES = −0.32).

From the studies of exceptional schools and teachers

12. Dedicate time to writing, including writing across the curriculum.

13. Involve students in various forms of writing over time.

14. Have students plan, draft, revise, edit, and share their work.

15. Keep students engaged and on task by involving them in thoughtful activities (such as planning a composition) versus activities that require little thoughtfulness (such as completing a workbook page that can be finished quickly).

16. Teach often to the whole class, in small groups, and with individual students; this includes teaching the process of writing, as well as more basic writing skills.

17. Model, explain, and provide guided assistance when teaching.

18. Provide just enough support so that students can make progress or carry out writing tasks and processes, but encourage students to act in a self-regulated fashion, doing as much as they can on their own.

19. Be enthusiastic about writing and create a positive environment in which students are constantly encouraged to try hard, to believe that what they are learning will permit them to write well, and to attribute success to effort and what they learned.

20. Set high expectations for students, encouraging them to surpass their previous efforts or accomplishments.

21. Adapt writing assignments and instruction to better meet the needs of individual students.

Note. ES, effect size.

earlier, these recommendations must be treated more cautiously than the first 11, as they are based on weaker evidence.

An important issue in implementing these recommendations is determining what is still missing to form a comprehensive writing program for the general education classroom. Prominent elements that we think are still missing include:

- Linking reading and writing instruction together to promote development of both skills.

- Teaching handwriting, spelling, and typing.
- Promoting vocabulary development as a means of enhancing writing.
- Working with web-based technologies and using writing software (beyond word processing).
- Teaching text structure and other elements of genre.
- Encouraging students to assess their own writing development and performance, facilitating rich discussion of the writing process and students' writing.
- Involving parents in the writing program and students' writing life.

WRITING INSTRUCTION FOR STUDENTS WITH LD: TIER II RECOMMENDATIONS

We placed our 11 Tier II recommendations for teaching writing to students with LD into three categories. The first category contains recommendations based on instructional procedures that have been studied in at least four or more true or quasi-experimental studies or four or more single-subject design studies conducted with students with LD. The second category contains recommendations based on two to four studies conducted with these students, whereas the third category includes recommendations based on two or more studies conducted mostly with struggling writers who were not identified with LD (i.e., promising practices). Requiring that the latter two categories include at least one replication provides some assurance that the findings were reliable. In each category, the recommendations are ordered by strength of impact. As noted earlier, effect sizes of 0.20, 0.50, and 0.80 are considered small, moderate, and strong, respectively, in true experimental research and quasi-experimental studies. For single-subject design studies, an effect size was calculated by determining the percentage of data points for a given treatment condition that exceeded the highest positive value obtained during baseline. This metric is called percentage of nonoverlapping data (PND). PND scores from 50 to 70% represent a small effect; scores between 70 and 90% a moderate effect; and scores above 90% a strong effect.

Tier II Recommendations Based on Data from Four or More Studies with Students with LD

1. *Teach students with LD strategies for planning, revising, and editing their compositions* (strong positive impact). Although explicitly teach-

ing students strategies for planning, revising, and/or editing has a strong positive impact on the quality of all students' writing (see Table 6.1), the effect is especially pronounced for students with LD and other struggling writers. This has been confirmed in more than 25 studies involving true experimental and quasi-experimental designs (effect size = 1.02; Graham, 2006b; Graham & Harris, 2003; Graham & Perin, 2007a), as well as single-subject designs (PND = 96%; Graham, 2006b).

One approach to teaching writing strategies to students with LD that has been particularly successful is the Self-Regulated Strategy Development model (SRSD; Harris & Graham, 1996; Graham & Harris, 2005). The average effect size for SRSD in experimental studies and quasi-experimental research is almost double the effect size for all other strategy approaches combined (Graham, 2006b; Graham & Perin, 2007a). SRSD includes five stages of instruction: Develop Background Knowledge (students are taught any background knowledge needed to use the strategy successfully), *Describe-It* (the strategy, as well as its purpose and benefits, are described and discussed; a mnemonic for remembering the steps of the strategy may be introduced), *Model-It* (the teacher models how to use the strategy), *Memorize-It* (the student memorizes the steps of the strategy and any accompanying mnemonic), *Support-It* (the teacher scaffolds student mastery of the strategy), and Independent Use (students use the strategy with little or no support). Instruction is characterized by explicit teaching, individualized instruction, and criterion-based versus time-based learning. Students are treated as active collaborators in the learning process, and they are taught a number of self-regulation skills (including goal setting, self-monitoring, self-instructions, and self-reinforcement) designed to help them manage the writing strategies, the writing process, and their writing behavior.

We provide an example of SRSD (Harris, Graham, & Mason, 2006) that was used with second graders who were experiencing difficulty with writing, including children with LD and those at risk for LD. The instruction was delivered to small groups of children outside of the regular classroom. Students receiving SRSD learned two planning and drafting strategies: one for story writing and the other for persuasive writing. Students were taught a general strategy, POW, that prompted them to Pick a topic, Organize their ideas (or plan) in advance of writing, and Write and say more while writing (i.e., to continue to plan as they wrote). For each genre, they were taught a more specific strategy for organizing their ideas (within the planning step just described) that involved generating, culling, and organizing ideas in terms of the basic structural features of a story or persuasive paper. For example, for story writing, students made notes on the following questions or story parts before writing: Who are the main characters? When does the story take place? Where does the story take place? *What* do the main characters of the story want to do? *What* happens when the main characters try to do it? *How* does the story end? *How* do the main characters feel? The mnemonic WWW, What = 2, How = 2 was used to help them remember the questions.

Instruction first focused on story writing, and then persuasive writing was taught. For each genre, the first stage of instruction involved introducing the general (POW) and the genre-specific strategy and making sure that students were familiar with the basic parts of a story or persuasive essay (Develop Background Knowledge). Next, the rationale for using the general and genre-specific strategies were established (*Discuss-It*) and students began memorizing (*Memorize-It*) the strategy mnemonics (e.g., POW and WWW, What = 2, How = 2). Students also assessed and graphed their performances on a story or essay written before the start of instruction. This established a baseline against which to compare later performance, which was also assessed and graphed (self-monitoring). Then the teacher modeled how to apply the general and genre-specific strategies (*Model-It*), making the process visible by thinking aloud. Before writing the composition, the teacher set a goal to use all of the basic parts for a story or essay (goal setting). Once the composition was finished, the teacher and students discussed what the teacher said that helped them while writing. Students then generated several self-statements to use while they wrote (self-instructions). The teacher and students collaboratively wrote the next paper, setting goals, using self-statements, and graphing their performance (*Support-It*). The teacher gradually withdrew instructional support until students could use the strategies and self-regulation procedures independently and successfully (Independent Use). Finally, students identified opportunities to apply what they were learning outside of their small group and then evaluated and discussed their successes in doing so. This instruction not only improved the quality of students' stories and persuasive essays but also resulted in improvements in two untaught genres: personal narrative and informative writing.

   2. *Use direct instruction to teach grammar skills to students with LD (moderate positive impact).* Although the data from two recent reviews suggest that grammar instruction does not improve the grammar or the quality of most students' writing (Andrews et al., 2006; Graham & Perin, 2007a), research with students with LD paints a somewhat different picture for these youngsters. The average PND (based on the correct use of various grammar skills in text) in five single-subject design studies in which direct instructional procedures were used to teach grammar to students with LD was 77% (see Rogers & Graham, in press). The effect of such instruction on the quality of these students' writing is unknown, however.

The grammar skills taught to students with LD have included capitalization, punctuation, dialogue, possessives, nouns, adjectives, adverbial phrases, and so forth. Direct instructional procedures have included modeling, guided practice, and review. A study by Dowis and Schloss (1992) provides a representative example of this approach. Four sixth-grade students with LD were taught the use of adverbial clauses and possessives in a regular education setting. The teacher taught the grammatical skills to a large group of both special education and general education students. The mini-lessons explicitly taught the definition of adverbial clauses or possessives and the rules that guide the use of these writing elements. The teacher modeled how to correctly use adverbial clauses and possessives. After learning these elements in the mini-lesson, all four students increased their ability to include adverbial clauses and possessives in written sentences.

Tier II Recommendations Based on Data from Two to Four Studies with Students with LD

These recommendations must be treated more cautiously than recommendations 1 and 2. The positive impact of these secondary interventions has not been replicated as frequently.

3. *Have students with LD work cooperatively with other struggling writers to plan, draft, revise, and edit their compositions (strong positive impact).* Two of the studies reviewed in *Writing Next* (Graham & Perin, 2007a) examined the impact of working together in a structured manner to plan, draft, and/or edit text on students with LD. The average effect size on the quality of students' text was 1.13 in the two investigations (Dailey, 1991; MacArthur, Schwartz, & Graham, 1991).

The MacArthur et al. (1991) investigation is used to illustrate this approach. Special education teachers taught fourth- through sixth-grade students with LD a peer revision strategy for 6 to 8 weeks within the context of a process writing approach. During instruction, students first individually wrote and revised a personal narrative on the computer. They then met with a peer to use a two-step revision strategy that they had been taught via the SRSD model (Harris & Graham, 1996) described earlier. In the first step, the two students worked together to read aloud and discuss each other's story. They then independently reread the other student's paper and made revision notes, focusing on unclear sections and the need for any additional details. After discussing each other's revision notes, students independently revised their narratives using the peer's suggestions. In the second step, the pair met again to discuss their substantive revisions and to edit each other's papers for mechanical errors (e.g., complete sentences, capitalization, punctuation, and spelling). Students then wrote their final drafts using the peers' suggestions. Compared with students with LD who received only process writing instruction, youngsters taught to use this cooperative arrangement saw improvements in correct spelling and punctuation, revising behavior, and quality of their narrative writing.

4. *Explicitly teach students with LD strategies for producing written summaries of reading material (strong positive impact).* One quasi-experimental study (Placke, 1987), reviewed in *Writing Next* (Graham & Perin, 2007a), and a single-subject design study by Nelson, Smith, and Dodd (1992) included in Rogers and Graham (in press) examined the effectiveness of teaching a summarization strategy to students with LD. In the first study, the effect size for the quality of written summaries was 1.12, and, in the second study, PND for including important information in summaries was 100%.

In the Nelson et al. (1992) investigation, five students with LD, ages 9–13, were taught a nine-step summarization strategy. Before teaching the strategy, the teacher ensured that students understood the general components of a summary (e.g., that a summary should contain only important information), cues in text that help identify the main idea (e.g., bold or underlined words, introductory sentences), and the steps in the strategy and the reasons for each step. The teacher and students worked in a group to apply the summary strategy steps using a summary writing guide. The guide visually provided the steps of the summarization strategy: (1) identifying the main idea, (2) noting important things about the main idea, (3) rereading to make sure the main idea and important ideas were correct, (4) writing a topic sentence, (5) grouping ideas, (6) determining whether any important ideas were missing or whether any unimportant ideas could be deleted, (7) writing the summary, (8) rereading the summary for unclear ideas, and (9) having a peer read the summary. After learning the summarization strategy, all five students wrote summaries that included more main ideas and important details from the text.

5. *Make the process writing approach more effective for students with LD by explicitly teaching them strategies for carrying out the processes of planning, revising, and editing (strong positive impact).* Although the process approach to writing had a small positive impact on the writing quality of students in general in *Writing Next* (see Table 6.1), the impact of this approach with youngsters with LD and other struggling writers is less certain. Three studies in *Writing Next* (Graham & Perin, 2007a) included students with LD or other poor writers, and only one of these studies yielded a positive impact (Curry, 1997). However, the study

by Curry (1997), the MacArthur et al. (1991) investigation reviewed earlier, and a single-subject design study by Danoff, Harris, and Graham (1993; Graham & Harris, 2003) revealed that explicitly teaching planning, revising, and/or editing strategies to students with LD in a process writing classroom via the SRSD model (Harris & Graham, 1996) had a strong impact on their writing. The average effect size for writing quality in the two group studies (Curry, 1997; MacArthur et al., 1991) was 0.89, and in the single-subject design study by Danoff et al. (1993), PND was 100% for the inclusion of basic story elements in students' narratives.

We illustrate the combination of the process approach and strategy instruction using the study by Curry (1997). In this investigation, fourth-grade students with LD in process writing classrooms were taught the story-writing strategy described earlier in recommendation 1 for students with LD (see the study by Harris et al., 2006). These teachers provided opportunities for sustained writing, allowed students to select their own topics, developed a community of learners, and taught the writing strategy through mini-lessons (teachers in the control condition did all of these except teach the writing strategy). During the mini-lessons, students were taught the essential components of narrative compositions using the story-grammar strategy (WWW, What = 2, How = 2). The addition of strategy instruction to the process writing approach improved the story-writing quality of the participating students with LD.

6. *Set clear and specific goals for what students with LD are to accomplish in their writing (moderate to strong positive impact).* Three of the five goal-setting studies reviewed in *Writing Next* (see Graham & Perin, 2007a) examined the impact of setting specific goals on the quality of text produced by students with LD. These three experimental studies produced an average effect size of 0.76.

Graham, MacArthur, and Schwartz (1995) provide one example of goal setting. After writing the first draft of a personal narrative, students with LD in grades 4–6 were given either a general revising goal to improve their papers (control condition) or to improve them by adding at least three things to make them better (the goal-setting condition). Students in the goal-setting condition made more meaning-changing revisions than students in the control condition, resulting in papers of better quality.

Ferretti, MacArthur, and Dowdy (2000) provide a second example of goal setting. In their study, fourth- and sixth-grade students with LD wrote a letter to persuade an audience to agree with their position on a controversial topic. Half of these students were given a set of specific product goals for their writing, which involved including a statement of belief, supporting reasons, and reasons that someone may disagree with this belief. In comparison with students who received a general goal, sixth-grade students with LD who were given the specific product goals for their writing included more elements of argumentative discourse and wrote qualitatively better persuasive letters.

Tier II Recommendations Based on Data from Two or More Studies with Struggling Writers Not Identified with LD

The recommendations in this section are based on studies involving students who experience difficulty with writing. Although some of these investigations included students with LD, most of the students across all the studies were poor writers who were not receiving special education services for LD. These recommendations should be viewed as promising practices, because their effectiveness with students with LD has not been established.

7. *Teach writing and reading together as a means of improving the writing of students with LD (strong positive impact).* We located two studies for which we were able to calculate an effect size for the impact of combined reading and writing instruction on the writing performances of struggling writers. One of these was a single-subject design investigation (Mason, Snyder, Sukhram, & Kedem, 2006) and the other a quasi-experimental study (Mason & Meadan, 2007). Both studies included some children with LD, but the majority of students were struggling writers without LD. Combining reading and writing instruction had a strong impact on writing, as in the first study PND for including main ideas from reading in written text was 92%, and the effect size in the second study was 0.72 for this same variable and 1.13 for length of compositions.

The study by Mason et al. (2006) provides an example of combined reading and writing instruction. They taught both a reading and a writing strategy to fourth-grade struggling writers, using the SRSD instructional model presented earlier (Harris & Graham, 1996). The reading comprehension strategy called TWA taught students to Think before reading (think about the author's purpose, what you want to know, and what you want to learn), to think While reading (think about reading speed, linking knowledge, and rereading parts), and to think After reading (think about the main idea, supporting details, and what you learned). Students outlined science and social studies texts and gave oral retellings to focus on the main idea and important details of the text. After students demonstrated that they could independently use TWA to generate a written outline and orally summarize a passage that was read, they were taught a writing strategy (PLANS) to incorporate the information they learned while reading an informative paper. This strategy helped break the writing into manageable subtasks by teaching the students to follow three steps. First, they used PLANS (Pick goals, List ways to meet goals, And make Notes and Sequence them). The second and third steps directed them to write and say more and to assess their goals to ensure they were met, respectively. After learning the TWA + PLANS strategy for reading and writing, all nine students included more main ideas from texts in their informative papers.

8. *Use word processing and related software as a primary tool for writing with students with LD (moderate to strong positive impact).* Seven true experimental and quasi-experimental studies in *Writing Next* (Graham & Perin, 2007a) examined the impact of word processing on the quality of writing produced by struggling writers (only one of these studies involved students with LD). The average effect size was 0.70, suggesting that word processing may be a promising tool for students with LD. Also, the findings from four single-subject design studies in Rogers and Graham (in press) suggest that software (such as word prediction, speech synthesis, and planning programs) can provide a small but positive boost to the effectiveness of word processing with students with LD (average PND across all measures = 60%). Even though all four of the studies from Rogers and Graham (in press) involved students with LD, we did not include them in previous sets of recommendations, because they did not involve replication for each of the separate software programs studied. We thought that these findings were important enough, however, to include them as promising practices.

Instead of providing an example that just focuses on the use of word processing, we present a study by MacArthur (1998) in which students with LD used a word processor plus speech synthesis and word prediction software. Five students, ages 9–10, wrote dialogue journals to communicate with their classroom teacher. During baseline, students wrote the dialogue journals using a word processor. They were then instructed in the use of speech synthesis and word prediction software. The speech synthesis software allowed the students to have the computer read aloud a particular word, sentence, or the entire journal entry. The word prediction software suggested possible words based on letters typed to that point. With this software, the student could click on any word to hear it pronounced and then double-click to insert the chosen word into the document. After instruction in using the speech synthesis and word prediction software, four of the five students wrote more legible words (correctly decoded out of context) and more correctly spelled words.

9. *Teach text transcription skills (handwriting, spelling, and typing) to students with LD (moderate positive impact).* Five experimental studies and one quasi-experimental study have examined the effects of teaching handwriting, spelling, or typing to students who experience difficul-

ties mastering these skills (see Graham, in press). Students in these studies were in grades 1, 2, 8, or 9. Teaching basic text transcription skills had a moderate effect on improving students' writing quality, as the average effect size across the six studies was .59.

An investigation by Graham, Harris, and Fink (2000) provides an example of how one text transcription skill, handwriting, can be taught to first-grade children who experience difficulty mastering handwriting. Instruction consisted of multiple activities designed to increase students' knowledge of letter names and letter formation and their handwriting fluency. Students first practiced letter names with games and songs. Next, they practiced letter formation by tracing letters with numbered arrows. They also independently copied letters and words containing the target letters. Students evaluated their own handwriting by circling their best formed letter or word. Finally, they completed exercises to improve handwriting fluency by copying sentences with multiple occurrences of the target letters under timed conditions. Students graphed their progress on these exercises.

A study by Graham, Harris, and Fink-Chorzempa (2002) provides an example of effective spelling instruction for young struggling writers. Instruction was designed to improve students' ability to spell words with different long and/or short vowel patterns. Spelling skills were taught through a variety of activities, including word sorts, games, word-making activities, and phonics instruction. Students also studied spelling words that used the targeted spelling patterns. The study procedure involved examining the letters in each word, visualizing and saying the letters of the word with closed eyes, reexamining the letters, writing each word three times without looking, and checking and correcting any misspellings. Students graphed their spelling performances over time.

   10. *Encourage students with LD to monitor one or more aspects of their writing performances (small positive impact).* Graham and Perin (2007c) calculated an average PND for five single-subject design studies that examined the effects of self-monitoring on the performance of struggling writers (some of the students had LD). Self-monitoring ranged from having students count how many words they generated each time they wrote to determining whether specific genre elements (e.g., story parts such as setting, plot, action, resolution) were included in their papers. The effects of such instruction were positive but small, as the average PND was 67%.

A study by Shimabukuro, Prater, Jenkins, and Edelen-Smith (1999) provides a good example of this intervention approach. Three students in grades 6 or 7 with LD or attention-deficit/hyperactivity disorder (ADHD) learned a self-monitoring strategy designed to improve their ability to accurately complete more independent writing assignments (sentence writing exercises). Students learned the importance of improving both the quality and quantity of their independent work and were taught how to manage this work time by graphing their progress at the end of each work session. This arrangement had a positive impact on both the quality and quantity of their sentences.

11. *Reinforce positive aspects of the writing of students with LD (small positive impact)*. Graham and Perin (2007c) calculated an average PND for four single-subject design studies examining the impact of reinforcement on students' writing performance (most of the students in these studies were struggling writers). Reinforcement involved social praise, tangible reinforcers, or both as a means of increasing specific writing behaviors. This approach had a small but positive impact on writing, as the average PND was 56%.

We draw on a study by Hopman and Glynn (1989) to provide an example of the use of reinforcement. In this investigation, reinforcement was tied to a goal-setting procedure, and the effects of each cannot be untangled. Nevertheless, the study illustrates how reinforcement can be tied to a specific instructional activity. Four students received social reinforcement designed to improve the number of words they wrote in their stories. Each student first wrote a story with no reinforcement and then negotiated with the teacher a target number of words to write in the next story. If the student successfully met or exceeded the number of words based on his or her individual target, then the teacher provided social reinforcement in the form of praise, smiles, and encouragement. Once students successfully met their targets for three consecutive stories, the teacher and students negotiated a higher target. Compared with writing with no reinforcement, all four students increased the number of words in their stories. Three of four students also improved the quality of their stories when receiving social reinforcement.

CONCLUDING COMMENTS

In this chapter, we presented a series of recommendations for teaching writing to students in general and students with LD in particular. These recommendations were scientifically based, as they were formed by examining empirical studies (true experiments, quasi-experiments, and single-subject studies) in which the impact of instruction was quantified for all students, writing was measured reliably, and the impact of instruction was replicated. The only exception involved the last 10 recommendations in Table 6.1; they were based on the study of exceptional teachers and schools and had to involve practices that were evident in the majority of the available qualitative studies (thus increasing the confidence that can be placed in these recommendations).

Of course, the faith that can be placed in any scientifically supported recommendation depends on the quality of the evidence on which it is based. For example, experiments provide a better source of evidence than quasi-experiments, as the former rules out more alternative explanations for the findings than the latter (Cambell & Stanley, 1963). Nevertheless, it is important to note that true experiments and quasi-experiments in other fields yield about the same average effect size, with greater variability in effect size for individual studies (Pressley, Graham, & Harris, 2006). Moreover, there was no difference between the average effect size for true experiments and quasi-experiments in the *Writing Next* meta-analysis (Graham & Perin, 2007a). It must further be emphasized that even though a practice yielded a positive impact on students' writing performance in two or more experimental studies, this does not imply that it will work in every classroom or with all students. When a doctor gives us a pill to cure our ills, there is no guarantee that it will work. Instead, both we and the doctor need to monitor its impact to see if the desired effects are obtained or if a different course of action is needed. Teachers should do the same thing with scientifically supported recommendations.

In closing, we address two additional factors that will likely influence the implementation of scientifically supported practices. First, implementation is dependent on teachers' willingness to apply these practices. This willingness is influenced by teachers' knowledge and beliefs about: (1) the suitability of an intervention, (2) its effectiveness, (3) how hard it is to implement, (4) possible negative effects of implementation, and (5) the adequacy of their knowledge about how to implement it. In a recent study (Graham, Papadopoulou, & Santoro, 2006), these five variables accounted for 30% of the variance in teachers' use of specific adaptations for struggling writers, after controlling for variance due to teaching experience, number of children in the classroom (including number of struggling writers and students receiving special education services), and teacher efficacy. If scientifically supported practices are to be applied widely, we must consider teachers' views about the acceptability of a Tier I or Tier II recommendation.

Second, the success of implementing scientifically supported practices also depends on different forms of support. This includes support from the administration and the building-level principal. Teachers' success in using new practices depends on adequate professional development, the purchase of needed resources (e.g., materials), and the allocation of time to plan, implement, evaluate, and modify the target practices. Likewise, teachers are more likely to devote energy and commitment to implemen-

184 TEACHING COMPOSING

tation if they work together as a team and have a voice in the decision-making process.

REFERENCES

Andrews, R., Torgerson, C., Beverton, S., Freeman, A., Locke, T., Low, G., et al. (2006). The effects of grammar teaching on writing development. *British Educational Research Journal, 32,* 39–55.

Atwell, N. (1987). *In the middle: Reading, writing, and learning from adolescents.* Portsmouth, NH: Heinemann.

Cambell, D., & Stanley, J. (1963). *Experimental and quasi-experimental designs for research.* Chicago: Rand McNally.

Curry, K. A. (1997). *A comparison of the writing products of students with learning disabilities in inclusive and resource room settings using different writing instruction approaches.* Unpublished doctoral dissertation, Florida Atlantic University, Boca Raton.

Dailey, E. M. (1991). *The relative efficacy of cooperative learning versus individualized learning on the written performance of adolescent students with writing problems.* Unpublished doctoral dissertation, John Hopkins University, Baltimore.

Danoff, B., Harris, K. R., & Graham, S. (1993). Incorporating strategy instruction within the writing process in the regular classroom: Effects on the writing of students with and without learning disabilities. *Journal of Reading Behavior, 25,* 295–322.

Dowis, C. L., & Schloss, P. (1992). The impact of mini-lessons on writing skills. *Remedial and Special Education, 13,* 34–42.

Ferretti, R. P., MacArthur, C. A., & Dowdy, N. S. (2000). The effects of an elaborated goal on the persuasive writing of students with learning disabilities and their normally achieving peers. *Journal of Educational Psychology, 92,* 694–702.

Graham, S. (in press). Teaching writing. In P. Hogan (Ed.), *Cambridge encyclopedia of the language sciences.* Cambridge, UK: Cambridge University Press.

Graham, S. (2006a). Writing. In P. A. Alexander & P. H. Winne (Eds.), *Handbook of educational psychology* (pp. 457–477). Mahwah, NJ: Erlbaum.

Graham, S. (2006b). Strategy instruction and the teaching of writing: A meta-analysis. In C. A. MacArthur, S. Graham, & J. Fitzgerald (Eds.), *Handbook of writing research* (pp. 187–207). New York: Guilford Press.

Graham, S., & Harris, K. R. (2002). Prevention and intervention for struggling writers. In M. Shinn, H. Walker, & G. Stoner (Eds.), *Interventions for academic and behavior problems: II. Preventive and remedial approaches* (pp. 589–610). Bethesda, MD: National Association of School Psychologists.

Graham, S., & Harris, K. R. (2003). Students with learning disabilities and the process of writing: A meta-analysis of SRSD studies. In L. Swanson, K. R.

Harris, & S. Graham (Eds.), *Handbook of research on learning disabilities* (pp. 383–402). New York: Guilford Press.

Graham, S., & Harris, K. R. (2005). *Writing better.* Baltimore: Brookes.

Graham, S., Harris, K. R., & Fink, B. (2000). Is handwriting causally related to learning to write? Treatment of handwriting problems in beginning writers. *Journal of Educational Psychology, 92,* 620–633.

Graham, S., Harris, K. R., & Fink-Chorzempa, B. (2002). Contributions of spelling instruction to the spelling, writing, and reading of poor spellers. *Journal of Educational Psychology, 94,* 669–686.

Graham, S., MacArthur, C. A., & Schwartz, S. (1995). Effects of goal setting and procedural facilitation on the revising behavior and writing performance of students with writing and learning problems. *Journal of Educational Psychology, 87,* 230–240.

Graham, S., Papadopoulou, E., & Santoro, J. (2006, April). *Elementary teachers' views about the use and acceptability of adaptations for struggling writers.* Paper presented at the annual meeting of the Council for Exceptional Children, Salt Lake City, UT.

Graham, S., & Perin, D. (2007a). *Writing next: Effective strategies to improve writing of adolescents in middle and high school.* Washington, DC: Alliance for Excellence in Education.

Graham, S., & Perin, D. (2007b). A meta-analysis of writing instruction for adolescent students. *Journal of Educational Psychology, 99,* 445–476.

Graham, S., & Perin, D. (2007c). What we know, what we still need to know: Teaching adolescents to write. *Scientific Studies of Reading, 11,* 313–336.

Graves, D. (1983). *Writing: Teachers and children at work.* Exeter, NH: Heinemann.

Harris, K. R., & Graham, S. (1996). *Making the writing process work: Strategies for composition and self-regulation* (2nd ed.). Cambridge, MA: Brookline Books.

Harris, K. R., Graham, S., & Mason, L. (2006). Improving the writing performance, knowledge, and motivation of young struggling writers in second grade. *American Educational Research Journal, 43,* 295–340.

Hopman, M., & Glynn, T. (1989). The effect of correspondence training on the rate and quality of written expression of four low achieving boys. *Educational Psychology, 9,* 197–213.

Horner, R., Carr, E., Halle, J., McGee, G., Odom, S., & Wolery, M. (2005). The use of single-subject research to identify evidence-based practice in special education. *Exceptional Children, 71,* 165–180.

MacArthur, C. A. (1998). Word processing with speech synthesis and word prediction: Effects on the dialogue journal writing of students with learning disabilities. *Learning Disability Quarterly, 21,* 151–166.

MacArthur, C. A., Schwartz, S., & Graham, S. (1991). Effects of a reciprocal peer revision strategy in special education classrooms. *Learning Disabilities Research and Practice, 6,* 201–210.

Mason, L. H., & Meadan, H. (2007, January). *A components analysis of a multiple strategy instructional approach for self-regulating expository reading comprehension and informative writing.* Paper presented at the annual Pacific Coast Research Conference, San Diego, CA.

Mason, L. H., Snyder, K. H., Sukhram, D. P., & Kedem, Y. (2006). TWA + PLANS strategies for expository reading and writing: Effects for nine fourth-grade students. *Exceptional Children, 73,* 69–89.

National Commission on Writing for America's Families, Schools, and Colleges. (2004, September). *Writing: A ticket to work … or a ticket out. A survey of business leaders.* New York: College Entrance Examination Board. Retrieved from *www.collegeboard.com.*

National Commission on Writing for America's Families, Schools, and Colleges. (2005, July). *Writing: A powerful message from state government.* New York: College Entrance Examination Board. Retrieved from *www. collegeboard.com.*

Nelson, R., Smith, D., & Dodd, J. (1992). The effects of teaching a summary skills strategy to students identified as learning disabled on their comprehension of science text. *Education and Treatment of Children, 15,* 228–243.

Persky, H. R., Daane, M. C., & Jin, Y. (2003). *The nation's report card: Writing 2002* (NCES No. 2003–529). Washington, DC: Government Printing Office.

Placke, E. (1987). *The effect of cognitive strategy instruction on learning disabled adolescents' reading comprehension and summary writing.* Unpublished doctoral dissertation, State University of New York, Albany.

Pressley, M., Graham, S., & Harris, K. R. (2006). The state of educational intervention research. *British Journal of Educational Psychology, 76,* 1–19.

Rogers, L., & Graham, S. (2007). *A meta-analysis of effective writing instruction: Evidence from single-subject design research.* Manuscript submitted for publication.

Saltzman, J. (1993). *If you can talk, you can write.* New York: Warner Books.

Shimabukuro, S. M., Prater, M. A., Jenkins, A., & Edelen-Smith, P. (1999). The effects of self-monitoring of academic performance on students with learning disabilities and ADD/ADHD. *Education and Treatment of Children, 22,* 397–414.

Troia, G. A. (2006). Writing instruction for students with learning disabilities. In C. A. MacArthur, S. Graham, & J. Fitzgerald (Eds.), *Handbook of writing research* (pp. 324–336). New York: Guilford Press.

CHAPTER 7

Written Composition Instruction and Intervention for Students with Language Impairment

NICKOLA W. NELSON
FROMA P. ROTH
ADELIA M. VAN METER

As noted throughout this book, composing is a multifaceted process. It draws on multiple levels of language knowledge to achieve communicative, affective, and intellectual purposes, and it is guided by metalinguistic knowledge and executive functions. Students with language impairment (LI) are multifaceted beings as well. Each brings a unique set of competencies to the task of composing. This chapter focuses on teaching children with LI to compose written texts. It describes how LI affects written composition and offers instructional and intervention methods for targeting language development across language levels (i.e., sound, word, sentence, discourse) and modalities (i.e., listening, speaking, reading, writing). Readers are referred to Chapter 6 in this volume, by Graham, Olinghouse, and Harris, for a systematic review and evaluation of the scientific evidence supporting instructional practices for teaching composition to students with special needs. A language-levels assessment model also is adopted in this chapter based on principles used by Scott in Chapter 15 of this volume to frame writing assessment.

Written composition is a relatively permanent but modifiable act of communication. This makes it an ideal context in which to help students develop metalinguistic and linguistic competence, as well as a sense of audience and a theory of mind (i.e., projecting what others might think, know, or need to know at a particular point in time; e.g., Baron-Cohen, 1995). Compositions may address a curricular requirement (e.g., stories, reports, time-lines, essays), serve social purposes (e.g., interactive journals, e-mails, instant messages), or function as mechanisms of self-reflection and communication (e.g., diaries, to-do lists, some poems). Each genre places unique demands on what an author knows and can apply in such domains as language, communication and social cognition, orthography, executive function, and self-regulation. Students who lack basic language abilities may not know how to begin a writing task. Students whose language abilities are tenuous or disconnected across domains may perform differently from day to day and task to task. Such problems may be magnified by limited instructional opportunities to learn to write.

Written composition contexts can be used to help students with impaired or weak language and communication skills develop more integrated, productive, and effective cognitive–linguistic and social–linguistic systems. When students with LI work on original written products using a writing process approach set in a social context, such as in a classroom-based writing lab (Nelson, Bahr, & Van Meter, 2004), intervention teams can target spoken, as well as written, language objectives. Students move recursively among the stages of planning, organizing, drafting, revising, and editing, periodically sharing their work and eliciting feedback from others. Within these activities, language intervention can target specific language development objectives at the linguistic levels of discourse, syntax, words, and sounds, while also emphasizing effective inter- and intrapersonal skills for social interaction and self-regulation. The nature of this individualized work is the focus of this chapter.

DEFINITIONAL ISSUES OF LI

LI is a primary disorder if no related condition is found to explain why children are slow in learning to talk and communicate using language. LI can emerge (or reach a threshold to be identified) at varied developmental stages. Longitudinal research shows that many late-talking toddlers appear to catch up with their peers around kindergarten (Bishop & Edmundson, 1987; Paul, Hernandez, Taylor, & Johnson, 1996) but that recovery may be "illusory" (Scarborough & Dobrich, 1990). Children with language delays are at risk of falling behind again when they face new challenges associated with learning to read and write (Fey, Catts, Proctor-Williams, Tomblin, & Zhang, 2004; Scarborough & Dobrich, 1990). Difficulty with written composition may be particularly challenging for children with underdeveloped language systems, although written composition rarely has been used as a diagnostic measure (Fey et al., 2004).

LI may be specific or nonspecific, depending on whether a discrepancy appears between language abilities and nonverbal cognitive development. When a discrepancy is documented, the condition is termed *specific language impairment* (SLI). When language and cognitive skills are both low, the condition may be termed *nonspecific language impairment* (NLI). Efforts to identify a specific phenotype for SLI have not resulted in a single profile (Rice & Warren, 2004; Watkins, 1994). A number of researchers (e.g., Aram & Nation, 1975; Bishop & Edmundson, 1987; Conti-Ramsden, Crutchly, & Botting, 2003), however, have reported evidence for LI subtypes. One subtype identified by all of these researchers involves deficits in the phonological system alone. This pattern affects sound–word-level skills such as nonword repetition, rapid automatic naming, phonemic awareness, reading decoding, and spelling. It is the pattern often associated with dyslexia and spelling difficulties. The other, more classic type of LI involves additional deficits in nonphonological language skills in the areas of morphology, syntax, and semantics. This pattern of morphosyntactic difficulty affects sentence- and discourse-level skills required for language comprehension and formulation in spoken and written language.

In addition to these two subtypes, Bishop (2000) described pragmatic language impairment (PLI) as a separate syndrome of LI that shared features in common with autism spectrum disorders but that did not represent classic autism. This PLI classification mirrored an earlier category suggested by Rapin and Allen (1983) and others, called semantic–pragmatic impairment. Tomblin, Zhang, Weiss, Catts, and Ellis Weismer (2004) used a variety of tests and found results similar to Bishop's (2000) by showing that pragmatic difficulties were dissociated from other phonological and syntactic–semantic language skills. That is, some children had relative strength in pragmatics in concert with weak abilities in phonology, syntax, and semantics, whereas others seemed to fit Bishop's definition of PLI in terms of weak pragmatic skills in the presence of basically intact phonology, syntax, and semantics.

Research evidence has not supported a categorical difference between children with SLI and with NLI. Based on their longitudinal research (e.g., Catts, Fey, Tomblin, & Zhang, 2002; Tomblin & Zhang, 1999), for example, Tomblin et al. (2004) concluded that children who meet the criteria for NLI have similar profiles to those who meet criteria for SLI and that any differences are more dimensional (i.e., related to severity) than categorical. Similar conclusions have been drawn for specific learning disabilities. Fletcher, Morris, and Lyon (2003), for example, concluded that "classification research over the past 10 to 15 years has provided little evidence that IQ discrepancy demarcates a specific type of LD that differs from other forms of underachievement" (p. 31). Such research is consistent with research on SLI in indicating that specific and nonspecific learning disabilities (LD) represent dimensional (i.e., a matter of degree) rather than categorical differences.

When symptoms of LI persist (or reappear), difficulty with literacy learning often is a central feature, so that problems of LI reemerge and may be relabeled as LD. Research has highlighted phonological awareness as the language skill most highly suspect when early reading problems are observed (e.g., Torgesen, Wagner, Rashotte, Burgess, & Hecht, 1997), but the subtyping studies mentioned earlier support the presence of other LI subtypes as well. The phonological hypothesis has some support as an explanation of specific reading difficulties (often called dyslexia), but it is too narrow to explain the profiles of students with LI, who also have difficulties at the sentence and discourse levels (Bishop & Edmundson, 1987; Catts, 1993; Gillam & Johnston, 1992; Scarborough, 2005; Scott & Windsor, 2000).

The identification of LI and LD overlaps in a number of ways. Decisions to identify a child as having LI or LD as a primary diagnosis may be more a matter of when, how, and by whom a diagnosis is made than of clearly demarked distinctions between the conditions. Either diagnosis can involve difficulties in spoken *or* in written language. To avoid the need to make artificial, or at least fuzzy, distinctions between students with LI or LD, some researchers and clinicians identify children as having language–learning disabilities (LLD; Scott, 2002; Silliman, Butler, & Wallach, 2002). Scott and Windsor (2000) noted that the lack of clarity and consistency in identifying the nature of groups of children participating in research on written composition makes it difficult to distinguish patterns across groups.

In addition to primary classifications of LI, LD, and LLD, secondary involvement of language and literacy systems occurs with almost all other developmental disorders and with the acquired disorders of childhood and adolescence. Language development, and particularly written composition, requires the integration of a number of cognitive–linguistic, sensory–motor, and social–emotional systems. As such, it is vulnerable to primary diagnosis involving any of those developmental systems. Students may need deliberate attention to their language and literacy learning needs, whether they are diagnosed with autism spectrum disorder, intellectual disability, hearing impairment, visual impairment, attention-deficit disorder, emotional impairment, behavioral disorder, or complex communicative needs associated with severe impairment of multiple systems. Although we do not address these populations directly in this chapter, many of the recommendations for language-levels instruction and intervention for students with LI can be extended across diagnostic groups.

DESIGNING INSTRUCTION AND INTERVENTION FOR STUDENTS WITH LI

A Language-Levels Model for Addressing Written Processes and Products

More critical than a particular student's diagnostic label is the nature of the language-learning difficulties the child experiences. Here we suggest an organizational framework for addressing students' composition needs that considers both processes and products, emphasizing language levels. It is compatible with the language-levels model used by Scott (Chapter 14, this volume) to outline measures of written language composition at the word, sentence, and discourse levels. Writing processes have been targeted and employed in instruction and intervention since Hayes and Flower (1987) brought to light the recursive acts authors use to plan, organize, draft, revise, and edit their written compositions. Composing processes include executive functions, as well as core language knowledge and working memory (Singer & Bashir, 2004). Students with LI may require direct teaching of executive function and self-regulatory aspects of writing processes, but it is basic knowledge of language components that is the focus of this chapter.

Language knowledge is a hidden competence that cannot be measured or targeted directly. All products, from formal test scores to original compositions, are influenced by the context in which they are produced and the student's motivation at the moment of observation. Within the limits of such performance factors, basic language knowledge is brought online when students attempt a range of academic and social interaction communication acts. Such acts may involve any of the four modalities—listening, speaking, reading, or writing. Language knowledge must be inferred by analyzing products generated as a student uses language in one or more of these modalities, all of which draw on inner knowledge of language sounds, words, sentences, and discourse.

The Nexus of Intervention and Instruction

Intervention may occur in inclusive instructional settings in classrooms with specialized or therapeutic scaffolding added or in one-on-one or small-group remedial sessions—hence the combined terms: language *instruction and intervention*. Many of the *instructional* techniques that are used to teach writing composition to *all* students are useful for students with LI as well. What this chapter adds is a focus on *intervention* techniques, which differ in their intensity, individualization, and concentration on specific problems of language development (Nelson et al., 2004; Ukrainetz, 2006).

Scaffolding is the instructor's primary tool for mediating a student's knowledge of language at the discourse, sentence, and word levels. The term *scaffolding* is attributed to Bruner (1975) but traced back to Vygotsky's (1978) earlier-20th-century view of learning as a socially mediated enterprise. *Scaffolding* is a term and concept used widely across disciplines (e.g., Englert, 1992; Hogan & Pressley, 1997; Johnston, 2004; Ukrainetz, 2006) to describe adult mediation as a means of helping children achieve higher levels of competence than they could demonstrate on their own. Like literal scaffolds, intervention scaffolds are designed to support development only until children can function at higher levels independently. Scaffolding language differs from other forms of teacher talk in the nature of the questions that are posed. Rather than relying on test-like questions to assess what students know, scaffolding questions frame key components to guide students to construct more advanced language knowledge and to support future learning.

A student's written work in progress provides a concrete sample of the student's self-generated language that can be an object of joint focus and revised by the student with intervention scaffolding. Such scaffolding assumes that an adult mediator: (1) has a sophisticated grasp of the complex nature of higher level, integrated, literate language abilities that are legitimate goals both of instruction and intervention; (2) has assessed the student's abilities across processes and products; (3) has identified appropriate individualized targets; and (4) has plans in place to ensure that the therapeutic focus is deliberate and not just coincidental. Such an approach views teachable moments, though valuable, as insufficient to constitute an intervention plan. Rather, intervention is guided by a set of specific individualized goals and objectives in which advances in language knowledge are targeted and instruction focuses directly on building language competence.

To combine written composition instruction with language intervention, a collaborative approach is essential. Rather than working in isolation, teachers, speech–language pathologists, special educators, and families can coordinate their expertise to target mutually shared compositional writing objectives (Nelson & Van Meter, 2006; Silliman, Ford, Beasman, & Evans, 1999). For example, if the curriculum calls for all third-grade students to write a report on animal migration, scaffolding might target language intervention for a child with LI to address reading comprehension objectives in the context of gathering information for the report. Reading for a purpose might be targeted in tandem with discourse-level objectives, in which a child is provided scaffolding in order to help him or her consider macrostructure elements while completing a planning sheet to address questions constructed by the collaborative team. Then syntactic difficulties might be addressed in the process of drafting and revising the report to use higher level syntactic structures to represent logical, causal, and temporal relationships among propositions. Word-level problems can be addressed through mini-lessons targeting particular orthographic word families and in editing to improve word choices to make them more interesting and to be certain that they convey the student's intended meaning. Parents and peers can serve as audience for works in progress and can ask questions that guide the student to add details to the report.

Collaborative efforts enhance the quality and generalizability of instruction and intervention gains because each team member possesses specialized knowledge and skills (Paul, Blosser, & Jakubovitz, 2006; Roth & Troia, 2006). Collaborative approaches also make it possible to balance purposes of language intervention with the realistic pressures of meeting academic timelines associated with language instruction in general education classrooms. When goals to complete a curricular project on schedule compete with a student's individualized goals to acquire a new skill and demonstrate it independently, interdisciplinary teams may need to decide to address growth in particular skill areas rather than completion of a fully developed product.

Sensitivity to children's cultural and linguistic backgrounds is critical at all points. Such variables directly influence choices of contexts for assessment of and intervention and instruction targeting writing processes, as well as products. For example, in some cultures, emphasis is placed on what a child can learn independently, whereas other cultures focus on what a learner can accomplish in collaboration with peers (Barrs, Ellis, Hester, & Thomas, 1989). Discourse macrostructures also differ across cultures (e.g., Pritchard, 1990; Westby, 1994). Culturally influenced learning styles and discourse structures can interact with children's individual learning styles and discourse knowledge and may necessitate different assessment and intervention strategies.

A combination of classroom-based instruction and relatively more direct individualized intervention may be best suited to achieve maximum benefits for all students. It is consistent with recommendations by Graham and Harris (2002) that instruction for students with writing disabilities should be based on a model that: "(a) emphasizes both prevention and intervention; (b) responds to the specific needs of each child; (c) maintains a healthy balance between meaning, process, and form; and (d) employs both formal and informal learning methods" (pp. 200–201). Those elements of balance and individualization are key components of a comprehensive program aimed at improving written composition for students with LI.

DISCOURSE-LEVEL INSTRUCTION AND INTERVENTION

Three major discourse genres—conversation, narration, and exposition— can be used to classify most other subgenres. For example, conversation may take many forms, including personal–social interaction, argument, instruction, or recounting of personal events (taking it into the realm of narratives); narration may take the form of fictional stories (mysteries, romance, fairy tales, fables), personal narratives, and accounts embedded in conversations, among others; exposition may take the form of reports, timelines, persuasive pieces, essays, opinion pieces, and many other forms. Beyond these three major genres, children may write poetry or other discourse forms of emotional expression. Conversation can be targeted in a written-composition intervention context (e.g., e-mails, text messaging, social notes, pen-pal letters, interactive journals), but it also occurs in a spoken-language intervention context within writing-process oral communication activities, such as peer conferencing and author groups. Narrative and expository genres are more frequently targeted in written composition. Narratives are found frequently in spoken as well as written language and emerge during the preschool years. Thus they are often used as an early instructional context. Expository discourse also offers appropriate writing composition contexts, even in those early years.

Narrative Contexts for Written Composition Instruction

Students with age-appropriate language performance at the single-sentence level may still have difficulties with the more advanced ability to structure extended written discourse units required by narration. Children who cannot tell, retell, or understand stories struggle to learn how to compose written narratives. Thus narrative knowledge is an important index of risk for language and literacy learning problems. For instance, Lewis, O'Donnell, Freebairn, and Taylor (1998) reported that students with earlier diagnosed LI revealed difficulties with written discourse organization when they reached school age. Fey et al. (2004) showed that children identified with LI in kindergarten generated stories in fourth grade that were judged generally weaker in overall quality based on evaluations of story content, organization, and style. They also found problems in storytelling to reemerge at fourth grade for students whose narrative skills had seemed to normalize by second grade. Nelson and Van Meter (2007) found both grade level and ability level differences in story grammar measures for a heterogeneous group of children with and without special needs across grades 1–6.

Intervention targets at the discourse level may address macrostructure organization, which focuses on overall text construction, and meaning, including the number of episodes or subplots and the completeness of those episodes or subplots. Many narrative structure analysis models use aspects of Stein and Glenn's (1979) story grammar analysis based on inclusion of story components, event sequences, and episodic structure. Applebee's (1978) description adds another dimension, emphasizing growth in ability to maintain a central theme while connecting plot elements both sequentially and logically, ending with resolution tied to the theme. Bruner's (1986) description emphasizes the ability of mature narrators to include a landscape of consciousness (characters' inner reactions, thoughts, and plans), as well as a landscape of action (the events of the story).

From a story grammar perspective, a set of elements or components represent the episode or plot structure of classic stories. Called the story schema, these components are outlined in Table 7.1. A story can contain one or more episodes or subplots, and episodes also may be embedded in highly complex stories. An episode is assessed as complete or incomplete based on its inclusion of story grammar components, with a complete episode containing all three major components: initiating event/response, attempt, and consequence. An episode that omits any of these three key elements is considered incomplete. Missing components (major or minor) can be targeted in intervention. Table 7.1 describes story grammar analysis based on episode components and illustrates scaffolding language to help move students to the next levels of narrative development.

A variety of procedural facilitators, such as graphic organizers, mnemonic acronyms, think sheets, and story grammar outlines or maps, are effective in enhancing the content, structure, and comprehension of students' written compositions (Deshler & Schumaker, 1996; Englert, Raphael, Anderson, Anthony, & Santos, 1991; Graham & Harris, 1989; Idol, 1987; Scardamalia & Bereiter, 1986). Such facilitators can assist students with LI and other learning problems in forming a concrete planning guide for writing a complete story and a mechanism for monitoring their progress while obtaining ongoing instructional feedback and support (Baker, Gersten, & Scanlon, 2002; Dimino, Gersten, Carnine, & Blake, 1990; Gurney, Gersten, Dimino, & Carnine, 1990). A graphic organizer for planning might take the form of a story guide, with scaffolding questions that guide students to incorporate the basic components of a complete episode, such as:

TABLE 7.1. Targeting Story Grammar Components in Intervention

Episode components	Related story maturity levels	Scaffolding possibilities
Setting Information about character description and story context (social, physical, temporal)	Is the story limited to description of disconnected elements? → *Heap* Is the story limited to a simple listing of events in no particular order? → *Isolated description/ descriptive sequence*	"You have a lot of good ideas here. Which one do you want to write about? Can you help the reader know how they fit together?" "I'm a little confused about what happened first. Oh, let's put a '1' next to that, and then what happened? How about if we put a '2' there so we can remember the order you want?"
Initiating event/problem Influences character to act	Is the story limited to a temporal sequence with no cause and effect? → *Temporal/action sequence*	"Does your story have a problem?" "What might happen if the boy forgets to feed his dog?"
Response Character's reaction to the initiating problem	Is the story limited to a partial episode with a causally related sequence of events but with no implied goal for addressing the problem? → *Causal sequence*	"It seems like your character has a big problem to face. I wonder what she is going to do about it."
Plan Character's strategy for attaining a goal related to the problem	Is the story limited to a primitive episode with a clearly stated problem and implied goal-directed behavior to address the problem but no explicit plan? → *Primitive/abbreviated episode*	"I see that your character knows that he needs to do something, but I wish I knew more about what he planned to do."
Attempt Character's actions to attain goal	Is the story limited to an episode with a clearly stated problem and implied goal-directed behavior but no intentional attempt by the character to address the problem? → *Primitive/ abbreviated episode*	"I love seeing your character thinking and planning about what to do about the mean fire-breathing dragon, but does she try out her plan? I want to know what she does next to try to solve the problem."
Consequence Character's success or failure to attain the goal	Is the story limited to an episode in which the character has an explicit plan and makes an attempt to address the problem, but the consequence is not clearly stated or related to the attempt? → *Primitive/ abbreviated episode*	"This is a wonderful story. You really grabbed my interest with how you told this story. It has a problem, and your character made a plan and tried to carry it out. I'm wondering, though, what happened. Did the plan work? Or did the character have to try something different?"

(continued)

TABLE 7.1. (*continued*)

Episode components	Related story maturity levels	Scaffolding possibilities
Resolution Character's thoughts or feelings regarding the consequence	Is the story limited to a complete episode with logical related events, a central theme, a problem, goal, attempt, and consequence, but the character's thoughts and feelings about the consequence are not clearly stated? → *Complete episode* (but needs elaboration)	"Your story really makes me think about what it takes to solve a problem like this. I loved that I knew exactly what your character was thinking when she made her plan and knowing how it came out. I think your audience still might want to know more about how your *character* felt about how her plan turned out, though. Do you see a place where you might add something about what she was thinking near the end?"

Note. Based on Nelson et al. (2004); Stein and Glenn (1979); and Westby (1991).

1. Setting: When does the story take place? Where does the story take place? Who is the story about?
2. Problem: What problem does the main character face?
3. Attempt: What does the main character do?
4. Consequence: How is the problem solved? What happens at the end of the story?

For example, Carl was an 8-year-old with LI who benefited from the story guide to build on a story he composed as an isolated description. Carl's initial draft included only setting (S) elements of characters and context. It had none of the three key components of the narrative schema. Carl wrote (punctuation and spelling have been corrected):

> Once there was a land with people (S). The people rode in spaceships (S). They found new lands (S). They saw mice (S). They saw a turtle with two heads (S). One of them had teeth (S).The end.

Carl received direct instruction in the narrative schema by using the story guide first to outline the components of a favorite storybook with a clear story grammar structure. As each question was posed, Carl was scaffolded to write the answer into the story guide template using his knowledge of the storybook. He completed this activity several times, with reduced scaffolding on each rereading. Then Carl used the questions and answers to compose his retold story. As Carl revised his telling of the story events, he was scaffolded to compose sentences orally first to connect the story parts logically, then to write them (thus combining a sentence-level and a discourse-level focus). On completion of the writing activity, Carl used the story guide as a monitoring strategy to compare his composition with the original story and then used it again to compose a new story. As Carl became more facile with basic story structure, additional questions were gradually introduced to stimulate story elaboration, for example, "What did the people look like? Where were the spaceships going? How did the people react to flying in a spaceship? Did they take along any supplies (e.g., food, tools) and why? Were the turtles and other animals friendly? If not, how did the people feel? What happened the day after? One month later?"

A story frame is similar to a story guide, but it uses a syntactic closure technique to make explicit the components of a story the student may be planning or revising:

> This story is about _____ . The problem starts when _____ .
> The first thing the main character did was _____.
> Then_____. The problem was solved when _____.

For example, the story frame technique helped Denise, an 8-year-old who struggled with written composition, to evaluate and elaborate her story. Denise's original story had more components than Carl's. Her story was parsed for inclusion of the story grammar elements, setting (S), problem (P), and conclusion (C), as follows:

> Once there was a dinosaur named Dino (S) who lived in the ice age (S). Dino liked to swim in the water (S). Along came a shark (P), and gulp, that was the end of Dino (C). The end.

In this story, Denise was beginning to convey causally related components, but the story was missing one of the key elements of a complete story. She had included no goal or attempt on the part of Dino to evade the shark. To encourage Denise to connect the problem with the consequence and to begin to think about the character as capable of goal setting, the story frame questions were used to help her generate ideas for the missing goal and attempt elements. The instructor in this example referred to the story frame while scaffolding: "You told your readers what the story is about and that the problem started when 'along came a shark.' But what was the first thing that Dino did when he saw the shark?" In response to this query, Denise thought of several attempt possibilities (*swam really fast*; *screamed*; *tried to hide*) and decided that Dino would swim really fast. Then the story frame was used to scaffold her in thinking about alternative consequences to the event, again using the story frame as a support. This time Denise decided that he might *sink*, *drown*, or *go under water*, but that her ending, " ... the shark went gulp, and that was the end of Dino," would still work with any of them. The story frame then was elaborated to encourage a resolution by asking, "What did Dino think when he saw his plan wasn't going to work? Did the shark react in any way?" As Denise gained mastery with the story frame, she learned to take increased ownership for generating a complete story on her own, and parts of the story frame were gradually faded.

Expository Contexts for Written Composition Instruction

Expository discourse writing projects can be incorporated into written composition instructional and intervention activities across the curriculum. Ukrainetz (2006) described the demands that varied expository genres make on students' organizational abilities, with nonacademic "daily life" examples of each, including: (1) description (classified ad); (2) enumeration (family genealogy); (3) procedure (driving directions); (4) explanation (investigative news report); (5) comparison–contrast (consumer report); and (6) persuasion (editorial). Interventions focused on expository discourse must consider the required structure and content of each and teach specific organizational patterns. Graphic organizers and other templates and scaffolding questions address this need. For example, a student learning to write a social studies or science report might be given specific guidelines on what to include. In the planning stage, scaffolding might focus on identifying main ideas and supporting details. Harris and Graham (1996) and colleagues have suggested a variety of mnemonic devices as part of their Self-Regulated Strategy Development (SRSD; see Chapter 5, this volume).

Planning frames also can be used to evaluate the completeness of expository discourse structures such as compare–contrast, descriptive, or persuasive texts using paper copies or computer-based software supports. Transitional terms (e.g., *first, next, then, finally*) can be incorporated in discourse frames that convey the temporal relationships across personal or historical timelines. During drafting and revising, scaffolding might focus on clarity of ideas and providing transitions among them. For example, a student with language difficulties used a template to plan an animal report that included the questions: "What is the animal's food source? When does the animal migrate? Where does it migrate to? What hazards (dangers) does the animal face?" This template guided students in a third-grade class to find information related to curricular objectives about migration and their selected animals. Students consulted resource books and the Internet and wrote notes they used later to compose their reports. The student with LI received additional scaffolding to complete the template and developed greater language competence in the process.

SENTENCE-LEVEL INSTRUCTION
AND INTERVENTION

Discourse abilities are problematic for many students with LI, but even greater difficulties at the sentence level may make their discourse generation and organization abilities appear to be relative areas of strength (Gillam & Johnston, 1992). Sentence-level difficulties can appear either as errors of grammatical form or as a limited variety and complexity of structures for conveying relationships among concepts and across sentence boundaries. Table 7.2 offers an outline of some of the difficulties that may be observed at the sentence level in the written compositions of students with LI. It also suggests examples of direct instructional and contextualized scaffolding techniques targeting syntactic formulation.

Students with LI show particular risks for grammatical error. Rice, Tomlin, Hoffman, Richman, and Marquis (2004) tracked grammatical tense marker use of 24 young children with SLI and NLI from kindergarten through fourth grade and found that the grammatical performance of children with NLI lagged behind the performance of children with SLI during grades 2 and 3 but reached the level of the other students by grade 4. Gillam and Johnston (1992) and Scott and Windsor (2000) both noted that the presence of grammatical errors in T-units (a unit of grammatical analysis that contains one main clause plus any subordinate clauses or nonclausal units) as a feature that differentiated students with LI from those with typical language (TL).

Grammatical error rates may be affected by sociolinguistic bias, however, when applied to compositions written by students whose spoken dialects allow variations in subject–verb agreement or plural forms. In such cases, the degree of sentence elaboration may be a better metric than syntactic "correctness" that is judged according to the norms of standard edited English. Nelson and Van Meter (2007), for example, compared original story samples from a diverse group of students, some of whom had special needs and some with TL, but most of whom used dialectal forms when talking. The results showed that mean length of T-units (MLTU) was significantly shorter for students with special needs compared with students with TL across racial and ethnic groups. Although grammatical errors per T-unit did not differentiate the students with TL from those with special needs, the proportion of simple incorrect sentences (i.e., those with grammatical errors but no coordinated or subordinated clausal elements) was significantly higher for students with special needs compared with those with TL.

Beyond grammatical errors, intervention targets illustrated in Table 7.2 at the sentence level include other structural elements identified as problematic in baseline samples or merely desirable as developmental

TABLE 7.2. Targeting Advancing Syntactic Complexity in Intervention

Current performance	Direct instruction possibilities	Contextualized scaffolding possibilities
Has difficulty generating sentences (even simple ones) in both spoken and written language.	Use sentence frame with story character in NP slot. Scaffold student in generating alternative actions in the VP slot, including need for object complements for transitive verbs—for example: Bats ... eat insects ... *fly*	"You have some interesting facts in your plan. Let's think about how to write them in sentences in your report. What sentence could you write about what bats eat?"
Uses mostly simple correct and incorrect sentences when composing in writing but more elaborate and correct forms when talking.	Scaffold the student in generating a list of descriptive words and phrases for key concepts (e.g., *furry bodies, dark caves*); then use the list to construct elaborated NPs. A similar mini-lesson can be used to generate a list of adverbs to elaborate the meaning of VPs—for example, how a bat flies (*softly, quietly*).	"Your plan says 'Bats eat insects.' It also says they drink the blood of large animals. I'm curious. Do all bats drink blood? Oh I see, you say, 'Some bats drink the blood of large animals.' Do you want to write it that way in your report?" Scaffold correctness by offering multiple choices of how a book author might say it. For example, "Would a book author say, 'a bat eat' or 'a bat eats'?"
Uses mostly simple sentences (both correct and incorrect), rarely combines sentences, even with coordinating conjunctions.	Present a personalized mini-lesson to illustrate the student's current simple sentences, with coordinating conjunctions listed at the top of the page, to help him or her select which word might fit best to show how two ideas (simple sentences) are related—for example: The child tried to ride his new bike ___ he fell off. The robin found a worm ___ she could feed her babies. The teacher took her class outside ___ she let them play.	Focus on opportunities to combine ideas logically as the student reads a work in progress. Provide feedback about pairs of sentences that show related ideas, with only enough scaffolding to allow the student to combine ideas into more complex sentences. Start with compound sentences, joining two independent clauses with *and*. Gradually ask about other relationships, for example, disjunctive relationships, which require the use of *but, although*, or *except*; causal relationships, which require the use of *because* or *therefore*; or logical relationships, which require the use of *if ... then, so that*.

(continued)

TABLE 7.2. (*continued*)

Current performance	Direct instruction possibilities	Contextualized scaffolding possibilities
Uses an appropriate balance of simple and compound sentences but shows limited variety in types of sentence embedding and combining.	Construct a personal mini-lesson to illustrate the student's current compound sentence-combining approach. Scaffold the student by offering alternative paraphrases to combine the ideas in different ways that mean the same thing but that sound more like what an author would say—for example: The girl ate dinner and she went home. → *The girl ate dinner and went home; After the girl ate dinner, she went home; When the girl finished dinner, she went home.* The walrus looked but he didn't catch a fish. → *Although the walrus looked for a fish, he didn't catch one; The walrus didn't catch a fish, even though he looked everywhere.*	During revising and editing, make a pass through the student's drafted composition, looking specifically for the conjunction *and*. In each case, scaffold the student in asking him- or herself two questions: 1. Do I need this *and* in this spot? 2. Is there a better way to show how the ideas fit together?

Note. NP, noun phrase; VP, verb phrase.

targets of instruction. Possible targets include increases in the MLTU or numbers of clauses per T-unit, as well as a reduction in the percentage of T-units with grammatical errors. Fey et al. (2004) reported that children who had been diagnosed with LI in kindergarten produced stories in second and fourth grades that contained shorter and less complex C-units (similar to a main clause but not always complete), in addition to more grammatical errors. Lewis et al. (1998) found that children with language difficulties across language levels (i.e., sentence-level difficulties, as well as phonological ones) used fewer morphemes and had shorter MLTU in their written compositions than siblings or students with phonological disorders only. Appropriate targets at the sentence level for addressing such concerns include greater variation in numbers of connectives or reduction in overuse of particular syntactic elements. An example of the latter would be run-on sentences, which consist of multiple independent clauses strung together with the coordinating conjunctions *and*, *but*, *or*, and *so*. Nelson and Van Meter (2007) reported that run-on sentences were common in the original compositions of students with TL at around second grade but that students with special needs in written language seemed to hit this point developmentally at around third grade.

At early points in development, students who struggle to generate text produce shorter works with less complex sentences in writing than they do in speaking (Gillam & Johnston, 1992; Scott & Windsor, 2000). Although this pattern shifts for most students some time during elementary school, when they begin to use more elaborate structures in writing than in talking, this may not be the case for some students with LI. For such students, intervention can take advantage of higher level skills in the spoken modality through lessons and scaffolding designed to increase awareness of syntactic skills and how to bring them online while writing. Students may be scaffolded to elaborate their syntax during the drafting or revising stage through questions that elicit added details, phrases, and clauses. Students may need to practice the skill of "dictating" their more elaborate spoken sentences to themselves a clause or phrase at a time as they transcribe the words. They can also learn to use the editing features of computer software programs to make the process of inserting, moving, and deleting text more manageable and less frustrating. It is important that they also practice proofreading their revised texts aloud to themselves and learn to identify any syntactic errors that may have crept in during editing.

Research has supported the necessity and effectiveness of direct instruction for students with special needs in combining multiple ideas using varied syntactic structures (Andrews et al., 2006; Saddler & Graham, 2005). For example, special educators, clinicians, and teachers may offer mini-lessons in sentence combining (Eisenberg, 2006), in which practice opportunities are provided for students to consider relationships across sentences and ways to create causal, temporal, and conditional links between ideas. Direct teaching and practice strategies might include paraphrasing, judging which of several sentence options sounds better, or mini-lessons on the use of adverbial and adjectival phrases or transitional terms (e.g., *although, however, thus, therefore*). Other sentence-combining instruction might focus on embedding by asking students to integrate information from two or more sentences. Students who learn to use paraphrasing and sentence combining in direct skills practice continue to need scaffolding in applying these new abilities to their individual work. For example, a student's attention might be focused on sentences in his or her written work that could be combined, and the instructor might scaffold more interesting and mature ways to present information: "Are there ideas you can combine here for a more interesting sentence? Maybe you could tell your reader *why* he did that."

Reading activities may be used to further hone a student's recognition of sentence complexity and can support the development of skills for parsing sentence elements. For example, when taking notes to complete an animal report, students must be able to paraphrase an original source while retaining the meaning and then be able to represent those ideas in writing in a way that fits smoothly into a larger piece of discourse. The third-grade student described previously, who planned an animal report on migration, drafted the following sentences based on the notes he took using his planning template:

> Bats are mammals them have 8 inch wing span. They have hair, floe [fur], fingers. Bats eat insects small animals eats blood log [large] animals.

Scaffolding focused on combining related ideas into more complex sentences. One technique involved asking him to select from paraphrased alternatives that combined the description of bats as mammals and also told the width of their wingspan. His final product included the following sentences:

> Bats are mammals that have an 8-inch wing span. They have hair, fur, and fingers. Bats eat insects, small animals, and drink the blood from big animals.

The concepts and language represented in these sentences were those of the student. Even though they were scaffolded, they represented his current level of understanding. Scaffolding does not mean telling the student what to write, nor does it involve correcting the student's errors or elaborating his or her ideas, but supporting the student's growing competence to do so independently.

WORD-LEVEL INSTRUCTION AND INTERVENTION

Language intervention targets at the word level generally include word knowledge in the dual areas of meaning and form. Because this book includes a section devoted specifically to intervention for spelling and word-form knowledge, we devote less attention to it here.

Errors of vocabulary and spelling both are common in the writing of students with LLD (Gillam & Johnston, 1992; Lewis et al., 1998), and they are related. Spelling and handwriting often are grouped together as transcription elements within the broader task of written composition (e.g., Berninger, 1999). Both spelling and handwriting are strong predictors of the amount and quality of written composition in the elementary grades (Graham, Berninger, Abbott, Abbott, & Whitaker, 1997), suggesting that they serve as limiting factors that justify direct attention to support composing, as well as for their own sake.

To the extent that children struggle with retrieving the sounds and other aspects of words, they have less cognitive capacity to devote to other demands of written composing (e.g., generating sentences and holding their ideas in working memory as they compose and transcribe their sentences within a larger segment of discourse). Beyond percentage correct, qualitative analysis of spelling patterns can provide a window into what a student knows about the alphabetic and orthographic principles (e.g., Ehri, 2000; Kamhi & Hinton, 2000). Students whose errors show incomplete knowledge of sound–symbol relationships need additional work in recognizing sounds and representing them with letters. Students who spell phonetically sound by sound but do not show conventional spelling patterns may need support in learning orthographic sound patterns represented in word families, such as the -*ight* pattern in *fight*, *right*, and *light* and sound pattern rules such as the use of silent -*e*. They additionally may need support in spelling morphemes that may sound different in different words but are always spelled the same, for example, -*ed* for past tense and word meaning families such as *real*, *really*, and *reality*. Missing or weak skills then can be targeted as a pathway in supporting word selection and transcription, thus allowing students to devote greater cognitive energy to sentence and discourse levels of written composition.

To investigate the degree to which spelling and handwriting might be intertwined, Masterson and Apel (2006) compared spelling with and without handwriting as the output mode. They found that output modality rarely affected spelling accuracy, even for highly complex words, and concluded that spelling knowledge draws on lexical representations stored in long-term memory and is relatively modality free. This supports a recommendation to teach students with LI directly about the nature of words, in terms of both grapheme–phoneme relationships (the alphabetic principle, which governs sound–symbol relationships) and orthographic–morphemic relationships (the orthographic principles governing syllabic patterns). It also supports a decision to allow students to use computer software to support their written composing, revising, and editing efforts.

Word Content and Form as Integrated Intervention Targets

One quantifiable target of content word knowledge (i.e., the ability to draw on an adequate vocabulary to convey meaning) is the number of different words (NDW) an author produces in a given time frame or sample length (Nelson & Van Meter, 2007; Scott & Windsor, 2000). The ability to think of an appropriate word to convey an intended concept and to know how to spell it correctly indicates much about what an author knows about language. Word knowledge is difficult to quantify, however. The NDW count is only a rough measure, which is influenced by such confounding variables as discourse length, whether a composition topic has been assigned or generated by the student, and time consumed by other aspects of the writing process.

The NDW measure does have the advantage of being sensitive to language abilities, however. Nelson and Van Meter (2007) found that NDW and percentage of words spelled correctly both differentiated children by grade and by special needs. Among typically developing students, first and second graders were similar, as were fourth and fifth graders, but third graders produced significantly more different words than second graders and significantly fewer different words than fourth graders. This suggests that third grade may be a transition year in literacy composition development, characterized by solidification of word-level transcription skills, similar to what happens when third graders transition from learning to read to reading to learn. Children with special needs produced significantly fewer different words at third grade than their typically developing peers. The mean (M) of 30.93 different words per story (SD = 20.73) for special needs students was more like that of typically developing second graders (M = 30.66; SD = 17.19) than of their same-age peers (M = 50.29; SD = 20.41). Fey et al. (2004) also found that fourth-grade students with LI produced stories with fewer different words than their peers did.

Examples of Language Intervention Focused on Word Knowledge

All children need instruction to learn to form letters by hand and to develop handwriting that is intelligible to others and appears appropriately mature (Berninger, 1999). Students with LI may need additional practice associating sounds and letters both perceptually and in production (Gillon, 2004; Torgesen et al., 1997). They also need to develop an awakened "ear" for interesting vocabulary they might incorporate into the compositions they write (Nelson & Van Meter, 2006). Word content and form can be assessed and intervention provided in tandem as students work on their written compositions.

Santos was one of these students. He had received speech–language pathology services as a preschooler for speech production difficulties and delayed expressive language, but he gradually caught up with his peers in early elementary school in these areas. Santos was referred again for services in fourth grade as he showed a continuing lag in his language development in reading and writing. Evaluation of Santos's skills at that point showed he had reduced skill in decoding words and overall poor comprehension of text. Observation of his approach to reading showed that he had adopted a "get it done fast" strategy. His response to timed fluency tests, which were common in his school, had been to increase his overall rate of speech but to glide over unknown words. Santos rarely stopped to check for meaning. In the area of writing, Santos was reluctant to begin and had significant difficulty generating topic ideas. Once he had a plan, he had difficulty generating spelling of words he wanted to use and showed difficulty using varied and descriptive word choices.

Intervention at the word level for Santos focused on reciprocal relationships between reading and writing. Goals included the ability to realize that he did not know a word while reading, to pronounce multisyllabic words correctly in all contexts, and to learn new orthographic patterns related to sound and meaning for use when composing. Scaffolding extended to connecting word meanings to comprehension of sentences and discourse. Some examples of print support questions printed on a bookmark included:

> What can I do when I don't know a word? I can ask myself:
> 1. Do I know this word?
> 2. What are the parts I recognize?
> 3. What makes sense here?
> 4. Should I look it up in the dictionary or ask someone for help?
> 5. What should I do to remember this word?

Santos was encouraged to write new words he thought he wanted to remember for later use in written composing in a personal dictionary. Sections were organized by alphabet, as well as by orthographic sound families (e.g., *fight, might, right*), semantically related words roots (e.g., *real, realism, reality*), and homophones (e.g., *there, their, they're*).

In the planning and revising stages of the writing process, scaffolding for Santos focused on adding descriptive words and finding synonyms for frequently used words, such as *said* (*reported, commented, argued, shouted, whispered*). He kept lists of brainstormed "new and improved" words in his personal dictionary. Santos began to identify unknown words more independently while reading and began to show evidence that he was working to comprehend text. As Santos's ability to decode and encode complex words increased, he began to check purposefully whether his meaning matched the teacher's. At that point, his overall fluency scores temporarily dipped, but his comprehension and reading pleasure increased. Returning after a week-long holiday break, he delightedly reported that he had read his first chapter book. At about the same point Santos began to demonstrate personal motivation to write, producing stories on his own that he shared with his family and teacher. He proudly pointed out interesting word choices in his own writing, as well as in the writing of others.

CONCLUSIONS

Individualized intervention can be embedded in more comprehensive activities that target written composition instruction as part of general education. Students with LI struggle with written language comprehension and expression, but they also can demonstrate relative strengths in some areas. For example, students with LI may have interesting story ideas even though their discourse lacks organization or detail. They may have relative strength in formulating spoken sentences although their written compositions are characterized by simple sentences with numerous grammatical errors. This chapter has emphasized an intervention approach that is based on individualized goals and objectives aimed at taking advantage of relative strengths and current levels of development to target increasingly mature abilities across the language levels of discourse, sentences, and words. This necessitates the use of multiple approaches and flexibility in strategy instruction with collaborative efforts among teachers and clinicians. By combining focus on process and product using a collaborative approach, the diverse needs of students with LI can be addressed.

ACKNOWLEDGMENTS

Portions of this chapter were presented on November 18, 2006, at the annual meeting of the American Speech–Language–Hearing Association in Miami, Florida. Cheryl M. Scott and Gary A. Troia participated in that presentation, and this chapter reflects their ideas, as well as our own. Preparation of this chapter was supported in part by Grant No. H324R980120 from the U.S. Department of Education, Office of Special Education Programs, to Western Michigan University.

REFERENCES

Andrews, R., Torgerson, C., Beverton, S., Freeman, A., Locke, R., Low, R., et al. (2006). The effect of grammar teaching on writing development. *British Education Research Journal, 32*(1), 39–55.

Applebee, A. N. (1978). *The child's concept of story: Ages two to seventeen.* Chicago: University of Chicago Press.

Aram, D. M., & Nation, J. (1975). Patterns of language behavior in children with developmental language disorders. *Journal of Speech and Hearing Research, 18*, 229–241.

Baker, S., Gersten, R., & Scanlon, D. (2002) Procedural facilitators and cognitive strategies: Tools for unraveling the mysteries of comprehension and the writing process, and for providing meaningful access to the general curriculum. *Learning Disabilities Research and Practice, 71,* 65–77.

Baron-Cohen, S. (1995). *Mindblindness: An essay on autism and theory of mind.* Cambridge, MA: MIT Press.

Barrs, M., Ellis, S., Hester, H., & Thomas, A. (1989). *The primary language record: Handbook for teachers.* London: London Education Authority.

Berninger, V. W. (1999). Coordinating transcription and text generation in working memory during composing: Automatic and constructive processes. *Learning Disability Quarterly, 22,* 99–112.

Bishop, D. V. M. (2000). Pragmatic language impairment: A correlate of SLI, a distinct subgroup, or part of the autistic continuum? In D. V. M. Bishop & L. B. Leonard (Eds.), *Speech and language impairments in children: Causes, characteristics, intervention, and outcome* (pp. 99–113). East Sussex, England: Psychology Press.

Bishop, D. V. M., & Edmundson, A. (1987). Language-impaired four-year-olds: Distinguishing transient from persistent impairment. *Journal of Speech and Hearing Disorders, 52,* 156–173.

Bruner, J. (1975). The ontogenesis of speech acts. *Journal of Child Language, 2,* 1–40.

Bruner, J. (1986). *Actual minds, possible worlds.* Cambridge, MA: Harvard University Press.

Catts, H. W. (1993). The relationship between speech–language impairments and reading disabilities. *Journal of Speech and Hearing Research, 36,* 948–958.

Catts, H. W., Fey, M. E., Tomblin, J. B., & Zhang, X. (2002). A longitudinal investigation of reading outcomes in children with language impairments. *Journal of Speech, Language, and Hearing Research, 45,* 1142–1157.

Conti-Ramsden, G., Crutchly, A., & Botting, N. (2003). The extent to which psychometric tests differentiate subgroups of children with SLI. *Journal of Speech, Language, and Hearing Research, 40,* 765–777.

Dimino, J., Gersten, R., Carnine, D., & Blake, G. (1990). Story grammar: An approach for promoting at-risk secondary students' comprehension of literature. *Elementary School Journal, 91,* 19–32.

Ehri, L. C. (2000) Learning to read and learning to spell: Two sides of a coin. *Topics in Language Disorders, 20*(3), 19–36.

Eisenberg, S. L. (2006). Grammar: How can I say that better? In T. A. Ukrainetz (Ed.), *Contextualized language intervention: Scaffolding pre-K–12 literacy achievement* (pp. 145–194). Eau Claire, WI: Thinking Publications.

Englert, C. S. (1992). Writing instruction from a sociocultural perspective: The holistic, dialogic, and social enterprise of writing. *Journal of Learning Disabilities, 25,* 153–172.

Englert, C. S., Raphael, T. E., Anderson, L. M., Anthony, H. M., & Santos, D. D. (1991). Making writing strategies and self-talk visible: Cognitive strategy instruction in regular and special education classrooms. *American Education Research Journal, 28,* 337–372.

Fey, M. E., Catts, H. W., Proctor-Williams, K., Tomblin, J. B., & Zhang, X. (2004). Oral and written story composition skills of children with language impairment. *Journal of Speech, Language, and Hearing Research*, 47, 1301–1318.

Fletcher, J. M., Morris, R. D., & Lyon, G. R. (2003). Classification and definition of learning disabilities: An integrative perspective. In H. L. Swanson, K. R. Harris, & S. Graham (Eds.), *Handbook of learning disabilities* (pp. 30–56). New York: Guilford Press.

Gillam, R., & Johnston, J. (1992). Spoken and written language relationships in language/learning impaired and normally achieving school-age children. *Journal of Speech and Hearing Research, 35*, 1303–1315.

Gillon, G. T. (2004). *Phonological awareness: From research to practice.* New York: Guilford Press.

Graham, S., Berninger, V. W., Abbott, R., Abbott, S., & Whitaker, D. (1997). The role of mechanics in composing of elementary school students: A new methodological approach. *Journal of Educational Psychology, 89*, 170–182.

Graham, S., & Harris, K. R. (1989). Components analysis of cognitive strategy instruction: Effects on learning disabled students' compositions and self-efficacy. *Journal of Educational Psychology, 81*, 353–361.

Graham, S., & Harris, K. R. (2002). The road less traveled: Prevention and intervention in written language. In K. G. Butler & E. R. Silliman (Eds.), *Speaking, reading, and writing in children with language learning disabilities* (pp. 199–217). Mahwah, NJ: Erlbaum.

Gurney, D., Gersten, R., Dimino, J., & Carnine, D. (1990). Story grammar: Effective literature instruction for high school students with learning disabilities. *Journal of Learning Disabilities, 23*, 335–342.

Harris, K. R., & Graham, S. (1996). *Making the writing process work: Strategies for composition and self-regulation* (2nd ed.). Cambridge, MA: Brookline Books.

Hayes, J., & Flower, L. (1987). On the structure of the writing process. *Topics in Language Disorders, 7*(4), 19–30.

Hogan, K., & Pressley, M. (Eds.). (1997). *Scaffolding student learning: Instructional approaches and issues.* Cambridge, MA: Brookline Books.

Idol, L. (1987). Group story mapping: A comprehension strategy for both skilled and unskilled readers. *Journal of Learning Disabilities, 20*, 196–205.

Johnston, P. H. (2004). *Choice words: How our language affects children's learning.* Portland, ME: Stenhouse.

Kamhi, A., & Hinton, L. (2000). Explaining individual differences in spelling ability. *Topics in Language Disorders, 20*(3), 37–49.

Lewis, B. A., O'Donnell, B., Freebairn, L. A., & Taylor, H. G. (1998). Spoken language and written expression: Interplay of delays. *American Journal of Speech–Language Pathology, 7*(3), 77–84.

Masterson, J. J., & Apel, K. (2006). Effect of modality on spelling words varying in linguistic demands. *Developmental Neuropsychology, 29*(1), 261–277.

Nelson, N. W., Bahr, C. M., & Van Meter, A. M. (2004). *The writing lab approach to language instruction and intervention.* Baltimore: Brookes.

Nelson, N. W., & Van Meter, A. M. (2006). The writing lab approach for building language, literacy, and communication abilities. In R. J. McCauley & M.

E. Fey (Eds.), *Treatment of language disorders in children* (pp. 383–422). Baltimore: Brookes.

Nelson, N. W., & Van Meter, A. M. (2007). Measuring written language ability in narrative samples. *Reading and Writing Quarterly, 23,* 287–309.

Paul, D. R., Blosser, J., & Jakubovitz, M. D. (2006). Principles and challenges for forming successful literacy partnerships. *Topics in Language Disorders, 26*(1), 5–23.

Paul, R., Hernandez, R., Taylor, L., & Johnson, K. (1996). Narrative development in late talkers: Early school age. *Journal of Speech and Hearing Research, 39,* 1295–1303.

Pritchard, R. (1990). The effects of cultural schemata on reading processing strategies. *Reading Research Quarterly, 25,* 273–295.

Rapin, I., & Allen, D. (1983). Developmental language disorders: Nosologic considerations. In U. Kirk (Ed.), *Neuropsychology of language, reading, and spelling* (pp. 155–184). New York: Academic Press.

Rice, M. L., Tomblin, J. B., Hoffman, L., Richman, W. A., & Marquis, J. (2004). Grammatical tense deficits in children with SLI and nonspecific language impairment: Relationships with nonverbal IQ over time. *Journal of Speech, Language, and Hearing Research, 47,* 816–834.

Rice, M. L., & Warren, S. F. (2004). Introduction. In M. L. Rice & S. F. Warren (Eds.), *Developmental language disorders: From phenotypes to etiologies* (pp. 1–3). Mahwah, NJ: Erlbaum.

Roth, F. P., & Troia, G. A. (2006). Collaborative efforts to promote emergent literacy and efficient word recognition skills. *Topics in Language Disorders, 26*(1), 24–41.

Saddler, B., & Graham, S. (2005). The effects of peer-assisted sentence combining instruction on the writing performance of more and less skilled young writers. *Journal of Educational Psychology, 97,* 43–54.

Scarborough, H. S. (2005). Developmental relationships between language and reading: Reconciling a beautiful hypothesis with some ugly facts. In H. W. Catts & A. G. Kamhi (Eds.), *The connections between language and reading disabilities* (pp. 3–24). Mahwah, NJ: Erlbaum.

Scarborough, H. S., & Dobrich, W. (1990). Development of children with early language delays. *Journal of Speech and Hearing Research, 33,* 70–83.

Scardamalia, M., & Bereiter, C. (1986). Written composition. In M. Wittrock (Ed.), *Handbook on research on teaching* (pp. 778–803). New York: Macmillan.

Scott, C. M. (2002). A fork in the road less traveled: Writing intervention based on language profile. In K. G. Butler & E. R. Silliman (Eds.), *Speaking, reading, and writing in children with language learning disabilities* (pp. 219–237). Mahwah, NJ: Erlbaum.

Scott, C. M., & Windsor, J. (2000). General language performance measures in spoken and written narrative and expository discourse of school-age children with language learning disabilities. *Journal of Speech, Language, and Hearing Research, 43,* 324–339.

Silliman, E. R., Butler, K. G., & Wallach, G. P. (2002). The time has come to talk of many things. In K. G. Butler & E. R. Silliman (Eds.), *Speaking, reading, and writing in children with language learning disabilities* (pp. 3–26). Mahwah, NJ: Erlbaum.

Silliman, E. R., Ford, C. S., Beasman, J., & Evans, D. (1999). An inclusion model for children with language learning disabilities: Building classroom partnerships. *Topics in Language Disorders, 19*(3), 1–18.

Singer, B. D., & Bashir, A. S. (2004). Developmental variations in writing composition skills. In C. A. Stone, E. R. Silliman, B. J. Ehren, & K. Apel (Eds.), *Handbook of language and literacy: Development and disorders* (pp. 559–582). New York: Guilford Press.

Stein, N. L., & Glenn, C. G. (1979). An analysis of story comprehension in elementary school children. In R. Freedle (Ed.), *New directions in discourse processing* (Vol. 2, pp. 53–120). Norwood, NJ: Ablex.

Tomblin, J. B., & Zhang, X. (1999). Are children with SLI a unique group of language learners? In H. Tager-Flusberg (Ed.), *Neurodevelopmental disorders: Contributions to a new framework from the cognitive neurosciences* (pp. 361–382). Cambridge, MA: MIT Press.

Tomblin, J. B., Zhang, X., Weiss, A., Catts, H., & Ellis Weismer, S. (2004). Dimensions of individual differences in communication skills among primary grade children. In M. L. Rice & S. F. Warren (Eds.), *Developmental language disorders: From phenotypes to etiologies* (pp. 53–76). Mahwah, NJ: Erlbaum.

Torgesen, J. K., Wagner, R. K., Rashotte, C. A., Burgess, S., & Hecht, S. (1997). Contributions of phonological awareness and automatic naming ability to the growth of word-reading skills in second- to fifth-grade children. *Scientific Studies of Reading, 1*, 161–185.

Ukrainetz, T. A. (2006). The many ways of exposition: A focus on discourse structure. In T. A. Ukrainetz (Ed.), *Contextualized language intervention: Scaffolding pre-K–12 literacy achievement* (pp. 247–288). Eau Claire, WI: Thinking Publications.

Vygotsky, L. S. (1978). *Mind in society: The development of higher psychological processes* (M. Cole, V. John-Steiner, & E. Souberman, Eds.). Cambridge, MA: Harvard University Press.

Watkins, R. V. (1994). Specific language impairment in children: An introduction. In R. V. Watkins & M. L. Rice (Eds.), *Specific language impairments in children* (pp. 1–16). Baltimore: Brookes.

Westby, C. E. (1991). Learning to talk—talking to learn: Oral–literate language differences. In C. S. Simon (Ed.), *Communication skills and classroom success* (pp. 181–218). San Diego, CA: College Hill.

Westby, C. E. (1994). The effects of culture on genre, structure, and type of oral and written texts. In G. P. Wallach & K. G. Butler (Eds.), *Language learning disabilities in school-age children and adolescents* (pp. 180–218). Boston: Allyn & Bacon.

CHAPTER 8

Teaching Written Expression to Culturally and Linguistically Diverse Learners

ANNE W. GRAVES
ROBERT RUEDA

A recent survey conducted by the U.S. Department of Education (Kindler, 2002) found that, during the 2000–2001 school year, English learners (ELs) accounted for over 1 in 10 students in elementary schools. Students of color, many of whom do not speak English as their first or native language, are likely to account for approximately one-third of the school population in the United States by 2010 (Grant & Gomez, 2001). ELs speak more than 460 different languages and, although native Spanish speakers continue to represent the largest group of ELs (79.2%), there are five other groups with large representation in this country: Vietnamese, Hmong, Korean, Creole (Haitian), and Cantonese. Combined, these five groups now account for approximately 7.7% of ELs in U.S. schools. Other languages are spoken by less than 1% of the national population, though there are urban areas with sizable populations of students speaking Arabic, Russian, Tagalog, Khmer (Cambodian), and Chinese dialects other than Cantonese (Kindler, 2002).

At the same time that diversity is increasing in American public schools, achievement differences between students from diverse backgrounds and their European American peers remain. For example, in 2002 the National Assessment of Educational Progress (NAEP) assessments of writing proficiency indicated that 28% of fourth graders, 31%

of eighth graders, and 24% of 12th graders performed at or above proficient levels, but fewer African Americans and Hispanics were in the "proficient" group than whites or Asian Pacific Islanders (National Center for Education Statistics [NCES], 2004).

These population data, combined with the writing proficiency data, appear to indicate that U.S. schools are in crisis with respect to literacy learning, particularly in urban centers where many ELs attend school. Compounding this problem, the No Child Left Behind (NCLB) Act of 2001 mandates that states use competency exams to prove that all students, including ELs, are proficient in reading, math, and science in grades 3 through 8 (Lewis, 2003). Some states have made passing such a competency exam a requirement for grade promotion and/or graduation (Chalk, Hagan-Burke, & Burke, 2005). Because existing data suggest a strong connection between reading comprehension and written expression (e.g., Baker, Gersten, & Graham, 2003; Graham & Harris, 2005; Shanahan, Chapter 4, this volume), one would anticipate that students who perform poorly on reading competency tests also will perform poorly on measures of written expression. Moreover, many states use exams that require students to demonstrate their competence in reading, math, and science through written expression. All said, the demands for written expression are perhaps at their highest in the history of U.S. education. The implications seem clear: For students who possess weak literacy skills, especially those who are from culturally and linguistically diverse (CLD) backgrounds, the odds of academic and, ultimately, life success are low. Thus the role of teachers in ensuring that students become proficient writers and literate students and citizens is critical (Graves, Gersten, & Haager, 2004). At the same time, the task is more complex because teachers face the daunting goal of simultaneously building content knowledge, developing writing ability, and enhancing English language growth (Baca & Cervantes, 2008; Torres, 2000).

The purpose of this chapter on writing instruction for CLD students is to discuss some of the special factors that need to be taken into account with this population. In addition, we propose a conceptual model that can be used to guide intervention efforts. Finally, suggestions and illustrations of various culturally relevant writing instruction practices are presented.

WHAT ARE THE SPECIAL NEEDS OF CLD STUDENTS?

One of the unfortunate characteristics of much past work on CLD students is the failure to take into account or "unpack" the myriad of factors that characterize these students. A host of related but separate factors can contribute independently, as well as interactively, to the developmental trajectories and school success of CLD students. These cover a range of domains, but some of the most important include language, culture, socioeconomic status (SES), and ethnic or racial background. Each of these contributes in unique ways to the opportunity to learn and to the individual learning characteristics of students and serves to distinguish among individuals within seemingly homogenous groups (often based on racial or ethnic labels). Although a complete review of all of these factors is beyond the scope of this chapter, we briefly discuss some of the major considerations in the paragraphs that follow.

Language Considerations

Students who are nonproficient in English often need special scaffolding to handle academic work in English. This does not mean that being a native speaker of a language other than English automatically creates a deficiency. Rather, it means that students who are not native speakers of English will need assistance in the *academic language* that characterizes school and specific disciplines such as science and math, such as specialized (e.g., *transpire*) and technical (e.g., *isotope*) vocabulary, complex syntactic constructions (e.g., embedded clauses and phrases), and decontextualized information (Beck, McKeown, & Kucan, 2008; Gersten & Jiménez, 1994; Graves et al., 2004).

In addition, developmental aspects of language acquisition need to be understood. For example, there is a relatively well-established pattern of second-language acquisition in which students first acquire the features of a new language that enable them to interact in informal social situations. Often this occurs in the course of a year or two of exposure to a new language. The second stage, in which the literate skills (reading and writing in formal contexts) that characterize the specialized language of schools and academic disciplines are developed, can take significantly longer, on the order of 5–10 years. Theories about language acquisition generally support native language instruction to facilitate underlying academic proficiency. The instruction can later be "transferred in" and applied to English-language learning (Baca & Cervantes, 2008; Chang, 2004; Cummins, 1992; Jiménez, 2003; Krashen, 1985).

Another important consideration is that low proficiency in English should not automatically be taken as a sign of diminished cognitive or academic ability without additional convincing evidence. Students are often able to engage in complex literacy tasks such as writing in their native language that they may not be able to do in English. An important principle is that language ability *in whatever language(s) students have acquired* should be used as a resource in instruction (Moll, 1988; Moll &

Diaz, 1987). The development of writing ability, once acquired, can be used in whatever language the writer deems appropriate. The important point here is that there is no convincing evidence that instruction in the native language in writing or any other area is harmful to students. While there is long-standing controversy about the language of instruction for non-native speakers of English, a more important consideration is quality of instruction (Graves et al., 2004; Graves, Plasencia-Pienato, Deno, & Johnson, 2005).

Cultural Considerations

Although students who are non-native speakers of English may be native-born or immigrants, it is equally possible that they come from homes and communities in which cultural beliefs, understandings, and conventions or everyday practices are different from those typically valued and rein-forced in school settings (Mehan, 1979; Monzó & Rueda, 2001). There is a long-standing hypothesis in the educational research literature that these cultural factors can serve to make the interactional and discourse features of many classrooms difficult for some students (Tharp, 1989). The nature of conversational patterns and public behavior, adult–child relationships, the role of siblings in child care, views of schooling in terms of later life achievement, the role of competition, and so forth, all may be different for some students from what is encouraged and reinforced in schools (Henderson & Landesman, 1994).

It is important to differentiate cultural *practices* (what people actu-ally do in their everyday lives) from the cultural *models* (general cultural beliefs and values) to which people may subscribe (Gallimore & Gold-enberg, 2001; Gutierrez & Rogoff, 2003). Even though individuals may espouse seemingly similar values and beliefs consistent with a particular cultural model (or attributed to a given ethnic or racial group), their actual cultural practices may vary. An additional caution is that it is problematic to make inferences about the cultural practices or the cultural models of an individual based on group labels such as ethnicity or in the absence of reliable evidence. It is important to understand family–home–community cultural practices, however, as they can be useful resources for instruc-tion. These *funds of knowledge* can help create meaningful connections for students between existing knowledge and competence and those tasks and activities valued in schools, including writing (Moll, 1986, 1990).

Socioeconomic Considerations

Although SES and ethnic or racial status are often confounded in discus-sions of CLD students, they are not identical. SES affects students in many important ways, especially with respect to opportunity to learn (Sirin, 2005). When families are in poverty, students may be affected by factors related to nutrition, child care, access to print, family job security, accumulation of school-relevant prior knowledge, and a host of other indices of social and cultural capital (Lee & Bowen, 2006). Complicating matters is the fact that many students are from families in which, due to poverty, the adults in the household have varying levels of schooling and of spoken English-language proficiency and English literacy. Thus opportunities for the student to practice the English language or to receive assistance with writing homework are limited. As Sirin (2005) points out, the relationships between socioeconomic factors are complex, and disagreements exist about the measures of SES used by researchers, but there is a consistent and moderate relationship between SES and achievement that must be addressed if students are to succeed.

In reality, all of the preceding characteristics do not occur randomly, but co-occur systematically. That is, a recent immigrant is likely to be nonproficient in English and less familiar with American cultural conventions and is more likely to be poor. This does not mean that these factors *always* coexist, however, so care must be taken not to infer things about students based on superficial knowledge inferred from global labels (e.g., immigrant status, English learner, etc.).

How do teachers and schools begin to address these complex issues in the domain of writing instruction? Obviously, it is a challenging undertaking to accommodate the cognitive, linguistic, cultural, and motivational diversity of ELs and to carefully design and implement instruction to successfully address these students' needs. It is helpful to have a conceptual model or framework that can guide decisions about which factors to emphasize with a particular student or group of students.

A CONCEPTUAL MODEL FOR ADDRESSING WRITING AT MULTIPLE LEVELS

In thinking about a comprehensive model that can help integrate the various considerations related to writing and literacy for CLD students, we draw heavily on sociocultural theory. Rather than being one theory, it is really a family of related theories. Although an extended treatment of this approach is beyond this chapter, the general common features of sociocultural approaches include the ideas that: (1) learning is social; (2) learning is facilitated by assisted performance that is responsive to individual needs; (3) learning is mediated by cultural tools and artifacts; and (4) learning takes place in communities of practice and is indexed by changes in participation within these communities (Rogoff, 2003).

Recent extensions of sociocultural theory provide a helpful way for educators to think conceptually about all of the factors that might be relevant to consider in writing instruction and other curricular domains for CLD students. In general, sociocultural approaches focus on cultural–historical factors in learning and conceptualize learning and development as a function of multiple interacting levels of influence (Rogoff, 2003). Although it is typical to consider only the individual in learning and development, the "multiple levels of analysis" approach includes the individual, the interpersonal, and the community–institutional focus of analysis (Rogoff, 2003). These levels can be seen as embedded concentric circles, with individual factors at the center, surrounded by interpersonal level factors, both surrounded by cultural–institutional factors.

Factors in the *individual plane* of learning include all of the characteristics that we normally focus on in education, including cognitive, linguistic, motivational, and other learning-related characteristics. Factors at this level might relate to specific cognitive-processing skills, learning strategies, and metacognitive and executive functions, as well as motivational variables such as self-efficacy beliefs, attributions for failure and success, and goal orientations. In terms of motivation, for example, when students experience negative events in school, their affective reactions often may be counterproductive to learning. Thus difficulties in acquiring English or feeling marginalized because of language or cultural differences may result in reduced interest and participation in school activities (Artiles, Rueda, Salazar, & Higareda, 2002; August & Hakuta, 1997; Baca & Cervantes, 2008; Gay, 2000; Jiménez, 2003; Obi, Obiakor, & Algozzine, 1999; Ogbu, 1992). Although these individual factors are critical to learning outcomes, sociocultural theory suggests that the other levels are just as critical.

Factors in the *interpersonal plane* of learning have to do with the characteristics of social relationships or the interactions between people in social settings, especially the classroom and related instructional contexts. Important aspects include the social organizational features of a given setting, which can have a major influence on engagement, participation, cooperative learning, and achievement. It is important to keep in mind that ELs and students of color are in school-based cultural settings in which the social organization and interactional dynamics are unfamiliar or strange. Moreover, they may not have access to support systems at home that might assist in successfully navigating these types of academic cultural settings (Echevarria & Graves, 2007; Faltis & Arias, 1993; Faltis & Hudelson, 1994). Thus, learning is more than just the result of individual cognitive, linguistic, or motivational dimensions. Because an important part of learning is social, the nature and quality of interpersonal interactions and the organization of social settings can have a major impact on student outcomes over time. One source of evidence for these effects is found in work based largely in educational anthropology that has focused on comparative studies between cultures in classrooms and home settings (e.g., Florio-Ruane & McVee, 2000). Studies in this tradition have documented differential treatment and access to learning activities such as writing based on such factors as race, language, ethnicity, and social class. Alternatively, studies such as those based on the Kamehameha Project with native Hawaiian students suggest that student participation and engagement can be facilitated by changing features of the social setting and interactional context (Au & Kawakami, 1994; Lucas, Henze, & Donato, 1990).

Finally, factors in the *community or institutional plane* have a bearing on learning as well. These may involve shared history, languages, rules, values, beliefs, identities, and even cultural tools such as writing that have been passed down and that allow us to engage in intellectual activities in new and different ways. Sociocultural approaches assume that learning is mediated by cultural–historical knowledge, tools, traditions, and so forth from the past as well as the present. Thus an important aspect of understanding learning outcomes is knowing something about the family and community values and supports that are available to individual students. Oftentimes students come from communities in which salient issues infiltrate and permeate student learning and classroom activities. These issues might include sociopolitical matters such as conflict over bilingual education, immigration, and economic resources (Monzó & Rueda, 2001). At a minimum, classroom instruction that capitalizes on the home and community resources for instructional purposes or that is able to tap into salient issues is more likely to foster student engagement and effort (Fitzgerald, 2003).

In short, a multidimensional or multilevel approach to writing instruction suggests the need to consider all of these levels simultaneously. Sociocultural theory holds that all three are interconnected in ways that cannot be easily disentangled. Whereas writing instruction is sometimes approached as the teaching of cognitive skills and strategies to individuals, this more comprehensive conceptual model suggests that instruction needs to be considered within the context of classroom, family, and the larger sociocultural spheres. Given the multilevel model described here, the following section examines strategies for and examples of how to approach instruction at each of the levels.

Writing Instruction Aimed at Individual Factors

Cognitive Strategy Instruction

Teachers must be sensitive to the fact that CLD learners may have extraordinary cognitive burdens when learning new information due to potential unfamiliarity with academic language and text structures. Students in these circumstances may be in a survival mode—attempting to manage demanding academic tasks and at the same time maintaining an egocentric concern for their own well-being (Baca & Cervantes, 2004; Walker de Felix, Waxman, Paige, & Huang, 1993). When students encounter new information or procedures in school that are unfamiliar and therefore difficult to learn, they are likely to resist teachers' efforts and may experience emotional blocks or trauma because they are simply overwhelmed beyond their coping capacity (Cummins, 1992). In these circumstances, students can be so overtaxed in attempting to derive meaning from English or content-oriented technical language that they may not spontaneously generate the strategies needed for efficient and effective learning (Ortiz & Graves, 2001; Yang, 1999). On the other hand, some students in these situations do develop learning strategies on their own (Echevarria & Graves, 2007; Fitzgerald, 1995). Consequently, cognitive strategy instruction is key to the success of many students in acquiring writing proficiency.

Explicit instruction in learning strategies can increase the comfort and learning potential of students needing support. It has a long history of research supporting its efficacy in the fields of educational psychology, special education, and general education with a variety of students, including ELs and other struggling learners (Chamot & O'Malley, 1994, 1996; Deshler & Schumaker, 1994; Echevarria & Graves, 2007; Fitzgerald & Graves, 2004; Genesee, Lindholm-Leary, Saunders, & Christian, 2005; Graham & Harris, 2005; Graves, 1986; Graves & Levin, 1989; Vaughn, Gersten, & Chard, 2000; Woolfolk, 2006). Additionally, studies have shown strategy instruction to be effective at both the elementary level (e.g., Baker et al., 2003; Sexton, Harris, & Graham, 1998; Troia & Graham, 2002) and secondary level (e.g., Chalk et al., 2005; De La Paz, 1999, 2001; Scanlon, Deshler, & Schumaker, 1996; Short, 1994).

Learning strategies are not a curriculum but cut across all curricular areas. Strategies that enhance access to content are used in literature, science, social studies, and math classes and facilitate knowledge acquisition. For example, the steps for writing about an experiment (see the following) can be taught in science to help students increase the knowledge they gain from science lessons and experiments, provided the steps of conducting an experiment are relatively automatic for them. This can be done in a series of mini-lessons (about 15 minutes) on the strategy (Ellis & Graves, 1990). Using mini-lessons allows students to learn the strategy in a controlled practice situation during a designated period of time. Teachers can provide opportunities to memorize and use the strategy during practice sessions before requiring strategy use in a science lesson (Rosebery, Warren, & Conant, 1992).

- Step 1: Write the purpose of the experiment and the expected outcomes.
- Step 2: Gather materials.
- Step 3: Write the procedures.
- Step 4: Carry out the experiment (observe and take notes).
- Step 5: Write the exact results.
- Step 6: Compare and contrast in writing expectations and actual results.
- Step 7: Write about what the results mean.

Such a learning strategy provides a series of steps for integrating language knowledge and content knowledge (Chamot & O'Malley, 1994, 1996; Fitzgerald & Graves, 2004; Gersten, Taylor, & Graves, 1999; Jiménez, 2003; Jiménez, García, & Pearson, 1996; Short, 1994).

In general, cognitive strategy instruction aims to shape behavior by teaching strategy steps, cognitive modeling, guided instruction, and self-regulation (Hallenbeck, 2002). One well-documented model for strategy instruction is the Self-Regulated Strategy Development (SRSD) model developed by Graham and Harris at the University of Maryland (Graham & Harris, 2005). The SRSD model is an approach in which students learn specific strategies and self-regulation procedures (e.g., goal setting, self-assessment, and coping self-talk) for using the strategies during writing activities. Teachers model the use of the strategies and provide diminishing amounts of scaffolding (e.g., guided collaborative practice with ample feedback) while the students master the skills to reach a criterion for learning. The findings of research conducted using SRSD and other strategy instruction studies show that, across content areas and differing student needs, strategy instruction is effective. When strategy instruction is used in an inclusive classroom, it can lead to positive outcomes for students with and without disabilities.

Although strategies are equally as effective for CLD students as they are for all students, given the earlier discussion of some of the possible characteristics of this population, certain considerations need to be kept in mind (Baker et al., 2003).

1. Examine the strategy for necessary prerequisite skills (i.e., concepts and rules) that must be taught first for successful and efficient mastery of the strategy.
2. Select strategies that are highly useful across many situations. For example, choose a strategy for "writing a paragraph" rather than one for completing a specific assignment.
3. Teach strategies when there is evidence of a student's history of difficulty in an area. Students who have already spontaneously

generated effective strategies should not be taught new or different ones.

4. Compare strategies to a scope and sequence of writing instruction and teach the strategies in an order that is logical and fits into the framework of the writing program.
5. Make language (e.g., wording of the steps of a strategy) and examples simple and comprehensible. The description and modeling of the strategy should be straightforward and transparent so that any student can readily see how to implement it.
6. Model the strategy for students frequently, using teacher think-aloud for each step.
7. Have the students collaboratively practice the strategy with teacher supervision and feedback before having them use it on their own.
8. Adapt the instruction and the application of the strategy to individual differences as students begin to use the strategy.
9. Embed strategies in writing activities that are personally relevant, challenging but not too difficult, and linked to specific and clearly communicated content-learning objectives.
10. Provide abundant practice and opportunities for students to apply the strategy to many different practical situations.

Process Writing Approaches

There is a growing body of research on writing instruction for students in special and general education in which strategy instruction is infused into the writing process (e.g., Graham & Harris, 2005; De La Paz, 2001; Englert et al., 1995; Ferreti, MacArthur, & Graham, 2003) as students iteratively and recursively plan, draft, revise, and edit their written products (see Figure 8.1). Several studies indicate that process writing instruction combined with strategy instruction and progress monitoring are effective in improving both the length and quality of students' compositions (Baker et al., 2003; Espin, De La Paz, Scierka, & Roelofs, 2005; Rapp, 1997). A few studies of process writing instruction for special education students who speak a first language other than English indicate similar results (Graves, Valles, & Rueda, 2000; Ruiz, 1995a, 1995b).

The Early Literacy Project (ELP) is a well-known example of a process approach to writing instruction for students with and without writing difficulties (Englert et al., 1995). The ELP includes an emphasis on the following four principles in the development of language skills to enhance learning: (1) meaningful and purposive activities, (2) self-regulated learning, (3) responsive instruction (that is, students who

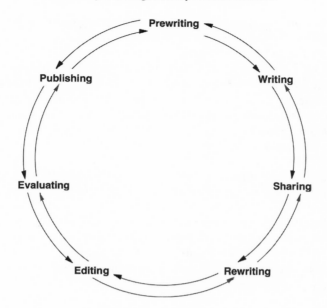

FIGURE 8.1. The writing process.

need assistance may receive direct instruction, strategy instruction, or less explicit instruction, but students who are working successfully are encouraged and allowed to work independently), and (4) building communities of learners through collaborative learning and problem solving. Within the framework, the ELP program includes some of the following elements: thematic units, unsupervised silent reading, partner reading and writing, sharing chair (which provides students with opportunities to ask questions and act as informants to peers and teachers), story discussions, author's center for writing projects, and morning news (which provides students with a language experience activity in which the teacher writes about students' personal experiences as the students dictate). Englert and her colleagues (1995) concluded that the ELP improved the reading and writing performance of students, particularly those students who were taught by teachers who had had 2 years of experience in the project.

Efficacious programs that are similar to the ELP have been developed for ELs specifically, including those with learning disabilities; one such example is the Optimal Learning Environment (OLE) program (Graves et al., 2000; Ruiz, 1995a, 1995b). OLE is similar to the ELP in that it is based on creating a contextualized environment for learning with a focus on thematic units, with the difference that it targets the unique learning needs of ELs. A major assumption in this approach is that native language work provides a bridge toward learning to read and write and that meaningful and purposeful use of language is critical to motivation and the acquisition of English language and literacy.

The OLE program, not unlike the ELP program, includes an integration of listening, speaking, reading, and writing in authentic activities. Both programs require abundant active involvement of students to develop communicative competence (Ruiz, 1995a). The learning environment is designed in a way that facilitates this development by including the following activities:

- Interactive journals in which the teacher responds to students' daily entries in writing to provide regular modeling of written discourse.
- Writer's workshop activities (mini-lessons, sustained writing, conferencing, and sharing) to help students become accustomed to the writing process (see Figure 8.1).
- Patterned reading and writing in which students read and copy key phrases from texts.
- Creating text for wordless books.
- Shared reading with predictable texts, followed by literature circle conversations.
- Literature study with response journals.
- Sustained silent reading.

Results from qualitative studies in which OLE was used with native Spanish speakers suggest not only that the approach increased the length and quality of the writing performances of ELs but also permitted nonreaders and nonwriters to improve their English- and Spanish-language competence (Ruiz, 1995a, 1995b). Two additional studies in which ELs with learning disabilities served as participants have corroborated these results. A descriptive case study that compared the writing instruction in four bilingual special education settings indicated marked improvement for students who were receiving the OLE instruction (Graves et al., 2000). In a second quasi-experimental study of Spanish-speaking students with learning disabilities, one group was provided with the OLE model for writing instruction and the other group used traditional instruction with a focus on spelling and journal writing. Results indicated a significant difference in writing quantity and quality using writing assessments developed by Graves and Montague (1991) and used again in several other studies (Graves & Montague, 1991; Graves, Montague, & Wong, 1990; Graves, Semmel, & Gerber, 1994; Lewis, Graves, Ashton, & Kieley, 1997).

Addressing Limited Prior Knowledge

Many students come to school with limited experiences or with experiences that do not map easily onto traditional school purposes and activities. Some students, especially those in urban settings, do not have opportunities to travel, visit museums, go to libraries, and so forth. It does not mean that they have *no* prior knowledge, however. Even the most "at-risk" families acquire a significant amount of knowledge in navigating the demands of everyday life. Moll (1987) writes extensively about the value of the funds of knowledge that students bring to the classroom from their homes and communities. Across grade levels, teachers understand that accessing these funds of knowledge is an important way to empower and motivate students. Drawing on topics with which all students have some experience is an important aspect of this approach. For example, one second-grade teacher provided each student with a spiral notebook to decorate and in which to respond to daily topic prompts or writing stems (e.g., "Today the weather is ... ") that were common enough to evoke a response from each student. Students were asked to write for 2 minutes in their notebooks and then turn to a partner and read the entry. Then the teacher asked for several of the students to read their entries to the class, keeping track each day of who had already shared with the class. In a sixth-grade class, the first author observed a teacher who planned a unit entitled, "Viva San Diego." Each student was to pick an area of the city they wanted to learn more about, such as Balboa Park; conduct research to learn as much as they could about the area they selected; and prepare a report and a drawing, map, or reproduction of the area. Students were encouraged to involve parents and family in preparing and gathering information. In another example, a high school teacher of students who were in sheltered English classes spent time in class explaining school activities, assisting the students as they completed applications for after-school clubs and programs, and advocating for the students by ensuring that decisions about participation in these activities were fairly made. This seemed to help students feel as much a part of the school community as everyone else. When the students learned that the teacher was their ally, they were more motivated to learn from her. From time to time, the teacher would raise questions about incidents that may have involved prejudice or stereotyping in after-school activities and encouraged students to write about these. This teacher not only helped develop students' background knowledge about the school community, but she also helped them connect this knowledge with personally relevant and meaningful issues in an academic task, namely writing. Another way to build prior knowledge that is meaningful to students is to have them share information about their own cultural and ethnic backgrounds (e.g., how stories are structured and told or how problems are solved) in a non-threatening context (Echevarria & Graves, 2007; Franklin & Thompson, 1994).

Addressing Motivational Factors

In the past, motivation was often considered to be a stable trait of students—students were either motivated or not. In this view, motivation is hard to influence, because it is seen as a fixed characteristic of the individual. Current theory, however, views motivation as a set of task-specific beliefs, which include perceived competence, expectations for success or failure, goals for performing the task, perceived value of the task, and reasons for success or failure (e.g., Pintrich, 2003). These beliefs can be influenced by factors such as past success or failure with academic tasks in a domain (e.g., writing), teacher feedback and expectations, and knowledge and use of self-regulated learning strategies.

Many CLD students may not have high levels of academic engagement because they lack good models of academic behavior or because they may not see its relevance to their out-of-school lives. This situation may be exacerbated when students are confronted with low expectations and/or unchallenging tasks and activities. In one illustrative study, Miller (1999) found that high school English teachers had low expectations of Latino students and that these students were incapable of completing complex literacy tasks such as writing a report or an essay. As part of an experiment, the teachers had their students conduct authentic research about salient topics in their community (e.g., immigration issues) and produce reports and other written materials documenting their research. The results of the experiment indicated that, when motivational factors were addressed by making connections between academic exercises and out-of-school experiences, the students could complete complex literacy projects.

Motivation can be addressed in other ways as well. For example, journal writing at the beginning of each class day or at the beginning of each unit can facilitate the development of secondary students' writing skills and can reinforce positive feelings toward school (Guthrie & Wigfield, 2000; Peyton, Jones, Vincent, & Greenblatt, 1994). Likewise, students are more likely to be motivated when presented with challenging tasks than with simplistic tasks in the context of authentic purpose and personal autonomy (Henze & Lucas, 1993). As an example, a middle school science teacher designated a weekly problem solver for the classroom (Echevarria & Graves, 2007). Any problem encountered during the week was assigned to the problem solver. The problem solver could work independently or use a self-selected committee to compose a written answer to the problem. One week, the student problem solver was faced with a situation in which the teacher had scheduled a field trip to the beach as part of a marine biology unit but the school could not supply enough adult supervision. The field trip was not approved. The principal told the teacher that if adult supervision was obtained by the class members, the class could still make the trip. The problem solver for the week proposed sending notes home to all the parents and to community members asking for field trip chaperones. The effort was entirely student initiated, and the notes were handwritten by the problem solver and her committee. The students were successful in obtaining enough adult supervision, and the field trip was approved. The students were pleased with their efforts and found their new responsibilities and independence rewarding and encouraging.

Writing Instruction Aimed at Interpersonal Factors

Although it is clear that many ELs need instruction related to their individual cognitive and motivational factors, many authors have written about the need for culturally and linguistically sensitive instruction (e.g., Baca & Cervantes, 2004; García, 1993; Gay, 2000; Gersten & Baker, 2000). Such instruction focuses simultaneously on developing content area knowledge, academic proficiency, and English-language proficiency (Chamot & O'Malley, 1994, 1996; Gersten, Baker, Haager, & Graves, 2005; Graves, 1998; Jiménez, 2003; Jiménez & Gersten, 1999) and attending to specific cultural and discourse norms. One consideration in this regard is the social organization of learning settings (how activities are structured, carried out, and regulated in the class). One aspect of social organization that has received considerable attention is grouping practices.

Grouping Practices

Peer tutoring and cooperative learning are grouping arrangements in which students at all grade levels can participate and feel valued (Greenwood, Arreaga-Mayer, Utley, Gavin, & Terry, 2001; Johnson & Johnson, 1989; King, 1990; Schunk & Hanson, 1985). One benefit of partner work and cooperative groups lies in the diversity of cultural and academic backgrounds brought together so that more competent students can act as bridges to academic content and activities when others' language, culture, or prior knowledge differences initially limit their participation and success. Another is that teachers can strategically group individuals together who have different academic talents so that they can learn from each other. Moreover, peer-mediated activities, if planned with ample forethought and explicitly modeled, can guarantee an equal opportunity for all students to participate actively. Specific and focused instruction can be provided by peer tutors, and both the tutors and tutees often show academic benefits from their interaction (see Greenwood et al., 2001, for a full review). Cooperative groups facilitate problem solving by allowing students to work together to achieve a common goal while maintaining individual accountability (e.g., Arreaga-Mayer, 1998; Klingner & Vaughn, 1996).

One example of peer partner groups was recently observed in a sixth-grade social studies setting. The teacher was beginning a unit on American Indians in the southwestern United States and randomly assigned her 32 students to 16 Native American tribes from the southwest, including Mexico and Central America, using a lottery drawing. Student teams were given instructions on how to prepare a poster and report on the tribe they were assigned. Each pair had to decide which portion of the task to complete independently and then come together and teach each other about what they had learned. Together they were to write the report and design the poster. The students worked on this for one whole class period per week for 4 weeks and were able to use the Internet and the library to complete the project. Partners checked the other's work, and the teacher checked the draft products to give recommendations to ensure an informative and well-crafted final project. The pairs gave a brief oral presentation of their work, and the posters were displayed in the school cafeteria.

Research indicates that forming small instructional groups for students who possess similar needs can be beneficial (Reyes, 1992). When all the students in a group need the same information, skills, or strategies, but the instruction requires more teacher attention than can be offered in a large group, small-group instruction may be beneficial (Vaughn, Gersten, & Chard, 2000). Teachers can promote more active student involvement in small groups by, for instance, asking individualized questions and requiring group responses to those questions in writing (Troia & Graham, 2003). When conferences on written products occur in small groups, teachers can provide informative feedback to a few students at a time. Then, when students have revised their work using this feedback, they can share it with their peers in small groups. Thus both teachers and students can provide modeling that may expand the knowledge base of young writers. It is crucial in small-group instruction that teachers' choices for placing students in groups are strategic, flexible, and well suited for the specific learning activities and objectives selected. One implication of making wise instructional decisions regarding grouping is that students do not remain in a stable group across academic domains or across time; continuous regrouping better meets students' needs and helps prevent stigma associated with fixed-group arrangements (McIntosh, Graves, & Gersten, 2007).

Other Interactional Considerations

Creating a sense of student autonomy and belonging is important from a motivational standpoint, and teachers are essential agents in creating a classroom climate in which independence, ownership, and meaningful affiliations are valued, encouraged, and reinforced. In one third-grade classroom, with approximately 85% ELs, the teacher had weekly individual conferences with students. In these conferences, she asked the student to retell either a part of a narrative the student was reading or a part of a content-area chapter being studied. The teacher wrote down the words spoken by the student, and then the student read that text to a peer to receive feedback for revision. Though the teacher wrote the words, the student was aware of his or her intellectual ownership of the text. Once a week students in the class read aloud their chapter summaries or stories and posted them on the "Work This Week" bulletin board. The teacher kept a portfolio of each student's work, and each week a new piece was added to the collection, ultimately leading to a substantial portfolio documenting growth in writing performance.

CLD students are likely to feel a greater sense of belonging, to feel more supported emotionally, and to have higher self-esteem to contribute to the community of writers in the classroom setting if teachers take the following actions (Echevarria & Graves, 2007):

- Provide activities that promote success in reading and writing.
- Focus on content and activities that are meaningful to students.
- Create roles for students in the classroom that capitalize on their strengths.
- Hold high expectations for *all* learners.
- Respond positively and productively to cultural and personal diversity.

Building a community of writers also can be accomplished when ELs are allowed to write for a common purpose, such as a class, grade, or school newsletter (Graves, Gersten, & Haager, 2004). Teachers can build this atmosphere progressively throughout the year. For example, one teacher created a sharing time at the beginning of the year in which students had 2 minutes to share something they had learned about a thematic unit on whales. Later in the year, as students grew more comfortable with one another and with sharing, the teacher changed the activity to "author's chair," and students read what they had written about how a local grocery store was operated, part of a thematic unit on community businesses. Additionally, building a community of writers involves the provision of mechanisms for abundant student recognition. All forms of sharing and publishing assist students in receiving attention and recognition for their work, as well as establishing purposes for it.

Finally, another way to create a rich and exciting classroom climate that promotes interaction is through the use of dialogue journals. Such journals include entries about content students are learning and responses to those entries by the teacher, peers, or family members. This interpersonal writing represents a language experience approach to literacy instruction and is quite appropriate for both elementary and secondary students (Anderson & Roit, 1996; Liang, Peterson, & Graves, 2005; Waldschmidt, Kim, Kim, Martinez, & Hale, 1999). For example, one middle school math teacher had students use a binder as a journal (Echevarria & Graves, 2007). For 3 minutes at the start of each math period, the students made journal entries about their thoughts and feelings concerning the math homework or about how the concepts they were learning applied to their lives. The students were asked to share their entries in small groups or to read anonymous entries to the class. Each week, the teacher collected the journals, read the entries, and provided written comments in the journals. The comments created a written interaction, or dialogue, with each student and established an opportunity for language development, even in a math class.

Writing Instruction Aimed at Community and Institutional Factors

The community or institutional plane is normally the least attended to of the three levels of learning and development considered here. Yet issues that are salient to families and communities outside of the school context affect students' perceptions about school, influence the relationships between teachers and students, and seep into learning activities in other ways. Some families may feel uncomfortable in their interactions with formal institutions such as schools because of their limited education and lack of (or negative) experience with similar institutions. Or some may perceive their role in school matters as passive, deferring to the expertise of teachers and administrators. As noted earlier, students naturally bring with them the cultural tools available to them from home and community: language, beliefs, ways of interacting with others, and so forth. Ideally, all of these can be appropriated for instructional purposes. Some of the most relevant aspects of this plane of learning are considered here.

Family Engagement

The superficial celebration of cultural and linguistic diversity in the schools is not likely to feel real to parents and community members until an authentic and comfortable place is created for the families of all students based on mutual trust (Baca & Cervantes, 2004; Chan, 1990; Chang, 2004; Gay, 2000; Goldenberg, Gallimore, Reese, & Garnier, 2001; Gonzalez et al., 1993). Teachers must establish relationships with family members and key community individuals and should invite them to participate in the classroom. Family members in the classroom might help students learn about other cultures and can serve as role models for all students. For example, a parent who claimed to have made over 100 piñatas was asked to guide a piñata art project in one second-grade class (Echevarria & Graves, 2007). On the other hand, classroom service does not have to be culturally specific. It is designed to bring parents and community members into the class on a regular basis to provide a multiplicity of cultural leadership. For example, any parent could be asked to share life experiences or job-related experiences (Hildebrand, Phenice, Gray, & Hines, 2000). This type of participation is likely to be more effective when it is strategic and directly tied to writing instruction (e.g., a news reporter discusses how to reduce bias in reporting events) rather than being superficial in nature.

Parents and family members can be encouraged to volunteer for many different roles in the classroom. Volunteers can read texts written by students and offer feedback or work with small collaborative writing groups. Parents or community members with special skills can occasionally teach classes. For example, one teacher invited a father who worked on a fishing boat to speak to the class about sea life. The student assisted his father in speaking English, and they worked together to present information and pictures to the class (Echevarria & Graves, 2007; Scarcella & Chin, 1993). In another example (discussed earlier), a fifth-grade teacher planned a unit entitled "Viva San Diego." The teacher invited parents to participate. Each student picked an area of the city he or she wanted to learn more about, and students and their parents did research about and visited their chosen areas to learn as much as they could about them, which aided students' planning efforts for an expository piece about their area. In the end, each student wrote a report about and made a representation (e.g., model) of the area selected. All of these artifacts were displayed in the school showcase. Such activities are most likely to be effective when they are leveraged to push students' competence with writing.

Chang (2004) describes a research project that established an after-school support group for low-achieving Asian American ELs in a middle school using sheltered instruction. The project illustrates how families and educators can be brought together to further develop the writing skills of ELs. Specifically, teachers and parents participated by attending workshops together and forming support teams. The teams were composed of parents, general educators, special educators, and English-language development teachers. After a year of work together, "Family Literacy Nights" were launched. The goals of these gatherings were to: (1) transfer classroom knowledge to the home; (2) have teachers, parents, and students work together to complete reading and writing assignments similar to those given in school; (3) have teams explore multiple paths to teaching and learning; and (4) give parents opportunities to discuss home practices and develop strategies for supervising their children's completion of homework assignments. Parents were taught to use a set of guiding principles developed by Chang (2001), which include the following:

1. Help your child productively use what he or she knows well.
2. Model language used in school.
3. Provide opportunities to use new vocabulary words at home.
4. Help your child relate what was learned in school to home life each day.
5. Give positive feedback frequently.
6. Help your child think of questions and see how ideas or concepts are related.
7. Talk about the importance of lifelong learning.
8. Value your child's abilities in multiple ways and help your child learn through multiple paths.

Buffering Negative Social Influences

Teachers have a responsibility to promote cross-cultural understanding throughout the school (Baca & Cervantes, 2004; Gay, 2000; Harry, 1996; Harry & Klingner, 2006; Jiménez, 2003). Students from ethnolinguistically diverse backgrounds may have experienced ignorance, prejudice, and disrespect and may even have been targets of abuse. A teacher plays an important role in promoting a positive social climate at school. School-wide implementation of rules for appropriate ways of interacting in a democratic, pluralistic community is essential.

To promote prosocial behavior among students and to increase positive feelings about written products, one sixth-grade teacher of students who were ELs also was the faculty advisor for a homework club (Echevarria & Graves, 2007). The teacher encouraged students from all cultural and linguistic groups to join the club and share examples of their writing and approaches to studying. During the daily lunchtime meeting, the students were allowed to eat lunch, play music, share their work, and receive help with their homework. The teacher created a safe atmosphere for social engagement and learning. Often, the teacher would either post students' writing or read excerpts from students' written work to other students. Parents were invited to attend the meetings when they could.

Resources and Time

Because of the accountability demands placed on schools, often the allocation of instructional time is a complex and divisive issue. In the worst case, writing is not taught or not taught systematically and comprehensively. Yet research supports the notion that allocating time for writing instruction and practice across content areas improves writing performance including the use of timed tasks (Deno, 1985; Espin et al., 2005). Teachers need to allocate ample time for writing each day so students become comfortable with the writing process and different genres, develop an awareness of how to manage the complexities of writing assignments, and welcome opportunities to produce written artifacts that represent meaningful personal and social contributions of superior quality.

One suggestion for thinking about how to manage time is to determine the amount of time during instruction and homework that can be devoted to writing. Once this amount of time is determined, it is recommended that students spend one-third of that time on sustained writing, one-third on prewriting activities and teacher-directed instruction or mini-lessons, and one-third on sharing and revising. With this approach, students are engaged in writing for essentially half of the time allotted (time devoted to revising is included). In secondary classrooms and resource programs in which students are working on content-area subject matter, it is recommended that they spend about one-third of the time in class in writing activities. For example, if students are learning about ecosystems in science and some of the students need practice with text composition, the teacher could set up a mini-writing workshop conducted over several class periods in which students plan, draft, revise, edit, and present a paragraph about the contrasting characteristics of two ecosystem models (e.g., fresh water and salt water ecosystems).

Professional Development and Instructional Support

One institutional factor that affects the lives of many CLD students is the lack of equity in the distribution of educational resources. This includes the resources available to teachers and related factors such as professional development and support. Many teachers, especially those in urban schools, work in isolation and have little professional development in areas such as writing. It is important that these factors be addressed so that teachers have adequate support in creating and sustaining effective instructional environments. In the same way that students need a community of learners to function optimally, teachers also need a community of practice in which understandings about writing development, assessment, instruction, teaching practices, instructional challenges, and plausible solutions are shared on an ongoing basis. The National Writing Project and its affiliates have been established with these purposes in mind (for more detail, see Troia et al., Chapter 3, this volume).

CONCLUDING REMARKS

Research and examples from expert teachers indicate that there are several principles and specific practices that make up a successful writing instruction program that accounts for the unique characteristics of CLD students. These include attending to students' (1) cognitive needs (explicit strategy instruction, teaching writing as a process, and making effective use of students' existing prior knowledge); (2) varied cultural understandings and practices; (3) language needs (scaffolding to make tasks and materials more comprehensible); (4) motivational needs (authentic, personally relevant, and challenging writing tasks); (5) social interactions (strategic grouping practices, creating opportunities for student autonomy, and building a learning and writing community); and (6) community and institutional needs (a supportive, safe, and welcoming learning environment for students, parents, and families; adequate time for writing each day; sustained and focused professional development). The conceptual framework proposed here permits consideration of the different factors that influence learning and development in writing; all levels need to be addressed in order to allow the students most in need of help to become proficient writers. In presenting a conceptual model, we are not attempting to build a set of practices to replicate in a rigid fashion. We wish for our ideas to be taken in the context of the other information presented in this book. Our purpose was to convey that the needs of individual students or groups of students, within a given classroom and community, need to be taken into account. Thus attention to one or more levels can be *foregrounded* or *backgrounded* as needed, keeping in mind that learning and development are functions of all three levels. Fortunately there is now a sizeable body of research that provides tools that can assist teachers as they nurture the writing proficiency of all students.

REFERENCES

Arreaga-Mayer, C. (1998). Language-sensitive peer-mediated instruction for language minority studies in the intermediate elementary grades. In R. Gersten & R. Jiménez (Eds.), *Promoting learning for culturally and linguistically diverse students: Classroom applications from contemporary research* (pp. 73–90). Belmont, CA: Wadsworth.

Artiles, A., Rueda, R., Salazar, J., & Higareda, I. (2002). English-language learner representation in special education in California urban school districts. In D. Losen & G. Orfield (Eds.), *Racial inequity in special education* (pp. 117–136). Cambridge, MA: Harvard Education Press.

Au, K. H., & Kawakami, A. J. (1994). Cultural congruence in instruction. In E. R. Hollins, J. E. King, & W. Hayman (Eds.), *Teaching diverse populations: Formulating a knowledge base* (pp. 5–23). New York: Albany State University Press.

August, D., & Hakuta, K. (Eds.). (1997). *Improving schooling for language minority children: A research agenda.* Washington, DC: National Academy Press.

Baca, L., & Cervantes, H. (2004). *The bilingual special education interface* (3rd ed.). Columbus, OH: Merrill.

Baker, S., Gersten, R., & Graham, S. (2003). Teaching expressive writing to students with learning disabilities: Research-based applications and examples. *Journal of Learning Disabilities, 36,* 109–124.

Beck, I., McKeown, M., & Kucan, L. (2008). *Bringing words to life: Robust vocabulary instruction* (2nd ed.). New York: Guilford Press.

Chalk, J. C., Hagan-Burke, S., & Burke, M. D. (2005). The effects of self-regulated strategy development on the writing process for high school students with learning disabilities. *Learning Disability Quarterly, 28,* 75–87.

Chamot, A. U., & O'Malley, J. M. (1994). *The CALLA handbook: Implementing the cognitive academic language learning approach.* Reading, MA: Addison-Wesley.

Chamot, A. U., & O'Malley, J. M. (1996). The cognitive academic language learning approach (CALLA): A model for linguistically diverse classrooms. *Elementary School Journal, 96,* 259–274.

Chang, J. M. (2001). *Scaffold for school–home collaboration: Enhancing reading and language development* (Research Report No. 9). Santa Cruz, CA: Center for Research on Education, Diversity, and Excellence.

Chang, J. M. (2004). *Family literacy nights: Building the circle of supporters within and beyond school for middle school English language learners* (Educational Practice Report No. 11). Santa Cruz, CA: Center for Research on Education, Diversity, and Excellence.

Cummins, J. (1992). Bilingual education and English immersion: The Ramirez report in theoretical perspective. *Bilingual Research Journal, 16,* 91–104.

De La Paz, S. (1999). Self-regulated strategy instruction in regular education settings: Improving outcomes for students with and without learning disabilities. *Learning Disabilities Research and Practice, 14,* 92–106.

De La Paz, S. (2001). Teaching writing to students with attention-deficit disorders and specific language impairment. *Journal of Educational Research*, 95, 37–47.

Deno, S. L. (1985). Curriculum-based measurement: The emerging alternative. *Exceptional Children*, 52, 219–232.

Deshler, D., & Schumaker, J. B. (1994). Strategy mastery by at-risk students: Not a simple matter. *Elementary School Journal*, 94, 153–167.

Echevarria, J., & Graves, A. A. (2007). *Sheltered content instruction: Teaching students with diverse needs* (3rd ed.). Los Angeles: Allyn & Bacon.

Ellis, E. S., & Graves, A. W. (1990). Teaching rural students with learning disabilities a paraphrasing strategy to increase comprehension of main ideas. *Rural Special Education Quarterly*, 10(2), 2–10.

Englert, C. S., Garmon, A., Mariage, T. V., Rozendal, M., Tarrant, K., & Urba, J. (1995). The Early Literacy Project: Connecting across the literacy curriculum. *Learning Disability Quarterly*, 18, 253–277.

Englert, C. S., & Mariage, T. V. (1992). Shared understandings: Structuring the writing experience through dialogue. In D. Carnine & E. Kame'enui (Eds.), *Higher-order thinking* (pp. 107–136). Austin, TX: PRO-ED.

Espin, C. A., De La Paz, S., Scierka, B. J., & Roelofs, L. (2005). The relationship between curriculum-based measures in written expression and quality and completeness of expository writing for middle school students. *Journal of Special Education*, 38, 208–217.

Faltis, C. J., & Arias, M. B. (1993). Speakers of languages other than English in the secondary school: Accomplishments and struggles. *Peabody Journal of Education: Trends in Bilingual Education at the Secondary School Level*, 69(1), 6–29.

Faltis, C. J., & Hudelson, S. (1994). Learning English as an additional language in K–12 schools. *TESOL Quarterly*, 28(3), 457–468.

Fitzgerald, J. (1995). English as a second language learners' cognitive reading processes: A review of research in the United States. *Review of Educational Research*, 65, 145–190.

Fitzgerald, J. (2003). New directions in multilingual literacy research: Multilingual reading theory. *Reading Research Quarterly*, 38, 118–122.

Fitzgerald, J., & Graves, M. F. (2004). *Scaffolding reading experiences for English-language learners*. Norwood, MA: Christopher-Gordon.

Florio-Ruane, S., & McVee, M. (2000). Ethnographic approaches to literacy research. In M. L. Kamil, P. B. Mosenthal, P. D. Pearson, & R. Barr (Eds.), *Handbook of reading research* (Vol. 3, pp. 153–162). Mahwah, NJ: Erlbaum.

Franklin, E., & Thompson, J. (1994). Describing students' collected works: Understanding American Indian children. *TESOL Quarterly*, 28(3), 489–506.

Gallimore, R., & Goldenberg, C. (2001). Analyzing cultural models and settings to connect minority achievement and school improvement research. *Educational Psychologist*, 36(1), 45–56.

García, E. (1993). Project THEME: Collaboration for school improvement at the middle school for language minority students. In *Proceedings of the Third National Research Symposium on Limited English Proficient Issues: Focus on middle and high school issues* (pp. 323–350). Washington, DC: U.S. Department of Education, Office of Bilingual Education and Minority Language Affairs.

Gay, G. (2000). *Culturally responsive teaching: Theory, research, and practice.* New York: Teachers College Press.

Genesee, F., Lindholm-Leary, K., Saunders, W., & Christian, D. (2005). English language learners in U.S. schools: An overview of research findings. *Journal of Education for Students Placed at Risk, 10*(4), 363–385.

Gersten, R., & Baker, S. (2000). What we know about effective instructional practices for English language learners. *Exceptional Children, 56,* 454–470.

Gersten, R., Baker, S., Haager, D., & Graves, A. W. (2005). Exploring the role of teacher quality in predicting reading outcomes for first grade English learners: An observational study. *Remedial and Special Education, 26*(4), 197–206.

Gersten, R., Baker, S., Haager, D., & Graves, A. W. (2005). Exploring the role of teacher quality in predicting reading outcomes for first grade English learners: An observational study. *Remedial and Special Education, 38,* 212–222.

Gersten, R., & Jiménez, R. (1994). A delicate balance: Enhancing literature instruction for students of English as a second language. *Reading Teacher, 47*(6), 438–449.

Gersten, R., Taylor, R., & Graves, A. W. (1999). Direct instruction and diversity. In R. Stevens (Ed.), *Teaching in American schools: A tribute to Barak Rosenshine.* Upper Saddle River, NJ: Merrill/Prentice Hall.

Goldenberg, C., Gallimore, R., Reese, L., & Garnier, H. (2001). Cause or effect? A longitudinal study of immigrant Latino parents' aspirations and expectations, and their children's school performance. *American Educational Research Journal, 38,* 547–582.

Gonzalez, N., Moll, L. C., Floyd-Tenery, M., Rivera, A., Rendon, P., Gonzales, R., et al. (1993). *Teacher research on funds of knowledge: Learning from households* (Educational Practice Report No. 6). Santa Cruz, CA: National Center for Research on Cultural Diversity and Second Language Learning.

Graham, S., & Harris, K. R. (2005). Self-Regulated Strategy Development: Helping students with learning problems develop as writers. *Elementary School Journal, 105,* 169–181.

Grant, C. A., & Gomez, M. L. (2001). *Campus and classroom: Making schooling multicultural* (2nd ed.). Columbus, OH: Merrill.

Graves, A. W. (1986). The effects of direct instruction and metacomprehension training on finding main ideas. *Learning Disabilities Research and Practice, 1,* 90–100.

Graves, A. W. (1998). Instructional strategies and techniques for students who are learning English. In R. Gersten & R. Jiménez (Eds.), *Promoting learning for culturally and linguistically diverse students: Classroom applications from contemporary research* (pp. 250–270). Belmont, CA: Wadsworth.

Graves, A. W., Gersten, R., & Haager, D. (2004). Literacy instruction in multiple-language first-grade classrooms: Linking student outcomes to observed instructional practice. *Learning Disabilities Research and Practice, 19,* 262–272.

Graves, A. W., & Levin, J. R. (1989). Comparison of monitoring and mnemonic text-processing strategies in learning disabled students. *Learning Disability Quarterly, 12,* 232–236.

Graves, A. W., & Montague, M. (1991). Using story grammar cueing to improve the writing of students with learning disabilities. *Learning Disabilities Research and Practice, 6,* 246–251.

Graves, A. W., Montague, M., & Wong, B. Y. L. (1990). The effects of procedural facilitation on story composition of learning disabled students. *Learning Disabilities Research and Practice, 5,* 88–93.

Graves, A. W., Plasencia-Peinado, J., Deno, S., & Johnson, J. (2005). Formatively evaluating the reading progress of first-grade English learners in multiple language classrooms. *Remedial and Special Education, 26*(4), 215–225.

Graves, A. W., Semmel, M., & Gerber, M. (1994). The effects of story prompts on the narrative production of students with and without learning disabilities. *Learning Disability Quarterly, 17,* 154–164.

Graves, A. W., Valles, E., & Rueda, R. (2000). Variations in interactive writing instruction: A study of four bilingual special education settings. *Learning Disabilities Research and Practice, 15,* 1–10.

Greenwood, C. R., Arreaga-Mayer, C., Utley, C. A., Gavin, K. M., & Terry, B. J. (2001). Class-wide peer tutoring learning management system: Applications with elementary-level English language learners. *Remedial and Special Education, 22,* 34–47.

Guthrie, J. T., & Wigfield, A. (2000). Engagement and motivation in reading. In M. Kimil, P. Mosenthal, D. Pearson, & R. Barr (Eds.), *Handbook of reading research* (Vol. 3, pp. 403–422). Mahwah, NJ: Erlbaum.

Gutierrez, K. D., & Rogoff, B. (2003). Cultural ways of learning: Individual styles or repertoires of practice. *Educational Researcher, 32*(5), 19–25.

Hallenbeck, M. J. (2002). Taking charge: Adolescents with learning disabilities assume responsibility for their own writing. *Learning Disability Quarterly, 25,* 227–246.

Harry, B. (1996). These families, those families: The impact of research identities on the research act. *Exceptional Children, 62,* 292–300.

Harry, B., & Klingner, J. K. (2006). *Why are so many minority students in special education? Understanding race and disability in schools.* New York: Teachers College Press.

Henderson, R. W., & Landesman, E. M. (1992). *Mathematics and middle school students of Mexican descent: The effects of thematically integrated instruction* (Research Report No. 5). Santa Cruz, CA: National Center for Research on Cultural Diversity and Second Language Learning.

Henze, R. C., & Lucas, T. (1993). Shaping instruction to promote the success of language minority students: An analysis of four high school classes. *Peabody Journal of Education: Trends in Bilingual Education at the Secondary Level, 69*(1), 54–81.

Herrell, A. L. (2000). *Fifty strategies for teaching English language learners.* Upper Saddle River, NJ: Prentice-Hall.

Hildebrand, V., Phenice, L. A., Gray, M. M., & Hines, R. P. (2000). *Knowing and serving diverse families* (2nd ed.). Columbus, OH: Merrill.

Jiménez, R. T. (2003). Literacy and Latino students in the United States: Some considerations, questions, and new directions. *Reading Research Quarterly, 38*, 122–128.

Jiménez, R. T., García, G. E., & Pearson, E. P. (1996). The reading strategies of bilingual Latina/o students who are successful English readers: Opportunities and obstacles. *Reading Research Quarterly, 31*, 90–112.

Jiménez, R. T., & Gersten, R. (1999). Lessons and dilemmas derived from the literacy instruction of two Latina/o teachers. *American Educational Research Journal, 36*, 111–123.

Johnson, D. W., & Johnson, R. T. (1989). Cooperative learning: What special educators need to know. *Pointer, 33*, 5–10.

Kindler, A. (2002). *survey of the states' limited English proficient students and available educational programs and services, 1999–2000 summary report.* Washington, DC: National Clearing House for English language Acquisition and Language Instruction Educational Programs.

King, A. (1990). Enhancing peer interaction and learning in the classroom through reciprocal questioning. *American Educational Research Journal, 27*, 664–687.

Klingner, J. K., & Vaughn, S. (1996). Reciprocal teaching of reading comprehension strategies for students with learning disabilities who use English as a second language. *Elementary School Journal, 96*, 275–293.

Krashen, S. D. (1985). *The input hypothesis: Issues and implications.* New York: Longman.

Lee, J., & Bowen, N. K. (2006). Parent involvement, cultural capital, and the achievement gap among elementary school children. *American Educational Research Journal, 43*, 193–218.

Lewis, A. C. (2003). Holes in NCLB. *Education Digest, 68*(6), 68–69.

Lewis, R. B., Graves, A. W., Ashton, T., & Kieley, C. (1997). Text entry strategies for improving writing fluency of students with learning disabilities. *Learning Disabilities Research and Practice, 13*, 95–108.

Liang, L. A., Peterson, C. A., & Graves, M. F. (2005). Investigating two approaches for fostering children's comprehension on literature. *Reading Psychology, 26*(4/5), 387–400.

Lucas, T., Henze, R., & Donato, R. (1990). Promoting the success of Latino language minority students: An exploratory study of six high schools. *Harvard Educational Review, 60*, 315–340.

McIntosh, A., Graves, A., & Gersten, R. (2007). The effects of response to intervention on literacy development in multiple language settings. *Learning Disability Quarterly, 30*(3), 212–222.

Mehan, H. (1979). *Learning lessons: Social organization in the classroom.* Cambridge, MA: Harvard University Press.

Miller, R. (1999). *Helping Mexican and Mexican-American students in the schools of the East Side Union High School District* (Report No. RC-022-140). Washington, DC: Office of Educational Research and Improvement, U.S. Department of Education. (ERIC Document Reproduction Service No. 435522)

Moll, L. C. (1986). Writing as communication: Creating strategic learning environments for students. *Theory into Practice, 25*(2), 102–108.

Moll, L. C. (1988). Some key issues in teaching Latino students. *Language Arts, 65,* 465–472.

Moll, L. C. (1990). *Vygotsky and education: Instructional implications and applications of socio-historical psychology.* Cambridge, UK: Cambridge University Press.

Moll, L. C., & Diaz, S. (1987). Change as the goal of educational research. *Anthropology and Education Quarterly, 18*(4), 300–311.

Monzó, L., & Rueda, R. (2001). *Constructing achievement orientations toward literacy: An analysis of sociocultural activity in Latino home and community contexts* (CIERA Report No. 1-011). Ann Arbor, MI: Center for the Improvement of Early Reading Achievement.

National Center for Education Statistics. (2004). *The condition of education: Writing performance of students in grades 4, 8, and 12.* Retrieved February 15, 2007, from *nces.ed.gov/programs/coe/2004/section2/indicator10.asp.*

Obi, S. O., Obiakor, F. E., & Algozzine, B. (1999). *Empowering culturally diverse exceptional learners in the 21st century: Imperatives for U.S. educators* (Report No. EC307730). Washington, DC: National Institute of Education. (ERIC Document Reproduction Service No. ED439551)

Ogbu, J. U. (1992). Understanding cultural diversity and learning. *Educational Researcher, 21*(8), 5–14.

Ortiz, A., & Graves, A. W. (2001). English language learners with literacy-related learning disabilities. *International Dyslexia Association Commemorative Booklet Series, 52,* 31–36.

Peyton, J. K., Jones, C., Vincent, A., & Greenblatt, L. (1994). Implementing writing workshop with ESOL students: Visions and realities. *TESOL Quarterly, 28*(3), 469–488.

Pintrich, P. R. (2003). A motivational science perspective on the role of student motivation in learning and teaching contexts. *Journal of Educational Psychology, 95,* 667–686.

Rapp, W. H. (1997). Success with a student with limited English proficiency: One teacher's experience. *Multiple Voices for Ethnically Diverse Exceptional Learners, 2,* 21–37.

Reyes, M. (1992). Challenging venerable assumptions: Literacy instruction for linguistically different students. *Harvard Educational Review, 64,* 427–446.

Rogoff, B. (2003). *The cultural nature of human development.* Oxford, UK: Oxford University Press.

Rosebery, A. S., Warren, B., & Conant, F. R. (1992). *Appropriating scientific discourse: Findings from language minority classrooms* (Research Report No. 3). Santa Cruz, CA: National Center for Research on Cultural Diversity and Second Language Learning.

Ruiz, N. T. (1995a). The social construction of ability and disability: I. Profile types of Latino children identified as language learning disabled. *Journal of Learning Disabilities, 28,* 476–490.

Ruiz, N. T. (1995b). The social construction of ability and disability: II. Optimal and at-risk lessons in a bilingual special education classroom. *Journal of Learning Disabilities, 28,* 491–502.

Scanlon, D., Deshler, D. D., & Schumaker, J. B. (1996). Can a strategy be taught and learned in secondary inclusive classrooms? *Learning Disabilities Research and Practice, 11,* 41–57.

Scarcella, R., & Chin, K. (1993). *Literacy practices in two Korean-American communities* (Research Report No. 8). Santa Cruz, CA: National Center for Research on Cultural Diversity and Second Language Learning.

Schunk, D. H., & Hanson, A. R. (1985). Peer models: Influence on children's self-efficacy and achievement. *Journal of Educational Psychology, 77,* 313–322.

Sexton, M., Harris, K. R., & Graham, S. (1998). Self-regulated strategy development and the writing process: Effects on essay writing and attributions. *Exceptional Children, 64,* 295–311.

Short, D. (1994). Expanding middle school horizons: Integrating language, culture, and social studies. *TESOL Quarterly, 28*(3), 581–608.

Sirin, S. R. (2005). Socioeconomic status and academic achievement: A meta-analytic review of research. *Review of Educational Research, 75,* 417–453.

Tharp, R. (1989). Psychocultural variables and constants: Effects on teaching and learning in schools. *American Psychologist, 44,* 349–359.

Torres, C. C. (2000). *Emerging Latino communities: A new challenge for the rural south* (Report No. RC 022 605). Chicago: ERIC Clearinghouse on Rural Education and Small Schools. (ERIC Document Reproduction Service No. ED 444806)

Troia, G. A., & Graham, S. (2002). The effectiveness of a highly explicit, teacher-directed strategy instruction routine: Changing the writing performance of students with learning disabilities. *Journal of Learning Disabilities, 35,* 290–305.

Vaughn, S., Gersten, R., & Chard, D. (2000). The underlying message in LD intervention research: Findings from research syntheses. *Exceptional Children, 67,* 99–114.

Waldschmidt, E. D., Kim, Y. M., Kim, J., Martinez, C., & Hale, A. (1999). *Teacher stories: Bilingual playwriting and puppetry with English language learners and students with special needs* (Report No. FL026293). Montreal, Quebec, Canada: ERIC Clearinghouse on Languages and Linguistics. (ERIC Document Reproduction Service No. ED 442288)

Walker de Felix, J., Waxman, H., Paige, S., & Huang, S. Y. (1993). A comparison of classroom instruction in bilingual and monolingual secondary school classrooms. *Peabody Journal of Education: Trends in Bilingual Education at the Secondary School Level*, 69(1), 102–116.

Woolfolk, A. (2006). *Educational psychology* (10th ed.). Boston: Allyn & Bacon.

Yang, N. D. (1999). The relationship between English as a foreign language learners' beliefs and learning strategy use. *System*, 27, 515–535.

CHAPTER 9

Using Technology
to Teach Composing
to Struggling Writers

CHARLES A. MACARTHUR

On saterday I wanet to my friends hoals and sleepover. We falled a cow sckatin we havint falled the sck yate but we falled a bunch of uthere bons. [Journal entry by a fifth-grade student with learning disabilities]

The student who wrote the preceding journal entry was excited to write in his journal and tell his teacher about the cow skeleton and other bones he had found at his friend's house (even though they hadn't found the skull yet). Unfortunately, his teacher had to ask for his help in deciphering his writing, and when his teacher wrote back to him in his journal, she had to help him read her response. This example, taken from a study on word prediction software discussed later in the chapter, illustrates a rather extreme case of the problems with spelling that many students with learning disabilities (LD) face. Students with LD, in general, struggle with all aspects of writing, with both the composing processes of planning and revising and with the transcription processes of getting language onto paper (for a review, see Troia, 2006). Compared with normally achieving students, they have less knowledge of the characteristics of good writing and the requirements of various text structures (Englert, Raphael, Anderson, Gregg, & Anthony, 1989). In addition, they engage in relatively little planning and have few strategies for generating or organizing content (Graham, Harris, MacArthur, & Schwartz, 1991). Furthermore, their revising is focused primarily on mechanics and is generally ineffective (MacArthur, Graham, & Schwartz, 1991). Finally, they have difficulty with the transcription processes of spelling, handwriting, capitalization, and punctuation. Consequently, their papers have more errors and are shorter, less complete and organized, and lower in overall quality than those of their average peers (Graham et al., 1991). These problems are amply discussed in many chapters in this volume.

The purpose of this chapter is to review ways in which technology can support the writing of students with LD. A wide range of computer applications have been developed to support writing, and many of them are especially helpful for struggling writers. Word processing, spelling-checking, word prediction, and speech recognition programs can offer support for transcription and revision. Outlining programs and concept mapping software can offer help in planning. At the same time, technology has expanded the types of writing that people create in school and out-of-school environments to include e-mail, blogs, Internet chat, hypertext, and multimedia. These new forms of writing have not been studied extensively, but they may offer both opportunities and challenges to struggling writers. Multimedia software may help struggling writers to express their ideas with less writing, and new opportunities for authentic communication online may motivate and guide writing. However, these new tools also present new requirements and skills to master.

In the first section of the chapter, I review the research on word processing and discuss what kinds of instruction are needed to take advantage of the power of word processing. The second section focuses on computer tools that may help students compensate for problems with basic transcription and sentence generation, including speech synthesis, word prediction, and speech recognition. In the third section, I consider tools that may support planning and revising processes, including programs that prompt planning and revising activities, outlining and concept mapping software, and automated essay scoring systems. These first three sections all focus on technology applications designed to support the production of traditional written compositions. In the final section, I consider how technology provides new environments and forms for writing, discussing hypermedia authoring and the use of the Internet to promote written communication. Research on technology and writing is somewhat limited, particularly with students with LD. Thus the review considers research conducted with students without disabilities and mentions promising technologies that have generated little research at this time.

WORD PROCESSING

Word processors are flexible writing tools that can be used to support all aspects of the writing process, both cognitive and social. They are well adapted to contemporary views of writing as a cognitive process involving recursive cycles of planning, drafting, and revising. They make it easy to extend, reorganize, and edit text without recopying. By facilitating revising, word processors may encourage students to concentrate on content and organization in early drafts, knowing that errors in conventions can be fixed later. The typing, editing, and spell checking capabilities are especially important for struggling writers who have difficulties with handwriting and spelling. In addition, word processing can support the social processes involved in writing by enhancing opportunities for collaborative writing and publication. Collaborative writing is facilitated by the visibility of the screen and the use of typing. Students can work together at the computer with a clear, legible view of the developing text without individual handwriting to show who wrote which sentences. Texts can be published in many forms. The ability to produce an attractive publication free of errors may be especially motivating for struggling writers.

A substantial number of studies have investigated the impact of word processing on writing. These studies have compared writing instruction with and without word processing across a range of ages and writing abilities and for periods of time ranging from a few weeks to a full year. Meta-analyses have found moderate positive effects on the length and quality of compositions, with larger effects for low-achieving students. The earliest meta-analysis (Bangert-Drowns, 1993) found small to moderate effect sizes (ESs) for length (0.36) and quality (0.27). No difference in ES was found across elementary, secondary, and college students. However, writing ability did matter. The small ES for quality is better viewed as a moderate ES (0.49) in nine studies of remedial instruction for struggling writers and a near-zero ES (0.06) in 11 studies with average writers. A review of research since that analysis (Goldberg, Russell, & Cook, 2003) found somewhat larger ESs for length (0.50) and quality (0.41). A recent meta-analysis of 19 studies, including some of those reviewed in the earlier analyses, limited to grades 4–12 (Graham & Perin, 2007), found an ES of 0.51 for writers in general but a larger ES of 0.70 for low-achieving writers (overall ES = 0.55). None of the studies provided specific results for students with LD. However, there is solid evidence that word processing is an effective instructional support, especially for low-achieving students.

One aspect of writing that may be directly affected by word processing is revision. The evidence indicates that simply having access to word processing does not help students with LD to revise effectively. Two studies (MacArthur & Graham, 1987; MacArthur, Graham, Schwartz, & Shafer, 1995) that compared text production using word processing and handwriting by students with LD in the absence of any specific instruction found no differences in their final papers in terms of length, syntactic complexity, vocabulary, errors of spelling and capitalization, or overall quality. MacArthur and Graham (1987) did find that students made more revisions while composing with word processing, but most of them were minor revisions that had no impact on quality. Word processing makes revising easier and thus may increase motivation to learn about revision. However, it does not directly help students learn how to evaluate their writing, diagnose problems, or fix those problems.

Research has demonstrated that a combination of word processing and instruction in revising strategies increases the amount of revision and improves the overall quality of writing by students with LD. MacArthur and his colleagues conducted three related studies on this combination. The first study evaluated a revising strategy for individual students (Graham & MacArthur, 1988). The other two studies investigated peer revising strategies with instruction provided by research assistants (Stoddard & MacArthur, 1993) and by teachers in classrooms (MacArthur, Schwartz, & Graham, 1991). Students wrote and revised all compositions on a word processor, including those compositions in the baseline or control conditions. Thus the contrast was between word processing with and without revising instruction. In all three studies, instruction had positive effects on the number and quality of revisions, improvement from first to final draft, and quality of the final draft. The results support a conclusion that specially designed instruction is needed to help students take advantage of the power of word processing to improve revision. The results do not demonstrate that the word processor is essential to the success of the instruction, but my experience in helping teachers implement the revising strategy without word processing indicates that there is substantial student resistance to frequent revision when recopying is needed.

An important practical issue when using word processing is typing skill. Handwriting fluency is correlated with writing quality (Graham, Berninger, Abbott, Abbott, & Whitaker, 1997); thus there are good theoretical reasons to believe that typing fluency would likewise affect quality. Russell (1999) compared word processing and handwriting for middle and high school students taking a statewide writing test; effects depended on typing skill. For students whose keyboarding speed was at least 0.5 standard deviation above the mean (20+ words per minute), word processing had a moderate positive effect (ES = 0.5) on writing quality. Conversely, for students whose keyboarding speed was 0.5 standard deviation below the mean, there was a moderate negative effect (ES = –0.4). Typing may be inherently easier than handwriting, especially for students with handwriting problems. However, it can also be a barrier. The practical implications are clear; students need typing instruction to use word processing effectively. In my experience, typing instruction software is an effective way to develop students' skill.

Spelling checkers provide significant support for students with spelling problems. In one study, middle school students with LD who had moderate to severe spelling problems corrected 37% of their errors with a spelling checker, compared with 9% unaided (MacArthur, Graham, Haynes, & De La Paz, 1996). College students with LD (McNaughton, Hughes, & Clark, 1997) used a spelling checker somewhat more effectively, correcting 60% of their errors compared with 11% unaided.

It is important for teachers and students to understand the limitations of spelling checkers and how to work around those limitations. One significant limitation is that they fail to detect spelling errors that produce other words, including homonyms (e.g., *mite* for *might*) and other similar-sounding words (e.g., *were* for *wear*). In the MacArthur et al. study (1996), 37% of students' misspellings were not detected for this reason. Students need to understand how significant this problem is and proofread specifically to look for incorrect words. Another important limitation is that the correct spelling may not appear in the list of suggestions, especially when words are severely misspelled. In the same study, this problem occurred for 42% of identified errors. Students need to learn to try alternate spellings if the intended word is not in the list; phonetic spellings will work with most current spelling checkers. Other potential problems are that students may not recognize the correct spelling in the list of suggestions and that proper names or slang may be falsely identified as errors. In the MacArthur et al. study (1996), these problems occurred less often.

Some word processors designed for use in schools or to support struggling writers have special features in their spelling checkers. For example, they may flag common homonyms and alert students to check them. They may permit users to select smaller dictionaries to reduce the problem of not identifying misused homonyms such as *mite* for *might* (a smaller dictionary would not have the uncommon word *mite*). Finally, they may include speech synthesis to pronounce the words in the list of suggestions. These features may be important for some students with more severe spelling (and reading) problems, though no research has investigated them.

One important practical issue is access. Although word processing is probably the most widely available and commonly used computer application, few schools have sufficient technology to permit students to do most of their writing on a computer. Students cannot get the real benefit of word processing unless they use it for the entire writing process, from drafting through revision and publication. Practical solutions include shared computer labs devoted to writing instruction or use of relatively inexpensive laptops dedicated to word processing (e.g., AlphaSmarts).

TOOLS TO SUPPORT TRANSCRIPTION

Speech Synthesis

Speech synthesis translates text into computer-generated speech. It is a critical component of assistive technology for reading (for a research review, see MacArthur, Ferretti, Okolo, & Cavalier, 2001). It may also assist struggling writers with revising. By listening to their text, students may be able to use their oral language skills to identify errors that they would miss when reading. For example, it might help them find errors in grammar, punctuation, and incorrect words not flagged by a spelling checker. Theoretical models of revising (Hayes, 1996) include reading skill as an important component; thus assisted reading might support the revising process in general. Speech synthesis capabilities are included on most computers, and common word processors (e.g., Microsoft Word) will read text. Word processors designed for use by struggling writers add features that may be important for editing; in particular, they highlight words as they are spoken.

Little research has addressed the effects of speech synthesis. In a study by Borgh and Dickson (1992), elementary students without disabilities used a special word processor that prompted them to check for errors; half of the students used speech synthesis along with the prompts. No differences were found in overall amount of revision or the length and quality of papers. Raskind and Higgins (1995) asked college students with LD to detect errors in their papers with and without speech synthesis. Students detected more errors in the speech synthesis condition, although the difference was not large (35% vs. 25% detection) and data on actual correction of errors were not reported.

Speech synthesis is one area in which the research provides little guidance. As with other assistive technology, the effects probably depend on instruction in how to use the tool. For example, if students are encouraged to reread their text several times with the support of speech synthesis and highlighting of text, it may help them to find errors and awkward sentences. Students might also try using speech synthesis in combination with other tools; for example, using speech synthesis to detect errors not flagged by a spelling checker or to detect errors created using speech recognition while dictating.

Word Prediction

A word processor with a spelling checker is an effective tool for many struggling writers. But some students with severe spelling problems may have difficulty with traditional spelling checkers. Their spelling may be so impaired that a spelling checker cannot suggest the correct words, and they may not be able to read their own writing. Consider, for example, the journal entry at the beginning of this chapter. No spelling checker would suggest the correct spelling for *hoals*, *skatin*, or *falled*. Other students are reluctant to ignore spelling errors on a first draft. These students may benefit from word prediction software.

Word prediction was originally developed for individuals with physical disabilities that make typing difficult. It "predicts" what word the user intends to type based on initial letters. For example, if I have typed, "My best f," the program might offer a list of predictions including "food," "friend," and "family." If I continue by adding *r* to the *f*, the program would update the list, eliminating words that do not start with *fr* and adding new words. When the intended word appears in the list, I can insert the word in the text by typing the number of the word or clicking on it. Most word prediction systems also provide speech synthesis to help students read the list of words. Depending on the sophistication of the program, predictions will be based on spelling alone or in combination with syntax and words or phrases recently used by the writer.

Newell, Booth, Arnott, and Beattie (1992) reported a series of case studies of word prediction use by 17 students with a range of disabilities, including cerebral palsy, visual and hearing impairments, developmental delay, and language and learning disabilities. Of the six students who had mild to moderate language and learning disabilities, five showed improvements in accuracy of spelling, quantity of writing, and motivation to write.

MacArthur (1998, 1999) investigated the use of word prediction with 9- and 10-year-old students with severe spelling problems, using single-subject designs to study the effects of treatment on individual students. In the first study (MacArthur, 1998), five students wrote dialogue journals with their teacher, using a word processor in the baseline condition and a simple word prediction program with speech synthesis in the treatment condition. The second study (MacArthur, 1999) used a more complex word prediction program with a larger vocabulary and a more sophisticated prediction algorithm that used information on syntax and frequency of word use by individual users. Students wrote journals in an alternating treatment design comparing handwriting, word processing, and word prediction. Across the two studies, six of eight students demonstrated dramatic improvements in the legibility of their writing and spelling when using word prediction. During baseline, their writing ranged from 55 to 85% legible words (i.e., readable in isolation) and 42 to 75% correctly spelled words. With word prediction, all six students increased their percentage of both legible and correctly spelled words to above 90%. A more recent study (Handley-More, Deitz, Billingsley, & Coggins, 2003) with similar students (ages 10–11, with LD and severe spelling problems), found similar effects; two of three students made substantial improvements in legibility and spelling. Thus the available research supports the use of word prediction software with students with severe spelling problems.

The research also revealed that design issues, such as the size of the dictionary, its match to the writing task, and subtleties in the design of the interface, make a difference in the impact. If the dictionary is too small, it will not help students with the most difficult words they use; if it is too large, there will be too many distracting words in the lists of suggestions. Programs offer two different kinds of solutions to the problem of dictionary size. One solution is a choice of general dictionaries of different sizes. Another solution is to provide or to give the teacher the option of adding topical dictionaries for particular writing assignments. Important issues in the interface design include how many words to display in the list of suggestions and whether the list includes close phonetic matches for students with spelling problems. In the best programs, both of these features can be adjusted by the user.

The research has addressed the use of word prediction only with students with severe spelling problems who might have difficulty using a standard spelling checker. However, it is possible that other students with writing problems might benefit, including students who are reluctant to ignore spelling errors on a first draft or students who find it difficult to learn to type. The use of topical dictionaries might also support vocabulary development if used creatively, a possibility that might be explored in future research.

Speech Recognition

Dictation has a long history as a means of composing for busy professionals and some authors. Winston Churchill, one of the more prolific writers of the first half of the 20th century, composed nearly all his work by dictating to secretaries (Manchester, 1988). Speech recognition software makes it possible to dictate directly to the computer without the assistance of another person. Early systems required the user to dictate a word at a time, called "discrete speech recognition." Current systems permit continuous dictation, although the user must dictate punctuation, and they require only a few minutes of training the system to adjust to an individual's voice.

Potentially, speech recognition offers a solution for students who struggle with handwriting and spelling. For students with learning disabilities and other poor writers, dictated compositions are both substantially longer and qualitatively superior to compositions written via handwriting or word processing (Graham, 1990; MacArthur & Graham, 1987; Reece & Cummings, 1996). In comparison with dictating to a tape recorder for later transcription, speech recognition has the additional advantage that the user can see and reread the emerging text. In a series of studies comparing handwriting, dictation to a tape recorder, and dictation to a typist working on a word processor so that the author could see the screen, Reece and Cummings (1996) demonstrated that seeing the screen improved the writing of average students. They also found that dictation in both forms improved the writing of struggling writers.

However, current speech recognition systems, despite dramatic improvements in the past decade, still have serious limitations. First, accuracy of speech recognition is limited. Although the systems never misspell words, they do not always recognize dictated words correctly. Reviews of software generally report accuracy for adults of 95% or better (e.g., Metz, 2006). A study with 10th-grade students (MacArthur & Cavalier, 2004) reported average accuracy of 87% after 2 hours of training and practice. Second, users must articulate carefully, must dictate punctuation and formatting, and must avoid extraneous vocalizations. Third, users must learn to recognize and correct new types of mistakes. Instead of the familiar spelling mistakes, users must find incorrect words. The popular speech recognition programs will support editing by reading back the user's actual dictation while highlighting the words.

Three studies of speech recognition with students with LD have been reported. Higgins and Raskind (1995) studied the effects of discrete speech recognition with college students with LD. Following 6 hours of training, students composed essays under three conditions: speech recognition, dictation to a scribe, and unassisted (i.e., handwriting or word processing without a spell checker). Quality ratings were significantly higher in the speech recognition than the unassisted condition. Quinlan (2004) worked with middle school students with and without problems in writing fluency. After 3 hours of training, students wrote four 10-minute papers, using handwriting and speech recognition with and without planning. Students with writing problems, but not the average writers, wrote longer papers and made fewer errors using speech recognition. However, speech recognition did not improve writing quality.

MacArthur and Cavalier (2004) investigated the use of speech recognition and dictation to a scribe as test accommodations. Many states permit the use of dictation to a scribe as a test accommodation under certain conditions, though, to my knowledge, none specifically mention speech recognition software. Tenth-grade students with and without LD received 6 hours of training and practice in the use of speech recognition and in the use of a simple planning procedure for writing persuasive essays. All students then wrote essays in three conditions: speech recognition, dictation to a scribe who typed on a visible screen, and handwriting. All 31 students (except 1 who dropped out of the study) were able to use speech recognition to compose and edit essays with acceptable accuracy. Students with LD made fewer errors using speech recognition than handwriting. Most important, students with LD produced higher quality essays using speech recognition than using handwriting and even better essays when dictating to a person. No statistically significant differences among conditions were found for students without LD. The results were interpreted to support the use of dictation as a test accommodation. It improved the performance of students with LD by removing transcription barriers to their composing.

Despite its potential, speech recognition raises many practical issues. It is difficult to use speech recognition in a school environment because the software requires a reasonably quiet environment for accurate recognition. Also, it makes composing a more public effort, which may be embarrassing, especially for struggling writers. It is probably most suitable for use in resource rooms or at home. In addition, students must make a commitment to learning to use the software effectively. No research results have been reported on students who have used the software long term. College students with LD, who are required to produce substantial amounts of written work, may benefit most from its use.

SUPPORT FOR PLANNING AND REVISING

Proficient writers devote considerable time to planning and revising. They set goals and subgoals based on audience and content, search their memories for relevant content or gather ideas from reading, and use knowledge of different genres of writing to organize their content (Hayes, 1996). Throughout the writing process, they evaluate and revise their writing, looking for problems and opportunities to improve their writing. In contrast, students with LD engage in relatively little planning (Troia, 2006). They often have problems generating sufficient content, and they have limited knowledge of common text structures that could help them in organizing their writing. Their revising is limited primarily to correction of errors and minor changes in wording that do not affect meaning (MacArthur et al., 1991). Often, they introduce new errors in the process of recopying a paper to fix previous errors.

From the early days of word processing, researchers and developers have attempted to design computer tools to support planning and revising processes. This section considers three types of tools: programs that prompt students in planning and revising processes, tools for outlining and concept mapping, and programs that automatically evaluate essays and provide feedback.

Prompting Programs

Prompting programs are designed to support writers by asking them a series of questions or presenting reminders to engage in various processes. The Writing Partner (Zellermayer, Salomon, Globerson, & Givon, 1991) was a good example. It provided metacognitive support for planning, drafting, and revising based on cognitive models of writing. The prompts were interactive in that later questions were based on students' answers to earlier questions. The planning tools asked students to answer questions about rhetorical purpose (e.g., "Are you trying to persuade or describe?"), topic, audience (e.g., "Is your audience experts or beginners on this topic?"), main ideas, and key words. While students worked on their drafts, prompting questions appeared in random order, asking students to consider purpose, organization, and elaboration. The revising questions included generic revising concerns but also drew on planning (e.g., asking about evidence if the purpose was persuasive). A research study with high school students produced mixed results. Students were randomly assigned to one of three groups: Writing Partner with solicited guidance (SG) or with unsolicited guidance (USG) or regular word processing control (C). The only difference between the two experimental groups was that the USG group saw the drafting prompts at random intervals without asking for them, whereas the SG group was directed to check the prompts by typing a special key. Planning and revising support were identical. Pretest and posttest essays were written by hand without support in order to test the theory that the metacognitive support would be internalized. Students in the USG group earned substantially higher quality ratings both on essays written with support and on handwritten posttest essays than the other two groups, which did not differ from each other. The reason for the difference between the SG and USG groups is not clear. Unfortunately, no further research was conducted with this tool to replicate or extend the findings.

Other research on prompting programs has been mixed as well. Reynolds and Bonk (1996; Bonk & Reynolds, 1992) found increases in revision and writing quality on an essay written with support for college students but no effects on revision or quality for essays written with support or on a transfer essay for middle school students. Englert, Wu, and Zhao (2005) conducted a study with students with LD using an Internet-delivered prompting program. The online system prompted students to generate a title, topic sentences, details, and a conclusion for a personal narrative. Students wrote papers with and without the prompting support. Personal narratives written with support were better organized and contained more relevant content. The study did not test whether students learned to write better papers once the support was withdrawn.

The rationale for prompting programs is reasonable. Research without computers has shown that text-structure planning prompts and prompts to set goals during planning can enhance the writing of students with LD (Ferretti & MacArthur, 2001; Montague, Graves, & Leavell, 1991). Additionally, brief goal-setting prompts to add content or consider audience can improve the revising of students with and without LD (Graham, MacArthur, & Schwartz, 1995; Midgette, Haria, & MacArthur, 2008). Future research should focus on the design of prompting software and on methods that integrate it with instruction.

Outlining and Concept Mapping

Outlining and concept mapping are widely used in writing instruction as planning tools. Concept maps are visual representations of relationships among different ideas using nodes and links. A recent meta-analysis of 55 studies (Nesbit & Adesope, 2006) found the use of concept maps to be associated with increased knowledge of content in the areas of science, psychology, statistics, and nursing. Graphic organizers, closely related to concept maps, are an important component of some planning strategies that have been shown to be effective (Graham, 2006). Common word processors include outlining capabilities, and one concept-mapping program, Inspiration, has become very common in schools.

Electronic concept maps and outlines have some advantages over paper-and-pencil versions. First, the electronic versions are easily revised and expanded; new ideas can be inserted and the sequence of information can be easily altered. Electronic concept maps can be expanded beyond the reasonable limits of paper ones. In addition, electronic outlines and maps can be displayed with details hidden to view the organization of higher level topics. Second, electronic maps can be automatically converted into outlines, and vice versa. One of the challenges of using concept maps in writing is developing a linear written product from a map with multiple nodes and links. Conversion of the map to an outline provides a linear organization; the sequence of that organization can then be altered as needed. Third, the contents of the electronic map or outline can be directly transferred to a rough draft in a word processor.

One way that educators use concept-mapping software is to provide students with template maps that represent the text structure of a particular genre. For example, a template for persuasive writing might include linked nodes for thesis, reasons, evidence, and conclusion. Students can insert content into the existing nodes and add and reorder nodes as needed. When the map is completed, they can automatically convert it into an outline. In mapping or outlining mode, they can draft the details of their writing before transferring the content to a word processor as a rough draft. In fact, Inspiration software comes with a variety of templates for various types of texts and content areas.

Unfortunately, despite the popularity of concept-mapping software, little research has investigated its effectiveness. Anderson-Inman and her colleagues (e.g., Anderson-Inman & Horney, 1998) have conducted a number of descriptive and qualitative studies of concept mapping as a tool to support reading and studying. Sturm and Rankin-Erickson (2002) investigated the effects of paper-and-pencil and electronic concept mapping on the writing of middle school students with LD. After receiving instruction in both mapping by hand and mapping on the computer, students wrote essays with no mapping, hand mapping, and computer mapping. No significant differences in the length or quality of essays were found among the three conditions, although both length and quality increased from pretest to posttest.

In summary, although there is little research on electronic concept mapping, the research on using noncomputer concept maps and graphic organizers as part of reading and writing instruction is generally positive. Clearly, more research is needed to explore the effectiveness of concept-mapping software and to develop effective instructional routines for using it. A variety of important instructional issues need to be addressed. One issue is how to design templates for concept maps. Another is how to make use of the capability to automatically generate outlines or rough drafts from concept maps. Overall, an important issue is how much and what type of instruction is needed to help students with LD make effective use of concept mapping.

Automated Essay Evaluation

A recent approach to supporting revising is the use of automated essay scoring (AES) systems to provide feedback to students on their writing. Several AES systems have demonstrated good interrater reliability with human raters (for a review, see Shermis, Burstein, & Leacock, 2006). Reading student papers and providing helpful feedback is a time-consuming task for teachers, which limits the amount of feedback students receive. AES systems can provide feedback within minutes, permitting students to revise and get feedback multiple times on a single paper. Systems that use AES in this way are now available to schools.

One such system, Summary Street (Wade-Stein & Kintsch, 2004), is based on latent semantic analysis, which evaluates the semantic content of writing and how well it matches criterion texts. The program evaluates students' summaries and provides feedback on how well the summaries represent the content in each section of a text, whether they meet length requirements, and which sentences might be redundant or irrelevant. Three studies with sixth- and eighth-grade students have investigated its effects on summary writing (Franzke, Kintsch, Caccamise, Johnson, & Dooley, 2005; Steinhart, 2001; Wade-Stein & Kintsch, 2004). Summary Street was compared with writing on a word processor that gave feedback only on length and spelling. In all three studies, students' summaries were judged higher in quality and content coverage. Franzke and colleagues (2005) found that the gains transferred to better performance on items from a statewide reading comprehension test that required writing summaries but not to other types of comprehension items. More research is needed that focuses on transfer of learning to improved summary writing without the tool and improved reading comprehension. No research has examined the use of such systems with students with LD or other struggling writers. Nonetheless, this is a promising area of research, because studies have shown that teaching summarization strategies improves students' reading comprehension and writing (Graham & Perin, 2007). In general, more research is needed on the use of AES systems to provide feedback on student writing.

NEW ENVIRONMENTS AND FORMS OF WRITING

So far, I have discussed tools and instruction focused on supporting the production of traditional written products. However, technology has a broader impact on literacy in the development of new environments for writing and new forms of written communication, which afford new opportunities for reading and writing but also new challenges for students with LD. Some scholars argue that technology will transform the nature of literacy (for a discussion, see the volume edited by Reinking, McKenna, Labbo, & Kieffer, 1998). Several key differences between traditional written text and new electronic forms of text are often cited (MacArthur, 2006). First, because hypertext or hypermedia is nonlinear, readers choose what they will read, and writers must anticipate the needs of different readers and their navigation of the text. Second, electronic texts integrate multiple media, including visual images and sound, which may transform the ways that knowledge is represented. Third, the Internet provides access to an immense amount of information, which requires the development of skills in comprehending hypermedia, searching for information, and critical evaluation (Coiro & Dobler, 2007). Thus the process of gathering information for writing is dramatically changed. Finally, the Internet opens up new possibilities for reaching audiences beyond the classroom and interacting with them, including e-mail, blogs, zines, Internet chats, personal web pages, and classroom Internet projects.

Despite widespread access to the Internet and theories about its effects on literacy activities, there is limited research on the impact of the Internet and related technologies on literacy, especially on writing and writing processes. Even less research has focused on students with LD. In this section, I briefly discuss research on two aspects of new forms of writing that have received some attention: composing hypermedia and the use of the Internet for written communication.

Composing Hypermedia

A substantial body of research has investigated the design of hypermedia, or multimedia, to enhance content learning (for a review, see Dillon & Gabbard, 1998). Far less work has focused on the effects of learning to compose hypermedia. Creating hypermedia and traditional text are similar in that both are composing processes with communicative purposes that require considering audience, setting goals, organizing content, presenting content clearly, and revising. They differ in two major ways: hypermedia uses links among content, in contrast to the linear nature of traditional text, and hypermedia uses multiple media to represent content. Both of these differences have an impact on the composing process. In fact, style guidelines for developers of hypermedia documents address many of the complexities of designing hypermedia. In addition, because of the complexities of creating it, hypermedia projects in classroom settings generally involve collaborative work among students, which brings additional support from peers but also further complexities related to collaboration.

Research on composing hypermedia in schools consists mostly of qualitative case studies. Erickson and Lehrer (1998, 2000) studied collaborative inquiry projects based on composing hypermedia in middle school social studies classes. They documented the development of cognitive design skills, including research skills, planning and management, audience consideration, organization, presentation, and evaluation. They showed how over time students moved from paying attention to superficial aspects of display and content links to a more rhetorical focus on designing links to communicate effectively with readers. They also reported positive effects on student engagement and collaboration. Baker (2001) reported an ethnographic case study of a fourth-grade class in an intensive technology environment. Students worked on collaborative multimedia projects in science and social studies. The composing process was highly recursive, with students brainstorming, searching for information, composing, and revising repeatedly. The process was supported by the visible nature of hypermedia projects, which supported high levels of peer interaction. However, the teacher expressed some concern that students were too focused on presentation to the detriment of content.

Ferretti and Okolo (1996) argued that multimedia design projects are especially appropriate for students with LD because they offer multiple ways for students to learn and demonstrate their knowledge rather than relying entirely on reading and writing. They designed and studied multimedia inquiry projects in upper elementary inclusive classrooms that were team-taught by special and general education teachers. In two studies, they found that students' knowledge of historical events increased and that students with LD learned as much as their nondisabled peers. Students' attitudes toward social studies and toward collaboration increased in one of the studies. They also reported numerous challenges in implementing multimedia design projects. Collaborative inquiry projects were time-consuming, and the need to provide training in technology and the generally poor typing skills of the students extended the time further. More substantively, detailed analysis of group interaction patterns revealed that some groups worked well together whereas in other groups the higher achieving students took over the project and essentially excluded the students with LD. Teachers need to provide instruction in the design skills for conducting research and in the social skills for effective collaboration.

Internet Communication

The Internet provides multiple opportunities for sharing student writing with audiences beyond the school walls and for collaborative writing with classes from other schools. Much of what we know about the effects of using the Internet for writing in school comes from qualitative studies of innovative teachers (Karchmer, 2001). One growing use of the Internet is for intercultural communication projects, in which classes from different parts of the country or the world collaborate on curriculum projects that involve shared inquiry and writing. In addition to developing cultural awareness and increasing targeted content knowledge, such projects may improve students' writing skills by enhancing motivation and by requiring them to write clearly to communicate with students who have different backgrounds and experiences. Garner and Gillingham (1996) conducted case studies of six teachers who used the Internet for intercultural communication projects. They found that teachers changed their teaching methods to devote more effort to inquiry projects that drew on student interests and authentic problems. They also found that the projects stimulated motivation to write and encouraged children to attempt to understand cultural differences and consider audience needs.

Karchmer (2001) studied 13 teachers in grades K–12 who made extensive use of the Internet. The elementary teachers made a practice of publishing their students' writing on class web pages, in collaborative projects with other schools, or at online writing sites. They reported that students were highly motivated by having a wider audience. The secondary teachers used the Internet more for access to information than for publication of student work.

None of the research has focused on students with LD. However, one early descriptive study used local area networks to support writing development of students who were deaf or hearing impaired (Batson, 1993). Students engaged in written discussion online using what we would now call Internet chat software. After some period spent discussing a topic, students wrote papers on the topic, with access to the script of the full written conversation. The purpose was to provide informal practice in English for students who communicated primarily via signing.

Although none of the research has focused on students with LD, the applications seem promising for struggling writers. Writing for real-world audiences on the Internet, particularly audiences who respond to one's writing, might motivate students to write more extensively and revise more carefully. Interactive writing using chat software as a prewriting technique might provide useful practice in writing and also help students to generate ideas to use in their writing.

CONCLUDING COMMENTS

In concluding, I stress a few points of importance to both practitioners and researchers. First, the one area in which there is enough research to support general recommendations is word processing. Using word processing in combination with writing instruction has a moderate positive impact on the quality of students' writing, especially for struggling writers. Schools should try to provide sufficient access to technology for students to use word processing throughout the writing process, from drafting to publication. Word processing should be available as a test accommodation for students with disabilities. In addition, other students who do most of their writing with word processors should also have access to them during testing because the research indicates that these students are disadvantaged by having to use handwriting.

Second, in areas other than word processing, the research demonstrates that technology can have a positive impact on writing under some circumstances. In the area of assistive technology for transcription problems, word prediction software may help students with severe spelling problems, and speech recognition software can help high school students with LD produce higher quality papers. But the research does not tell us which students are most likely to benefit or whether these tools would have the same impact in typical school settings. The research on software to support planning and revising shows promise, but the findings are either mixed or limited, and little research has focused on struggling writers. The new possibilities for using automated essay scoring to provide repeated feedback to students is promising, but research is just beginning. Research on new environments and forms of writing is likewise limited. Considerable research has investigated the impact of hypermedia, or multimedia, on reading, but less has addressed the problems and potentials of composing hypermedia. Research on using the Internet in literacy instruction has included both reading and writing activities, but most of the work to date consists of case studies of innovative teachers. Of course, we need more research. For practitioners, the message is to try applications with individual students or in particular class settings while carefully assessing whether they work.

Third, technology applications by themselves are not necessarily effective. The effects depend on how the technology is used in a particular context; this is true both for instructional and noninstructional real-world applications. In instruction, the effects depend on how technology is combined with teaching methods designed to take advantage of the tool's power. The extensive research on word processing has studied the use of technology in combination with instruction. Despite expectations that word processing would dramatically affect revising, researchers found that it had little impact on the quality of revising by struggling writers until it was combined with instruction in strategies for evaluation and revision. As researchers, staff developers, and teachers, we need to keep this point in mind. For example, researchers should investigate not only the effects of concept mapping but also the effects of using it with a planning strategy. Staff developers would be better advised to help teachers learn to participate in a particular intercultural communication project than to provide general training on using the Internet. The developers of MySpace made a fortune because they had a great idea about how to use technology to support a particular social need. Educators need to have great ideas about how to use technology in instruction. In many cases, practitioners are leading the way in technology applications. Researchers and teachers need to work together to advance our understanding in this always changing field.

REFERENCES

Anderson-Inman, L., & Horney, M. A. (1998). Transforming text for at-risk readers. In D. Reinking, M. C. McKenna, L. D. Labbo, & R. D. Kieffer (Eds.), *Handbook of literacy and technology* (pp. 15–44). Mahwah, NJ: Erlbaum.

Baker, E. A. (2001). The nature of literacy in a technology-rich, fourth-grade classroom. *Reading Research and Instruction, 40,* 159–184.

Bangert-Drowns, R. L. (1993). The word processor as an instructional tool: A meta-analysis of word processing in writing instruction. *Review of Educational Research, 63*(1), 69–93.

Batson, T. (1993). The origins of ENFI. In B. C. Bruce, J. K. Peyton, & T. Batson (Eds.), *Network-based classrooms: Promises and realities* (pp. 87–112). New York: Cambridge University Press.

Bonk, C. J., & Reynolds, T. H. (1992). Early adolescent composing within a generative–evaluative computerized prompting framework. *Computers in Human Behavior, 8,* 39–62.

Borgh, K., & Dickson, W. P. (1992). The effects on children's writing of adding speech synthesis to a word processor. *Journal of Research on Computing in Education, 24*(4), 533–544.

Coiro, J., & Dobler, E. (2007). Exploring the online reading comprehension strategies used by sixth-grade skilled readers to search for and locate information on the Internet. *Reading Research Quarterly, 42,* 214–257.

Dillon, A., & Gabbard, R. (1998). Hypermedia as an educational technology. *Review of Educational Research, 68,* 322–349.

Englert, C. S., Raphael, T. E., Anderson, L. M., Gregg, S. L., & Anthony, H. M. (1989). Exposition: Reading, writing, and the metacognitive knowledge of learning disabled students. *Learning Disabilities Research and Practice, 5,* 5–24.

Englert, C. S., Wu, X., & Zhao, Y. (2005). Cognitive tools for writing: Scaffolding the performance of students through technology. *Learning Disabilities Research and Practice, 20,* 184–198.

Erickson, J., & Lehrer, R. (1998). The evolution of critical standards as students design hypermedia documents. *Journal of the Learning Sciences, 7,* 351–386.

Erickson, J., & Lehrer, R. (2000). What's in a link? Student conceptions of the rhetoric of association in hypermedia composition. In S. P. Lajoie (Ed.), *Computers as cognitive tools: No more walls* (Vol. 2, pp. 197–226). Mahwah, NJ: Erlbaum.

Ferretti, R. P., & MacArthur, C. A. (2001). The effects of elaborated goals on the argumentative writing of students with learning disabilities and their normally achieving peers. *Journal of Educational Psychology, 92,* 694–702.

Ferretti, R. P., & Okolo, C. M. (1996). Authenticity in learning: Multimedia design projects in the social studies for students with disabilities. *Journal of Learning Disabilities, 29,* 450–460.

Franzke, M., Kintsch, E., Caccamise, D., Johnson, M., & Dooley, S. (2005). Summary Street: Computer support for comprehension and writing. *Journal of Educational Computing Research, 33,* 53–80.

Garner, R., & Gillingham, M. G. (1996). *Internet communication in six classrooms: Conversations across time, space, and culture.* Mahwah, NJ: Erlbaum.

Goldberg, A., Russell, M., & Cook, A. (2003). The effect of computers on student writing: A meta-analysis of studies from 1992 to 2002. *Journal of Technology, Learning, and Assessment, 2*(1), 1–51.

Graham, S. (1990). The role of production factors in learning disabled students' compositions. *Journal of Educational Psychology, 82,* 781–791.

Graham, S. (2006). Strategy instruction and the teaching of writing: A meta-analysis. In C. A. MacArthur, S. Graham, & J. Fitzgerald (Eds.), *Handbook of writing research* (pp. 187–207). New York: Guilford Press.

Graham, S., Berninger, V. W., Abbott, R. D., Abbott, S. P., & Whitaker, D. (1997). Role of mechanics in composing of elementary school students: A new methodological approach. *Journal of Educational Psychology, 89,* 170–182.

Graham, S., Harris, K. R., MacArthur, C. A., & Schwartz, S. S. (1991). Writing and writing instruction with students with learning disabilities: A review of a program of research. *Learning Disability Quarterly, 14,* 89–114.

Graham, S., & MacArthur, C. A. (1988). Improving learning disabled students' skills at revising essays produced on a word processor: Self-instructional strategy training. *Journal of Special Education, 22,* 133–152.

Graham, S., MacArthur, C. A., & Schwartz, S. S. (1995). Effects of goal setting and procedural facilitation on the revising behavior and writing performance of students with writing and learning problems. *Journal of Educational Psychology, 87,* 230–240.

Graham, S., & Perin, D. (2007). *Writing next: Effective strategies to improve writing of adolescents in middle and high schools.* Washington, DC: Alliance for Excellent Education.

Handley-More, D., Deitz, J., Billingsley, F. F., & Coggins, T. E. (2003). Facilitating written work using computer word processing and word prediction. *American Journal of Occupational Therapy, 57,* 139–151.

Hayes, J. R. (1996). A new framework for understanding cognition and affect in writing. In C. M. Levy & S. Ransdell (Eds.), *The science of writing* (pp. 1–27). Mahwah, NJ: Erlbaum.

Higgins, E. L., & Raskind, M. H. (1995). Compensatory effectiveness of speech recognition on the written composition performance of postsecondary students with learning disabilities. *Learning Disability Quarterly, 18*, 159–174.

Karchmer, R. (2001). The journey ahead: Thirteen teachers report how the Internet influences literacy and literacy instruction in their K–12 classrooms. *Reading Research Quarterly, 36*, 442–466.

MacArthur, C. A. (1998). Word processing with speech synthesis and word prediction: Effects on the dialogue journal writing of students with learning disabilities. *Learning Disability Quarterly, 21*, 1–16.

MacArthur, C. A. (1999). Word prediction for students with severe spelling problems. *Learning Disability Quarterly, 22*, 158–172.

MacArthur, C. A. (2006). The effects of new technologies on writing and writing processes. In C. A. MacArthur, S. Graham, & J. Fitzgerald (Eds.), *Handbook of writing research* (pp. 248–262). New York: Guilford Press.

MacArthur, C. A., & Cavalier, A. (2004). Dictation and speech recognition technology as accommodations in large-scale assessments for students with learning disabilities. *Exceptional Children, 71*, 43–58.

MacArthur, C. A., Ferretti, R. P., Okolo, C. M., & Cavalier, A. R. (2001). Technology applications for students with literacy problems: A critical review. *Elementary School Journal, 101*, 273–301.

MacArthur, C. A., & Graham, S. (1987). Learning disabled students' composing under three methods of text production: Handwriting, word processing, and dictation. *Journal of Special Education, 21*, 22–42.

MacArthur, C. A., Graham, S., Haynes, J. B., & De La Paz, S. (1996). Spelling checkers and students with learning disabilities: Performance comparisons and impact on spelling. *Journal of Special Education, 30*, 35–57.

MacArthur, C. A., Graham, S., & Schwartz, S. S. (1991). Knowledge of revision and revising behavior among learning disabled students. *Learning Disability Quarterly, 14*, 61–73.

MacArthur, C. A., Graham, S., Schwartz, S. S., & Shafer, W. (1995). Evaluation of a writing instruction model that integrated a process approach, strategy instruction, and word processing. *Learning Disability Quarterly, 18*, 278–291.

MacArthur, C. A., Schwartz, S. S., & Graham, S. (1991). Effects of a reciprocal peer revision strategy in special education classrooms. *Learning Disabilities Research and Practice, 6*, 201–210.

Manchester, W. (1988). *The last lion: Winston Spencer Churchill, alone 1932–1940*. New York: Little, Brown.

McNaughton, D., Hughes, C., & Clark, K. (1997). The effect of five proofreading conditions on the spelling performance of college students with learning disabilities. *Journal of Learning Disabilities, 30*, 643–651.

Metz, C. (2006). Dragon Naturally Speaking, 9.0 Professional. *PC Magazine Online*. Retrieved February 7, 2007, from *www.pcmag.com/article2/0,1895,1996759,00.asp*.

Midgette, E., Haria, P., & MacArthur, C. A. (2008). The effects of content and audience awareness goals for revision on the persuasive essays of fifth- and eighth-grade students. *Reading and Writing, 21*, 131–151.

Montague, M., Graves, A., & Leavell, A. (1991). Planning, procedural facilitation, and narrative composition of junior high students with learning disabilities. *Learning Disabilities Research and Practice, 6*, 219–224.

Nesbit, J. C., & Adesope, O. O. (2006). Learning with concept and knowledge maps: A meta-analysis. *Review of Educational Research, 76*, 413–448.

Newell, A. F., Booth, L., Arnott, J., & Beattie, W. (1992). Increasing literacy levels by the use of linguistic prediction. *Child Language Teaching and Therapy, 8*, 138–187.

Quinlan, T. (2004). Speech recognition technology and students with writing difficulties: Improving fluency. *Journal of Educational Psychology, 96*, 337–346.

Raskind, M. H., & Higgins, E. (1995). Effects of speech synthesis on the proofreading efficiency of postsecondary students with learning disabilities. *Learning Disability Quarterly, 18*, 141–158.

Reece, J. E., & Cummings, G. (1996). Evaluating speech-based composition methods: Planning, dictation, and the listening word processor. In C. M. Levy & S. Ransdell (Eds.), *The science of writing* (pp. 361–380). Mahwah, NJ: Erlbaum.

Reinking, D., McKenna, M. C., Labbo, L. D., & Kieffer, R. D. (Eds.). (1998). *Handbook of literacy and technology.* Mahwah, NJ: Erlbaum.

Reynolds, T. H., & Bonk, C. J. (1996). Facilitating college writers' revisions within a generative–evaluative computerized prompting framework. *Computers and Composition, 13*(1), 93–108.

Russell, M. (1999). Testing writing on computers: A follow-up study comparing performance on computer and on paper. *Educational Policy Analysis Archives, 7*(20). Retrieved June 4, 2008, from *epaa.asu.edu/epaa/v7n20/*.

Shermis, M., Burstein, J., & Leacock, C. (2006). Applications of computers in assessment and analysis of writing. In C. A. MacArthur, S. Graham, & J. Fitzgerald (Eds.), *Handbook of writing research* (pp. 403–416). New York: Guilford Press.

Steinhart, D. (2001). *Summary Street: An intelligent tutoring system for improving student writing through the use of latent semantic analysis.* Unpublished doctoral dissertation, Institute of Cognitive Science, University of Colorado, Boulder.

Stoddard, B., & MacArthur, C. A. (1993). A peer editor strategy: Guiding learning disabled students in response and revision. *Research in the Teaching of English, 27*, 76–103.

Sturm, J. M., & Rankin-Erickson, J. L. (2002). Effects of hand-drawn and computer-generated concept mapping on the expository writing of students with learning disabilities. *Learning Disabilities Research and Practice, 17*, 124–139.

Troia, G. A. (2006). Writing instruction for students with learning disabilities. In C. A. MacArthur, S. Graham, & J. Fitzgerald (Eds.), *Handbook of writing research* (pp. 324–336). New York: Guilford Press.

Wade-Stein, D., & Kintsch, E. (2004). Summary Street: Interactive computer support for writing. *Cognition and Instruction, 22*, 333–362.

Zellermayer, M., Salomon, G., Globerson, T., & Givon, H. (1991). Enhancing writing-related metacognitions through a computerized writing partner. *American Educational Research Journal, 28*, 373–391.

Part IV
TEACHING SPELLING TO STRUGGLING WRITERS

CHAPTER 10

Teaching Spelling to Students with Language and Learning Disabilities

LOUISA C. MOATS

THE NATURE OF POOR SPELLING

Spelling Problems Are Common

Poor spelling is a feature of most language-based learning disabilities (LD), such as dyslexia, and sometimes exists in people who read reasonably well. Poor spelling, therefore, is one of the most ubiquitous of all learning difficulties. Contrary to the common belief that spelling is a simple and basic academic ability, learning to spell depends on the integrity of multiple underlying skills (Aaron, Wilczynski, & Keetay, 1998; Ehri, 1989; Treiman & Bourassa, 2000). Poor spelling can originate with weaknesses in any of several aspects of language processing, attention, self-regulation, and graphomotor coordination.

The consequences of spelling disability, in addition to frustration and embarrassment, include poor note taking and impoverished and ineffective written expression. Students who spell poorly write fewer words, divert their attention from the content and cohesion of their compositions, and restrict their word choice (Moats, Foorman, & Taylor, 2006; Re, Pedron, & Cornoldi, 2007). The written compositions of poor spellers, moreover, may be judged more harshly than those of students who can present neat, correctly spelled work. Poor spelling, therefore, has more significant social and academic consequences than might be apparent from the small amount of attention usually given this subject in research, testing, and instruction.

Dyslexia, meaning "difficulty with language," is currently defined as follows by the International Dyslexia Association (Lyon, Shaywitz, & Shaywitz, 2003, p. 1):

> Dyslexia is one of several distinct learning disabilities. It is a specific language-based disorder of constitutional origin characterized by difficulties in single-word decoding, usually reflecting insufficient phonological processing. These difficulties in single-word decoding are often unexpected in relation to age and other cognitive and academic abilities: they are not the result of generalized developmental disability or sensory impairment. Dyslexia is manifest by variable difficulty with different forms of language, often including, in addition to problems with reading, a conspicuous problem with acquiring proficiency in writing and spelling.

This current definition explicitly states that spelling difficulty is a symptom of dyslexia or specific reading disability. Dyslexia, in its milder forms, may be manifested primarily as a spelling, writing, or reading fluency problem (Joshi & Aaron, 2005; Lefly & Pennington, 1991), and dyslexia in all its forms may affect as many as 20% of all students (Shaywitz, 2004). Current classification research on learning disorders (Fletcher, Lyon, Fuchs, & Barnes, 2007; Morris et al., 1998) subsumes spelling disability within other subtypes of reading and language disabilities, indicating that it is commonly associated with most forms of LD. Spelling and writing problems also characterize many students with attention-deficit/ hyperactivity disorder (ADHD; Re et al., 2007). Moreover, ADHD and LD overlap in about 30% of the population (Olson, 2006). Students with ADHD may be inattentive to the letter sequences they are generating, may have trouble with letter formation and control of written output, and may have particular difficulty with proofreading and self-correction. Strategies for improving the self-monitoring aspects of spelling and writing will be critical in teaching this population.

Good spelling requires knowledge of language structures at many levels, including phonological awareness, awareness of morphemes (e.g., *un-*, *desir*[e], *-able*) and their combinations, awareness of the syntactic role that a word is assigned (e.g., *attacked* is a past-tense verb because of *-ed* at the end), and awareness of orthographic patterns (e.g., *ight* as in *light* and *frightened*). These aspects of spelling are addressed in detail later in this chapter, but the main point is that spelling requires much more than rote visual memory. Evidence for spelling being dependent on language proficiency comes from studies in which spelling and reading comprehension share common variance (Ehri, 2000; Mehta, Foorman, Branum-Martin, & Taylor, 2005) and studies showing that spelling problems are associated with specific linguistic deficiencies (Kamhi & Hinton, 2000; Lennox & Siegel, 1998; Moats, 1995). The more limited a child's overall language abilities are, the more limited spelling achievement will tend to be. Instruction, moreover, will need to address many aspects of language that contribute to accurate spelling.

Graphomotor coordination is necessary for letter formation and fluent production of letter sequences. Habits for correctly spelling words are developed by hand, as well as by ear and eye (Berninger & Graham, 1998). *Dysgraphic* is the term sometimes used for students whose problems with letter formation and legible, fluent handwriting are prominent. Rarely, students are dysgraphic without being dyslexic, but more commonly, the graphomotor skills involved in writing are strongly interconnected with other aspects of language processing (Berninger et al., 2006). Teachers of students with spelling problems should ensure that the students can form letters and write them with sufficient fluency and automaticity.

Spelling is related to reading but is more difficult. The development of spelling is intimately connected with the development of reading (Ehri, 2000). We generally cannot accurately spell words that we have not read; on the other hand, we read many more words than we typically spell, and poor spellers need dozens of opportunities to write problematic words before they can remember them. Good spellers are almost always good readers; in fact, in the mid-1800s, books for reading instruction were called spellers. Several studies have reported that teaching phoneme awareness and phonetic spelling generalizes to better reading in young children (Blachman, Tangel, Ball, Black, & McGraw, 1999; Uhry & Shepherd, 1993). The lingering problems with spelling that "remediated" or "compensated" individuals with dyslexia demonstrate suggest that spelling is more difficult to master than reading.

Spelling is more difficult than word recognition because we must encode or generate from memory all the letters that correspond to the spoken word. To read, however, we can name a word without consciously or accurately processing the exact details of the letter sequence. Most people, for example, can read the word *accommodate*; many leave out the double "m," however, while spelling it. Spelling makes unique demands on orthographic memory; therefore, it is unreasonable to expect that students will be able to spell simply by looking at words in texts. Spelling instruction must aim to enhance students' memories for all the letters in words they study by using strategies to enhance understanding of the words' structures and by increasing attention to the internal details of the orthography.

Phonological, orthographic, and morphological processes all mediate spelling. Phonological awareness is a genetically influenced underlying language skill found to mediate both reading and spelling development (Olson, 2006). Students with the most severe phonological processing problems tend to have the most severe problems with spelling (Cassar, Treiman, Moats, Pollo, & Kessler, 2005; Lindamood, 1994; Moats, 1996; Olson, 2006). If students cannot detect the identity of the phonemes in words and hold their sequence in memory while spelling is being generated, they will delete sounds, misperceive and confuse sounds, and fail to recall the symbols that represent the sounds (Kamhi & Hinton, 2000). Spelling requires phonological precision, such as that involved in comparing and differentiating words such as *flush*, *flesh*, *fresh*, and *thresh*. Remediation for students with severe phonological processing difficulties must address this problem directly, and many students with phonological impairments make only small gains in relative standing on spelling achievement tests even with excellent teaching (Moats, 1996).

Phonological awareness is necessary but not sufficient for accurate spelling of a basic writing vocabulary. Students must also become familiar with the patterns and constraints of English orthography (Apel, Wolter, & Masterson, 2006) and use that knowledge to help them remember specific letters in specific words. To that end, English spelling is more regular than many of us think (Balmuth, 1992; Bryson, 1990; Hanna, Hanna, Hodges, & Rudorf, 1966; King, 2000; Henry, 2003; Moats, 2000; Sacks, 2003). Five major principles explain why English orthography is pattern based and how it represents spoken language:

- Every speech sound in a word is represented in spelling by a grapheme, and many graphemes are letter combinations rather than single letters (e.g., *snow* has three graphemes—*s*, *n*, *ow*; *eight* has two graphemes—*eigh*, *t*; *blotch* has four graphemes—*b*, *l*, *o*, *tch*.

- Many phonemes have more than one spelling, but these are often determined by the position of a sound in a word, as well as by the sounds that precede and follow the target phoneme (e.g., the long -*i* vowel is usually spelled with a single letter in open syllables such as *rival*; *igh* before /t/, as in *fight*; and *y* at the end of one-syllable words, such as *cry*.

- There are rules, or orthographic conventions, determining how certain letters can be used and what sequences of letters are permitted in written words (e.g., some letters are never doubled, and no word in English ends in a *v* or a *j*).

- Spelling in English often represents morphemes, or meaningful parts of words (e.g., *mnemonic*, *amnesty*, and *amnesia* are all derived from the Greek root *mne*, which means memory or mind).
- Most spellings can be explained according to a word's history and language of origin. Anglo-Saxon, Old French, Latin, and Greek all have contributed to most modern English spellings.

In two recent studies (Moats et al., 2006; Cassar et al., 2005), I and my colleagues obtained evidence that poor spellers in the intermediate and middle grades have trouble understanding and using orthographic knowledge at all these levels. Cassar et al. (2005) asked whether the types of errors made by children with LD between third and seventh grades could be distinguished from the types of errors made by normally developing younger children. The spelling of the older students with dyslexia was very poor but was not qualitatively distinguishable from that of younger students who were learning to spell more easily. This finding led us to conclude that students with severe dyslexia were similar to normally progressing students in the processes by which they learned to spell but that they were learning much more slowly. Certain linguistic challenges in the spelling system were too difficult for many to overcome, such as mastery of the various ways to spell vowels, the spelling of consonant clusters, and the spelling of unaccented syllables and grammatical endings that did not sound the way they were spelled.

In the writing samples of a group of fourth graders in high-poverty schools who did not qualify for special education (Moats et al., 2006), spelling errors were numerous. They included some speech sound substitutions and omissions that indicated inadequate phoneme awareness. Even more common, however, were omitted and misspelled inflectional endings (-*ed*, -*s*, -*ing*), misspellings of common but irregular words, misspelled vowels, and errors involving the addition of endings to base words. In this population, reading fluency was also below average, even though the children as a group were scoring satisfactorily on untimed reading comprehension measures. Their underlying difficulties with language affected both reading and spelling.

Spelling instruction presents an opportunity—and perhaps an obligation—to teach all children about the structure of their language, even as specific words are being chosen for emphasis and practice. The principles described in the next section are especially important for poor spellers who are dependent on systematic, direct instruction to make progress in spelling and ultimately in written composition.

HOW TO TEACH A POOR SPELLER

Several reviews of research on spelling instruction with students with LD have been carried out over the past decade (Bailet, 2004; Graham, 1999; Wanzek et al., 2006) and several older reviews exist as well (e.g., Fulk & Stormont-Spurgin, 1995; Moats, 1995). Although much less research exists on spelling instruction than on reading instruction, the body of work on spelling intervention converges on several important principles:

- Instruction should emphasize multisensory techniques, such as saying words while tracing and writing them, raising a finger for each phoneme spoken in a segmented syllable before spelling the syllable, or constructing words with letter tiles before writing the word (Graham, 1999).
- The content of instruction should emphasize the patterns in language. For example, students benefit from instruction in phoneme–grapheme correspondences and common rime units (Berninger et al., 1998), in syllable patterns and their spellings (Bhattacharya & Ehri, 2004), and in morphological units such as inflectional and derivational affixes and roots (Bryant, Nunes, & Bindman, 1997; Carlisle, 1994).
- Instruction should limit the number of nonpattern words taught at any one time and provide immediate corrective feedback on specific errors. Very poor spellers, for example, may be able to handle only three new irregular words at a time (Wanzek et al., 2006) while they are learning regular spelling patterns.
- Systematic and explicit instruction must be provided in which words learned are immediately practiced and generalized to writing. Systematic instruction teaches spelling patterns within and in relation to the entire system of orthographic representation and provides comprehensive coverage of the content domain. Explicit instruction occurs when a teacher tells the student a new concept and models its use, helps the student through several practice items, and provides guided practice sufficient to support independent application of the spelling or spelling pattern. This form of instruction is associated with meaningful gains in spelling performance (Berninger et al., 1998; Graham, 2000; Johnston & Watson, 2006).

Thus a good spelling lesson will help the student remember words for writing through two major avenues: heightened consciousness of the conventions of English spelling listed earlier and automatic recall of specific letter sequences that can be achieved through a great deal of multisensory practice. Generalization into written composition will not occur automatically but must be engineered through scaffolding and self-monitoring strategies, such as supported proofreading and editing, dictations with immediate feedback, and rewards for using reference materials to self-correct.

Following is a more detailed description of each strand in a multicomponent lesson. The content and emphasis of each strand, as well as the selection of strands in each lesson, will vary according a student's level of spelling development. For example, students who are not able to spell phonetically will need more work on phoneme segmentation than students who do spell phonetically. Students who spell phonetically but who do not remember the letters used for vowels may benefit from more practice understanding and using the multiple vowel spelling patterns that characterize English. Students who can spell longer words phonetically should benefit from greater emphasis on word structure at the morpheme level. Students who are inattentive to what they have written will need instruction focused on orthographic detail and proofreading.

Letter Formation and Handwriting Fluency

Although this chapter is about spelling, the production of written words depends on accurate and fluent letter formation (Treiman, 2006). This "old-fashioned" skill has often been shortchanged in classrooms that emphasize personal expression in writing before students have developed letter formation habits. Berninger and Graham (1998) and other researchers, however, have shown that spelling and composition improve when students have developed habits of legible letter formation and can write the alphabet accurately from memory with adequate speed. Experienced educators and clinicians (Allen, 2005; Carreker, 2005) often take time to teach students with dyslexia how to form letters, reporting that most cases of "dysgraphia" can be cured or ameliorated with direct instruction in how to write letters and daily practice for a few weeks.

Pronunciation and Speech Sound Identification

The poorest spellers are those who cannot take the sounds of words apart and put them back together again (Goswami, 1992). Segmenting speech sounds in spoken words is the first step to successful spelling—a skill that most children learn in kindergarten and first grade. Older students who are very poor spellers often need additional work on phoneme identification and segmentation before they can progress. All students should be encouraged to say words aloud when they are learning to spell a new word, because they and the teacher need to know whether they can accurately perceive and remember the phonological features (sounds, syllables, stress patterns) of the word they are writing. Raising a finger for each sound pronounced or moving a penny into a "sound box" as each phoneme is produced are helpful multisensory techniques.

Speech sounds are more easily perceived if their features have been identified explicitly (Lindamood, 1994). The identity of vowels and consonants can be demystified if simple charts of these speech sounds are used as reference points (Moats, 2000). The two major categories of speech sounds (consonants and vowels) should be distinguished, and confusable sounds should be differentiated by their articulatory features, such as voicing, nasality, or stopping. Children tend to confuse spellings of speech sounds that have overlapping features (i.e., that are similar in articulatory properties), such as /f/ and /v/ in *half* and *have*, respectively.

Vowel phonemes are open speech sounds that form the nucleus of any syllable. Awareness of vowel sounds in speech is important for spelling progress, as the majority of children's phoneme–grapheme mapping errors occur on vowels. There are three types of vowel phonemes: long (tense), short (lax), and diphthong (sliders). Instruction should highlight difficult contrasts such as front short vowels (/ĭ/, /ĕ/, /ă/) and low middle vowels /ŏ/, /aw/. These phonemes should be separated when first introduced and later contrasted explicitly.

Phoneme–Grapheme Correspondences

Graphemes are the functional spelling units that represent phonemes. In English, they may be one (*i*), two (*ie*), three (*igh*), or four (*eigh*) letters in length. At least several hundred graphemes are used fairly predictably to spell 43 or so phonemes (Kessler & Treiman, 2001). Teaching the more predictable phoneme–grapheme associations and requiring students to be both accurate and fast with these elements has a positive effect on reading and spelling (Ehri, 1998, 2004; Berninger et al., 1998). Consonant graphemes include single letters, digraphs (two letters representing one unique sound, such as *th* and *ng*); trigraphs (three letters representing one unique sound, such as *tch* and *dge*) and silent letter spellings such as *kn* (*knot*) and *ps* (*psychology*). Vowel spellings are numerous and more variable than consonant spellings. Figure 10.1 shows the most common spellings for the vowel sounds by proportion of use in English words. To assist students in learning the correspondence system between phonemes and graphemes, an activity called *phoneme–grapheme mapping* (Grace, 2006) is helpful. One box in a grid represents each phoneme in a word. The graphemes that spell each phoneme are identified and written and the structure of the word is discussed. For example, the grid of "sound

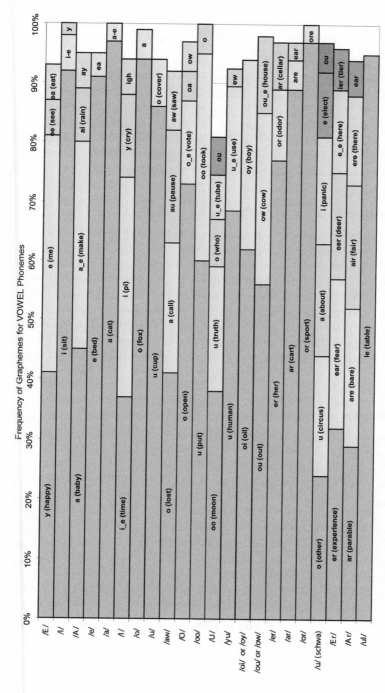

FIGURE 10.1. Frequency of graphemes used for spelling the vowel sounds of English. Based on Hanna et al. (1966) and Moats (2008).

boxes" shown here enables the teacher to demonstrate how digraphs are different from blends and how *r*-controlled vowel (vowel + *r*) combinations work.

s	t	a	ff	
ch	ir	p		
s	c	r	a	tch
s	l	ee	ve	
d	o	dge		

Conditional Spelling Correspondences

Many phoneme–grapheme correspondences are conditional. The spelling of a given phoneme depends on the speech sounds that come before or after the target phoneme–grapheme correspondence. For instance, doubled consonants often follow short vowels in closed syllables: *stuff, doll, mess, jazz*. This pattern is an orthographic convention; the extra letters do not correspond to extra sounds. Each of these example words has only one consonant phoneme at the end of the word. Word-pattern sorting, as emphasized in Bear, Invernizzi, Templeton, and Johnston (2005), is especially valuable in helping students learn about these "choice" spellings.

Other Orthographic Rules

Although much about orthography is predictable or pattern based, the correspondence system is complex. Spellings of base words often change when an ending is added, for example. A doubled consonant or its substitute must come between a stressed short vowel syllable and an inflection beginning with a vowel (e.g., *grabbing, drugged*). The complex spellings *ck, dge, tch,* and *x* replace or act as doubled consonants after short vowels in words such as *picnicking, dodger, pitching,* and *boxer* and signal that the vowel is short (of course, there are exceptions; some words with /ch/ after a short vowel, which by rule should be spelled with *tch*, do not conform to this generalization: *much, rich, which, such, bachelor*). Long vowel sounds can never be spelled with single vowel letters before these complex consonant units.

The letter *e* has several uses in orthography. Sometimes it acts as a relational unit by itself; that is, it represents phonemes directly (e.g., *bet, fetal*). Sometimes it acts as a marker within a larger orthographic pattern. The letter *e* indicates that a vowel is long, as in *drape* and *probe*. It indicates that a *c* or a *g* should have its "soft" sound, as in *stooge, receive,* and *nice*. It is also placed at the ends of words with *s* to keep them from looking like plurals rather than to mark the vowel (e.g., *please*, not *pleas*; *horse*, not *hors*).

These and other orthographic conventions are part of what a good speller knows. Good spellers extract these patterns from exposure to multiple examples or from direct teaching. Poor spellers, however, may not detect such patterns easily even when shown multiple examples. In addition, students with dyslexia might learn a rule such as *i* before *e* except after *c* but are unable to generalize that rule to their own spelling. They do not easily or rapidly recognize to which words the rule should be applied. This reality—that rules and patterns just do not "compute" in children who are very poor spellers—suggests that words prioritized for instruction should be those most often used in writing (Graham, Harris, & Loynachan, 1994), even when word lists are organized by orthographic pattern.

Irregular, High-Frequency Words

Odd and truly unpredictable spellings, such as *of*, *isle*, and *does*, constitute a small percentage of English words and are generally descendants of Old English or Anglo-Saxon words. Unfortunately, these words are overrepresented among the words most often used in writing and are a continuing source of frustration for poor spellers. Traditionally, these words have been called "outlaw," "lookout," "red," or "tricky" words. Irregular, high-frequency words should be taught a few at a time and then practiced over extended periods until correct spelling habits are formed. When words cannot be taught by pattern, visual orthographic images can be reinforced with these five steps:

1. Spell the word with letter tiles.
2. Ask students to say the letters and form an image of the word with their mental "cameras."
3. Turn over the tiles so that the letters are facing down. Ask students to identify the letters in random order. Turn each tile right side up as a student names the letter.
4. Turn over the tiles and hide the letters again. Ask students to identify the letters in reverse order. Turn each tile right side up as a student names the letter.
5. Finally, ask students to spell the word correctly and write it from memory.

Another standard multisensory technique involves tracing, saying, and then writing the letters in a word (Fernald, 1943). Students write first with their fingers on a rough surface, such as a masonite board or carpet square, saying each letter name in the word. Then they write the word on paper with a pencil. Immediately after two or three words are practiced, students write them in dictated phrases and sentences. When the student recalls the word correctly 3 days in a row, the word is put into a "learned" file for periodic review. Some programs make use of mnemonic clues for high-frequency, irregular words; examples are provided in Table 10.1.

Multisyllabic Words

There are six regular syllable spelling types in English that can be used to organize instruction in analysis and recall of longer words. A seventh category can be added for odd syllables that are typically unaccented syllables at the ends of words (e.g., -*ture*, -*ive*, -*ic*, -*age*). Identification of the six syllable types can help students break longer words into manageable pieces for spelling and understand how long and short vowels are represented. After the syllable types have been taught and students can recognize, pronounce, and sort them, longer words can be tackled. When engaged in guided spelling activities, the teacher should dictate words slowly, syllable by syllable, and ask students to pronounce each syllable clearly. Then the teacher should ask students to write separate syllables (*ac-com-plish-ment*) on rectangular squares of paper or small masonite boards. Finally, the teacher should ask students to write the whole word on a white board or paper and use it in a sentence. Programs derived from Orton–Gillingham teaching principles emphasize this approach (Birsh, 2005). They move gradually through a progression that begins

TABLE 10.1. Examples of Mnemonic Clues for High-Frequency Irregular Words

High-frequency irregular word	Mnemonic clue
they	They went to the Y.
what	What hat will you wear?
said	Mom said, "Sally's apple is delicious!"
some	So, give some to me!
been	A bee has been here.
only	There was only one bird on the nest.
where	Where is it? Here it is.
friend	I am your friend to the end.
family	Father and mother, I love you.

Note. Adapted from Javernick and Moats (2007). Copyright 2007 by Sopris West. Adapted by permission.

with closed-syllable words (e.g., *webcast, laptop, napkin*) and then combine closed syllables with other syllable configurations, all of which are listed in Table 10.2.

Morphology and Orthography

The English spelling system represents morphemes, or meaningful parts of words, in addition to phonemes (Chomsky & Halle, 1968; Venezky, 1999). The analyses by Henry (2003) and by Templeton and Morris (2000), among others, have focused on the importance of teaching students about compounds, prefixes, suffixes, roots, and word origins. Meaning is preserved in spelling, although pronunciation of morphemes may vary. We spell *health* using the pattern in *heal* and *anxious* using the pattern in *anxiety*, although pronunciation differences are marked in those words. Many other related words look similar in spelling but are

TABLE 10.2. Six Types of Syllables in English Orthography

Syllable type	Examples	Definition
Closed	*dap*ple *hos*tel *bev*erage	A syllable with a short vowel sound ending in one or more consonants; the vowel sound is spelled with one vowel letter
Open	*pro*gram *ta*ble *re*cent	A syllable that ends with a long vowel sound, spelled with a single vowel letter
Consonant–*le*	bi*ble* bea*gle* lit*tle*	An unaccented final syllable containing a consonant before /l/ followed by a silent *e*
Vowel team and diphthong	*awe*some *train*er con*geal* *spoil*age	Syllables with long or short vowel sound spellings that use a vowel combination; diphthongs such as *ou/ow* and *oi/oy* are included in this category
R-controlled (vowel–*r*)	*spur*ious con*sort* *char*ter	A syllable in which a single vowel is followed by an /r/; the vowel pronunciation often changes before /r/
V–C–*e* (magic *e*)	com*pete* des*pite*	Syllable has a long vowel spelled with a vowel–consonant–silent *e*

Note. Some unstressed and odd syllables do not fit into these categories, such as *-age* in *verbiage*, *-ture* in *sculpture*, and *-tion* in *adoration*.

pronounced differently, such as *advantage/advantageous, express/expression, machine/mechanic,* and *medic/medicine.*

The spelling of inflectional morphemes or grammatical word endings (*-ed, -s, -es, -er, -est, -ing*) deserves attention early and often in instruction for poor spellers. As the study by Moats et al. (2006) showed, errors on these endings are extremely common even in students with reading and language weaknesses who have not been identified for special education services. English words use consistent spellings for inflections, including the past tense *-ed* and the plural *-s* and *-es,* even though the pronunciation of these endings varies depending on the final phoneme of the word to which the endings are added. For instance, the past tense is pronounced variously as /t/, /d/, and /ed/, and only the last form constitutes a syllable. Thus the words *talked* (/t/), *spelled* (/d/), and *wanted* (/ed/) all have a different-sounding past-tense form. These linguistic complexities must be demystified before students can be expected to develop insight into word structure that will help them recognize when to use *-ed.* Many times over, students at the late primary and intermediate levels should follow these steps:

1. Decompose affixed words into their root and affix (e.g., *shamed* = *shame* + *ed*).
2. Sort past-tense (or plural) words by the sounds of their endings (e.g., /t/, /d/, /ed/).
3. Find more words that follow each pattern.
4. Learn the orthotactic rules that prescribe how an affix is pronounced (e.g., voiceless /t/ is the sound for *-ed* when it follows a voiceless consonant, and voiced /d/ is the sound for *-ed* when it follows a voiced consonant).
5. Write past-tense words from dictation in phrases and sentences.
6. Receive immediate corrective feedback on errors made in writing.

Students with mild dyslexia can advance to the study of derivational morphology. For example, the prefix–root–suffix structure of many Latin-based words accounts for the prevalence of doubled consonants where first and second syllables are joined. Many Latin prefixes are "chameleons"; they appear in alternate forms in order to blend into the root that follows. These changes have occurred for ease of pronunciation; it is much easier to say "ap-proached" than "ad-proached" or "sup-pose" than "sub-pose." The process of changing the consonant at the end of a prefix to match the consonant at the beginning of a Latin or Greek root is called *assimilation.* Doubled consonants between the first and second syllable of a Latin-based word often, but not always, signify an assimilated prefix. Other examples are *aggressive, irregular, suffix,* and *connection*. More advanced students with reading and spelling problems who have good oral vocabularies can benefit from instruction at this level, even though they may still struggle with the spelling of *their* or *does*.

Language of Word Origin

Not only does spelling represent meaningful word parts (morphemes) and meaningful relationships among words with a common root, but it also often reflects the language from which a word originated. Henry (2003), for example, emphasizes the importance of organizing word study by layers of language (see Table 10.3). Some spellings are simply borrowed directly from another language and do not fit the rules and patterns of English. Orthography may make more sense to students with

TABLE 10.3. Layers of English Orthography

Layers of English	Sound–symbol correspondences	Syllable patterns	Morpheme structures
Anglo-Saxon words	Consonants • Singleton • Digraphs • Blends Vowels • Single short/long • V–C–*e* • Vowel team • *R*-controlled	Closed Open Magic *e* Vowel-*r* Vowel team • Consonant-*le*	Compounds Inflections Base words Suffixes (e.g., *-hood, -ly, -ward*)
Latin (Romance) words			Prefixes Roots Suffixes Latin plurals (e.g., *alumni, minutiae, curricula*)
Greek words	*ph* for /f/ (*graph*) *ch* for /k/ (*chorus*) *y* for /i/ (*gym*)		Combining forms (e.g., *neuropsychology, photographer*) Plurals (e.g., *crises, parentheses*)

Note. Based on Henry (2003).

learning disabilities if borrowings are explained and classified by the language of origin. Examples of foreign words that retained non-English spellings when they were borrowed include *petite, baguette, fatigue, boutique* (French); *plaza, tortilla, fiesta, mesa* (Spanish); *pizza, solo, piano, bravo* (Italian); *chutzpah, shlep* (Yiddish). One practical application of this principle is that words with a non-English spelling pattern, such as those with *ch* for /sh/ (*charlatan, cache, chaise, machine, Charlotte*), can be put aside for separate treatment in a phonics lesson.

Helpful Strategies

Even with the best instruction, students with dyslexia, language disorders, ADHD, or graphomotor coordination problems may respond slowly to instruction. Accommodations and coping strategies are very important in the overall treatment program for students with learning disabilities, as are the cultivation of tolerant attitudes from teachers, family members, and employers. After all, many accomplished leaders (Woodrow Wilson), artists (Leonardo da Vinci), actors (Whoopi Goldberg), athletes (Greg Louganis), writers (John Irving), and inventors (Thomas Edison) have been notoriously poor spellers. Better approximations of accurate spellings, better use of a spelling checker, or adoption of more adaptive coping strategies may be the most realistic goals for many students with learning disabilities. Accommodations that are often necessary to help students meet academic requirements include the following:

• Poor spelling on regular schoolwork or spontaneously written material (e.g., in-class tests) is not counted off from the content grade.
• Students are allowed a "cheat sheet" of key content word or name spellings as they take written tests.
• Proofreading checklists are provided that direct the student toward specific words or patterns that have been studied.
• Some written work is done with the help of technology, such as a speech-to-text software.
• When spelling accuracy is essential, proofreading help is provided or allowed.

Preventive scaffolding is often the best strategy for young children with spelling disabilities. Before students are asked to write, they can talk through their ideas with a partner or adult who can write down some key words for them that will be used in the composition. Composing one sentence at a time until greater skill is acquired is also helpful. Students can then coach themselves with self-talk, such as "What I can say, I can write." Immediate, corrective feedback should be provided for incorrect words with patterns that have been studied.

Proofreading is often an overwhelming task for students who are poor spellers. They do need structured practice locating and correcting errors, however, so that they are not totally dependent on outside proofreading help or a computer spelling checker. A proofreading checklist that lists some commonly misspelled words and a personal spelling dictionary of learned words helps to make the task more manageable. Individualizing spelling instruction is easier for teachers with the advent of computer-based diagnostic tools. Three such tools that enable a teacher to pinpoint each student's spelling weaknesses are Spell Doctor (*www.spelldoctor.com*), Spelling Performance Evaluation for Language and Literacy, second edition (SPELL-2; *www.learningbydesign.com*), and Super-Spell Assessment Disk (*www.4mation.co.uk*).

Spelling checkers are useful aids, but, ironically, they are more useful to people who spell fairly well than to people who spell poorly (MacArthur, Graham, Haynes, & De La Paz, 1996). Students who spell at less than a fifth-grade level may not use a spelling checker effectively for several reasons. First, spelling checkers may not recognize the intended word if it is spelled with little phonetic regularity. Second, spelling checkers do not correct homophone errors or substitutions of real words for one another. Finally, spellcheckers offer the writer several alternatives from which the intended word must be selected, and the writer must already know what the word looks like to pick out the spelling that is needed. So spelling checkers, although helpful, will not obviate the need for proofreading assistance. Such assistance may come in the form of a combination of speech synthesis and word prediction software (which enables the student to hear text read aloud to locate errors more easily and to eliminate or reduce the need to spell words fully).

To conclude, spelling instruction, even for poor spellers, is an opportunity to teach children about language—its sounds, meanings, and history. Memory for orthographic images may be enhanced when a word's spelling makes sense. Certainly, interest in language and motivation to master it can be bolstered if lessons are designed to teach spelling as more than a rote memorization skill. Accurate spelling is very difficult for students with LD, ADHD, and other language disabilities, and achievement gains are often modest. A combination of interesting and effective instruction, realistic expectations for accuracy and proofreading competence, a sense of humor, and accommodations such as technological aids will work best for the student who is a poor speller.

REFERENCES

Aaron, P. G., Wilczynski, S., & Keetay, V. (1998). The anatomy of word-specific memory. In C. Hulme & R. M. Joshi (Eds.), *Reading and spelling: Development and disorders* (pp. 405–419). Mahwah, NJ: Erlbaum.

Allen, K. (2005). Alphabet knowledge: Letter recognition, naming, and sequencing. In J. Birsh (Ed.), *Multisensory teaching of basic language skills* (2nd ed., pp. 113–150). Baltimore: Brookes.

Apel, K., Wolter, J. A., & Masterson, J. J. (2006). Effects of phonotactic and orthotactic probabilities during fast mapping on 5-year-olds' learning to spell. *Developmental Neuropsychology, 29,* 21–42.

Bailet, L. (2004). Spelling instructional and intervention frameworks. In C. A. Stone, E. R. Silliman, B. J. Ehren, & K. Apel (Eds.), *Handbook of language and literacy: Development and disorders* (pp. 661–678). New York: Guilford Press.

Balmuth, M. (1992). *The roots of phonics: A historical introduction.* Baltimore: York Press.

Bear, D. R., Invernizzi, M., Templeton, S., & Johnston, F. (2005). *Words their way: Word study, phonics, vocabulary, and spelling instruction* (3rd ed.). Upper Saddle River, NJ: Merrill.

Berninger, V. W., Abbott, R. D., Jones, J., Wolf, B. J., Gould, L., Anderson-Youngstrom, M., et al. (2006). Early development of language by hand: Composing, reading, listening, and speaking connections; three letter-writing modes; and fast mapping in spelling. *Developmental Neuropsychology, 29,* 61–92.

Berninger, V. W., & Graham, S. (1998). Language by hand: A synthesis of a decade of research on handwriting. *Handwriting Review, 12,* 11–25.

Berninger, V. W., Vaughan, K., Abbott, R. D., Brooks, A., Abbott, S., Reed, E., et al. (1998). Early intervention for spelling problems: Teaching spelling units of varying size within a multiple connections framework. *Journal of Educational Psychology, 90,* 587–605.

Bhattacharya, A., & Ehri, L. (2004). Graphosyllabic analysis helps adolescent struggling readers read and spell words. *Journal of Learning Disabilities, 37,* 331–348.

Birsh, J. R. (2005). *Multisensory teaching of basic language skills* (2nd ed.). Baltimore: Paul Brookes.

Blachman, B. A., Tangel, D. M., Ball, E. W., Black, R., & McGraw, C. K. (1999). Developing phonological awareness and word recognition skills: A two-year intervention with low-income, inner-city children. *Reading and Writing: An Interdisciplinary Journal, 11,* 239–273.

Bryant, P., Nunes, T., & Bindman, M. (1997). Children's understanding of the connection between grammar and spelling. In B. A. Blachman (Ed.), *Foundations of reading acquisition and dyslexia* (pp. 219–240). Mahwah, NJ: Erlbaum.

Bryson, B. (1990). *The mother tongue: English and how it got that way.* New York: Avon Books.

Carlisle, J. (1994). Morphological awareness, spelling, and story writing: Possible relationships for elementary-age children with and without learning disabilities. In N. Jordan & J. Goldsmith-Phillips (Eds.), *Learning disabilities: New directions for assessment and intervention* (pp. 123–145). Boston: Allyn & Bacon.

Carreker, S. (2005). Teaching spelling. In J. Birsh (Ed.), *Multisensory teaching of basic language skills* (2nd ed., pp. 257–295). Baltimore: Brookes.

Cassar, M., Treiman, R., Moats, L. C., Pollo, T. C., & Kessler, B. (2005). How do the spellings of children with dyslexia compare with those of nondyslexic children? *Reading and Writing: An Interdisciplinary Journal, 18*, 27–49.

Chomsky, N., & Halle, M. (1968). *The sound pattern of English.* New York: Harper & Row.

Ehri, L. C. (1989). The development of spelling knowledge and its role in reading acquisition and reading disability. *Journal of Learning Disabilities, 22*, 356–365.

Ehri, L. C. (1998). Grapheme–phoneme knowledge is essential for learning to read words in English. In J. L. Metsala & L. C. Ehri (Eds.), *Word recognition in beginning literacy* (pp. 3–40). Mahwah, NJ: Erlbaum.

Ehri, L. C. (2000). Learning to read and learning to spell: Two sides of a coin. *Topics in Language Disorders, 20*(3), 19–49.

Ehri, L. C. (2004). Teaching phonemic awareness and phonics. In P. McCardle & V. Chhabra (Eds.), *The voice of evidence in reading research* (pp. 153–186). Baltimore: Brookes.

Fernald, G. (1943). *Remedial techniques in basic school subjects.* New York: McGraw-Hill.

Fletcher, J. M., Lyon, G. R., Fuchs, L. S., & Barnes, M. A. (2007). *Learning disabilities: From identification to intervention.* New York: Guilford Press.

Fulk, B. M., & Stormont-Spurgin, M. (1995). Spelling interventions for students with disabilities: A review. *Journal of Special Education, 28*, 488–513.

Goswami, U. (1992). Phonological factors in spelling development. *Journal of Child Psychology and Psychiatry and Allied Disciplines, 33*, 967–975.

Grace, K. (2006). *Phonics and spelling through phoneme–grapheme mapping.* Longmont, CO: Sopris West.

Graham, S. (1999). Handwriting and spelling instruction for students with learning disabilities: A review. *Learning Disability Quarterly, 22*, 78–98.

Graham, S. (2000). Should the natural learning approach replace spelling instruction? *Journal of Educational Psychology, 92*, 235–247.

Graham, S., Harris, K. R., & Loynachan, C. (1994). The spelling for writing list. *Journal of Learning Disabilities, 27*, 210–214.

Hanna, P. R., Hanna, J. S., Hodges, R. E., & Rudorf, E. H., Jr. (1966). *Phoneme–grapheme correspondences as cues to spelling improvement* (U.S. Department of Education Publication No. 32008). Washington, DC: Government Printing Office.

Henry, M. (2003). *Unlocking literacy.* Baltimore: Brookes.

Javernick, E., & Moats, L. C. (2007). *Primary spelling by pattern, level 1.* Longmont, CO: Sopris West.

Johnston, R. S., & Watson, J. E. (2006). The effectiveness of synthetic phonics teaching in developing reading and spelling skills in English-speaking boys and girls. In R. M. Joshi & P. G. Aaron (Eds.), *Handbook of orthography and literacy* (pp. 679–691). Mahwah, NJ: Erlbaum.

Joshi, R. M., & Aaron, P. G. (2005). Spelling: Assessment and instructional recommendations. *Perspectives, 31*(3), 38–41.

Kamhi, A., & Hinton, L. N. (2000). Explaining individual differences in spelling ability. *Topics in Language Disorders, 20*(3), 37–49.

Kessler, B., & Treiman, R. (2001). Relationships between sounds and letters in English monosyllables. *Journal of Memory and Language, 44,* 592–617.

King, D. (2000). *English isn't crazy.* Baltimore: York Press.

Lefly, D., & Pennington, B. (1991). Spelling errors and reading fluency in compensated adult dyslexics. *Annals of Dyslexia, 41,* 143–162.

Lennox, C., & Siegel, L. (1998). Phonological and orthographic processes in good and poor spellers. In C. Hulme & R. M. Joshi (Eds.), *Reading and spelling: Development and disorders* (pp. 395–404). Mahwah, NJ: Erlbaum.

Lindamood, P. (1994). Issues in researching the link between phonological awareness, learning disabilities, and spelling. In G. R. Lyon (Ed.), *Frames of reference for the assessment of learning disabilities: New views on measurement issues* (pp. 351–373). Baltimore: Brookes.

Lyon, G. R., Shaywitz, S. E., & Shaywitz, B. A. (2003). A definition of dyslexia. *Annals of Dyslexia, 53,* 1–14.

MacArthur, C. A., Graham, S., Haynes, J. A., & De La Paz, S. (1996). Spell checkers and students with learning disabilities: Performance comparisons and impact on spelling. *Journal of Special Education, 30,* 35–57.

Mehta, P., Foorman, B. R., Branum-Martin, L., & Taylor, P. W. (2005). Literacy as a unidimensional construct: Validation, sources of influence, and implications in a longitudinal study in grades 1 to 4. *Scientific Studies of Reading, 9*(2), 85–116.

Moats, L. C. (1995). *Spelling: Development, disability, and instruction.* Baltimore: York Press.

Moats, L. C. (1996). Phonological spelling errors in the writing of dyslexic adolescents. *Reading and Writing: An Interdisciplinary Journal, 8,* 105–119.

Moats, L. C. (2000). *Speech to print: Language essentials for teachers.* Baltimore: Brookes.

Moats, L. C. (2008). *Language essentials for teachers of reading and spelling (LETRS, Second edition).* Longmont, CO: Sopris West.

Moats, L. C., Foorman, B. R., & Taylor, W. P. (2006). How quality of writing instruction impacts high-risk fourth graders' writing. *Reading and Writing: An Interdisciplinary Journal, 19,* 363–391.

Morris, R. D., Stuebing, K. K., Fletcher, J. M., Shaywitz, S. E., Lyon, G. R., Shankweiler, D. P., et al. (1998). Subtypes of reading disability: Variability around a phonological core. *Journal of Educational Psychology, 90,* 347–373.

Olson, R. K. (2006). Genes, environment, and dyslexia. *Annals of Dyslexia, 56,* 205–238.

Re, A. M., Pedron, M., & Cornoldi, C. (2007). Expressive writing difficulties in children described as exhibiting ADHD symptoms. *Journal of Learning Disabilities, 40,* 244–255.

Sacks, D. (2003). *Language visible: Unraveling the mystery of the alphabet from A to Z.* New York: Broadway Books.

Shaywitz, S. E. (2004). *Overcoming dyslexia.* New York: Knopf.

Templeton, S., & Morris, D. (2000). Spelling. In M. L. Kamil, P. B. Mosenthal, P. D. Pearson, & R. Barr (Eds.), *Handbook of reading research* (Vol. 3, pp. 525–543). Mahwah, NJ: Erlbaum.

Treiman, R. (2006). Knowledge about letters as a foundation for reading and spelling. In R. M. Joshi & P. G. Aaron (Eds.), *Handbook of orthography and literacy* (pp. 581–599). Mahwah, NJ: Erlbaum.

Treiman, R., & Bourassa, D. (2000). The development of spelling skill. *Topics in Language Disorders, 20*(3), 1–18.

Uhry, J. K., & Shepherd, M. J. (1993). Segmentation and spelling instruction as part of a first-grade reading program: Effects on several measures of reading. *Reading Research Quarterly, 28,* 219–233.

Venezky, R. L. (1999). *The American way of spelling: The structure and origins of American English orthography.* New York: Guilford Press.

Wanzek, J., Vaughn, S., Wexler, J., Swanson, E. A., Edmonds, M., & Kim, A. (2006). A synthesis of spelling and reading interventions and their effects on the spelling outcomes of students with LD. *Journal of Learning Disabilities, 39,* 528–543.

CHAPTER 11

Spelling and English Language Learning

PAULINE B. LOW
LINDA S. SIEGEL

Orthographies vary in how sounds are translated to print. Alphabetic orthographies utilize grapheme–phoneme correspondences, whereas nonalphabetic orthographies do not. This chapter examines the role of children's first languages in the ease or difficulty with which English spelling is acquired, with a particular emphasis on spelling achievement as it is influenced by the adherence of children's native language (L1) orthography to the alphabetic principle. The chapter begins with a review of the current literature on spelling acquisition in English language learning (ELL), followed by an empirical example of how educators and researchers can utilize spelling error analyses to examine the processes used in learning English spelling. It is important that we preface this chapter by noting the difficulty of isolating the task of spelling from the tasks of reading and vocabulary acquisition. Although this chapter is predominately focused on spelling, the three tasks—spelling, reading, and vocabulary—are all extensions of language and are acquired simultaneously and interactively.

Reading and writing are two of the important (perhaps the most important) vehicles for the dissemination of knowledge in literate cultures. For ELL students, the development of literacy involves not only an understanding of alphabetic script but also the manipulation of symbols that represent the values and beliefs of a culture with which they are still developing familiarity (Martin & Stuart-Smith, 1998). In Canada, immigration alone accounted for more than three-quarters of the population increase in the province of British Columbia from 1996 to 2001, and similar trends appear across other Canadian provinces (Statistics Canada, 2001). In the United States, 47 million people speak a non-English language at home (U.S. Census Bureau, 2000), with almost 9.8 million of those individuals being school-age children. In fact, the total population of non-English speakers has almost doubled since 1990 (U.S. Census Bureau, 2003). In turn, an increasing number of children are entering the North American school systems with minimal formal instruction in English and are immersed in English classrooms. It is often the case that children from immigrant families speak one language at home and are instructed in a second language at school. The children themselves may or may not be immigrants. Alternatively, parents may elect to speak their native language at home to their children, assuming that English will eventually be acquired in school.

This trend toward bi/multilingualism raises questions as to whether current educational practices are appropriate for children with diverse first languages. Even while valuing the diversity in children, educators should aim at developing comprehensive instructional strategies for a wide range of learners. To achieve such a goal, an increased awareness by educators is needed of children's language experience and how this may influence their understanding of reading and spelling in English. Previous research has produced mixed results, suggesting that bilingualism can be either an impediment to or a facilitator of the development of reading and spelling skills in a second language (Jarvis, 2000). Hence an increasing emphasis must be placed on clarifying those particular aspects inherent in the first language that contribute to the ease with which English spelling is acquired by young children.

ENGLISH ORTHOGRAPHY
AND THE ALPHABETIC PRINCIPLE

Orthographies represent speech in different ways, often reflecting the differences in the availability of sounds in the language. As such, writing systems vary in how they translate sounds to print. Fluent reading and spelling in alphabetic languages require the mastery of two processes: a phonological process based on the awareness of sounds in spoken words and an orthographic process based on the visual patterns of the written language (Lennox & Siegel, 1996; Vellutino, Fletcher, Snowling, & Scanlon, 2004). Orthographic knowledge refers to an understanding of the rules of the writing system, including letter sequencing and positional cues on letter pronunciation and spelling (Cassar & Treiman, 2004).

Early learners of an alphabetic orthography must understand that letters (graphemes) represent the smallest units of language sounds (phonemes), and that there are predictable grapheme–phoneme correspondences and phoneme–grapheme correspondences. This is called the *alphabetic principle.*

Alphabetic scripts, however, are not all alike. A framework for discussing differences in reading and spelling among alphabetic orthographies is the orthographic depth hypothesis. Shallow (or transparent) orthographies, such as Finnish and Italian, have more predictable grapheme–phoneme mappings. In contrast, deep (or opaque) orthographies, such as French and English, have complex grapheme–phoneme mappings. In English, for instance, a single grapheme may represent several phonemes (e.g., *ch* as in *choir* and *child*), and several graphemes may represent a single phoneme (e.g., *ea* as in *easy* and *ee* as in *bleed* for the phoneme /i/). In addition, the complexity of phoneme–grapheme mappings may differ across reading and spelling. Whereas there is typically one possible phonetic reading of an English word using grapheme–phoneme correspondences, there are multiple possible phonetic spellings of an English word using phoneme–grapheme correspondences, suggesting an asymmetry between grapheme–phoneme and phoneme–grapheme correspondences (Sprenger-Charolles, Siegel, & Bonnet, 1998; Stanovich, 1991). In order to correctly spell a word, a child must first segment the word into its individual phonemes and then decide which graphemes adequately represent these phonemes. Even more perplexing are the irregular words to which applying phoneme–grapheme rules actually result in an incorrect spelling (e.g., /məræŋ/ for *meringue*). Hence accessibility of the mental lexicon, or lexical access, is also important in spelling. However, there is much more to spelling than rote memory. Children with developed phonological and orthographic awareness will look for cues within the word to help them with this grapheme selection process. The first cue is the position of the phoneme within the word, and the second cue is the neighboring phoneme(s).

Most of the English consonants have regular reading and spelling correspondences, although there are a handful of variations. For instance, most consonant letters correspond to only one sound (e.g., *d, m, p, t*). A few consonant letters can correspond to one sound or be silent (e.g., *bad/ bomb, he/hour, kit/knee*) or correspond to more than one sound (e.g., *cat/cell/cello, go/cage*). Some combinations of letters represent one sound (e.g., *pick, grapheme, watch*), whereas some combinations of letters represent two possible sounds (e.g., *choice/choir*). The vowels, however, vary depending on the position of the vowel within the word and the syllabic and morphemic structure of the word (e.g., the sound of the letter *a* in the adjective *able* versus the suffix *-able* as in *capable*).

CROSS-LINGUISTIC THEORIES

Two major theoretical positions underlie ELL research. The universalist hypothesis, or linguistic-interdependence hypothesis, proposes that the development of literacy skills in different languages is shaped by common underlying cognitive and linguistic processes (Cummins, 1979). Hence skills learned in the native language (L1) will readily transfer to the learning of a second language. Evidence supporting the universalist perspective comes from a variety of studies. For instance, Durgunoglu, Nagy, and Hancin-Bhatt (1993) found that Spanish phonological awareness and Spanish word recognition were predictive of English word reading performance in a group of first-grade Spanish ELL students. Also according to the universalist perspective, children with difficulties in the processes involved with literacy acquisition in the first language should show the same difficulties in the second language. In a study of bilingual Portuguese–English-speaking children, Da Fontoura and Siegel (1995) found that there was a significant relationship between the acquisition of word reading, decoding, working memory, and syntactic awareness in the two languages. Furthermore, the bilingual children who had lower reading scores in one language also had lower reading scores in the other language.

The script-dependent hypothesis posits that success in learning to read and spell in a second language is significantly influenced by the differences between the two orthographies, such as shallow versus deep or alphabetic versus nonalphabetic. However, the presence of L1 effects on second-language literacy does not imply that second-language processes are adversely affected. Rather, it suggests that there may be qualitative differences in the skills or strategies that underlie second-language literacy processes and that these differences may be due to differences in orthographic elements of the L1. The script-dependent perspective has also received some support (e.g., Ryan & Meara, 1991; Wang, Koda, & Perfetti, 2003). Using visual word shape distortion in reading (e.g., cAsE aLtErNaTiOn), Akatmatsu (1999, 2003) demonstrated that the differences in the alphabetic sensitivity of fluent ELL adult readers could be attributed to whether the L1 orthography was alphabetic (Persian) or nonalphabetic (Chinese and Japanese). The Persian ELL readers were more successful than the Chinese and Japanese ELL readers in reading case-alternated words in isolation (Akatmatsu, 1999) and in reading case-alternated words in passages (Akatmatsu, 2003), suggesting that the Persian ELL readers were more efficient at preserving the spelling patterns, despite visual shape distortion, to come to a correct reading of the word. Also, in a study of Chinese ELL children, Wang and Geva (2003) found that although Chinese ELL children were less accurate at spelling pseudowords than English L1 children, they were better at determining legitimate and illegitimate letter strings. The authors concluded that the Chinese ELL children were more likely to use visual, holistic information based on orthographic patterns rather than the phonological strategy used by their English L1 peers.

COGNITIVE PROCESSES OF SPELLING

Spelling is a cognitive skill. Phonological processing, syntactic awareness, working memory, and orthographic processing are significant in the development of spelling and reading in English (for a review, see Siegel, 1993). The influences of these processes are so robust that many psychoeducational assessments for children at risk for learning disabilities typically assess some or all of these processes (e.g., Scanlon & Vellutino, 1997).

Phonological Processing

Phonological processing loosely refers to a variety of skills involving the processing of speech sounds. It is well established that phonological processing plays an important role in early literacy acquisition for native speakers of many languages, ranging from English (Perfetti, 1985) to Spanish (Durgunoglu et al., 1993) to Dutch (Patel, Snowling, & de Jong, 2004) to Chinese (Tan & Perfetti, 1998). In fact, core deficits in phonological processing are associated with persistent difficulties in the acquisition of literacy skills (Siegel, 1993). Of particular interest is phonological awareness, or the ability to discriminate and manipulate the sounds of the language. Phonological awareness is measured through a variety of techniques, including rhyming, segmenting sounds, blending sounds, and deleting sounds (Yopp, 1988). A related skill is phonological coding, or the application of grapheme–phoneme and phoneme–grapheme correspondences. Whereas phonological awareness refers to an oral language skill, phonological coding refers to the association of sounds to print. Phonological coding is measured by the accuracy of reading or spelling pseudowords, made-up words that follow predictable grapheme–phoneme correspondences. Phonological coding difficulties are also implicated in reading disability (Da Fontoura & Siegel, 1995; Geva & Siegel, 2000).

ELL speakers, by definition, experience delayed exposure to the phonological structures of the English language compared with native English speakers. Yet ELL speakers are not necessarily at a disadvantage in gaining early English literacy skills (Lesaux & Siegel, 2003). Phonological processing skills learned in the L1 can be relatively strong predictors of concurrent and subsequent literacy skills in the second language regardless of orthographic differences between languages (Campbell & Sais, 1995; Chow, McBride-Chang, & Burgess, 2005; Gottardo, Yan, Siegel, & Wade-Woolley, 2001). Studies show that the similarities between the languages may positively influence cross-linguistic transfer (e.g., Bialystok, Majumder, & Martin, 2003).

Syntactic Awareness

In addition to phonological processing, syntactic awareness is a significant cognitive correlate of reading and spelling acquisition. Syntactic awareness, or grammatical sensitivity, refers to the ability to understand the way in which linguistic elements of a specific language are put together to form grammatically correct words and phrases. In studies of ELL children, both L1 and English syntactic skills were found to be significantly correlated with reading skills across languages (e.g., Portuguese, Da Fontoura & Siegel, 1995; Hebrew, Geva & Siegel, 2000; Arabic, Abu-Rabia & Siegel, 2002). Similarly, syntactic awareness is a predictor of spelling performance. Muter and Snowling (1997) found that grammatical awareness, rather than phonological awareness, helped children to distinguish the orthographic aspects of spelling (e.g., choosing the correct spelling among word pairs that sound alike, as in *skait* vs. *skate*). In addition, Bryant, Nunes, and Bindman (2000) found that children's grammatical awareness influenced their spelling of regular past tense verbs ending in *-ed*. The importance of syntactic awareness to spelling performance is also evident in other alphabetic orthographies, such as French (Plaza & Cohen, 2003) and Danish (Juul, 2005).

Working Memory

Working memory refers to the ability to hold information in short-term storage while transforming or manipulating it in some way. According to Baddeley and Hitch's original model (1974), working memory consists of three components. The central executive is a limited-capacity attentional system responsible for the coordination of information from two subsidiary storage systems: the visual–spatial sketch pad and the phonological loop. The visual–spatial sketch pad temporarily stores visual and/or spatial information, and the phonological loop temporarily stores phonological or linguistic information. More recently, a third subsidiary system, the episodic buffer, has been proposed as a temporary storage system capable of integrating information from the central executive and the other two subsidiary systems with long-term memory (Baddeley, 2000).

Working memory is vital for encoding and decoding words using grapheme–phoneme correspondences while retrieving information about syntax and semantics. Moreover, certain tasks place greater demands on working memory than others. For instance, spelling an unfamiliar or made-up word requires first the segmentation of the orally dictated word into its individual phonemes, then the selection among several possible graphemes, and finally the application of orthographic knowledge of positional constraints. All of this occurs simultaneously in working memory.

Visual/Orthographic Processing

Orthographic awareness refers to an understanding of writing conventions, including which spelling patterns are legitimate or illegitimate in that language. English words are not always phonetic, so phonological processing and phonological coding skills alone are not sufficient. For instance, irregular words can be correctly spelled only by remembering letter strings (e.g., *yacht, colonel*). Spelling error analyses would help to determine which errors are phonetic errors and which are orthographic errors. For instance, the word *anxiety* spelled as *angziety* is phonetically correct but orthographically incorrect, as it contains an illegitimate letter combination.

ILLUSTRATION OF THE INFLUENCE OF ORTHOGRAPHY ON SPELLING STRATEGIES

English language learners who speak languages with alphabetic and nonalphabetic orthographies present a unique opportunity to examine whether the transfer of skills from the L1 to the second language differ according to the degree to which the L1 adheres to the alphabetic principle. According to the universalist hypothesis, if learning to spell in a second language involves processes that are shared across languages, then ELL speakers will benefit from cross-language transfer and show patterns of spelling that are similar to those of English L1 speakers. Meanwhile, the script-dependent hypothesis would suggest that the orthographic differences in children's linguistic backgrounds would lead to differences in the processes and outcomes for spelling. We conducted a detailed examination of the spelling skills of two groups of ELL children (Persian and Chinese) and a group of demographically matched English L1 children, and our results support the conclusion that English language learners are not at a disadvantage compared with English L1 learners, although the strategies employed may differ.

Persian is an alphabetic language with predictable grapheme–phoneme correspondences (i.e., a shallow orthography). Persian is a modified version of Arabic, with the letters written from right to left. There are 29 letters representing consonants and three letters representing long vowels. The three short vowels are represented by diacritics, not letters. The diacritics appear above or below the letter associated with the short vowel sound. However, diacritics are used only for beginning readers and are later omitted. Whereas in English the visual form of each letter remains constant regardless of position within the word, in Persian the visual form of the letter may vary depending on its position in the word. For instance, consider the letter "ﺕ," which corresponds to the sound /tʃ/. It appears as "ﺕ" when written as a solo letter and at the end of a word, but as "ﭺ" at the beginning and the middle of a word. Similar to English, a single Persian phoneme can be represented by several graphemes.

Although grapheme–phoneme correspondences do not apply in nonalphabetic languages, phonological processing is still important in learning to read and spell. For instance, the Chinese script was long believed to be completely logographic (visual), and the contributions of phonology to the learning of Chinese received little attention. Recent research has shown that the Chinese language is more phonetic and less visually based than initially believed, although the available phonetic information is much more imprecise than in alphabetic languages (e.g., Jackson, Chen, Goldsberry, Ahyoung, & Vanderwerff, 1999; Tan & Perfetti, 1998). The phonological information is represented at the level of the syllable rather than the phoneme (Leong, 1997; Perfetti & Zhang, 1995). As such, the Chinese script has been described as morphosyllabic, because each Chinese character is a morpheme as well as a syllable. Approximately 80% of Chinese characters are phonetic compounds that have a semantic radical to provide meaning and a phonetic component to guide pronunciation (Chan & Siegel, 2001; Huang & Hanley, 1994). However, the phonetic component guides pronunciation only about 40% of the time. Given the unreliability of phonetic information, other strategies may become particularly salient for reading and spelling, such as memory for the visual word form (Huang & Hanley, 1994).

The present research was conducted in a school district that is committed to the intervention and prevention of literacy difficulties. Universal screening of prereading skills and direct instruction in phonological awareness are part of the kindergarten program, followed by phonics instruction in grade 1. ELL students within the school district received the same classroom instruction as their English L1-speaking peers. The participants were 122 third-grade children (63 males and 59 females) from 25 schools in a single school district in Canada. The mean age of the children was 8.88 years (SD = 0.32). The children in this study were part of a larger longitudinal study that began in their kindergarten year. The participants were classified as ELL if they spoke a language other than English at home to parents, siblings, and grandparents. Within the sample, there were 45 English L1 speakers and 77 ELL speakers (32 Persian L1 and 45 Chinese L1). Among the Chinese L1 speakers, 14 were Mandarin speakers, 18 were Cantonese speakers, and 13 were speakers of an alternate Chinese dialect.

Most of the ELL speakers immigrated to Canada at an early age, although some were born in Canada and did not begin to speak English until school entry. All of the ELL speakers in this study had had at least 2 years of full-time English classroom instruction, with the majority of the children having received schooling in English since kindergarten. As the sample represented an entire school district, the participants also represented a wide range of socioeconomic status (SES) backgrounds. The children were (1) given the spelling subtest of the Wide Range Achievement Test—3 (WRAT-3; Wilkinson, 1993), a standardized measure of single-word spelling on which the child was asked to spell dictated words of increasing difficulty (the child could correctly spell a word using memory, knowledge of phonetics, or a combination of both), and (2) asked to generate plausible spellings of 15 orally presented pseudowords selected from the Goldman–Fristoe–Woodcock Sound–Symbol Tests: Spelling (Goldman, Fristoe, & Woodcock, 1974) in order to isolate their skill in applying phoneme–grapheme correspondences to spelling.

The performances of the language groups on measures of spelling are shown in Table 11.1. Although there were no significant differences between the language groups on the WRAT-3 spelling subtest, $F(2, 119)$ = 1.47, ns, η^2 = 0.02, there was a significant effect of L1 language on the pseudoword spelling task, $F(2, 119)$ = 5.56, $p < .01$, η^2 = 0.09. Post-hoc Tukey HSD pairwise comparisons revealed that, although there was no difference between the two alphabetic L1 groups (English, Persian) and

TABLE 11.1. Mean Scores on Spelling Measures by First Language

	English L1 (n = 45)	Persian L1 (n = 32)	Chinese L1 (n = 45)	Post hoc
WRAT-3 spelling subtest percentile				
M	69.73	69.94	76.38	
SD	21.79	21.23	18.24	
Pseudoword spelling (max. = 15)				
M	10.13	9.56	8.09	E = P
SD	2.61	3.02	3.30	P = C
				C < E*

*$p < .01$.

no difference between the two ELL groups (Persian, Chinese), the Chinese L1 group was less accurate than the English L1 group at spelling pseudowords ($p < .01$).

Generally, items on norm-referenced standardized tests and criterion-referenced classroom tests of spelling are scored as either correct or incorrect. Although misspellings lack complete accuracy, they are not without value and can be accurate to some degree. Misspelling error analysis provides a window into the strategies used when a child encounters spelling challenges. In order to examine the influences of L1 spelling strategies on English spelling, the first 10 spelling errors on the WRAT-3 spelling subtest for each child were analyzed. Three scores were constructed for each misspelling based on a system used by Lennox and Siegel (1996). Two of the scores were based on the phonological similarity of the misspelling to the target word, and one of the scores was based on visual similarity.

Phonemic accuracy refers to the number of phonemes correctly represented in the misspelling. For instance, the word *brief* has four phonemes (/b/ /r/ /i/ /f/). The item misspelled as BREFE receives a full score of 100% because all of the phonemes are represented, although the spelling is incorrect; whereas the word misspelled as BRF or BREF receives a score of 75%, as only three phonemes are correctly represented. The letter *E* in BREF is not considered phonemically accurate according to this scoring system because a vowel digraph (e.g., BREEF, BREAF) or a silent-*e* ending (e.g., BREFE) is required for the long *e* sound. It was also permissible for words to be orthographically illegitimate (e.g., CKWAN-TITY for *quantity*). For each child, the phonemic accuracy scores calculated for the 10 misspellings were summed and divided by 10 to yield an average score per child.

Phonetic plausibility refers to whether the misspelling sounds identical to the target word when read according to grapheme–phoneme correspondences. Correct responses in the phonetic plausibility category require accurate representations of all phonemes in their correct positions. As such, each phonetically plausible misspelling is also a 100% phonemically accurate misspelling (e.g., BREFE). Each misspelling received a score of 0 (incorrect) or 1 (correct). For each child, the phonetic plausibility scores calculated for the 10 misspellings were summed and divided by 10 to yield an average score per child. A measure of interrater agreement was calculated for the phonological similarity scores by comparing the ratings between two independent raters. Any disagreements among the scoring of items were resolved through discussion. The interrater agreement was 90% for the phonemic accuracy scores and 98% for the phonetic plausibility scores.

The *visual similarity* score reflects the amount of visual overlap between the letters in the misspelling and in the target word. The visual similarity score takes into consideration the percentage of correctly sequenced letters (percentage of bigrams) and the number of correctly represented letters. For instance, the word *brief* has 4 bigrams (*b-r*, *r-i*, *i-e*, *e-f*) and 5 letters, resulting in a total possible score of 9. The misspelling *BREF* has 2 correct bigrams (i.e., *b-r* and *e-f*) and 4 correct letters, resulting in a score of 6. The misspelling would then receive a score of 6 out of 9, or a visual similarity score of 67%. For each child, the visual similarity scores calculated for the 10 misspellings were summed and divided by 10 to yield an average score per child.

The performance of the language groups is shown in Table 11.2. Although the results of the phonemic accuracy scores revealed that the three language groups were comparably successful at correctly representing the individual phonemes within the misspellings, $F(2, 119) = 3.64$, *ns*, $\eta^2 = 0.06$, the three language groups differed on generating misspellings with phonetic plausibility at the word level, $F(2, 119) = 12.94$, $p < .001$, $\eta^2 = 0.18$. Post-hoc Tukey HSD comparisons revealed that the nonalphabetic Chinese L1 group was less proficient than the two alphabetic groups at generating phonetically plausible misspellings that can be read to sound like the target word (English, $p < .001$; Persian, $p < .01$).

In terms of visual similarity, the results of the analysis of variance (ANOVA) revealed that the three language groups did not differ in their accuracy at representing the target letters within the misspellings. The amount of visual overlap between the misspellings and the target spellings were similar across the three language groups, $F(2, 119) = 0.497$, *ns*, $\eta^2 = 0.01$.

An important finding was the differential use of strategies for spelling

TABLE 11.2. Spelling Error Analyses for WRAT-3 Spelling by First Language

	English ($n = 45$)	Persian ($n = 32$)	Chinese ($n = 45$)	Post hoc
Phonemic accuracy				
M	87.99	86.12	84.11	
SD	7.45	6.73	6.22	
Phonetic plausibility				
M	44.67	39.06	24.44	E = P
SD	19.26	17.66	20.51	P > C*
				C < E**
Visual similarity				
M	67.29	65.70	66.72	
SD	7.24	6.20	7.13	

$^*p < .01$; $^{**}p < .001$.

despite similar spelling achievement across language groups. Although the spelling outcomes for known "real" words (WRAT-3 spelling subtest) did not show variations that could be attributable to L1 language experience, the use of strategies for spelling unknown words did, as summarized in Figure 11.1.

The nonalphabetic Chinese group was less accurate than the English group at spelling pseudowords. Although the WRAT-3 subtest contained only real words, an "unknown" real word has no lexical entry in memory and, hence, will function as a pseudoword. Accordingly, the nonalphabetic Chinese L1 group was also less likely than both alphabetic groups to generate misspellings that can be read to sound exactly like the target word (phonetic plausibility). The results are consistent with those reported by Wang and Geva (2003), who found that Chinese L1 children were less accurate at spelling English pseudowords than English L1 children, suggesting that Chinese L1 children were less likely than English L1 peers to use a phonological strategy to spell. Overall, there is converging evidence to indicate that grapheme–phoneme mapping experience in a child's L1 is a potential influence on the use of strategies to spell in an alphabetic language such as English.

However, the misspelling error analyses also revealed that the three language groups were equally likely to generate misspellings that resembled the target word in visual form (visual similarity) and in individual phonemic units (phonemic accuracy). Combined, the findings of the spelling error analyses suggest that, although the Chinese L1 speakers had the requisite knowledge to apply phoneme–grapheme correspondences to represent sounds at the phonemic level, they were less efficient in applying rules in such a way as to come up with a completely phonetic misspelling. Given the visual emphasis of the Chinese script, one might expect that the Chinese L1 speakers would show a higher degree of visual accuracy in their misspellings. Yet we did not find evidence for the increased use of visual strategies, as indicated by the visual similarity scores. Although not directly tested in this study, it is plausible to suggest that the Chinese L1 speakers might be more likely to use a visual strategy to spell words that have some representation in memory. This would explain why the Chinese L1 speakers were able to spell as many real words as the alphabetic L1 speakers despite less efficiency in applying phoneme–grapheme mapping rules to spell pseudowords. However, for unknown words, using a visual strategy is not as advantageous, and consequently they shift to a phonologically based strategy, resulting in misspellings that are not more visually accurate than those of the alphabetic speakers.

The findings of the error analyses suggest that the strategies developed in an L1 are transferred to learning English spelling. Furthermore, the nature of L1 orthographic structures may have an influence on the

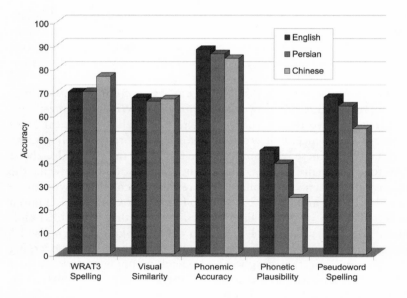

FIGURE 11.1. Spelling measures by first language (percent accuracy scores are reported, except for WRAT-3 percentile scores).

kind of cognitive processes that are transferred to learning English spelling. More specifically, although Chinese speakers with a nonalphabetic L1 are less efficient at the application of phoneme–grapheme correspondences to spell, they are able to spell real words as accurately as alphabetic L1 speakers, suggesting the involvement of other strategies such as memory for visual word form. This is an important finding, as it suggests that although there may be qualitative differences in strategies, the spelling outcomes do not necessarily differ for children with diverse language backgrounds.

RECOMMENDATIONS

There is a clear influence of one's first language on learning English spelling. However, this should not be confused with the idea that English language learners will necessarily be struggling with spelling. We should not approach the study of learning English spelling from a deficit perspective. In fact, the research illustrated in this chapter shows a similar degree of achievement in spelling among ELL and English L1 children when children are provided with an equal opportunity to gain literacy skills. All children, including those who are English language learners and those who have learning difficulties, benefit from direct and systematic spelling instruction that is rooted in a program with the integrated components of phonological and orthographic awareness, the alphabetic principle, phonics, text reading and writing, and rich vocabulary development.

Based on our preceding illustration, a qualitative analysis of spelling errors is strongly recommended should an educator wish to consider individualized spelling goals. Spelling should not be confused with writing, as a composition can be thoughtfully written but contain many spelling errors. Although our research study reported here emphasized spelling from dictation, spelling knowledge can be evaluated within the context of composing or spelling recognition tasks. For instance, a spelling recognition task that involves differentiating a real word from a pseudohomophone (e.g., *heat* vs. *heet*) can be used to assess knowledge of orthographic patterns. Similarly, a task that involves differentiating an orthographically legitimate pseudoword from one that is not (e.g., *filk* vs. *filv*) can be used to assess knowledge of orthographic regularity. Error analysis should be conducted considering the context and cognitive load required for the tasks. For instance, spelling from dictation is context-free and asks the child to focus specifically on the target word. In analyzing writing samples, the child's cognitive resources are divided among spelling and writing. Hence, comparing a spelling test and a writing sample may give clues as to a child's spelling habits in cases in which focused attention to spelling is required and in which it is not.

As noted at the start of this chapter, we emphasized the difficulty of discussing spelling without speaking of reading and vocabulary instruction. When children are learning about grapheme–phoneme mappings for reading, they should also be learning about phoneme–grapheme mappings for spelling. Understanding how sounds are linked to letters will aid in the spelling and reading of words that are phonetically regular. Learning to spell and read words that are phonetically irregular will require some rote memorization, although it can be argued that even within sight words, there is some regularity. For instance, although the final syllable in the word "meringue" cannot be predicted by letter–sound correspondences, the first syllable can. To facilitate the cross-transfer of knowledge acquired through reading and spelling, reading and writing curricula can be augmented by deriving spelling lists from classroom reading materials. The more exposure a child has to words through reading, spelling, and writing, the stronger his or her memory trace will be for the phonological, orthographical, and semantic properties of the word and subsequent retrieval.

For English language learners, vocabulary development is especially critical, as they will have had less exposure to the English vocabulary than their English-speaking peers. Hence the learning of spelling will be more meaningful when paralleled with vocabulary instruction. The English language learner will gain an understanding of not just the orthographic and phonological properties of the word but also its semantic properties. Embedded within this vocabulary instruction could be a focus on the morphological properties of words, such as prefixes, suffixes, and roots. Morphological awareness is particularly important for understanding the organization and spelling of multisyllabic words. For instance, knowing the prefix re- or the suffix -ed facilitates the understanding of subsequent words that also share the same prefix or suffix. Hence, by way of analyzing word parts, English language learners have a way of predicting the meaning of a word, the spelling of a word, and even the pronunciation of a word. Take, for instance, the pseudoword "gloping." One can predict to some degree the phonological and semantic properties of the word based on its spelling. The -ing at the end indicates that this word is potentially a verb set in the present tense. In addition, English orthographic spelling rules would dictate that the "o" is read as a long vowel sound.

CONCLUDING REMARKS

The term "English language learning" comes with it an assumption that the average ELL speaker will have less English oral language proficiency than the average native English speaker. However, we must be careful not to use oral language proficiency as an indicator of academic literacy. Clearly, ELL students are not at a disadvantage when it comes to learning to spell in English. In fact, the same instructional practices used with native English speaking children can be applied with ELL children (Lesaux & Siegel, 2003). The key to spelling success for ELL children is the quality of instruction, as opposed to differentiated instruction. Children are not passive recipients of teaching; rather, they incorporate what is taught into their cognitive toolkit, including the use of spelling strategies that may be appropriate for a particular word, sometimes based on how the word looks and sometimes on how it sounds. What is clear is that explicit and systematic instruction within a universal program of prevention will help all children, regardless of language background, develop their spelling tools and strategies.

ACKNOWLEDGMENTS

Preparation of this chapter was supported by a grant from the Natural Sciences and Engineering Research Council of Canada to Linda S. Siegel and a fellowship from the Social Sciences and Humanities Research Council of Canada to Pauline B. Low. We wish to thank the students, principals, teachers, parents, and administrators in the North Vancouver school district and our research assistants for their assistance with the study presented in this chapter.

REFERENCES

Abu-Rabia, S., & Siegel, L. S. (2002). Reading, syntactic, orthographic, and working memory skills of bilingual Arabic–English speaking Canadian children. *Journal of Psycholinguistic Research, 31,* 661–678.

Akatmatsu, N. (1999). The effects of first language orthographic features on word recognition processing in English as a second language. *Reading and Writing: An Interdisciplinary Journal, 11,* 381–403.

Akatmatsu, N. (2003). The effects of first language orthographic features on second language reading in text. *Language Learning, 53,* 207–231.

Baddeley, A. (2000). The episodic buffer: A new component of working memory? *Trends in Cognitive Sciences, 4,* 417–423.

Baddeley, A. D., & Hitch, G. J. (1974). Working memory. In G. A. Bower (Ed.), *Recent advances in learning and motivation* (Vol. 8, pp. 47–90). New York: Academic Press.

Bialystok, E., Majumder, S., & Martin, M. M. (2003). Developing phonological awareness: Is there a bilingual advantage? *Applied Psycholinguistics, 24,* 27–44.

Bryant, B., Nunes, T., & Bindman, M. (2000). The relations between children's linguistic awareness and spelling: The case of the apostrophe. *Reading and Writing: An Interdisciplinary Journal, 12,* 253–276.

Campbell, R., & Sais, E. (1995). Accelerated metalinguistic (phonological) awareness in bilingual children. *British Journal of Developmental Psychology, 13,* 61–68.

Cassar, M., & Treiman, R. (2004). Developmental variations in spelling: Comparing typical and poor spellers. In C. A. Stone, E. R. Silliman, B. Ehren, & K. Apel (Eds.), *Handbook of language and literacy: Development and disorders* (pp. 627–660). New York: Guilford Press.

Chan, C., & Siegel, L. S. (2001). Phonological processing in reading Chinese among normally achieving and poor readers. *Journal of Experimental Child Psychology, 80,* 23–43.

Chow, B. W. Y., McBride-Chang, C., & Burgess, S. (2005). Phonological processing skills and early reading abilities in Hong Kong Chinese kindergarteners learning to read English as a second language. *Journal of Educational Psychology, 97,* 81–87.

Cummins, J. (1979). Linguistic interdependence and the educational development of bilingual children. *Review of Educational Research, 49,* 222–251.

Da Fontoura, H. A., & Siegel, L. S. (1995). Reading, syntactic, and working memory skills of bilingual Portuguese–English Canadian children. *Reading and Writing: An Interdisciplinary Journal, 7,* 139–153.

Durgunoglu, A., Nagy, W. E., & Hancin-Bhatt, B. J. (1993). Cross-language transfer of phonological awareness. *Journal of Educational Psychology, 85,* 453–465.

Geva, E., & Siegel, L. S. (2000). Orthographic and cognitive factors in the concurrent development of basic reading skills in two languages. *Reading and Writing: An Interdisciplinary Journal, 12,* 1–30.

Goldman, R., Fristoe, M., & Woodcock, R. W. (1974). *GFW sound–symbol tests.* Circle Pines, MN: American Guidance Service.

Gottardo, A., Yan, B., Siegel, L. S., & Wade-Woolley, L. (2001). Factors related to English reading performance in children with Chinese as a first language: More evidence of cross-language transfer of phonological processing. *Journal of Educational Psychology, 93,* 530–542.

Huang, H. S., & Hanley, R. (1994). Phonological awareness and visual skills in learning to read Chinese and English. *Cognition, 54,* 73–98.

Jackson, N., Chen, H., Goldsberry, L., Ahyoung, K., & Vanderwerff, C. (1999). Effects of variations in orthographic information on Asian and American readers' English text reading. *Reading and Writing: An Interdisciplinary Journal, 11,* 345–379.

Jarvis, S. (2000). Methodological rigor in the study of transfer: Identifying L1 influence in the interlanguage lexicon. *Language Learning, 50,* 245–309.

Juul, H. (2005). Grammatical awareness and the spelling of inflectional morphemes in Danish. *International Journal of Applied Linguistics, 15,* 87–112.

Lennox, C., & Siegel, L. S. (1996). The development of phonological rules and visual strategies in average and poor spellers. *Journal of Experimental Child Psychology, 62,* 60–83.

Leong, C. K. (1997). Paradigmatic analysis of Chinese word reading: Research findings and classroom practices. In C. K. Leong & R. M. Joshi (Eds.), *Cross-language studies of learning to read and spell: Phonological and orthographic processing* (pp. 378–417). Dordrecht: Kluwer Academic.

Lesaux, N., & Siegel, L. S. (2003). The development of reading in children who speak English as a second language. *Developmental Psychology, 39,* 1005–1019.

Martin, D., & Stuart-Smith, J. (1998). Exploring bilingual children's perceptions of being bilingual and biliterate: Implications for educational provision. *British Journal of Sociology of Education, 19,* 237–254.

Muter, V., & Snowling, M. (1997). Grammar and phonology predict spelling in middle childhood. *Reading and Writing: An Interdisciplinary Journal, 9,* 407–425.

Patel, T. K., Snowling, M. J., & de Jong, P. F. (2004). A cross-linguistic comparison of children learning to read in English and Dutch. *Journal of Educational Psychology, 96,* 785–797.

Perfetti, C. A. (1985). *Reading ability.* Oxford, UK: Oxford University Press.

Perfetti, C. A., & Zhang, S. (1995). Very early phonological activation in Chinese reading. *Journal of Experimental Psychology: Learning, Memory, and Cognition, 21,* 24–33.

Plaza, M., & Cohen, H. (2003). The interaction between phonological processing, syntactic awareness, and naming speed in the reading and spelling performance of first-grade children. *Brain and Cognition, 53,* 287–292.

Ryan, A., & Meara, P. (1991). The case of the invisible vowels: Arabic speakers reading English words. *Reading in a Foreign Language, 7,* 531–540.

Scanlon, D. M., & Vellutino, F. R. (1997). A comparison of the instructional backgrounds and cognitive profiles of poor, average, and good readers who were initially identified as at risk for reading failure. *Scientific Studies of Reading, 1,* 191–215.

Siegel, L. S. (1993). The development of reading. In H. W. Reese (Ed.), *Advances in child development and behavior* (Vol. 24, pp. 63–97). San Diego, CA: Academic Press.

Sprenger-Charolles, L., Siegel, L. S., & Bonnet, P. (1998). Phonological mediation and orthographic factors in reading and spelling. *Journal of Experimental Child Psychology, 68,* 134–165.

Stanovich, K. E. (1991). Changing models of reading and reading acquisition. In L. Rieben & C. A. Perfetti (Eds.), *Learning to read* (pp. 19–32). Hillsdale, NJ: Erlbaum.

Statistics Canada. (2001). *Profile of languages in Canada: English, French and many others, 2001 Census.* Ottawa, Ontario: Statistics Canada.

Tan, L. H., & Perfetti, C. A. (1998). Phonological codes as early sources of constraint in Chinese word identification: A review of current discoveries and theoretical accounts. *Reading and Writing: An Interdisciplinary Journal, 10,* 165–200.

U.S. Census Bureau. (2000). *America speaks: A demographic profile of foreign-language speakers for the United States: 2000.* Retrieved February 21, 2007, from *www.census.gov/population/www/socdemo/hh-fam/AmSpks.html.*

U.S. Census Bureau. (2003). *Census 2000 report: Language use and English-speaking ability: 2000.* Retrieved February 21, 2007, from *www.census. gov/prod/2003pubs/c2kbr-29.pdf.*

Vellutino, F. R., Fletcher, J., Snowling, M. J., & Scanlon, D. M. (2004). Specific reading disability (dyslexia): What have we learned in the past four decades? *Journal of Child Psychology and Psychiatry, 45,* 2–40.

Wang, M., & Geva, E. (2003). Spelling performance of Chinese children using English as a second language: Lexical and visual–orthographic processes. *Applied Psycholinguistics, 24,* 1–25.

Wang, M., Koda, K., & Perfetti, C. A. (2003). Alphabetic and nonalphabetic L1 effects in English word identification: A comparison of Korean and Chinese English L2 learners. *Cognition, 87,* 129–149.

Wilkinson, G. (1993). *The Wide Range Achievement Test—Third Edition.* Lutz, FL: Psychological Assessment Resources.

Yopp, H. K. (1988). The validity and reliability of phonemic awareness tests. *Reading Research Quarterly, 23,* 159–177.

Part V

ASSESSMENT OF WRITING BY STRUGGLING WRITERS

CHAPTER 12

Classroom Portfolio Assessment for Writing

MARYL GEARHART

The term *portfolio assessment* was coined during the quest for authentic alternatives to standardized testing, yet, as Murphy and Underwood (2000) discuss, the notion has a longer history in educational practice. Elementary educators, for example, have long documented children's writing development by collecting and reviewing samples of children's work (Carini, 1986; Seidel et al., 1997). Although the image of an artist's portfolio is often cited as the inspiration for portfolio assessment, that image was not the only conceptual resource for the movement. In the 1990s, widespread interest in portfolios developed from a convergence of factors, including reader response theories of literacy and literacy learning (e.g., Rosenblatt, 1978), research on the cognitive and social processes of writing development (e.g., Dyson & Freedman, 1991), whole language views of instruction (e.g., Calkins, 1986; Graves, 1983), and arguments that assessments need to support sound instructional decision making (Frederiksen & Collins, 1989; Hiebert & Calfee, 1992; Wiggins, 1989). These influences reframed the ways educators thought about writing, writing instruction, and writing assessment in both general education and special education (Camp, 1993). Eager to provide students with authentic purposes for their writing and feedback from interested readers, educators saw portfolio assessment as a way to integrate reform methods of writing instruction and assessment and to engage teachers, students, and parents in the process (Calfee & Perfumo, 1993).

Writing portfolios have been used in many ways, and this chapter provides an overview of methods of portfolio assessment for supporting and evaluating the progress of struggling writers, focusing on uses in classrooms and resource rooms.[1] Unfortunately, evidence supporting the benefits of these portfolio methods is limited; in many cases we only have teachers' impressions of the usefulness of portfolios for evaluation or the benefits of portfolios for supporting student learning and motivation. The few empirical studies that exist use nonexperimental designs without a comparison group; without a comparison group we cannot differentiate the effects of portfolio use from the effects of other components of the writing curriculum and pedagogy. Because the research base is limited, I also draw on a wider range of publications, including conceptual discussions of portfolio assessment models and practitioner cases of portfolios used for assessment of struggling writers. The goal is to sort out various models and purposes of portfolio assessment to guide educators of struggling writers in portfolio design and implementation. A theme is that clarity in purpose is essential. Portfolios are flexible ways to support and assess students' writing progress, but their breadth and versatility can limit their usefulness if teachers and students use them for unclear or competing purposes.

This chapter begins with a historical and conceptual overview of frameworks for portfolio assessment of writing as used in both general and special education. The next section is a review of uses of portfolio assessment with students who have special needs. In this section, my criteria for selecting examples were flexible and pragmatic. Along with uses of writing portfolios that are aligned with models in general education, I include specialized uses that depart from prevailing views but that have value for the assessment of students with writing disabilities or students acquiring English as a second language. For example, special education teachers may collect evidence to monitor student progress toward writing goals identified in students' individualized education programs (IEPs) without engaging students in selecting or reviewing writing samples; although an evidentiary folder may not be a "portfolio" by some definitions, it is a useful way for teachers to support and communicate their evaluations to students, parents, and other teachers (e.g., Carpenter, Ray, & Bloom, 1995; Center on Disability and Community Inclusion, 2007). What is important is that the portfolio assessment method is appropriate for a clearly specified assessment purpose that supports sound instructional decisions and benefits students as emerging writers. In the final section, I reflect on tensions and trade-offs among different portfolio assessment models for struggling writers.

FRAMEWORKS FOR PORTFOLIO ASSESSMENT: HISTORICAL AND CONCEPTUAL OVERVIEW

Definitions of portfolio assessment differ greatly (Tierney, 2002), and it is not surprising that some scholars have written on the topic with the sole purpose of conceptualizing portfolio models and practices (e.g., Calfee & Freedman, 1996). A reasonable working definition is that a student's writing portfolio contains a body of writing, and portfolio assessment is the practice of judging the body of work. Yet even this definition is limited, particularly in classrooms serving struggling writers. In addition to student writing, portfolios may contain different phases of the writing process (planning sheets, drafts, revisions that may be scaffolded with revising checklists), students' reflections on their writing products and processes, teachers' evaluations or commentaries, and parents' observations. The versatility of portfolio assessment can make understanding the approach elusive.

In general education in the 1980s and 1990s, converging influences elevated portfolio assessment as the assessment strategy of choice for many literacy educators. Next I consider the roles of the whole language movement, assessment reforms, research on writing development, and cognitive research on writing processes and strategies.

Whole Language

Influenced by the whole language movement of the 1980s (Calkins, 1986; Graves, 1983), the authors of the International Reading Association (IRA) and National Council of Teachers of English (NCTE; 1994) standards for literacy assessment argued that views of writing as rhetoric and technical skill should be replaced with views of writing as a process of composing meaning with language. The whole language movement framed the redesign of writing assessment in several ways. First, writing was portrayed as a process of establishing a purpose for written communication and drawing on resources, models, and invention to accomplish that purpose. An implication for assessment was that writers need feedback appropriate to their purposes. Second, writing was recognized as creative work that required perseverance through several phases, starting with an initial brainstorm and proceeding through drafts, revisions, and final editing. This focus on the writing process drew attention to the importance of assessing students' progress through processes as well as the progress evidenced in their completed work. Third, writing was viewed as a transaction between a writer and reader (Rosenblatt, 1978). From this perspective, assessment should not impose unilateral judgments but should instead take the form of "assessment conversations"

(Davies & Le Mahieu, 2003) between students and teachers, or between students and their peers, that provide writers the opportunity to consider readers' interpretations. Writers also need to read their own writing from the perspectives of potential readers, a position that motivates the value of self-assessment (Hillyer & Ley, 1996).

Portfolio assessment is potentially aligned with these views when portfolios contain evidence of writing processes and serve as sites for interaction and reflection (Fu, 1992; Fu & Lamme, 2002; Graves, 1992). Portfolios provide opportunities for students, teachers, and parents to review samples of writing at various phases of completion, and the transportability of portfolios allows for commentary by a range of readers across a range of contexts. Reader feedback and assessment conversations can facilitate the progress of all student writers, including English language learners and students with special needs.

Authentic Assessment

During the reforms of the 1980s and 1990s, educators expressed concern that standardized testing was misaligned with the new instructional focus on higher level thinking and problem solving (Wolf, Bixby, Glenn, & Gardner, 1991). Reformers urged the development of "authentic" assessments that captured students' competence with complex tasks valued in our society, such as varied and purposeful genres of writing rather than multiple-choice assessment tasks or writing samples produced in response to decontextualized prompts created only for purposes of assessment (Wiggins, 1989). Portfolio assessment was the most radical and ambitious evaluation strategy to emerge from this period of assessment reform, as it encompassed both authentic assessment tasks and authentic assessment practices (Camp, 1993). Visionaries argued for a "portfolio culture ... replacing the entire envelope of assessment ... with extended, iterative processes, agreeing that we are interested in what students produce when they are given access to models, criticism, and the option to revise" (Wolf, 1993, p. 221).

The 1990s spawned widespread uses of portfolios for classroom assessment in both general and special education. In this millennium, advocates continue to argue that portfolio assessment, as a method deeply integrated with daily classroom instruction, serves as an essential balance to the potentially damaging impact of testing programs on students' opportunities for authentic authoring and assessment (Dudley, 2001; Williams, 2005). Special educators and other related service providers, as well as general education teachers, recognize the value of writing samples composed for authentic purposes and audiences to complement targeted assessments of specific writing skills.

Research on Writing Development

Research on writing development draws our attention to connections between oral and written composition (Dyson & Freedman, 1991; Gearhart, 2002; Hall, 1997). If we think of writing as composing meaning with language, then in an important sense writing development begins as soon as children compose text through their stories, songs, pretend play, and everyday conversations. Children develop understandings of writing genres as they listen to others read and begin to read themselves, and, once they can write text, they continue to construct understandings of rhetorical possibilities from readers' responses. As students gain appreciation for readers' perspectives, young writers gradually shift from writer-based to reader-based texts (Flower & Hayes, 1981). An implication of research on children's writing development is that writing assessment should not focus exclusively on writing mechanics or rhetorical skills, because skills mastery does not ensure that students can compose text for a variety of purposes and a range of audiences.

Developing writers need opportunities to develop their voices as writers with the help of readers who provide formative feedback. Of course, when a student struggles with vocabulary, grammar, spelling, or punctuation, the teacher's and the student's attention are drawn to these aspects of written expression, because they interfere with fluency and comprehension. Although teachers must assess students' progress with these skills, they must also encourage and monitor students' progress with composition. Portfolio assessment may have a unique role in writing assessment, because portfolios can contain records of oral compositions (audiotapes, videotapes, dictations) to balance written evidence.

Expert–novice research has validated the whole language view of writing as a cyclical process that shifts a writer back and forth from the perspective of writer and reader (Dyson & Freedman, 1991; Flower & Hayes, 1981). Writing is a process of problem solving and metacognitive monitoring, and, although many teachers teach the writing process as a series of steps, writing processes are rarely linear. Expert writers repeatedly revise their original purpose and their approach to accomplishing that purpose as they evaluate the effectiveness of their writing. Three implications of this research for assessment are that: (1) writing processes are important to assess; (2) assessment should include formative feedback from readers at key points in the progress of a piece; and (3) students need to learn how to identify and monitor their writing goals and strategies to achieve those goals.

Studies of expert and novice writers have provided a useful framework for research on instruction for struggling writers. A well-established body of research shows that students with learning disabilities (LD) benefit from instruction that promotes self-regulation of processes for planning, drafting, and revising. For example, students with LD who are explicitly taught strategies for planning and writing essays and narratives make greater progress than students who participate in writers' workshop (or some other form of process writing instruction) without explicit writing strategies instruction (De La Paz, 1997; De La Paz & Graham, 1997; Hallenbeck, 1996; Harris, Graham, & Mason, 2006; Saddler, Moran, Graham, & Harris, 2004; Sexton, Harris, & Graham, 1998; Troia & Graham, 2002). Although these studies did not use portfolio assessment as a component of their interventions, portfolio assessment is a compatible assessment approach. Portfolios could contain samples showing students' progress with specific writing strategies, and, with the support of the portfolio evidence, students could participate in monitoring their own progress.

The portfolio assessment movement was guided as much by instructional reforms as by assessment reforms. Portfolios were not just new kinds of assessments in the old assessment paradigm; portfolio tasks reflected new interpretations of writing, and portfolio practices became ways to support the growth of young writers. With multiple influences guiding the portfolio assessment movement and the potential richness of what a portfolio can contain and how it can be used, it is hardly surprising that multiple models emerged.

MODELS OF PORTFOLIO ASSESSMENT

Sorting out the many purposes and practices of portfolio assessment is challenging, particularly for classroom portfolios that serve both instructional and assessment functions. With a plethora of portfolio models available, teachers may confuse them, and, in their efforts to sort them out, focus more on portfolio content and procedure than on purpose (Herman, Gearhart, & Aschbacher, 1996). Teachers may ask what they should include in the portfolio, how the portfolio should be organized, or who should select the writing samples. In so doing, they may lose sight of their assessment needs and the ways portfolio assessment can serve those needs, and they may neglect the role of portfolios in practices such as reflection and conferencing.

What Does a Portfolio Contain?

In a useful article written by a special education researcher in the heyday of portfolio assessment, Nolet (1992) outlines five common characteristics of portfolios. First, portfolios generally contain samples of work constructed at various points in time. Second, they include writing produced within a range of contexts that vary in resources and support. Third, many of the samples represent "authentic" work, such as letters written to real people or "published" folk tales placed in the classroom library. Fourth, portfolios contain both "raw" samples of student work and summaries or reflections on that work and on student progress (written by students, teachers, or parents). Fifth, students have some role in constructing the portfolio—perhaps in the selection of writing samples, reflections on progress, or inclusion of an autobiography of their development as young writers. These five features are fairly comprehensive and capture the early vision in many ways.

What Purposes Do Writing Portfolios Serve?

Learner-Centered Portfolios

Beyond what portfolios contain, it is essential to clarify the purpose of portfolios (Nolet, 1992). Nolet distinguishes between "instructional portfolios" and "assessment portfolios," and O'Malley and Pierce (1996) make a similar distinction for portfolios used with English language learners. Although classroom writing portfolios often serve both functions, the term *instructional portfolio* draws attention to ways that portfolios can support learning opportunities for students. Other authors have used the terms *portfolio pedagogy, portfolio culture, assessment conversations,* or *learner-centered portfolios* (Paris & Ayres, 1994; Wolf et al., 1991) to represent classroom practices that promote student ownership and engage students in reflection, revision, and conferencing with the support of their portfolios (Keefe, 1995). The emphasis is on assessment *for* learning (Davies & Le Mahieu, 2003; Shepard, 2000; Stiggins, 2002). In learner-centered-portfolio classrooms, students set goals for writing improvement, record those goals in their portfolios, periodically review the writing in their portfolios, and reflect in writing about their progress. To enhance students' understandings of evaluation criteria, teachers may involve students in the construction of rubrics and in the analysis of writing samples, including their own writing (Hillyer & Ley, 1996). Students may also make decisions about the samples that best display particular writing achievements and organize them in their showcase portfolios (Moening & Bhavnagri, 1996).

Learner-centered portfolios can serve both instructional and assessment functions, though understanding how that is possible requires us to broaden our conception of assessment. According to *Webster's New International Dictionary* (2002), someone who assesses "sits beside" and "assists in the office of judge." This definition embraces both instructional and assessment functions and draws our attention to the social contexts of assessment in which someone sits beside a student and helps him or her judge his or her own writing. Formative assessment takes precedence over summative assessment (Nolet, 1992; Shepard, 2000).

Consider, for example, the roles of working portfolios and showcase portfolios in learner-centered-portfolio classrooms (e.g., Richter, 1997; Tierney, Carter, & Desai, 1991). A *working portfolio* (sometimes referred to as a *collection*) is a folder or bin in which students maintain their ongoing classroom writing in various stages of progress; collections have instructional utility as learner-centered places where students can pull, review, or revise earlier work. A *showcase portfolio* is a set of samples from the working folder, usually selected by students with guidance from their teacher, to showcase specific accomplishments. For example, to demonstrate writing in a range of genres, a student might select a poem, a personal narrative, a persuasive letter, and a science report. To demonstrate growing competence with the writing process, a student could select two sets of drafts and revisions; to convey growth within a genre, an earlier and a later sample of that genre could be selected. Students typically organize the samples, prepare a table of contents, and then write a letter of introduction to the reader, contextualizing the collection in an autobiographical account of their development as writers.

Showcase portfolios are evidence of students' writing achievements and, in that sense, a summative assessment, but O'Malley and Pierce (1996) argue (regarding portfolio assessment for English language learners) that showcase portfolios are more appropriately viewed as learning opportunities than as assessments. Students' understandings of the criteria for showcase selections may vary, and their selections are constrained by what is available in their working folders, and thus the contents of showcase portfolios are unlikely to be sufficiently systematic to support sound inferences about students' achievements and progress.

The benefit of showcase portfolios is that students learn about the characteristics of effective writing from the teacher's guidance in choosing their selections, the opportunity to self-assess, and the conferences that consolidate their understandings of their writing development. Two studies provide support for this view, at least for students in regular classrooms. Using a pre–post design, Moening and Bhavnagri (1996) reported that, after 9 weeks of developing and using showcase portfolios, 18 first graders wrote longer pieces and made more visits to the writing center and that their writing improved in quality based on holistic scoring. In another study based on periodic interviews and analyses of children's writing over 9 months, Hillyer and Ley (1996) reported positive outcomes in two classrooms of second graders who were using portfolios for self-assessment, conferencing, and showcasing; students developed a more positive view of themselves as writers, more enjoyment of writing, and more detailed critiques of the strengths and weaknesses in their writing. Although neither of these studies included a comparison group of students who were provided similar writing instruction but without portfolios, the findings are consistent with the arguments made for the benefits of showcase portfolios.

Showcase portfolios are often used to support teacher–student conferences or student-led conferences, in which students show their best writing and progress to parents' and then the student, parents, and teacher together set goals for further improvement (e.g., Davies, Cameron, Politano, & Gregory, 1992; Gearhart, 2002; Salend, 1998). As the findings from the Hillyer and Ley (1996) study demonstrate, it is critical that conferences are more than a celebration of students' achievements. If students are to grow as writers, they need supportive and specific feedback.

Assessment Portfolios

Assessment portfolios (Nolet, 1992; O'Malley & Pierce, 1996) or evaluation portfolios (Mueller, 2006) are intentionally constructed for the purpose of gauging students' progress and achievement. They typically serve purposes of grading, requests for special services or evaluations, and promotion and transition decisions. An assessment portfolio may contain writing samples as well as additional assessments and teacher documentation that provide targeted evidence to support a particular inference or decision. When portfolios serve an assessment function, the teacher (sometimes in consultation with the student) establishes clearly specified learning goals and systematically selects materials that provide evidence of achievement or progress. Assessment constructs need to be clearly defined to help teachers identify relevant evidence and exclude irrelevant evidence, and criteria for evaluating the evidence need to be developed in conjunction with decision rules about the evidence to be used when making a particular judgment. Integrating information from diverse samples and assessments is a particular challenge for portfolio assessment. Herman, Gearhart, and Baker (1993) report, for example, that teachers who scored writing collections tended to base their overall judgments on pieces of higher quality.

Assessment portfolios are promising methods for monitoring the progress of students who are struggling with writing due to disability or fluency in English. Current policy requires multiple sources of evidence to support referrals for evaluation by various specialists, placement in special education settings, and provision of a variety of specialized services, including English language support. The IEPs of students with special needs identify the specific knowledge and competencies that students are working toward, and portfolios can provide evidence of progress (e.g., Jochum, Curran, & Reetz, 1998; Nolet, 1992; Schutt & McCabe, 1994). Portfolios also can supplement standard measures of English language development (O'Malley & Pierce, 1996). Even if the contents of the portfolio provide insufficient evidence for a given decision, portfolios can help to validate and contextualize findings from other assessments, and the student work and student reflections contained in portfolios are often more readily understood by a wider range of stakeholders (Jochum et al., 1998). Including writing samples in an assessment portfolio also serves as a means of encouraging more authentic writing goals, such as writing in multiple genres and using writing as a creative and communicative tool.

The preceding summary does not capture the many varieties of portfolio assessment models described in the literature (e.g., Carpenter et al., 1995; Jochum et al., 1998). Process portfolios, for example, contain evidence of students' approaches to the writing process (Wolf et al., 1991). Students may select artifacts from all phases of a writing assignment, including brainstorming (graphic organizers, jottings), outlining, drafting, revising, editing, and publishing. Cumulative portfolios contain evidence of writing accomplishments and progress over a period of time (often a year) and can be passed on to the next grade. This kind of portfolio highlights how portfolios can serve as archives of evidence collected over an extended period of time. There are still more models, and one soon finds that models overlap and that labels for these models are used inconsistently. Providing an exhaustive list of writing portfolio models is less important than clearly understanding the instructional and assessment purposes of portfolio assessment.

CRITERIA FOR EVALUATING WRITING ASSESSMENT PORTFOLIOS

As Herman et al. (1996) comment, "a portfolio becomes an assessment when someone weighs its contents against criteria in order to reach judgments about the value or quality of performance" (p. 28). The authors argue that evaluative criteria should be (1) appropriate to the purpose of the assessment, (2) designed to measure students' progress toward important learning goals and developmentally appropriate "conceptions of excellence" (cf. National Research Council, 2001), (3) meaningful to a range of stakeholders, (4) clear, and (5) fair.

In writing assessment, criteria are commonly organized as rubrics, though there are certainly other methods for evaluating writing (Gearhart, 2002). Rubrics are generally organized as performance continua, with higher levels more closely fitting the characteristics of effective writing (Salinger, 2002). Decisions about rubric scales and levels are determined by the kind of information needed from the judgment. Analytic, multidimensional rubrics (sometimes referred to as analytical trait rubrics; Arter & McTighe, 2001) are generally more appropriate for students with special needs and English language learners, whose competencies in different aspects of writing are uneven (Wiig, 2000). The six-trait model (Spandel, 2004) is a widely used example of an analytic scoring rubric in which the traits of ideas, organization, voice, word choice, sentence fluency, and conventions are separately evaluated. The information produced by a rubric should identify strengths and weaknesses in the writing and guide appropriate interventions to support growth. Examples of rubrics specially designed for struggling writers can be found in Jochum et al. (1998; first grade), Collins (1996; grades 5–12), Garcia (2000; English language learners), O'Malley and Pierce (1996; English language learners), and Schirmer and Bailey (2000; deaf students).

When portfolios are designed as learner-centered opportunities, rubrics communicate what is expected of quality writing and serve as resources for students as they reflect on their work in progress. If a teacher's learning objectives include developmentally appropriate mastery of particular genres, then the rubrics should contain genre-specific criteria to provide students with guidance and feedback. For many writing genres, general criteria such as "begins each paragraph with a topic sentence" may not fit. Moreover, rubric levels defined in comparative terms ("some supporting detail" or "few transition words") may leave students and teachers uncertain about these features in a particular piece of writing. Thus it is desirable to specify the characteristics of writing quality at each level in objective terms whenever possible. As an example, Wolf and Gearhart (1994) developed an analytic rubric for narrative writing that contains genre-specific dimensions (theme, character, setting, plot, and communication); for each dimension, the performance levels describe writing characteristics in ways that minimize the vagueness of terms such as *more, less, greater,* and *fewer.* The first three (of six) levels of the plot dimension are: (1) one or two events with little or no conflict; (2) beginning sequence of events but occasional out-of-sequence occurrences; events without problem, problem without resolution, or little emotional response; and (3) single, linear episode with clear beginning, middle, and end; the episode contains the four critical elements of problem, emotional response, action, and outcome.

When portfolios serve an assessment function, it is necessary to specify the evidence that supports a particular judgment—the entire collection, a subset of pieces, or a single piece? If the judgment is based on several pieces, it also is necessary to establish whether separate scores are to be assigned to each piece and then aggregated or whether one judgment is applied to the set of evidence. An added challenge is determining whose work is contained in the portfolio; portfolios contain diverse samples written and selected under different conditions of support, making inferences complex to construct and judgments difficult to interpret (Gearhart & Herman, 1998). Establishing and implementing portfolio scoring procedures is challenging, and research on the technical quality of portfolios used in large-scale assessment programs has raised concerns about the reliability and validity of portfolio judgments (Herman, 1997). Fortunately, these concerns are reduced in the context of the general education classroom or special education resource room, because teachers have a greater understanding of the history of the portfolio samples, and they also gather and utilize a variety of formative evidence regarding student progress (Wesson & King, 1996). In the classroom, the more appropriate notions of validity may be those that emphasize instructional utility as a criterion (Frederiksen & Collins, 1989).

ISSUES FOR USES OF PORTFOLIO ASSESSMENT WITH STRUGGLING WRITERS

Effective use of portfolios requires thoughtful planning, as well as the recognition that broad and fundamental issues underlie specific decisions about the design of the model (Calfee & Perfumo, 1993; Herman et al., 1996). A conceptual framework is essential and should address the following questions, which serve to frame the next section of the chapter:

1. What are the assumptions about writing and writing development for the targeted population or individual student, and how do these assumptions inform the writing goals, tasks, and criteria for evaluating student progress?
2. In what ways are portfolios serving as sites for student learning, and in what ways are they serving more traditional assessment functions? If portfolios are serving an assessment function, is the information to be used for formative or summative purposes?
3. What is contained in the writing portfolios, and who constructs them? How are the portfolios evaluated and by whom?

Portfolio Assessment for Struggling Writers

Interest in portfolio assessment for students with special needs remains strong despite the current requirements of accountability testing. Literacy educators continue to believe that most students, regardless of their challenges, can "have a *voice*" (Jones, as quoted in Walter-Thomas & Brownell, 2001, p. 226) and participate in collecting, organizing, and reflecting on their writing, as well as the collaborative design of criteria for evaluating their writing. The flexibility of portfolio assessment makes it an especially attractive option. For example, in a resource room, portfolio assessment can incorporate curriculum-based measurement (e.g., Espin, Weissenburger, & Benson, 2004) once the teacher has established clear assessment targets and tasks aligned with students' IEPs. In a heterogeneous classroom, the conceptual framework for a mainstreamed student's portfolio can meld the IEP with the learning goals of the class (Wesson & King, 1996). Portfolios can organize records of student progress, and their portability can support collaboration among special educators and general educators and among parents, students, and teachers. The rich range of information in a portfolio provides a sound basis for instructional decision making. Indeed, in a study of the role of literacy portfolios in instructional decisions for English language learners with disabilities, Rueda and Garcia (1997) found that educators (teachers, special educators, and school psychologists) made more differentiated evaluations and instructional recommendations when provided portfolio evidence compared with standardized literacy measures.

In the following examples, uses of portfolios for students with writing disabilities are clustered separately from uses for English language learners. In both sections, I consider how portfolios may serve either as sites for learning and reflection or as evidence for assessment.

Portfolio Assessment for Students with Learning Disabilities

Learner-Centered Portfolios

This section illustrates uses of learner-centered writing portfolios. Although the portfolios in the examples may serve selected assessment functions as well, the focus here is on ways that teachers can use portfolios to support student learning. The examples span several grade levels and settings, including inclusion classrooms, as well as resource rooms.

Jochum and colleagues (1998) value the capacity of portfolios to help teachers create authentic writing assessments that guide students with learning disabilities to become self-directed writers as they learn to use writing as a tool for communication. In their model, students' IEPs are sources for goal setting, and most students can reflect on their writing progress toward those goals, but they generally need guidance with both goal setting and reflection. For example, students can reflect in a pictorial response or dictate their reflections; as students begin to write reflections, sentence starters can structure the writing (Salend, 1998, suggests addi-tional strategies to support reflection).

For her third-grade special education class, Susan Richter (1997) uses writing portfolios as a context for student learning and as a supple-ment to other assessments of written language. Students establish their goals for writing improvement in consultation with Richter. The nature of students' goals differs greatly, in part because Richter aims to use port-folios to promote student ownership. For example, one student wanted to learn to "slow down" his writing and focus more on the quality of each piece and less on the number of words in each piece. Every quar-ter, students construct showcase portfolios to illustrate their progress toward their self-chosen goals. Richter confers with each student, adds a summary of their conversation to the showcase portfolio, and then invites parents to contribute comments as well. Then students, parents, and Richter review the portfolios together in a joint conference as a way to construct new insights about students' progress. Through her experi-ence with portfolios and portfolio conferencing, Richter made discover-ies about her students. She learned, for example, that her students often need more time to plan, draft, and revise their writing and that they need her ongoing assistance in critiquing their strengths and weaknesses in writing. Richter's case illustrates how portfolios can be sites for teacher learning and instructional improvement.

A resource teacher, Lisa Boerum (2000), views literacy portfolios as an equitable way to support and assess the growth of each of her sixth-grade students with learning disabilities. Boerum's approach is indi-vidualized and criterion based but within a broader framework for the growth of all students. The core components of portfolio assessment are comparable across students—goal setting, collections of ongoing work, rubrics or assessment checklists for evaluation of projects, and oppor-tunities for reflection—but each student's goals are set based on the stu-dent's IEP. Boerum describes several student cases in detail and includes samples of their work and excerpts of their reflections written as let-ters to parents and Boerum. Ryan, for example, writes (original spelling retained), " ... I usually research more than I write information. Then I don't have enough time to write things down. There for my goal for the future for a researcher is to write things down more than I research. I can accomplish my researching goal by staying on task, staying focused, and writing down information" (p. 229). Adam writes, "I felt I did not have a very good introduction in my [Egypt] project. My thesis statement did not sound good and I did not follow it in my report. I feel that I improved this skill in my Einstien report" (p. 230). Boerum's detailed cases provide compelling evidence of the value of student engagement in goal setting and ongoing reflection.

Assessment Portfolios

The complexity of writing development requires multiple kinds of measures. Portfolio assessment could provide a way to integrate multiple sources; indeed, Nolet (1992) views portfolio assessment as "a process of collecting multiple forms of data to support inferences about student performance in a skill or content area that cannot be sampled directly by a single measure" (p. 5). However, the uses of portfolio assessment described in the special education literature incorporate portfolios as one valuable component within a more comprehensive assessment system for monitoring student progress in writing (Easley & Mitchell, 2003). The following examples span both classrooms and resource rooms.

Jochum et al. (1998) provide a model of the "individual education portfolio" for students with learning disabilities to complement and validate results from standardized assessments and observation records. Portfolios, they suggest, can be particularly useful in conveying a student's strengths, often obscured by typical tests. Multiple stakeholders, including the student, special educator, general educator, related service providers, and parents, should be engaged in setting goals and monitoring each child's progress. The authors provide a useful table outlining the potential roles, as well as a sample portfolio organization and sample documents to support student reflection, teacher evaluation, and year-end summary. The teacher might include statements of the student's writing goals and evidence of progress (teacher checklists or summaries and teacher-selected writing samples), and these could be differentiated for writing content (e.g., specific genres, vocabulary usage) or writing process (evidence from different phases of the development of pieces, student reflections on process). Students could include their personal goals, samples of what they regard as their best work, and reflections on those samples or on their progress throughout the year. Parents could complete surveys or written comments on their views of the student's writing goals and progress. The model is founded on the principle that students grow as writers when members of the portfolio team work together to support students' progress (for a similar model, see Schutt & McCabe, 1994).

Rachael Hobbs (1993) describes her portfolio reporting system for middle school students in her learning disabilities resource room. As a complement to information from standardized tests and grades, portfolio evidence is organized around each student's IEP and includes students' writing, audio and video recordings of oral reading and discussions, and Hobbs's anecdotal records. The writing samples help Hobbs document progress and areas that need strengthening to share with students' classroom teachers and other professionals, and she values writing samples as direct and accessible evidence of student progress. For example, the samples of a student with epilepsy revealed that she was declining in the organization of her writing and in mechanics, and that evidence helped to convince her physician that her medication needed adjustment. Another student's struggles with handwriting and spelling became apparent in his writing samples, prompting Hobbs to provide him with a computer, an adaptation that resulted in rapid improvement in the quality of his compositions. These examples underscore the value of writing samples as accessible evidence when it becomes important to communicate with parents or professionals who are not educators.

Wesson and King (1992) recommend portfolio assessment as a complement to curriculum-based measurement (CBM), an approach that other educators endorse as well (Jones, as cited in Walter-Thomas & Brownell, 2001). A teacher using CBM administers structured writing tasks to track progress over time with specific writing skills. Although CBM tasks are not complex "authentic" tasks that provide opportunities for student voice and choice, they provide useful structured evidence that complements portfolio writing samples. With this melded approach, portfolio records of students' progress with CBM tasks could provide students with feedback on their progress and motivation to continue progressing toward their goals (Wesson & King, 1992).[2]

Portfolio assessment models in special education are essentially those used in general education, and, as a result, teachers working with students with disabilities have access to resources beyond those specialized for their fields (e.g., Danielson & Abrutyn, 1997; Easley & Mitchell, 2003; Hebert, 2001; Tierney et al., 1991). What distinguishes portfolio assessment in special education is the role of the IEP as the conceptual framework for goal setting and ongoing monitoring. How teachers conceptualize writing and writing development for struggling writers will shape their choices of learning goals, portfolio tasks, and portfolio rubrics. How teachers conceptualize the roles of students, teachers, and parents in writing development will shape the ways portfolio practices serve as assessments for learning.

Portfolios for English Language Learners

English language development is complex, and monitoring students' progress requires multiple measures of oral and written literacy, as well as ongoing assessment. Learner-centered portfolios can help students clarify their goals and monitor their progress with the support of teachers and parents. Assessment portfolios can help teachers monitor students' progress with authentic writing. The following examples illustrate both learner-centered and assessment functions.

Learner-Centered Portfolios

In an extended chapter on classroom portfolio assessment for English language learners, O'Malley and Pierce (1996) provide teachers with detailed recommendations, including suggestions for portfolio forms and conferencing techniques. The authors praise portfolio assessment as an assessment method that is deeply integrated with instruction and that therefore has greater content validity than many external measures of student achievement. Emphasis is placed on the importance of student self-assessment and its value in both oral and written language development. English language learners should have roles in developing criteria for writing in each genre, in evaluating samples of exemplary writing, and in applying criteria to their own and their peers' writing. Evaluating the portfolios as a whole also requires portfolio criteria, and the authors provide examples. When reviewing the overall portfolio, a teacher might choose to use a rubric to evaluate the student's progress or to write comments on the student's strengths and needs, along with possible instructional options to address student's needs. The authors provide samples of questions to guide reviews of completed portfolios and teacher–student or teacher–student–parent conferences.

Portfolios can be learner-centered sites for parents and teachers as well as students, as illustrated by a unique portfolio approach developed by Paratore, Hindin, Krol-Sinclair, and Duran (1999). In this study, classroom teachers maintained files of student writing, and parents constructed portfolios of their children's home literacy practices. Parents and teachers then met for parent–teacher conferences, and the researchers analyzed the conversations. The analysis showed that parents and teachers considered evidence from both the children's home portfolios and the classroom portfolios, and, through joint discussion of both sources, the participants revised their perceptions of students' competencies and opportunities to learn at home and at school. In exit interviews, teachers and parents reported feeling engaged in a more collaborative approach to children's literacy development.

Assessment Portfolios

Moya and O'Malley (1994) describe a portfolio assessment model that provides a systematic assessment tool for students of English as a second language. Although the authors are concerned with portfolios for assessment at the school or district level, their recommendations have relevance to assessment portfolios in the classroom. Moya and O'Malley identify a number of principles for portfolio assessment design that suggest they view portfolios as vehicles for integrating multiple sources of information; the portfolios should be comprehensive (containing multiple kinds of evidence); predetermined and systematic; informative to all stakeholders; tailored to meet the needs of all stakeholders; and authentic (evidence of oral and written language development from a range of settings and for a range of purposes). Six steps are recommended for thoughtful design of a model that is well aligned with learning goals, instruction, and other assessments (also see Herman et al., 1996):

1. Identify purpose and focus.
2. Plan portfolio contents.
3. Design portfolio analysis.
4. Prepare for instruction.
5. Plan verification of procedures.
6. Implement the model.

There are resources for assessing students' progress with English literacy that have not been incorporated in portfolio assessment but certainly could be. Garcia and his colleagues, for example, developed the Authentic Literacy Assessment (ALA) to assess bilingual students' progress with writing in English, Spanish, and Chinese in a dual-immersion elementary school (Garcia, 2000). The assessments are designed in the tradition of direct writing assessment; students write to prompts, and then teachers score their writing with an analytic rubric that contains dimensions for topic, organization, style and voice, and conventions. The rubrics (provided in Garcia, 2000) span grades 1–5 to enable teachers to evaluate students' progress repeatedly across grade levels. Portfolios could be very useful places to maintain records of student scores, samples of students' responses, and comments from teachers, students, and parents.

PORTFOLIO ASSESSMENT: ADVANTAGES AND DISADVANTAGES FOR STUDENTS WITH SPECIAL NEEDS

Portfolio assessment is an inviting approach to writing assessment for students with special needs. As an archive of students' accomplishments, portfolios can be resources for student goal setting and self-assessment and for teacher and parent participation in students' journeys toward more effective writing. Students, teachers, and parents can have roles in selecting and reviewing key samples of writing, reflecting on areas of strength and weakness, and identifying needs for further growth. There may be other benefits, too. Because portfolios contain writing samples and not just students' scores on standardized assessments, portfolios encourage teachers to engage students of all abilities in writing for authentic audiences and purposes. Opportunities for authentic writing, accompanied with feedback from interested readers, can help students with special needs develop their voices as young writers who truly own their written work. For students struggling with written expression, the flexible design of portfolios provides a way to document students' progress with oral as well as written composition; recordings or dictations can represent progress in making meaning with language as complements to written assessments.

Although the research base is thin, the voices of portfolio advocates are compelling. Portfolio assessment has promise for students with writing challenges, yet the very flexibility and versatility of portfolio assessment may render the approach confusing to understand and somewhat daunting to implement. There are many models in general and special education—California teachers in the Bay Area Writing Project listed 34 different uses for writing portfolio assessment (Carpenter et al., 1995)! The risk with all these options is that teachers may find it difficult to identify an appropriate model for particular instructional or assessment purposes or may use a portfolio model for an inappropriate purpose. As a simple example, if students are asked to select pieces that illustrate their best work for a showcase portfolio, those pieces should not be used as evidence of progress, because a student's personal narrative in September cannot be easily compared with a folk tale in November or a poem in February. Even proponents of portfolio assessment raise concerns about the challenges of portfolio design and implementation and the risks "when bad things happen to good ideas" (Dudley, 2001, p. 19).

As discussed in this chapter, the distinction between learner-centered and assessment portfolios helps to sort out the confusion. Nevertheless, because portfolios often serve both functions in the classroom, there are acknowledged tensions between them (Davies & Le Mahieu, 2003; Tierney et al., 1998). At one pole of this tension, the need for summative measures propels portfolio assessment toward standardization of objectives, content, and criteria, reducing learner-centered opportunities for student initiative and authentic reader response (Davies & Le Mahieu, 2003). Conventional assessment paradigms assume an outside perspective and press for standardization of tasks and reporting, an essential element in establishing reliability and a benefit for communication of information across contexts, but a potential limitation for individualized evaluation and support. Conversely, attempts to enhance the learning value of portfolios press for flexible design to support each student's emerging authorship and voice. Learner-centered paradigms assume a contextualized perspective and value student-initiated writing and assessment conversations that provide individualized feedback and guidance. Although learner-centered portfolios do serve assessment functions if we view assessment as formative, as "sitting beside" the young writer, assessments negotiated in teacher–student conferences are highly contextualized in ways that can make it difficult for other stakeholders to interpret inferences and decisions. The tensions between the learning and assessment functions of portfolios can never be fully resolved, but they can be managed if teachers recognize these potential conflicts in purposes as they design and use portfolios in their classrooms.

Certainly the portfolio literature has its cautionary tales, but it is important to recognize that many of the published concerns focus on the technical issues of large-scale portfolio assessment, not on classroom implementation of portfolios. One issue in the large-scale literature, for example, is that of whose work is contained in a portfolio that travels from the classroom to the scoring table (Gearhart & Herman, 1998). Portfolios contain student writing composed in the social life of the classroom, and, because different students inevitably receive different kinds and levels of assistance, samples of writing in one portfolio are not likely to be comparable to samples in another portfolio as evidence of student achievement. A related issue is that of whose voice is represented in the selections. Portfolio samples can be organized by the student, teacher, or both to represent a student's achievements, and the selections may differ, perhaps because of differing understandings of the selection and scoring criteria or perhaps because different kinds of writing are available for the selections. Additional issues pertain to scoring—the challenge of evaluating a collection of diverse kinds of writing and the conundrum of scoring writing processes based on writing products (Gearhart & Wolf, 1997). All of these challenges to reliability of portfolio scoring and validity of results are thorny in the large-scale context but of less concern in the classroom context, in which teachers have access to multiple sources of evidence to ground their judgments. Nevertheless, teachers may need to build their assessment expertise to address issues as they become relevant to particular assessment purposes. As Nolet (1992) suggests, portfolio assessment is a "paradigm that is technically and theoretically much more complicated than procedures previously used in classrooms" (p. 18).

This chapter has reviewed models of portfolio assessment for students with learning disabilities and English language learners. We have discussed learner-centered ways in which portfolios can support individualized goal setting, reflection, and progress, as well as assessment models in which portfolios complement more standardized writing assessments. Up to this point, I have been silent about the thorny issue of feasibility, and of course it must be acknowledged. Portfolios, whatever their function and however they are used, do require considerable time from teachers, students, and parents, as well as special resources (Jones as cited in Walter-Thomas & Brownell, 2001; Wesson & King, 1996). Time is needed for organizing and reviewing material in the portfolios and for written reflections, evaluation, and regular conferencing; materials and space are required to maintain the portfolios. These challenges may be especially notable in inclusive classrooms in which teachers are supporting a large number of students with a considerable range of needs. Yet any innovation requires time and commitment, and the issue is whether portfolio assessment benefits struggling writers and all those who support them. The many authors cited in this article express great enthusiasm and deep belief in the capacity of portfolios to support their student writers. For these educators, writing portfolios are a worthwhile burden.

NOTES

1. This chapter focuses on classroom and resource room applications. Murphy and Underwood (2000) provide an extensive and scholarly review of research on portfolio programs developed by schools, districts, and states for purposes of accountability, although their book does not address specific issues concerning the large-scale assessment of struggling writers.

2. Berninger and Stage (1996) provide examples of specific assessments that might be useful in portfolio assessment, although the assessments are not described as curriculum-based measurement. A teacher might collect repeated process measures of handwriting fluency, defined by Berninger and Stage as the number of letters that can be written legibly in a particular amount of time. Repeated spelling assessments are another option; struggling writers generally have greater difficulty than general education students coordinating spelling (and punctuation and grammar) with composing meaning, and it is therefore important to track students' spelling progress. "Compositional fluency" is another potential measure; it is the number of words written to a prompt within a specified time without concern for mechanics.

REFERENCES

Arter, J., & McTighe, J. (2001). *Scoring rubrics in the classroom: Using performance criteria for assessing and improving student performance.* Thousand Oaks, CA: Corwin Press.

Berninger, V. W., & Stage, S. A. (1996). Assessment and intervention for writing problems of students with learning disabilities or behavioral disabilities. *British Columbia Journal of Special Education, 20*(2), 5–23.

Boerum, L. J. (2000). Developing portfolios with learning disabled students. *Reading and Writing Quarterly: Overcoming Learning Difficulties, 26,* 211–238.

Calfee, R. C., & Freedman, S. (1996). Classroom writing portfolios: Old, new, borrowed, blue. In R. C. Calfee & P. Perfumo (Eds.), *Writing portfolios in the classroom: Policy and practice, promise and peril* (pp. 3–26). Mahwah, NJ: Erlbaum.

Calfee, R. C., & Perfumo, P. (1993). Student portfolios: Opportunities for a revolution in assessment. *Journal of Reading, 36,* 532–537.

Calkins, L. (1986). *The art of teaching writing.* Portsmouth, NH: Heinemann.

Camp, R. (1993). The place of portfolios in our changing views of writing assessment. In R. E. Bennett & W. C. Ward (Eds.), *Construction versus choice in cognitive measurement: Issues in constructed response, performance testing, and portfolio assessment* (pp. 183–212). Hillsdale, NJ: Erlbaum.

Carini, P. F. (1986). Building from children's strengths. *Journal of Education, 168*(3), 13–24.

Carpenter, C. D., Ray, M. S., & Bloom, L. A. (1995). Portfolio assessment: Opportunities and challenges. *Intervention in School and Clinic, 31*(1), 34–41.

Center on Disability and Community Inclusion. *Portfolios and special education: Building a better IEP.* Retrieved March 29, 2007, from *www.uvm.edu/~cdci/programs/assess/why/interest/port.html.*

Collins, J. E. (1996). *Strategies for struggling writers.* New York: Guilford Press.

Danielson, C., & Abrutyn, L. (1997). *An introduction to using portfolios in the classroom.* Alexandria, VA: Association for Supervision and Curriculum Development.

Davies, A., Cameron, C., Politano, C., & Gregory, K. (1992). *Together is better: Collaborative assessment, evaluation and reporting.* Winnipeg, Manitoba, Canada: Portage & Main.

Davies, A., & Le Mahieu, P. (2003). Assessment for learning: Reconsidering portfolios and research evidence. In M. Segers, F. Dochy, & E. Cascallar (Eds.), *Innovation and change in professional education. Optimising new modes of assessment: In search of qualities and standards* (pp. 141–169). Dordrecht, Netherlands: Kluwer.

De La Paz, S. (1997). Strategy instruction in planning: Teaching students with learning and writing disabilities to compose persuasive and expository essays. *Learning Disability Quarterly, 20,* 227–248.

De La Paz, S., & Graham, S. (1997). Strategy instruction in planning: Effects on the writing performance and behavior of students with learning difficulties. *Exceptional Children, 63,* 167–181.

Dudley, M. (2001). Portfolio assessment: When bad things happen to good ideas. *English Journal, 90*(6), 19–20.

Dyson, A. H., & Freedman, S. W. (1991). Writing. In J. Flood, D. Lapp, J. R. Squire, & J. M. Jensen (Eds.), *Handbook of research on teaching the English language arts* (2nd ed., pp. 967–992). Mahwah, NJ: Erlbaum.

Easley, S. D., & Mitchell, K. (2003). *Portfolios matter: What, where, when, why and how to use them.* Markham, Ontario, Canada: Pembroke.

Espin, C. A., Weissenburger, J. W., & Benson, B. J. (2004). Assessing the writing performance of students in special education. *Exceptionality, 12,* 55–66.

Flower, L., & Hayes, J. R. (1981). A cognitive process theory of writing. *College English*, *44*, 765–777.

Frederiksen, J. R., & Collins, A. (1989). A systems approach to educational testing. *Educational Researcher*, *18*(9), 27–32.

Fu, D. L. (1992). One bilingual child talks about his portfolio. In D. H. Graves & B. S. Sunstein (Eds.), *Portfolio portraits* (pp. 171–184). Portsmouth, NH: Heinemann.

Fu, D. L., & Lamme, L. (2002). Assessment through conversation. *Language Arts*, *79*, 241–250.

Garcia, E. (2000). *Student cultural diversity: Understanding and meeting the challenge* (3rd ed.). Boston: Houghton Mifflin.

Gearhart, M. (2002). Classroom writing assessment. In B. J. Guzzetti (Ed.), *Literacy in America; An encyclopedia of history, theory, and practice* (pp. 66–72). Santa Barbara, CA: ABC CLIO.

Gearhart, M., & Herman, J. L. (1998). Portfolio assessment: Whose work is it? Issues in the use of classroom assignments for accountability. *Educational Assessment*, *5*, 41–56.

Gearhart, M., & Wolf, S. A. (1997). Issues in portfolio assessment: Assessing writing processes from their products. *Educational Assessment*, *4*, 265–296.

Graves, D. H. (1983). *Writing: Teachers and children at work*. Portsmouth, NH: Heinemann.

Graves, D. H. (1992). Help students learn to read their portfolios. In D. H. Graves & B. S. Sunstein (Eds.), *Portfolio portraits* (pp. 85–95). Portsmouth, NH: Heinemann.

Hall, N. (1997). The development of young children as authors. In V. Edwards & D. Corson (Eds.), *Encyclopedia of language and education* (Vol. 2, pp. 69–76). Dordrecht, Netherlands: Kluwer.

Hallenbeck, M. J. (1996). The cognitive strategy in writing: Welcome relief for adolescents with learning disabilities. *Learning Disabilities Research and Practice*, *11*, 107–119.

Harris, K. R., Graham, S., & Mason, L. H. (2006). Improving the writing, knowledge, and motivation of struggling young writers: Effects of self-regulated strategy development with and without peer support. *American Educational Research Journal*, *43*, 295–340.

Hebert, E. A. (2001). *The power of portfolios: What children can teach us about learning and assessment*. San Francisco: Jossey-Bass.

Herman, J. (1997). *Large-scale assessment in support of school reform: Lessons in the search for alternative measures*. CSE Technical Report 446, University of California, Los Angeles.

Herman, J. L., Gearhart, M., & Aschbacher, P. R. (1996). Developing portfolios for classroom assessment: Technical design and implementation issues. In R. C. Calfee & P. Perfumo (Eds.), *Writing portfolios in the classroom: Policy and practice, promise and peril* (pp. 27–59). Hillsdale, NJ: Erlbaum.

Herman, J. L., Gearhart, M., & Baker, E. L. (1993). Assessing writing portfolios: Issues in the validity and meaning of scores. *Educational Assessment*, *1*, 201–224.

Hiebert, F., & Calfee, R. C. (1992). Assessment of literacy: From standardized tests to performances and portfolios. In A. E. Fastrup & S. J. Samuels (Eds.), *What research says about reading instruction* (pp. 70–100). Newark, DE: International Reading Association.

Hillyer, J., & Ley, T. C. (1996). Portfolios and second graders' self-assessments of their development as writers. *Reading Improvement, 33,* 148–159.

Hobbs, R. (1993). Portfolio use in a learning disabilities resource room. *Reading and Writing Quarterly: Overcoming Learning Difficulties, 9,* 249–261.

International Reading Association and National Council of Teachers of English. (1994). *Standards for the assessment of reading and writing.* Newark, DE, Urbana, IL: International Reading Association and National Council of Teachers of English.

Jochum, J., Curran, C., & Reetz, L. (1998). Creating individual educational portfolios in written language. *Reading and Writing Quarterly: Overcoming Learning Difficulties, 14,* 283–306.

Keefe, C. H. (1995). Portfolios: Mirrors of learning. *Teaching Exceptional Children, 27,* 66–67.

Moening, A., & Bhavnagri, N. P. (1996). Effects of the showcase writing portfolio process on first graders' writing. *Early Education and Development, 7,* 179–199.

Moya, S. S., & O'Malley, M. (1994). A portfolio model for ESL. *Journal of Educational Issues of Language Minority Students, 13,* 13–36.

Mueller, J. (2006). *Authentic assessment toolbox: Portfolios.* Retrieved March 30, 2007, from *jonathan.mueller.faculty.noctrl.edu/toolbox/portfolios.htm.*

Murphy, S., & Underwood, T. (2000). *Portfolio practices: Lessons from schools, districts and states.* Norwood, MA: Christopher-Gordon.

National Research Council. (2001). *Knowing what students know: The science and design of educational assessment.* Washington, DC: National Academy Press.

Nolet, V. (1992). Classroom-based measurement and portfolio assessment. *Diagnostique, 18,* 5–26.

O'Malley, J. M., & Pierce, L. V. (1996). *Authentic assessment for English language learners: Practical approaches for teachers.* Boston: Addison-Wesley.

Paratore, J. R., Hindin, A., Krol-Sinclair, B., & Duran, P. (1999). Discourse between teachers and Latino parents during conferences based on home literacy portfolios. *Education and Urban Society, 32,* 58–82.

Paris, S. G., & Ayres, L. R. (1994). *Becoming reflective students and teachers with portfolios and authentic assessment.* Washington, DC: American Psychological Association.

Richter, S. E. (1997). Using portfolios as an additional means of assessing written language in a special education classroom. *Teaching and Change, 5*(1), 58–70.

Rosenblatt, L. (1978). Towards a transactional theory of reading. *Journal of Reading Behavior, 1,* 31–51.

Rueda, R., & Garcia, E. (1997). Do portfolios make a difference for diverse students? The influence of type of data on making instructional decisions. *Learning Disabilities Research and Practice, 12*, 114–122.

Saddler, B., Moran, S., Graham, S., & Harris, K. R. (2004). Preventing writing difficulties: The effects of planning strategy instruction on the writing performance of struggling writers. *Exceptionality, 12*, 3–18.

Salend, S. J. (1998). Using portfolios to assess student performance. *Teaching Exceptional Children, 31*(2), 36–43.

Salinger, T. (2002). Writing assessment. In B. J. Guzzetti (Ed.), *Literacy in America: An encyclopedia of history, theory, and practice* (pp. 688–693). Santa Barbara, CA: ABC CLIO.

Schirmer, B. F., & Bailey, J. (2000). Writing assessment rubric: An instructional approach for struggling writers. *Teaching Exceptional Children, 33*(1), 52–58.

Schutt, P. W., & McCabe, V. M. (1994). Portfolio assessment for students with learning disabilities. *Journal of Learning Disabilities, 5*, 81–85.

Seidel, S., Walters, J., Kirby, E., Olff, N., Powell, K., & Scripp, L. (1997). *Portfolio practices: Thinking through the assessment of children's work.* Washington, DC: National Education Association.

Sexton, M., Harris, K. R., & Graham, S. (1998). Self-regulated strategy development and the writing process: Effects on essay writing and attributions. *Exceptional Children, 64*, 295–311.

Shepard, L. S. (2000). The role of assessment in a learning culture. *Educational Researcher, 29*(7), 4–14.

Spandel, V. (2004). *Creating young writers: Using the six traits to enrich writing process in primary classrooms.* Boston: Pearson Education Inc.

Stiggins, R. J. (2002). Assessment crisis: The absence of assessment FOR learning. *Phi Delta Kappan, 83*, 758–765.

Tierney, R. (2002). Portfolios. In B. J. Guzzetti (Ed.), *Literacy in America; An encyclopedia of history, theory, and practice* (pp. 443–445). Santa Barbara, CA: ABC CLIO.

Tierney, R., Clark, C., Fenner, L., Herter, R., Simpson, C. S., & Wiser, B. (1998). Portfolios: Assumptions, tensions, and possibilities. *Reading Research Quarterly, 33*, 474–486.

Tierney, R. J., Carter, M. A., & Desai, L. E. (1991). *Portfolio assessment in the classroom.* Norwood, MA: Christopher-Gordon.

Troia, G. A., & Graham, S. (2002). The effectiveness of a highly explicit, teacher-directed strategy instruction routine: Changing the writing performance of students with learning disabilities. *Journal of Learning Disabilities, 35*, 290–305.

Walter-Thomas, C., & Brownell, M. T. (2001). Bonnie Jones: Using student portfolios effectively. *Intervention in School and Clinic, 36*, 225–229.

Webster's third new international dictionary of the English language unabridged. (2002). Springfield, MA: Merriam-Webster.

Wesson, C. L., & King, R. P. (1992). The role of curriculum-based measurement in portfolio assessment. *Diagnostique, 18*, 27–37.

Wesson, C. L., & King, R. P. (1996). Portfolio assessment and special education. *Teaching Exceptional Children, 28*(2), 44–48.

Wiggins, G. (1989). Teaching to the (authentic) test. *Educational Leadership*, *48*(7), 41–47.

Wiig, E. H. (2000). Authentic and other assessments of language disabilities: When is fair fair? *Reading and Writing Quarterly: Overcoming Learning Difficulties*, *18*, 179–210.

Williams, B. T. (2005). Standardized students: The problems with writing for tests instead of people. *Journal of Adolescent and Adult Literacy*, *49*, 152–158.

Wolf, D. P. (1993). Assessment as an episode of learning. In R. Bennett & W. Ward (Eds.), *Construction versus choice in cognitive measurement: Issues in constructed response, performance testing, and portfolio assessment* (pp. 213–240). Hillsdale, NJ: Erlbaum.

Wolf, D. P., Bixby, J., Glenn, J., & Gardner, H. (1991). To use their minds well: Investigating new forms of student assessment. *Review of Research in Education*, *17*, 31–74.

Wolf, S. A., & Gearhart, M. (1994). Writing what you read: Assessment as a learning event. *Language Arts*, *71*, 425–444.

CHAPTER 13

Assessment of Student Writing with Curriculum-Based Measurement

Betty J. Benson
Heather M. Campbell

Lee is an entering sixth-grade student identified by her fifth-grade teacher as needing additional assistance in writing. Lee has a history of struggling with writing; she has consistently scored below other students in her class on standardized tests and each year falls farther behind her peers. Her progress in most content areas has been affected by her difficulty with writing. Lee's current teacher has experienced frustration in assessing the writing proficiency of all her students. She is looking for an assessment procedure that will provide her with indicators of writing proficiency and that will allow her to track and measure student progress in her writing curriculum. She would also like to use assessment results as one means of monitoring the effectiveness of her teaching.

One of the most challenging skills to help students develop is the skill of writing. As illustrated in Lee's composite case study, student work in many content areas can be affected by poor writing skill development, especially as the demands of writing increase with each grade level. There are high-quality, research-based writing instruction methods and strategies for struggling young writers (see the chapters on writing instruction in this book); however, determining sound methods of writing assessment can be a challenging task for the classroom teacher.

In this chapter we discuss some of the challenges associated with the assessment of writing, including those issues that are of special interest to classroom teachers who teach writing. We review one research-based method of assessment, curriculum-based measurement (CBM), that has yielded valid and reliable indicators of writing performance. Using Lee's case to guide our discussion, we illustrate how these indicators can be used by classroom teachers to assess writing proficiency, to support instructional decisions, and to monitor student progress in the curriculum. In addition, practical, step-by-step information is provided to guide the classroom teacher in implementing CBM assessment procedures.

ASSESSMENT OF WRITING

The assessment of writing is a challenging task for several reasons. First, defining proficiency in writing is itself difficult. Proficient writing has been conceptualized from a number of perspectives: as a successful blending of complex, goal-directed thinking processes (Flower & Hayes, 1981); as the effective use of self-monitoring strategies (Gersten & Baker, 2001); and as a demonstration of language skills (Mellon, 1969). Fundamentally, writing is communication involving the interaction between writer, text, and audiences (Moran, 1987); however, it is the satisfactory integration of written language components that supports successful written communication. In a 1984 review and synthesis of language theories, Isaacson identified five core components of the written domain: (1) *fluency*; (2) *syntactic maturity*, the production of complex sentences; (3) *vocabulary*; (4) *content*, the organization of thought, originality, and style; and (5) *conventions*, the mechanical aspects of writing (1984, p. 103). Of course, other skills, such as idea development, planning, and revision, also play an important role in proficient writing. As a result, competent writing is a multifaceted integration of skills and processes, many of which are difficult to quantify.

Therefore, a second difficulty with writing assessment is deciding how these components of writing can be measured (Deno & Fuchs, 1987). Traditionally, two methods of assessment have emerged: indirect methods and direct methods (Breland, Camp, Jones, Morris, & Rock, 1987). Indirect methods of assessment generally follow a multiple-choice format and require students to identify errors, correct errors in text, or make judgments about the correctness of text written by someone else. The strengths of indirect writing assessment methods include ease in scoring and allowing large-scale comparisons across student populations. Indirect methods of assessment also have strong interscorer agreement (Charney, 1984) and internal consistency that designers of norm-referenced tests cite as evidence of their reliability (Isaacson, 1984). However, indirect methods have been criticized for their lack of content validity, narrow focus, and weak reflection of authentic writing demands (Bridgeman & Carlson, 1984; Yancey, 1999). Indirect methods probably are more attuned to the background knowledge that students bring to the task rather than to students' application of that knowledge to actual writing tasks (Moran, 1987). As a result, indirect methods are limited in what they can assess and how the assessment results can be applied to real classroom situations.

On the other hand, direct methods of writing assessment require students to produce an original piece of writing, usually in response to a prompt (Miller & Crocker, 1990). One strength of this method is that students can actually be involved in the writing process and create a product that is reflective of that process. However, scoring reliability can be difficult to establish in direct writing assessment, though reliability can be increased by controlling the systematic error associated with variability in how writing prompts are selected, administered, and scored (Raymond & Houston, 1990). What this means for the classroom teacher is that reliability can be increased by establishing and following consistent procedures for both the administration and the scoring of writing samples.

A third difficulty with writing assessment is deciding which of the components of writing can be reliably and validly measured and which components should be measured (Deno & Fuchs, 1987). In other words, measures must be chosen that produce results that are consistent, highly correlated with other assessments known to measure writing proficiency, and informative. Because writing is such a complex process, making the choice about what to measure is especially difficult. Basic proficiency in writing is demonstrated when students are able to generate a product that adheres to conventions of spelling, punctuation, capitalization, and formatting (Odell, 1981). Certainly, mastery of conventions does not indicate writing competency per se (Charney, 1984); however, the successful demonstration of such basic skills may be an important indicator of competency. For students at the elementary level, an assessment of these basic building blocks of writing provides one indication of proficiency level in these skill areas, as well as a baseline measure of competency in global writing performance. The assessment of these emerging skills is a starting point for drawing conclusions about individuals' writing—conclusions that can affect instructional decisions and outcomes for students.

Fourth and finally, writing assessment is problematic because most available writing measures are not tied to a specific curriculum. Consequently, teachers tend to rely on their own observations of student performance, rather than on assessment data, to make instructional decisions. Unfortunately, teacher observation may be neither a reliable nor a valid method for making instructional and curricular decisions because it tends to be biased (Deno, 1985). Although good instructional decisions are important for all students, these decisions are even more critical for those who struggle with the curriculum, fail to make progress, and ultimately fall behind their peers. Thus finding a direct measurement procedure that is tied to a teacher's own writing curriculum and that is simple to use and easy to interpret is vital. One such procedure is CBM, which is a standardized way to quantify student performance, track student progress in developing general writing proficiency, and inform classroom instruction (Deno, 1989).

> Lee's teacher is using research-based instructional methods in her classroom; to measure Lee's progress and the effectiveness of her teaching, she decides to use a direct method of writing assessment that can act as an indicator of Lee's general writing proficiency. She chooses CBM as that method and collects baseline data on three 5-minute narrative writing prompts. The prompts are scored for correct minus incorrect word sequences. Lee's scores are 30, 25, and 28 (see Figure 13.1, box 1). The teacher plots these baseline scores on a graph, drawing a solid vertical line from the top to the bottom of the graph to separate baseline data from the first phase of instruction (see Figure 13.1, box 2). The teacher notices that Lee's baseline data indicate that she is performing well below the average for other sixth-grade students in this class.

OVERVIEW OF CBM

CBM, a formative assessment tool that acts as a "vital sign" or "indicator" of proficiency in basic skill areas, was developed by Stan Deno and his colleagues at the University of Minnesota (Deno, 1985). He describes CBM as a method to measure student progress that is (1) reliable and valid, (2) simple and efficient to administer and score, (3) easily understood by parents, students, and teachers, and (4) inexpensive to use. In the current era of No Child Left Behind, in which all students must participate in high-stakes accountability testing, CBM is one evidence-based innovation that may serve to help teachers identify students who struggle with writing proficiency and monitor those students' progress toward meeting rigorous educational standards. CBM procedures have been implemented by several school districts to help them collect data to use within a responsiveness-to-intervention (RTI) model for identification of learning disabilities, a centerpiece of the 2004 Individuals with Disabilities Education Improvement Act (e.g., Fuchs, Mock, Morgan, & Young, 2003; Marston, 2005). In fact, the Heartland Area Educational Agency and Minneapolis Public Schools have both utilized CBM progress moni-

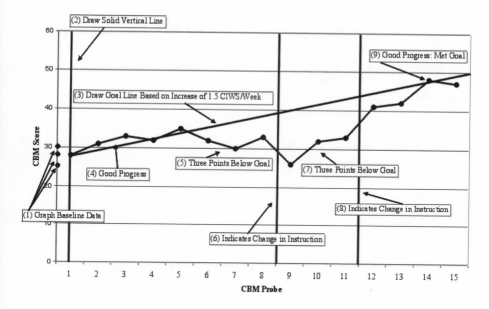

FIGURE 13.1. Writing CBM progress monitoring graph.

toring for more than 10 years as one aspect of their problem-solving models, designed to more accurately identify students in need of remedial services and special education (Marston, 2005; Mellard, Byrd, Johnson, Tollefson, & Boesche, 2004).

The administration of CBM writing measures is simple. Students are given a prompt (typically a story prompt) and are asked to write a composition based on that prompt. Students are given 30 seconds to think about the response they are going to write and then 3–7 minutes (depending on grade level) to generate the text. Students are instructed to continue writing for the entire time and to stop immediately when time is called. The teacher then scores the writing samples using a scoring system created and refined by researchers at the University of Minnesota. This CBM score should be considered an "indicator" of general proficiency in writing, alerting a teacher to the need for further skill development for students who score significantly below their peers or who fail to make adequate progress.

The technical adequacy of several types of CBM scoring methods have been investigated; research describing these methods follows this section, which describes the scoring procedures. The scoring process for CBM procedures is straightforward and follows a series of scoring rules (see Appendix 13.1). These rules provide teachers with a consistent scoring framework that supports reliability. Scoring begins when the teacher reads the entire sample through once, marking the end of each sentence with a vertical line. If correct punctuation is not used, the teacher marks the end of a logical phrase containing a subject and a verb. Depending on grade level, the teacher may then score a writing sample for words written (WW), words spelled correctly (WSC), correct word sequences (CWS), incorrect word sequences (IWS), or correct minus incorrect word sequences (CIWS). WW is simply the total number of words a student writes in the allotted time period, and WSC is the number of correctly spelled words. However, CWS consists of two adjacent words that are "acceptable," within the context of the phrase, to a native speaker of English (Videen, Deno, & Marston, 1982). Acceptable words are those words that are spelled correctly, used correctly (e.g., correct verb tense), and follow the scoring rules that appear in Appendix 13.1 at the end of this chapter. Unacceptable words are underlined as the teacher reads through the sample.

After the first reading, the teacher continues the scoring and marks an upward-facing carat between all acceptable adjacent words. The teacher also reviews the underlined unacceptable words and marks a downward-facing carat between adjacent words that are not acceptable. The final count of upward-facing carats is CWS; the final count of downward-facing carats is IWS. CIWS can then be determined. After scoring, the teacher plots the totals on a graph and uses the graph for progress monitoring. CBM scoring procedures are most easily understood by reviewing a sample of student writing. What follows is an illustration of how the teacher scored Lee's third baseline writing prompt and reached a score of 28 CIWS (see Figure 13.1, box 1).

> Lee's teacher uses CBM scoring procedures to determine the data points for Lee's baseline. She scores the 5-minute writing samples. She reads through the samples once and identifies each logical sentence with a vertical line; she also underlines incorrectly used words. She then marks CWS and IWS and calculates CIWS. Lee has 47 CWS and 19 IWS on her third baseline writing sample; this results in 28 CIWS. This score is plotted on the graph. The writing sample and the teacher's scoring follow:
>
> ^ It ^ was ^ a ^ dark ^ and ^ stormy ^ night^. | ^ The ^ lights ∨ _was_ ∨ out ^ all ^ over ^ the ^ city^. | ^ It ^ was ∨ _quite_ ∨ | ∨ it ^ was ∨ _to_ ∨ _quite_∨. | ^ I ^ was ^ in ^ my ∨ _palice_ ∨ car ^ when ^ across ^ the ^ radio ^ came ^ a ^ call ^ for ^ help^ . | ^ The ∨ _dispacsker_ ∨ _tole_ ∨ me ^ what ^ was ^ going ^ on ∨ | ∨ after ^ that ^ it ^ was ^ as ^ if ^ the ∨ _flushing_ ∨ red ^ lights ^ had ^ turned ^ on ∨ _themselfs_ ∨. |

On the graph the teacher draws a goal line corresponding to a weekly increase of 1.5 correct minus incorrect word sequences for the 15-week instructional period (see Figure 13.1, box 3). The goal line begins with Lee's median score from the baseline data, which is 28. This goal line will enable the teacher to monitor whether Lee is making satisfactory progress as her scores on the weekly writing prompts are plotted. The teacher will use the data to make informed decisions about instruction. If Lee scores below the goal line for 3 consecutive weeks, the teacher will change the instructional approach. If Lee scores above the goal line for 6 consecutive weeks, the teacher will raise the goal.

Students who struggle with writing proficiency may be monitored weekly or monthly during the course of a school year, and their scores can be graphed. After three baseline writing prompts are scored, teachers and students set a goal line based on typical student progress for that particular CBM scoring procedure and grade level. Involving students in the goal-setting process has been shown to increase student performance (Fuchs, Fuchs, & Deno, 1985), as well as to help students better understand their goals (Fuchs, Butterworth, & Fuchs, 1989). If a student continually scores above the goal line, the teacher may raise the goal. If the student's scores fall below the goal line three consecutive times, the teacher should implement a change in instruction for that student based on writing sample scoring information as well as information from other writing samples collected in class. For example, if the student seems to struggle with organization, a strategy could be taught to help him or her set goals for improving organization and monitoring his or her use of the writing process; in particular, effective planning for content and genre structure could be helpful in addressing these difficulties (e.g., Harris & Graham, 1999).

As the teacher monitors Lee's progress, she asks herself whether Lee is indeed making adequate progress to meet the grade-level writing standards and expectations of the curriculum and whether the instruction is effective. The answers to these questions are positive, as Lee makes good progress for the first several weeks of instruction (see Figure 13.1, box 4). However, by early October, Lee's progress slows; it is obvious from the data on the graph that her scores fall below the goal line and that she will not meet the goal by the end of the 15-week instructional period. So the teacher modifies the instructional approach (box 6). Lee's scores continue to decline for an additional 3 weeks (box 7), and the teacher once again modifies the instructional approach (box 8). This time, Lee's scores rebound, and she is back on track to meet her long-range goal.

RESEARCH ON CBM

Although the research base on CBM writing measures is not expansive, approximately 40 published studies highlight their technical adequacy. Fuchs (2004) described the stages involved in the 30-year CBM research history, including stage 1 (technical features of single CBM scores), stage 2 (technical features of student progress monitoring data), and stage 3 (the usefulness of CBM for instructional purposes). To date, most of the CBM research on writing has focused on stage 1, finding the most reliable and valid measures that correlate with or could be used to predict performance on standardized or teacher-created writing measures. However, a few studies have focused on determining which measures can best be used to monitor student progress in general writing proficiency.

Stage 1 Studies

Stage 1 studies dominate the extant research and provide evidence for four important generalizations about CBM research in writing. First, the simple scoring procedures that were thought to be valid for young students (WW and WSC) may not be the best CBM measures for use with older students. Early in CBM development, researchers at the Institute for Research on Learning Disabilities at the University of Minnesota compiled evidence that WW and WSC were reliable and valid measures of writing proficiency for students in grades 1–6 (Marston, 1989). In these early studies, reliability coefficients for WW and WSC (test–retest and parallel form) ranged from .42 to .99. Validity coefficients for WW with the Test of Written Language (TOWL) ranged from .41 to .81; validity coefficients for WSC ranged from .45 to .92. Correlations of CBM measures with holistic teacher ratings were .85 for WW and .84 for WSC. Subsequently, researchers were unable to duplicate these results and have found that more complex scoring measures produce stronger reliability and validity coefficients. For example, Parker, Tindal, and Hasbrouck (1991) found that correlations between teacher holistic ratings of writing and CBM measures for elementary students were generally strongest for CWS (r = .52–.61), whereas correlations for WW were the weakest (r = .36–.49). Gansle, Noell, VanDerHeyden, Naquin, and Slider (2002) found that WW was not the strongest predictor of writing competence for third and fourth graders, as measured by the Iowa Test of Basic Skills subscale (r = .15). However, more complex scoring procedures were better predictors, such as CWS (r = .43) or correct punctuation marks (r = .44). Gansle, Noell, VanDerHeyden, Slider, Hoffpauir, and Whitmarsh (2004) noted that the correlations between the Woodcock–Johnson Tests of Achievement—Revised Writing Samples subtest for third and fourth graders were stronger for CWS (r = .36) than for WW (r = .23). Weissenburger and Espin (2005) found that, for fourth-grade students, WW, CWS, and CIWS all produced statistically significant validity coefficients with a district writing test for 3-minute writing samples but that WW had the lowest validity coefficients among the three scoring procedures (rs = .45, .62, and .68, respectively). Similarly, Jewell and Malecki (2005) found that WW had some of the lowest validity coefficients for second, fourth, and sixth graders when correlated with the Scholastic Achievement Test and analytic trait scores. Whereas validity coefficients for WW ranged from .12 to .45, correlations for CWS were higher (r = .23–.58), as were coefficients for the percentage of CWS (r = .40–.67).

The results of several studies provide evidence for the need to increase complexity in scoring, particularly with older students' CBM writing samples. Espin et al. (2000) instructed seventh- and eighth-grade students to write on computers for 5 minutes (marking their progress at 3 minutes) in response to two story starters and two descriptive essay starters. Criterion variables were teacher ratings of writing competence and student performance on the district writing test. By far, CIWS produced the strongest validity coefficients with teacher ratings (r = .65–.70) and the district test (r = .69–.75). In a study involving a range of grade levels, Weissenburger and Espin (2005) asked fourth, eighth, and tenth graders to complete narrative writing samples in response to two story starters. The criterion variable was a district writing test. Students wrote for 10 minutes, marking their progress at 3-, 5-, and 10-minute intervals. Whereas for fourth-grade students WW, CWS, and CIWS all produced strong reliability (rs > .80) and statistically significant validity coefficients at 3 minutes (rs = .45, .62, and .68, respectively); the researchers found that for tenth graders, only a 10-minute writing sample scored for CIWS produced a reliability coefficient above .80 and yielded a statistically significant, though low-moderate in magnitude, validity coefficient of r = .36. Espin et al. (2008) administered story prompts to 10th-grade students. Students wrote for 10 minutes in response to each prompt. Students marked their progress at 3, 5, and 7 minutes. The criterion variable was a Minnesota high-stakes writing assessment. They found that, although WW, WSC, CWS and CIWS produced similar reliability coefficients at 5, 7, and 10 minutes, CIWS produced the largest validity coefficients (r = .57–.60), providing further evidence that simple scoring procedures may not be the best for older students.

The second generalization is that, in order to obtain a reliable and valid sample, older students need increased writing time (up to 10 minutes) compared with younger students (3–5 minutes). In the Espin et al. (2000) study, the researchers found that, in general, 5-minute samples scored for CIWS ($r = .78$) produced more reliable CBM writing scores for seventh and eighth graders than 3-minute samples ($r = .72–.74$). Validity coefficients also increased with time; 3-minute samples produced correlations for CIWS ranging from .66 to .69, whereas 5-minute samples produced correlations of .65 to .75. In the Weissenburger and Espin (2005) study, researchers found that reliability increased with sample duration across grades and scoring procedures. For the fourth graders, 3 minutes was sufficient for moderately strong validity ($r = .68$), whereas 8th graders had the highest validity coefficient at 5 minutes ($r = .63$) and 10th graders at 10 minutes ($r = .36$). Espin et al. (2008) found that, when 10th-grade students wrote for 10 minutes and marked their progress at 3, 5, and 7 minutes, both reliability and validity coefficients increased with time; in addition, only 7 and 10 minutes of writing produced CIWS alternate-form reliability coefficients above .80. Validity coefficients ranged from .56 to .60, with the highest coefficients obtained for a 10-minute sample. Thus, in order to obtain a reliable and valid sample score, researchers suggest that older students write for at least 7 minutes.

Third, it does not appear that the type of prompt (picture, story, or expository) has much impact on technical adequacy, but research continues in this area. Deno, Mirkin, and Marston (1980) found similar validity coefficients for story, topic sentence, and picture CBM writing prompts for students in grades 3–6. In Espin et al. (2000), seventh- and eighth-grade students performed similarly in response to two story starters and two descriptive starters. However, McMaster and Campbell (in press) found some evidence that, within grade level, the type of CBM writing prompt appeared to vary in technical adequacy; the strongest reliability and validity coefficients were obtained with picture prompts in mid-elementary grades and story or expository prompts in late elementary to middle school grades. Studies targeting English language learners (Campbell, 2004, 2006) have found effects based on type of prompt, with technical adequacy evidence supporting both picture and story prompts.

Finally, there is some evidence that the validity of CBM measures decreases with grade level, particularly among high school students. Parker et al. (1991) investigated the use of CBM writing for special education eligibility across grade levels (grades 2–6, 8, and 11). Students wrote for 6 minutes in response to a story starter. CWS generally had the highest correlations with holistic ratings ($r = .48–.61$); the lowest correlations were found at grade 11. Likewise, Weissenburger and Espin (2005) found that the magnitude of validity coefficients decreased across grade, with the strongest coefficients obtained for 3 minutes of writing for fourth graders ($r = .68$), whereas the highest eighth-grade coefficient was obtained at 5 minutes ($r = .63$) and for 10th graders at 10 minutes

(r = .36). McMaster and Campbell (in press) noted that in third-grade validity coefficients obtained for CWS and CIWS with the TOWL were relatively strong (r = .60–.75). Fifth-grade validity coefficients ranged from .57 to .65, but in seventh grade few of the validity coefficients were above .50.

Stage 2 Studies

Stage 2 studies, addressing the technical adequacy of CBM writing measures for progress monitoring, are more limited in number. Most growth studies have focused on student scores obtained from CBM writing measures administered in the fall and then again in the spring. Marston, Lowry, Deno, and Mirkin (1981) found that first through sixth graders made statistically significant fall-to-spring gains in WW and WSC. Similarly, Deno et al. (1980) noted gains in first through fifth graders from fall to spring in WW, WSC, and correct letter sequences (CLS). At a 10-week interval, Marston, Deno, and Tindal (1983) found that students made gains in WW, WSC, and CLS but did not demonstrate gains on the Scholastic Achievement Test. The researchers noted that whereas the CBM measures reflected gains, standardized achievement tests may not have been sensitive enough to capture small gains in writing. Parker et al. (1991) found that sixth, eighth, and eleventh graders all increased their CWS production from fall to spring. Similarly, Malecki and Jewell (2003) noted improvement in fall-to-spring CIWS scores for first through eighth graders.

Stage 3 Studies

To date, there have been few published stage 3 studies for CBM writing measures that have focused on the regular, weekly monitoring of struggling writers or that have tracked teacher changes in instructional methodologies in response to graphed CBM writing scores. Due to the fact that the technical adequacy of CBM writing measures is still being investigated, the use of such measures to monitor weekly writing progress has not been the subject of much research. Wallace et al. (2004) presented the results of a 20-week writing progress monitoring study. At a Minnesota urban high school, 72 students who were at risk of failing or who had already failed the Minnesota Basic Skills Test in writing participated in regular progress monitoring by four teachers over the course of 20 weeks. Each week, students wrote for 7 minutes in response to a story starter. Thirty-six students were regularly monitored by their teachers (the teachers scored students' writing samples for CIWS, graphed the data, and followed decision rules for making instructional changes). The other 36 students participated in weekly writing, but the teachers neither scored the data nor saw the graphs. Over the course of 20 weeks, the CIWS scores for the monitored group increased from 63 to 92 (an increase of about 1.5 CIWS per week). The CIWS scores for the group that was not monitored increased from 61 to 67 (an increase of about .30 CIWS per week). There were differential effects based on teacher—some teachers saw larger gains in their students' scores over the course of the study. Interestingly, there was little indication that any of the teachers actually made substantial instructional changes in response to their monitored students' data.

> The 15-week instructional period ends in December, and Lee has met the goal of an average weekly increase of 1.5 CIWS (see Figure 13.1, box 9). The teacher monitored Lee's progress toward this goal on a weekly basis; twice in this time period she implemented a change in instructional approach based on the CBM data. However, Lee is still performing below the average as compared with other sixth-grade students in this class. In looking ahead to the next instructional period, the teacher will continue to collect data, monitor Lee's progress, modify instruction, and set new instructional goals for her. The teacher will base decisions about the instructional approach on the data. Scoring writing samples for CIWS provides her with measures that are indicators of small changes in performance, so that she has the information she needs to make informed instructional changes.

LIMITATIONS OF CBM

Although CBM holds great promise for teachers who wish to assess and monitor student progress toward meeting writing goals and district- and state-mandated writing standards, there are questions unanswered by research. First, CBM writing measures have only moderate validity when compared with CBM reading measures. Whereas CWS and CIWS have validity correlation coefficients generally ranging from .35 to .70, correlation coefficients for CBM oral reading fluency generally range from .60 to .80 (Good & Jefferson, 1998). This could be due to the fact that in order to calculate criterion validity coefficients, CBM writing scores must be correlated with generally accepted standardized assessments of writing. However, most such assessments (e.g., TOWL) have only moderate criterion validity themselves (Hammill & Larsen, 1996). Other criteria frequently utilized to validate CBM writing measures, such as holistic writing scores, analytic trait scores, and teacher ratings, present different reliability and validity challenges, including the limited score range of rubrics and rater bias inherent in the scoring process.

Most research has focused on the technical adequacy of CBM writing scores, but research on using such data for progress monitoring, performance goal setting, and intervention planning has occurred less frequently (Fuchs, 2004). If CBM is to be used in the future to monitor student progress in writing, more research must be conducted on how often the measures should be administered, how much growth can be expected, what interventions are chosen, and how teachers' interventions affect student progress.

Due to these limitations, teachers and administrators should be cautioned about the misuse of CBM writing data. CBM writing data should not be used in isolation to assess student writing when making high-stakes decisions regarding educational placement or performance. Some districts collect CBM writing scores to use as a screening measure, and many teachers use CBM data to help with instructional decision making; both of these uses are appropriate given the current state of the extant research.

Although there are still many important questions about the use of CBM in making educational decisions in the domain of writing, research is ongoing. The Research Institute on Progress Monitoring (RIPM) at the University of Minnesota (*www.progressmonitoring.net*) is charged with establishing a cohesive research plan to address many of the remaining CBM questions. The Institute's main goal is to develop a seamless progress monitoring system that would be useful for K–12 students in both special and general education. The first RIPM CBM writing studies focused on technical adequacy, finding reliable and valid writing prompts and measures that could be used across and within grades. McMaster and Campbell (in press) found that writing for 3–7 minutes in response to a story prompt appeared to have the strongest technical adequacy across grade levels. Developing measures for early literacy has been a focus of recent RIPM research. McMaster, Du, and Petursdottir (2007) investigated the technical adequacy of a variety of CBM tasks with first graders; sentence copying, story prompts, and photo prompts scored for CLS or CWS/CIWS appear to hold promise. Further research continues on other writing measures, including research with high school students and computer-generated student writing versus handwriting.

SUMMARY

Writing is an amalgamation of complex skills and processes resulting in a product that is difficult for classroom teachers to evaluate. CBM is one method of formative evaluation that can provide teachers with useful individual student data that can be used to support the evaluation and monitoring of student progress in writing. On a practical level, technically adequate CBM procedures are easy to use and provide data that can inform instructional decisions. A growing research base has provided credible evidence that CBM can be used by classroom teachers to evaluate student writing performance. As the CBM research base continues to develop, studies are underway to determine how to increase the reliability and validity coefficients of CBM writing data, to refine measures for indexing student growth over time, and to link measures to instructional methods. The future contributions of CBM research to writing assessment are promising; the current contributions allow classroom teachers to assess student writing and make data-based instructional decisions that support student progress in the curriculum.

REFERENCES

Breland, H. M., Camp, R., Jones, R. J., Morris, M. M., & Rock, D. A. (1987). *Assessing writing skill*. New York: College Entrance Examination Board.

Bridgeman, B., & Carlson, S. S. (1984). Survey of academic writing tasks. *Written Communication, 1*(2), 247–280.

Campbell, H. (2004). *Curriculum-based measurement in written expression for students who are English language learners*. Unpublished manuscript, University of Minnesota.

Campbell, H. (2006). The reliability and validity of curriculum-based measures in written expression for English language learners. (Doctoral dissertation, University of Minnesota, 2006). *Dissertation Abstracts International, 67*, 2019.

Charney, D. (1984). The validity of using holistic scoring to evaluate writing: A critical review. *Research in the Teaching of English, 18*(1), 65–81.

Deno, S. L. (1985). Curriculum-based measurement: The emerging alternative. *Exceptional Children, 52*, 219–232.

Deno, S. L. (1989). Curriculum-based measurement and special education services: A fundamental and direct relationship. In M. R. Shinn (Ed.), *Curriculum-based measurement: Assessing special children* (pp. 18–78). New York: Guilford Press.

Deno, S. L., & Fuchs, L. S. (1987). Developing curriculum-based measurement systems for data-based special education problem solving. *Focus on Exceptional Children, 19*(8), 1–16.

Deno, S. L., Mirkin, P., & Marston, D. (1980). *Relationships among simple measures of written expression and performance on standardized achievement tests* (Vol. IRLD-RR-22). Minneapolis: University of Minnesota, Institute for Research on Learning Disabilities.

Espin, C. A., Shin, J., Deno, S. L., Skare, S., Robinson, S., & Benner, B. (2000).

Identifying indicators of written expression proficiency for middle school students. *Journal of Special Education, 34,* 140–153.

Espin, C. A., Wallace, T., Campbell, H., Lembke, E. S., Long, J., & Ticha, R. (2008). Curriculum-based measurement in writing: Predicting the success of high-school students on state standards tests. *Exceptional Children, 74*(2), 174–193.

Flower, L., & Hayes, J. R. (1981). A cognitive process theory of writing. *College Composition and Communication, 32,* 365–387.

Fuchs, D., Mock, D., Morgan, P. L., & Young, C. L. (2003). Responsiveness-to-intervention: Definitions, evidence, and implications for the learning disabilities construct. *Learning Disabilities Research and Practice, 18,* 157–171.

Fuchs, L. (2004). The past, present, and future of curriculum-based measurement research. *School Psychology Review, 33,* 188–192.

Fuchs, L., Butterworth, J., & Fuchs, D. (1989). Effects of ongoing curriculum-based measurement on student awareness of goals and progress. *Education and Treatment of Children, 12,* 63–72.

Fuchs, L., Fuchs, D., & Deno, S. L. (1985). Importance of goal ambitiousness and goal mastery to student achievement. *Exceptional Children, 52,* 63–71.

Gansle, K., Noell, G., VanDerHeyden, A., Naquin, G., & Slider, N. (2002). Moving beyond total words written: The reliability, criterion validity, and time cost of alternate measures for curriculum-based measurement in writing. *School Psychology Review, 31,* 477–497.

Gansle, K., Noell, G., VanDerHeyden, A., Slider, N., Hoffpauir, L., & Whitmarsh, E. (2004). An examination of the criterion validity and sensitivity to brief intervention of alternate curriculum-based measures of writing skill. *Psychology in the Schools, 41,* 291–300.

Gersten, R., & Baker, S. (2001). Teaching expressive writing to students with learning disabilities: A meta-analysis. *Elementary School Journal, 101,* 251–272.

Good, R., & Jefferson, G. (1998). Contemporary perspectives on curriculum-based measurement validity. In M. R. Shinn (Ed.), *Advanced applications of curriculum-based measurement* (pp. 61–88). New York: Guilford Press.

Hammill, D., & Larsen, S. (1996). *Test of Written Language—Third Edition: Examiner's Manual.* Austin, TX: PRO-ED.

Harris, K. R., & Graham, S. (1999). Programmatic intervention research: Illustrations from the evolution of self-regulated strategy development. *Learning Disability Quarterly, 22,* 251–262.

Isaacson, S. (1984). Evaluation of written expression: Issues of reliability, validity, and instructional utility. *Diagnostique, 9,* 96–116.

Jewell, J., & Malecki, C. K. (2005). The utility of CBM written language indices: An investigation of production-dependent, production-independent, and accurate production scores. *School Psychology Review, 34,* 27–44.

Malecki, C. K., & Jewell, J. (2003). Developmental, gender, and practical considerations in scoring curriculum-based measurement writing probes. *Psychology in the Schools, 40,* 379–390.

Marston, D. (1989). A curriculum-based measurement approach to assessing academic performance: What it is and why do it. In M. Shinn (Ed.), *Curriculum-based measurement: Assessing special children* (pp. 18–78). New York: Guilford Press.

Marston, D. (2005). Tiers of intervention in responsiveness to intervention: Prevention outcomes and learning disabilities identification patterns. *Journal of Learning Disabilities, 38,* 539–544.

Marston, D., Deno, S. L., & Tindal, G. (1983). *A comparison of standardized achievement tests and direct measurement techniques in measuring pupil progress* (Vol. IRLD-RR-126). Minneapolis: University of Minnesota, Institute for Research on Learning Disabilities.

Marston, D., Lowry, L., Deno, S. L., & Mirkin, P. (1981). *An analysis of learning trends in simple measure of reading, spelling, and written expression: A longitudinal study* (Vol. IRLD-RR-49). Minneapolis: University of Minnesota, Institute for Research on Learning Disabilities.

McMaster, K., & Campbell, H. (in press). New and existing curriculum-based writing measures: Technical features within and across grades. *School Psychology Review.*

McMaster, K. L., Du, S., & Petursdottir, A. L. (2007, February). *Technical adequacy studies in written expression.* Paper presented at the Pacific Coast Research Conference, San Diego, CA.

Mellard, D., Byrd, S., Johnson, E., Tollefson, J., & Boesche, L. (2004). Foundations and research on identifying model responsiveness-to-intervention sites. *Learning Disability Quarterly, 27,* 243–256.

Mellon, J. (1969). *Transformational sentence combining* (NCTE Research Report No. 10). Champaign, IL: National Council of Teachers of English.

Miller, M. D., & Crocker, L. (1990). Validation methods for direct writing assessment. *Applied Measurement in Education, 3*(3), 285–296.

Moran, M. R. (1987). Options for written language assessment. *Focus on Exceptional Children, 19*(5), 1–10.

Odell, L. (1981). Defining and assessing competence in writing. In C. Cooper (Ed.), *The nature and measurement of competency in English* (pp. 95–138). Urbana, IL: National Council of Teachers of English.

Parker, R. I., Tindal, G., & Hasbrouck, J. (1991). Progress monitoring with objective measures of writing performance for students with mild disabilities. *Exceptional Children, 58*(1), 61–73.

Raymond, M. R., & Houston, W. M. (1990). *Detecting and correcting for rater effects in performance assessment* (ACT Research Rep. No. 90-14). Iowa City, IA: American College Testing.

Research Institute on Progress Monitoring. (2006). *RIPM Research.* Retrieved October 1, 2006 from *www.progressmonitoring.net.*

Videen, J., Deno, S. L., & Marston, D. (1982). *Correct word sequences: A valid indicator of proficiency in written expression* (Research Rep. No. 84). Minneapolis: University of Minnesota, Institute for Research on Learning Disabilities.

Wallace, T., Espin, C. A., Long, J., Campbell, H., Ticha, R., & Lembke, E. (2004, March). *Creating a progress monitoring system: Preparing secondary stu-*

dents for success on Minnesota Basic Skills Tests. Paper presented at the Pacific Coast Research Conference, San Diego, CA.

Weissenburger, J. W., & Espin, C. A. (2005). Curriculum-based measures of writing across grade levels. *Journal of School Psychology, 43,* 153–169.

Yancey, K. B. (1999). Looking back as we look forward: Historicizing writing assessment. *College Composition and Communication, 50*(3), 483–503.

APPENDIX 13.1. Procedures for Scoring CBM Writing Samples

1. Read the entire writing sample before scoring.
2. In red, underline any incorrectly spelled words or words that are grammatically incorrect.
3. Mark the end of each sentence with a vertical line. If correct punctuation is not used, place a vertical line at the logical end of each phrase containing a subject and verb.
4. Using the following rules, identify correct word sequences (CWS) and incorrect word sequences (IWS). A CWS consists of two adjacent words that are acceptable, within the context of the phrase, to a native speaker of English (Videen, Deno, & Marston, 1982). Acceptable words are those words that are spelled correctly and used correctly (e.g., correct verb tense), and that follow the scoring rules.

SCORING RULES

Correct Word Sequences

Place a blue "up" carat (CWS) between adjacent words that are acceptable.

^ I ^ worked ^ hard ^ to ^ get ^ a ^ scholarship^.

Incorrect Word Sequences

Place a red "down" carat (IWS) between adjacent words that are not acceptable.

^ I ^ have ∨ *acomplished* ∨ many ^ things^.

Capitalization

Score a CWS at the beginning of a sentence if the word is capitalized and spelled correctly. The pronoun "I" should be capitalized, as should proper nouns (names and places). Beginning sentence capitalization should be scored as a CWS if the word is spelled correctly. Ignore all other capital letters.

> ^ She ^ rode ^ a ^ bus^. | ∨ she ^ liked ^ the ^ bus^. |
> ^She ^rode ^ to ∨ *alaska* ∨.

Punctuation

Score a CWS at the end of a sentence if the last word is correct and end punctuation is used. Ignore all internal punctuation except apostrophes. Score an incorrectly used apostrophe as IWS because the word is incorrectly spelled without the apostrophe.

> ^ He ∨ *didnt* ∨ take, ^ the ^ quiz ^ today ^.

Spelling

Common slang words (e.g., "gonna") should be scored as CWS. Variations in the spelling of proper names should be scored as CWS (e.g., "Salleye" rather than the more common "Sally"). Incorrect use of homophones should be scored as IWS ("hear" instead of "here").

> ^ Put ^ your ^ schedule ∨ *hear* ∨ on ^ the ^ desk ^.

Word Usage

Incorrect verb tenses, verb tense changes, and incorrect word endings are scored as IWS.

> ^ Back ^ in ^ high ^ school ^ I ∨ *receive* ∨ the ^ highest ^ award ^.

Score a personal pronoun as IWS when it is not in agreement with its antecedent.

> ^ Each ^ of ^ the ^ students ^ needs ^ to ^ buy ∨ *their* ∨ books ^.

Score the verb as IWS when it is not in agreement with the subject.

> ^ He ∨ *buy* ∨ lunch ^ every ^ day ^.

Score incorrect pronoun case as IWS.

> ∨ *Me* ∨ and ∨ *him* ∨ are ^ in ^ the ^ same ^ biology ^ class ^.

Score incorrect possessives as IWS.

^ My ∨ _roommates_ ∨ computer ^ is ^ not ^ working ^.

Run-On Sentences

Score run-on sentences as IWS where the sentence should logically end. Score an IWS for the missing end punctuation and for the missing capitalization of the second sentence.

^ They ^ brought ^ us ^ good ^ news ∨ | ∨ class ^ was ^ cancelled ^.

Run-on sentences should be divided by the scorer when more than two sentences are connected by a conjunction. The scorer should mark the logical end of the sentence with a vertical line and cross out the extra conjunction.

^ We ^ wanted ^ to ^ go ^ to ^ class ^ and ^ we ^ wanted ^ to ^ talk ^ with ^ our
^ group ∨ | ∨ ~~and~~ ∨ we ^ wanted ^ to ^ start ^ our ^ project ^.

Sentence Fragments

For a sentence fragment, either the beginning or the end of the phrase should be scored with IWS. For the following example, the phrase "They wear" is missing from the fragment.

^ Kids ^ wear ^ all ^ types ^ of ^ clothes ^ . | ∨ Baggy ^ clothes ^ like ^ Levis ^ .

Miscellaneous

Score the following as IWS: illegible words (one IWS on either side of the word), repeated words (all repeated words are incorrect), omitted words (one IWS). Score abbreviated words as IWS except: AM, PM, TV, OK, or t-shirts. Hyphenated words should be scored as one word. The symbol for "and" (&) should not be an IWS. Foreign words should not be counted as IWS. Incorrectly divided words, including compound words, should be scored as IWS.

^ She ^ finished ^ her ∨ _home_ ∨ _work_ ∨ yesterday. ^

SAMPLE PASSAGE FOR SCORING

It was Wednesday morning. Mr. Lee 4th hour class is getting started. Jenny was one of talkative girl. She was telling the fight with benji & Peter from her last class Mr. Lee waited for while to let her finish her story. But Jenny doesn't seem she is going to stop. Mr. Lee tried to teach the other students. Scince Jenny is talking loud in left corner no body paid any attention to Mr. Lee. Mr. Lee said "Class, let settle down and get ready to begin working."

SCORED PASSAGE

^ It ^ was ^ Wednesday^ morning^. | ^Mr. ∨ _Lee_¹ ∨ 4th^ hour ^ class ∨ _is_² ∨ getting ^started ^. | ^ Jenny^ was^ one^ of ∨ ³talkative ∨ _girl_⁴ ∨. | ^She^ was^ telling ∨ ⁵ the ^fight ^with ∨ _benji_⁶ ∨ & ^Peter^ from ^her ^last ^class ∨ ⁷ | ^Mr. ^Lee ^waited ^for ∨ _while_⁸ ∨ to ^let^ her^ finish^ her ^story^. | ∨ Jenny ∨ _Jenny_ ⁹ _doesn't_ ¹⁰ ∨ seem ¹¹ ∨ she ∨ _is_ ¹² ∨ going^ to ^stop^. | ^Mr. ^ Lee ^tried ^to ^teach^ the^ other^ students^. | ∨ _Scince_ ¹³ ∨ Jenny ∨ _is_¹⁴ ∨ talking ∨ _loud_¹⁵ ∨ in ∨ ¹⁶ left ∨ corner ∨ _no_ ∨ _body_¹⁷ ∨ paid ^any ^attention ^to ^Mr. ^Lee^. | ^Mr. ^Lee^ said ^ "Class, ∨ _let_¹⁸ ∨ settle^ down^ and^ get^ ready^ to^ begin^ working^." |

Scoring Explanation

1. Should be _Lee's_.

2. This is written in the past tense, so the _is_ should be _was_.

3. Omitted words—_the most_

4. _Girl_ needs to be plural.

5. Omitted word—_about_

6. _benji_ should be capitalized.

7. No end punctuation.

8. Should be _awhile_, not _while_.

9. Repeated word _Jenny_.

10. Should be past tense: _didn't_.

11. Omitted word—_like_.

12. Should be past tense: _was_.

13. Incorrect spelling.

14. Should be past tense: _was_.

15. Loud modifies a verb; should use an adverb: _loudly_.

16. Omitted word—_the_.

17. _No body_ is incorrect; should be _nobody_.

18. Should be conjunction—_let's_.

CHAPTER 14

Language-Based Assessment of Written Expression

CHERYL M. SCOTT

According to a panel recently convened to study the teaching of writing in schools, the problem is not that students cannot write; it is that they do not write well (National Commission on Writing, 2003, p. 16). The thought captured in this statement is a fitting backdrop for this chapter because it assumes that writing has been assessed and found wanting, not in an all-or-none fashion but by degrees. Although the panel's bleak conclusion might imply that we are confident in how to measure writing competence, to the contrary, they identified assessment as a major area of concern in terms of authenticity, alignment with standards, and adoption of best practices. Unfortunately, assessment has been one of the least researched topics, particularly for middle and high school students, according to an examination of writing research topics covered between 1999 and 2004 conducted by Juzwik and colleagues (2006).

Writing assessment is a broad term for a variety of tasks and measures. At the most basic level, writers could be evaluated on their execution of the process of writing, that is, how they planned, generated, and revised a text. Alternatively, writers could be evaluated on the words, sentences, and text they put on paper—their product. This chapter concentrates on the latter, the linguistic characteristics of written texts. Assessment tasks concerned with products run the gamut from machine-scored multiple-choice judgment tasks that do not require writing per se to those that prompt a multipage written product with embedded opportunities for planning and revision. Between those extremes are tasks that ask a student to write single sentences in response to various prompts (e.g., a word or several words plus a picture), as found in several norm-referenced tests of writing. Measures could be quantitative but broad, such as a calculation of average sentence length in words, or more detailed, such as the frequency of particular types of syntactic structures or words. Measures could also be qualitative, requiring an assessor to rate a text as a whole (holistic assessment) or to rate several traits of a text (organization, sentence fluency, etc.) according to a predetermined rubric.

The type of writing task and the measures used are usually tied to the purpose of assessment. The focus of a writing assessment could be to help an entire system—a classroom, a school district, or a state—determine how well a group of students are meeting a set of writing standards. In contrast, the focus could be an individual child or adolescent. In this case the writing assessment could be one part of a broader evaluation contributing to an identification of a language or learning disorder and/ or eligibility decision for special services. Or the goal could be to help the student become a more accomplished writer through refined instruction. Researchers in developmental writing and those studying struggling writers have used a broad array of measures and are challenged to find measures that have face validity for the particular questions being asked.

Language-based writing assessments that inform both instruction/ intervention and research are the focus of this chapter. For both purposes, children and adolescents are usually asked to compose an entire text, which can then be examined at several linguistic levels, namely *word* (lexical), *sentence* (semantic relations, sentential syntax), and *discourse* (overall productivity, cohesion, text macrostructure) levels. At each level, commonly used measures are discussed from the standpoint of what they convey or do not convey about written language. Measures are also critiqued on their robustness generally and on their applicability to specific assessment purposes. Under ideal circumstances, a rich body of methodological research could be consulted—research that speaks to the reliability and validity of each measure inclusive for the ages and characteristics of the writer(s) of interest. Not surprisingly, there are gaps in our knowledge about language measures in writing, so the critique is limited at points. At each linguistic level, I discuss additional or alternative linguistic measures or observations that do not yet appear routinely in the extant literature on writing but could potentially fill some of the assessment gaps faced by educators, clinicians, and researchers alike. Although it is well known that text composition suffers when transcription processes demand considerable attention and energy (Graham & Harris, 2000), spelling and handwriting are not addressed.

I have chosen five writing samples from a research database (Scott & Windsor, 2000) to illustrate key points throughout the chapter. The writers who produced these samples range in age from 10 years, 6 months to 13 years, 8 months. Three have been diagnosed with language learning disabilities (LLD) and also qualify as having specific language impairments (SLI), with oral language difficulties; two are typically developing (TD) students. All writers watched a 15-minute educational videotape about the southwestern desert in the United States in which a narrator described how the desert was formed and how plants and animals have adapted to the harsh conditions. They were asked to write a summary of the film and were given 20 minutes (or longer if needed) to do so. They were not prompted to either plan or revise. The expository samples are reproduced verbatim as consecutively numbered sentences in Figure 14.1. Spelling has been normalized and punctuation has been ignored for purposes of this chapter.

WORD-LEVEL MEASURES

Global Lexical Measures

Probably the most widely used broad, quantitative measure of writing at the word level is lexical diversity, or the number of different words written in the text. The idea behind this measure is that lexical diversity reflects vocabulary size and control. Given two individuals performing the same writing task, the one who knows more words will use a wider variety of words, allowing for greater specificity and wider breadth as needed to address the topic. Although not measured directly, lexical diversity is frequently represented in rubrics associated with state writing assessments (e.g., varied sentence structure and word choice). With roots in the analysis of spoken language samples, measures of lexical diversity have been adopted for the analysis of written language and are easily calculated in language analysis software (e.g., Systematic Analysis of Language Transcripts [SALT], Miller & Chapman, 2000). The most widely used measures are: (1) a simple count of the number of different words (usually word roots) in a sample (NDW) and (2) type–token ratio (TTR), a ratio of different words (types) to overall words (tokens). Both measures, unfortunately, are confounded by sample size. As the number of words in a sample increases, NDW increases as well, so the writer who wrote more words will almost always have a higher NDW. TTR, on the other hand, decreases due to the repetition of closed-class words (e.g., *the, a, this, in*) and the recurrence of content words via lexical cohesion as a topic continues to be developed.

These sample-size effects are evident for the five samples in Figure 14.1. As shown in Table 14.1, the two shortest samples in terms of total words (nos. 1 and 2) have the highest TTRs, and the two longest samples

Sample 1: LLD, age 13 years, 6 months

1. The desert is a dry and hot place.
2. It is very hard to live there because there is very little water.
3. If it does rain the water runs quickly because the ground is too dry.
4. So there is very little water absorbed by the plants.
5. Moist air from the coast passes through the mountains and drops rain or snow.
6. Then it drops down the slopes.
7. And warm dry air winds blow across the desert.
8. Animal life is hard because there is very little water.
9. Sometimes when it rains some homes get flooded.
10. Most animals come out at night because it is cooler out.
11. Most animals have holes in the ground because it's about 23 degrees lower than the surface.
12. A [EW] plants have needles that give protection against predators from getting their moisture.
13. Some animals build home [EW: homes] in the plants for protection.

Sample 2: LLD, age 13 years, 4 months

1. It's about a desert.
2. They have rain storms.
3. They destroy the animal's homes.
4. They try to save their lives by climbing on the cactuses.
5. They have rainfalls sometimes undergrounds [EW: underground].
6. The birds build their homes in dead cactuses for [EW: so] animals don't eat the babies or them.
7. There is a food chains [EW: chain] in the desert.
8. When there is a rainfall the trees and plants and animals get enough water to survive the hot days.
9. And at the beginning they show pictures.
10. There were all types of animals.
11. There were ants, spiders, rabbits, birds, [*and] pigs,
12. There were [EW: was] this dog.
13. But it wasn't a regular dog.
14. At the night it was cooler than the morning.
15. Some of the animals hunt or eat at night.
16. And some animals sleep during the days.
17. Then they get up at night when it's cooler.
18. The animals and plants drink water for their food and animals [EU].
19. They [*have] adapted to the environment.

Sample 3: LLD, age 11 years, 9 months

1. The desert is home to a lot of animals such as the scorpion.
2. The scorpion is a smaller creature that has a stinging tail that holds poison.
3. The scorpion hides during some of the hotter days under rocks and in holes.
4. The most common thing in the desert is the cactus.
5. The cactus has spikes to keep animals from biting into it.

FIGURE 14.1. (*continued*)

FIGURE 14.1. (continued)

6. But a pig that lives in the desert can bite it.
7. The tarantula lives in the desert.
8. And that lives under rocks and in holes.
9. The rain doesn't rain over the deserts that much.
10. But when it does it is normally a rainstorm.
11. And that is when the animals and the plants get their water.
12. The lizard lives in the desert.
13. And it eats the bugs that try to eat the cactus.
14. The coyote lives in the desert.
15. And it hides in caves.
16. Snakes live in the desert.
17. And they try to each whatever they can find.
18. Snakes live under rocks, in holes, and in caves as well.
19. Birds make nests in the cactuses so snakes and skunks don't eat the eggs.
20. Birds live in the cactuses for warmth.
21. The animals that live underground are 20° cooler than they would be outside in the sunshine.

Sample 4: TD, age 10 years, 6 months

1. The movie that I just watched was The desert 3rd edition!
2. At first they were explaining how most people think the desert is a dry barren uninhabitable place.
3. In this movie they don't like that.
4. They want you to see the many different plants and animals of the United States southwestern desert.
5. In the desert flash flooding and wind cause erosion on the landscape.
6. Rarely is there rain.
7. But when they get it [*it] comes in torrents.
8. It comes with high speed winds and harsh blowing water.
9. Many rodents and insects get flooded out.
10. And many of those drown.
11. In the desert when these waters come the dry sun baked soil and rocks cannot absorb all of the wetness.
12. So all of a sudden they have flash flooding which is good for many plants and few animals.
13. But in turn it is also bad for many small animals and small plants.
14. Plants like the saguaro cactus can spread their roots out over far ranges as to absorb and collect as much water as they can.
15. The saguaro cactus stores tons of water from flash floods.
16. So many animals would like to bite in and suck out water.
17. But they have spikes to protect them from most animals.
18. But a couple of animals are being a tortoise.
19. [*they] can bite in.
20. And the spikes don't hurt them.
21. Some plants can have their roots go down more than 30 meters over 100 feet.

22. Their roots go down so far to suck up water deep down.
23. After flash flooding plants bloom with many flowers and leaves.

Sample 5: TD, age 13 years, 8 months

1. The video I watched was about the desert.
2. The desert is formed by erosion.
3. There is little rainfall and intense heat conditions.
4. The desert may look like it is lifeless and empty.
5. But there are lots of organisms and plants that are adapted to the climate.
6. Some plants adapt to the desert mainly by having a horizontal root systems [EW: system] which lets them take in more water while others have tap roots that go down as much as thirty meters into the earth to get water.
7. Plants like cactuses form huge ribs around them that go upward and collect water.
8. When it rains, cactuses store the water inside them.
9. They are protected by thorns that cover them from predators with one or two exceptions.
10. The desert boar can eat cactuses and not get hurt.
11. Most plants grow pretty far away from each other because they are in a competition to get water all the time.
12. In some cases little plants will grow under big plants for shelter and coolness.
13. Organisms are all over the place in the desert.
14. But most of them are nocturnal meaning they sleep in the day and are active in the night.
15. Some organisms eat bugs to survive.
16. And they are eaten.
17. And it keeps going on.
18. This is called the food chain.
19. Lots of prey dig holes in the ground to get away from predators and get away from the blazing sun.
20. Sometimes it is twenty five degrees below the temperature outside in a hole.
21. Even though the prey digs holes in the ground predators still know where to find them.
22. All of the organisms in the desert adapt to the conditions also.
23. Water is scarce in the desert.
24. There is [EW: are] river [EW: rivers] above and underground which are usually surrounded by canyons and the occasional oasis.
25. Sometimes the ground cannot absorb all of the water in a rainfall so the result is flooding.
26. A desert is a very complex place where thousands of living things live.
27. They are just a little shy.

FIGURE 14.1. Samples of expository summaries by five writers in the Scott and Windsor (2000) database; ages, language status, and discourse, sentence, and word measures appear in Table 14.1. EW denotes an error at the word level. EU denotes an error at the utterance level. An asterisk signifies a word that was omitted by the writer.

TABLE 14.1. Global Quantitative Word- and Sentence-Level Measures for Five Written Language Samples Shown in Figure 14.1

Sample	Age (yr; mo)	Total T-units	Total words	TTR	NDW	TTR/ 140	NDW/ 140	Letters/ word	MLTU	Clause density
1-LLD	13;6	13	140	.59	82	.59	82	4.3	10.85	2.08
2-LLD	13;4	19	152	.53	80	.55	77	4.3	8.21	1.37
3-LLD	11;9	21	210	.43	91	.46	64	4.0	10.10	1.67
4-TD	10;6	23	262	.51	134	.64	90	4.2	11.48	1.70
5-TD	13;8	27	335	.50	169	.68	95	4.3	12.41	1.81

Note. TTR, type–token ratio for entire sample; NDW, number of different word roots in entire sample; TTR/140, type-token ratio for the first 140 words of the sample; NDW/140, number of different wrd roots for the first 140 words of the sample; MLTU, mean length of T-units (in words); Clause density, number of clauses (main and subordinate) divided by number of T-units.

(nos. 4 and 5) have lower TTRs, even though these were written by TD students, who would be predicted to show greater lexical diversity. NDW shows substantial increases with increasing sample size, as seen in Table 14.1. The result is that any one writer's score (NDW or TTR) cannot be easily interpreted unless comparison scores are from samples of exactly the same length and, ideally, the same discourse genre and writing task. To remove sample-size effects, I recalculated NDW and TTR using only the first 140 words of each sample. The number 140 was a constraint imposed by the size of the shortest sample (no. 1), which was 140 words long in its entirety. The resulting figures (in Table 14.1) show a very different picture for both NWD and TTR. Now, both NDW and TTR values for the two students with typical language (nos. 4 and 5) show higher diversity than those of the three students with LLD. Controlling sample size for these types of comparisons is obviously critical.[1]

Although controlling text length eliminates one methodological concern for measures of lexical diversity, others remain, among them the fact that researchers do not agree on an ideal sample size (Owen & Leonard, 2002). Also, some students may not be able to meet a predetermined sample size cutoff. One way around the text length limitation is the vocabulary diversity (VOCD), or "D" measure (McKee, Malvern, & Richards, 2000). Using a computer algorithm that predicts decline in vocabulary diversity with increased text length, the actual decline in diversity in a text is compared with the predicted decline. VOCD was the lexical diversity measure used by Strömqvist and colleagues (2002) in a large-scale, cross-linguistic study of speaking and writing in individuals ages 9 through young adult. They found that lexical diversity is a sensitive indicator of modality (speaking vs. writing). The online constraints imposed by speaking limited lexical diversity, but in writing, lexical diversity and individual variation increased. There were also clear developmental trends in both modalities. To date, VOCD has not been widely applied to writing assessment, but it would appear to have potential when sample size is hard to control and the effects of sample size on measures of diversity are uncertain.

In addition to diversity, two other lexical measures are often used in studies of writing. The measure of word length, operationalized as the number of letters in a word, capitalizes on the fact that word length and frequency are inversely related; as length increases, frequency decreases (Zipf, 1932). The use of lower frequency words as a developmental measure of more mature writing is reflected in the scoring rubrics of several norm-referenced writing tests and in readability formulas. A measure of the average number of letters (characters) per word is easily calculated by word processing programs. However, the calculations for the five samples highlighted in this chapter (Table 14.1) show that the range was quite narrow, from 4.0 to 4.3 letters per word. Further, the measure did not distinguish between the LLD and TD samples, nor did it vary along with diversity measures of TTR/140 and NDW/140. We are left with some questions, then, about the interpretation of word length. Lexical density is another global quantitative lexical measure used in studies of writing, albeit less frequently. This measure refers to the proportion of content words (usually defined as nouns, verbs, and adjectives) to total words, a ratio that is greater for writing than speaking (Halliday, 1985).

The interpretation and use of word-level measures of writing in educational and clinical circles depends in part on the availability of data showing whether and how these measures change with development and as a function of language ability. Measures of lexical diversity have a more extensive research base in spoken language; for written language, there are many gaps in the literature for all three measures (diversity, word length, and density), particularly in comparing students with and without language and learning disabilities.

As part of a broader cross-linguistic study, Strömqvist et al. (2002) measured lexical diversity, length, and density in texts produced by Swedish writers (10-, 13-, and 17-year-olds and adults), collapsing across narrative and expository samples. Each lexical measure was higher for writing compared with speaking. For both speaking and writing, there were significant main effects for age. Post-hoc testing revealed that age effects in writing for each of the three measures were limited to the developmental window between the ages of 13 and 17 and, for the measure of word length, to an increase in the proportion of very long words (i.e., > 10 letters) between age 17 and adult. Houck and Billingsley (1989) posted a similar finding for the timing of developmental effects on word length for English writers in grades 4, 8, and 11. There were significant differences for the number of words with seven or more letters between 4th and 11th grades (but not between 4th and 8th or between 8th and 11th grades). These results point to the fact that lexical measures may be sensitive only in certain developmental windows. Before early adolescence, the many demands that must be consciously coordinated to write well (e.g., transcription, generation of grammatical sentences, organizing content) may conspire to cap lexical growth. Perhaps only after a certain fluency threshold is reached can writers show their true lexical capabilities.

Although it is certain that lexical measures are developmentally meaningful, at least in certain age ranges, less is known about the sensitivity of these measures in terms of language ability. For the sparse group of studies available, there are conflicting findings. For example, significant differences in the number of words with seven or more letters were reported by Houck and Billingsley (1989) in a comparison of normally achieving students and those with learning disabilities (LD) but not in another study using the same measure (Barenbaum, Newcomer, & Nodine, 1987). Likewise, for the measure of lexical diversity, TTR distinguished between students ages 9 to 15 with and without LD in a study by Morris and Crump (1982), but NDW per 100 words was not a distinguishing feature of narrative or expository writing for children between 11 and 13 years of age, as reported by Scott and Windsor (2000).

In spite of general guidelines provided by group studies, interpreting the significance of global lexical measures for any one child remains problematic. If two writers produce texts with TTRs of 0.55 and 0.45, respectively, is that an important (practical) difference, one that would bring the child with the 0.45 TTR to the attention of a clinician or teacher? Even if the measures had sufficient sensitivity to identify struggling writers, the measures do not, by themselves, address the types of words that might be targeted in writing instruction or intervention. For this purpose, direct examination of the types of words used in writing samples is more helpful.

Types of Words

In their discussion of writing assessment at the word level, Nelson and Van Meter (2006) recommend analyzing word choice with a focus on maturity, interest, and variety. Various treatments of the development of both closed- and open-class words in older children and adolescents provide guidelines for choosing word categories (e.g., Nippold, 1998; Scott, 1988), and several developmental studies of writing demonstrate increased use of these types of words with age. For example, Nippold,

Ward-Lonergan, and Fanning (2005) reported significant increases in the use of adverbial conjuncts, abstract nouns, and metacognitive verbs in persuasive writing between ages 11 and 24. Strömqvist, Nordqvist, and Wengelin (2004) reported increases in speech-act verbs (those used for indirect and direct speech references in narrative writing, e.g., *propose, jeer, mutter*) across a similar age span. Drawing from these and similar resources, Table 14.2 lists several types of words that appear to be good candidates for both assessment and instruction.

I searched the five samples shown in Figure 14.1 for these types of advanced words. Sample 1 contained several earlier developing adverbs of magnitude (*very, too, sometimes*) and the abstract, derived noun *protection*, but little else of note. In sample 2, I identified the abstract,

TABLE 14.2. Types of Words (Categories) Used Increasingly with Age in Later Language Development

Lexical categories	Examples
Abstract nouns: those that do not have a physical presence (cannot be pointed to)	*economy, knowledge, contribution, love, situation, idea, vacation, theory, system, understanding*
Derived words: those with derivational prefixes and/or suffixes	*difference, unkind, kindness, advertisement, medicinal, comprehension, consumer, reality, gracious, ability, considerable, oppression*
Polysemous terms: words that have more than one meaning	The water is *warm*/she has a *warm* expression; the knife has a *keen* edge/his mind is very *keen*; he *fought* in Korea/he *fought* loneliness/those colors *fought* each other.
Adverbs of likelihood and magnitude: words that indicate the level of certainty, probability, or degree	*very, kind of, really, probably, definitely, extremely, possibly, very predictably, hugely, slightly, sort of, usually, certainly*
Metalinguistic verbs: those indicating some act of speaking (or writing)	*tell, discuss, whisper, intimate, imply, whimper, yell, exclaim, announce, reply, shout, propose*
Metacognitive verbs: those indicating some type of thought process	*decide, infer, conclude, think, remember, observe, assume, reason, believe, know, understand*
Subordinate conjunctions (later developing)	*unless, until, provided that, even though, whereupon, although*
Adverbial conjuncts (later developing)	*moreover, similarly, nevertheless, on the other hand, rather, however, for example, in addition, furthermore, for instance, actually, in conclusion, consequently*

Note. Based on Nippold (1998) and Scott (1988).

derived noun *environment*. Advanced words in sample 3 included adverbs of likelihood (*normally*, *as well*). There were no advanced subordinate conjunctions or adverbial conjuncts in any of the three texts produced by children with LLD. Inspection of samples 4 and 5, written by TD students, yielded many more advanced words, including the derived words *edition*, *barren*, *uninhabitable*, *different*, *erosion*, *wetness*, *organism*, *horizontal*, *exception*, *competition*, *coolness*, and *nocturnal*; the adverbs of likelihood *rarely*, *in some cases*, *usually*, and *just a little*; and the later-developing subordinate conjunctions *after*, *while*, and *even though*. I then decided to see how closely my list would correlate with a list of low-frequency words generated by an online word-frequency text profiler (*www.edict.com.hk/textanalyser*). The results are shown in Table 14.3. Words listed for each sample are those that do not appear among the 2,000 most frequent words of English (Brown Corpus; Francis & Kucera, 1982).[2] Words in bolded italics are those identified by the profiler that I had not picked. Words shown in parentheses at the end of the list are ones that I singled out but that were not identified by the profiler. Although there was considerable overlap in the two systems for identifying mature words, I overlooked several shorter words (many were verbs) identified by the profiler. On the other hand, words I chose that were not on the profiler list tended to be longer words. Nevertheless, the number of words identified as advanced by both systems—my judgment and the strict word frequency method used by the profiler—correlates well with the diversity measures TTR and NDW (for controlled sample sizes). The writers of samples 4 and 5, which had higher lexical diversity values, used many more advanced words.

SENTENCE-LEVEL MEASURES

The sentence is the domain of syntax, or grammar, and the associated semantic relations constructed when words are sequenced under a hierarchical system of grammatical rules. I address only syntax in this section, but my assumption is that syntax is the medium for underlying semantic relationships that are paramount to communication. Thus, if an analysis of sentential syntax shows that a child's written sentences are too simple (i.e., that most sentences are just one clause), then it is assumed that one area of semantics in which the child is also behind developmentally is in the expression of logical semantic relationships made possible by the use of subordinate clauses of reason, purpose, time, and so forth. A second assumption is that sentential syntax is also the medium for important text-level functions, for example, pointing backward or forward in

TABLE 14.3. Low-Frequency Words (Brown Corpus) Identified by a Text Profiler Program

Sample	Number of word types that do *not* appear in 2,000 most frequent list/ percentage of all words	Low-frequency words
1	11 7.8%	*absorbed, moist,* **passes, drops,** *slopes,* **blow,** *cooler,* **holes,** *degrees, predators, moisture* (*protection*)
2	10 6.6%	*storms, destroy,* **climbing,** *rainfalls, underground, survive, cooler,* **hunt,** *adapted, environment* (*regular*)
3	19 9.0%	*creature, stinging, tail,* **holds,** *poison,* **hides,** *hotter,* **rocks, holes,** *spikes, biting, normally, rainstorm, caves, nests, warmth, underground, cooler, sunshine*
4	35 13.3%	**movie,** *edition, explaining, barren, uninhabitable, southwestern, flash, flooding, erosion, landscape, rarely, torrents, harsh, blowing,* **drown,** *baked, soil,* **rocks,** *absorb, wetness, sudden, saguaro, roots, ranges, collect,* **stores, tons, bite, suck,** *spikes, protect,* **hurt,** *meters, bloom,* **leaves**
5	40 11.9%	**video,** *erosion, rainfall, intense, lifeless, organisms, adapted, climate, mainly, horizontal, root, tap, meters,* **huge,** *ribs, upward, collect, protected, thorns, predators, exceptions,* **hurt,** *coolness, nocturnal, survive, prey,* **dig, holes,** *blazing, degrees, scarce, underground, surrounded, canyons, occasional, oasis, absorb, rainfall, thousands,* **shy** (*conditions, systems, competition, temperature*)

Note. Words shown in **bold italics** were not among those I identified in an independent list of perceived low-frequency words; words in parentheses at the end of each list are those identified by me but not by the text profiling program.

the text, as required particularly in discourse monologues (such as writing). The student who writes the sentence, "*His father, who had watched Yanis's growing discontent, decided to talk to the village elders,*" shows syntactic acumen but also important discourse skills, including the ability to point backward in the text by using the past perfect form of the verb *watch* and supplying just the right amount of information needed by readers to make sense of the text (with the relative clause *who had watched Yanis's growing discontent*). The point for emphasis is that mastery of complex syntax is one of the tools necessary for full participation as a writer. Ravid and Tolchinksy (2002) discussed the development of "linguistic literacy" as the ability to use, as needed, the wide variety of features characteristic of different registers and genres. As applied specifically to syntax, Scott (2004) conceived of linguistic literacy as a system in which writers are successful at deploying a full range of syntactic (and associated semantic) structures in the service of many genres and, ultimately, communication needs.

Global Measures of Syntactic Complexity

Within the sentence are clauses, phrases, and words, each with its own grammar. When a new sentence begins, the same rules apply all over again. Sentences may consist of a single clause, which, minimally, must have a subject and a predicate. A simple sentence could be as short as two words (e.g., *Birds sing*). Sentences also can be very long and complex, with multiple clauses at different depths of subordination (i.e., one clause is subordinate to another clause, which is itself subordinate ... and so on) and 30 or more words. Sentence complexity has a long history of study by linguists in terms of abstract grammatical representations and by psychologists and others with interests in how such sentences are processed. In studies of spoken and written language development, sentence complexity at a global level is most often operationalized as a measure of average sentence length (in morphemes or words). As sentence length increases, complexity also increases with the addition of syntactic operations. In the following illustration, the second sentence shows additions of (1) a premodifier (*next*) in the slot before the head noun of the subject noun phrase of the main clause, (2) a modal auxiliary (*could*) to the verb phrase of the main clause, and (3) a subordinate adverbial clause, resulting in seven additional words (as underlined):

1. *The game is on TV.* (5 words)
2. *The <u>next</u> game <u>could</u> be on TV <u>if they win this one</u>.* (12 words)

The most common metric of sentence length in developmental writing studies is a calculation of the average number of words per T-unit (mean length of T-unit, MLTU), in which T-unit stands for terminable unit, as originally defined by Hunt in 1965.[3] MLTU for the five writing samples in Figure 14.1 are reported in Table 14.1; values for the texts produced by the three students with LLD are below those of the TD students.

A second common way to measure sentence complexity at a global level is to count clauses. A simple way to determine the number of clauses in a sentence is to count the verb phrases in the sentence (because each clause, by definition, must have a verb). Thus, in sample 5 (Figure 14.1), the sixth T-unit has seven verb phrases (*adapt, having, lets, take in, have, go down, to get*) and seven clauses. For a written text, the total number of clauses is divided by the total number of T-units, yielding the average number of clauses per sentence. This measure is termed the *subordination index* in some studies and *clause density* in others. Calculations of clause density for the five samples are shown in Table 14.1. A comparison of MLTU and clause density across the five samples shows an inconsistency. Sample 1, written by a student with LLD, posts the highest clause density, higher even than sample 5, written by a TD writer with a much higher MLTU. When the samples are examined more closely, the reason for the high clause density in sample 1 is apparent. This writer used many short, dependent clauses of causation (see T-units 2, 3, 8, and 10 for clauses beginning with *because*) that are among the early developing types of adverbial subordinate clauses. The result is a somewhat artificial inflation of clause density. This example underscores the fact that the interpretation of these measures requires a deeper understanding of the syntactic and semantic systems and their development that underlie the numbers.

The use of sentence length and clause density in writing assessment has a long history, dating back to early studies by Hunt (1965) and Loban (1976). Both measures show steady increases over the entire range of elementary and secondary grades and beyond to adult writers. However, increases are modest, and standard deviations are large in cross-sectional studies, complicating interpretation with any one child. To illustrate, Loban (1976) reported MLTUs of 7.60 at third grade, 8.02 at fourth grade, and 8.76 at fifth grade, an increase of just over one word per sentence (on average) over a 2-year period of development. An increase of one word could just as easily be engineered by asking a child to write on two different topics, or in two different genres, or on two different days, and so forth. These and other interpretation issues have been discussed previously by Scott and colleagues (Scott, 1988; Scott & Stokes, 1995), who concluded that the measures are sensitive to developmental changes, but only when several years intervene between comparisons and only when the confound of text genre, which has a substantial impact on sentence length, is controlled. Two recent reports cast some doubt about MLTU and clause density as developmental metrics in writing. In a recent study of persuasive writing, Nippold et al. (2005) failed to uncover developmental changes in clause density across a 13-year age span in 11-, 17-, and 24-year-old writers. Likewise, Nelson and Van Meter (2003) did not find any evidence that MLTU is a sensitive measure of sentence complexity in narratives written by children in grades 1 through 5.

Researchers have also used these measures to determine whether the writing of students with typical language development and school achievement differs from that of children with LLD. Several studies report no difference in MLTU between normally achieving students and those with LD or language impairments (e.g., Bishop & Clarkson, 2003; Cragg & Nation, 2006; Fey, Catts, Proctor-Williams, Tomblin, & Zhang, 2004; Houck & Billingsley, 1989; Morris & Crump, 1982). Other studies report significant differences in MLTU (Nelson & Van Meter, 2007; Scott & Windsor, 2000). Although fewer studies have measured clause density, both positive (Fey et al., 2004) and negative (Scott & Windsor, 2000) findings of significance have been reported.

Other Syntax Measures and Observations

As early as 1991, after reviewing evidence available to date, Newcomer and Barenbaum (1991) called for better measures of syntactic maturity than T-unit length. Although MLTU and clause density measures enjoy continued use up to the present, researchers have devised other quantitative measures of sentence complexity based on multiclause T-units; for instance:

• *Number of propositions per T-unit*: A proposition is a predicate and associated arguments, basically the semantic equivalent of a clause (Gillam & Johnston, 1992, p. 1307).

• *Percent of complex correct T-units*: A complex T-unit contains a main clause and one or more coordinating, subordinating, complementing, or relative clauses (Gillam & Johnston, 1992, p. 1306). Children with language and reading impairments exhibited more complex T-units in spoken compared with written stories, but the opposite was true for TD children. More important, the types of sentences that contributed the most to group differences were ones that contained several *different* types of subordinate clauses (Gillam & Johnston, 1992). Children free of language impairments generated significantly more of these types of sentences. In a related study, Scott (2003) showed that the ability to combine several different types of subordinate and coordinate clauses within the same T-unit was a distinguishing feature of children with and without LLD, a finding that agreed with that reported by Gillam and Johnston (1992). This is a promising finding in the search for sentence-level measures that are more sensitive to differences in language ability. Nippold et al. (2005) reported that relative clauses were the only type of subordinate clause used more frequently with age by 11-, 17-, and 24-year olds in persuasive essays; adverbial and complement clauses did not distinguish the groups. Taken together, these results indicate that finer-grained analyses of the *types of dependent clauses and their combinations within the*

T-unit may be more sensitive to developmental changes in writing and more useful in studies of writers with other language differences.

- *Connectives per T-unit*: This is a measure of the number of causal (*because, since, in order to*), conditional (*but, instead, however*), and temporal (*then, after, until, finally*) connectives (Gillam & Johnston, 1992). Children without disabilities used more T-units that combined various connectives in written (and spoken) stories than did those with language and reading impairments.

- *Simple correct, simple incorrect, complex correct, complex incorrect*: T-units are coded according to whether they contain one clause (simple) or more than one clause (complex) and whether there are any grammatical errors (Nelson & Van Meter, 2007). Significant grade effects (first through fifth) were found for all measures in narrative writing except for complex incorrect; of particular note, complex correct T-units accounted for 21% of all T-units in first grade, but this proportion doubled by fifth grade (42%). The measure was less successful in distinguishing between normally achieving and special-needs students.

Scott and colleagues are currently investigating additional sentence-level measures that involve finer-grained analyses of grammatical phenomena in written texts. The motivation is to find more sensitive measures of group differences by exploring structures and systems identified in the developmental literature as indicative of writing growth. For instance, it is well established that there are grammatical differences in spoken and written texts (see reviews by Biber, 1988; Chafe & Danielewicz, 1987; Halliday, 1985, 1987). Grammar and word choice in children's writing begins to become more distinctly "written" by the age of 8–10 years (Kroll, 1981; Perera, 1984, 1986; Scott, 2005). In a comparison of spoken and written versions of the same writing assignment, Scott (2002b) identified examples of "written" forms reported in the literature. Tallies of these structures distinguished language ability groups; 11-year-old students with LLD used fewer written forms than age peers, but their writing was comparable to that of language-matched writers who were 2 years younger. The following two sentences from Scott (2002b) illustrate spoken and written structural differences. It is interesting that the written version is actually shorter in number of words:

Spoken: And once cactuses die animals move into the cactus to live.

Written: Animals make homes out of dead plants.

Scott and Nelson (2006) reported results of a preliminary study exploring a weighted index of syntactic complexity in several tasks that required text-level writing by second, fourth, sixth, and ninth graders. They coded not only the type of subordinate clause and whether these were early or late developing but also clause depth (whether the dependent clause is subordinate to the main clause or to another subordinate clause) and position (left or right branching) and assigned weights accordingly. There were robust grade effects for the index, and it was less affected by task than MLTU. Theirs is not the first attempt to develop a weighted syntax index for measuring syntactic complexity in writing, but their weighting system incorporates more recent developmental findings in written forms of discourse.

Grammatical Accuracy

Researchers and clinicians are interested in grammatical accuracy, in addition to sentence complexity. Once students have reached a level at which they are reasonably fluent transcribers, usually by mid-elementary years, grammatical errors should be minimal. Scott and Windsor (2000) reported an overall error rate of 12% (errors/T-units) for TD 11-year-olds in narrative writing and 15% in expository writing. In practical terms, this means that a teacher reading a story would encounter a grammatical error approximately once in every nine sentences, or once in every seven sentences in a report. Errors included those in morphosyntax (inaccurate verb tense, verb aspect, noun–verb agreement, number, possession), pronoun usage (incorrect case, number, gender), noun phrase structure (e.g., omission/substitution of articles), clause structure (e.g., omission of obligatory arguments), word substitutions, and errors that spanned wider parts of the sentence (across clauses). Morphosyntactic errors, particularly verb tense omissions, accounted for the largest proportion of all errors (over half) in the written output of children between the ages of 9 and 13 (Scott, Windsor, & Gray, 1998).

Like complexity, accuracy has been measured and reported in a variety of ways. Accuracy assessments have sometimes been limited to a tally of fragments and/or run-ons, considered two of the grammar "demons" in language arts materials, but this practice confuses grammatical errors and punctuation (e.g., as punctuated by the writer, "*He wanted to see the ocean. Because he had never seen it before*" is a punctuation error rather than a grammatical error). Many studies have reported error rates but, unfortunately, no further details about the types of errors tallied. Two recent studies found no effect of age (Bishop & Clarkson, 2003) or grade (Nelson & Van Meter, 2007) on error rates in writing over the course of the elementary school years. Although on the surface this is a surprising finding, it is an interesting one and may indicate that typically developing writers obtain control of grammatical accuracy fairly early as they develop transcription fluency. The finding is also in keeping with the high level of accuracy in the spelling of verbs marked for past tense -*ed* in the narrative writing of second- and third-grade children (Carlisle, 1996).

Two studies demonstrated that grammatical error rates in writing constitute a true clinical marker for children and adolescents with specific language impairments (Mackie & Dockrell, 2004; Scott & Windsor, 2000). Both investigations compared writers with SLI with age peers and language peers. Children who were language peers were younger than the children with SLI, but their language was normal. In each investigation, writers with SLI had a higher error rate than both age peers (as expected) *and* language-matched children. This finding is particularly interesting because the more typical finding for a wide variety of language measures is that children with language impairments are distinguished from age peers but are similar to language peers. Indeed, in a comparison of morphosyntactic errors in speaking and writing, Windsor, Scott, and Street (2000) showed that children with LLD (who also met standard criteria for SLI) made verb errors (tense, number) in 13.9% of all opportunities (obligatory contexts) when writing compared with 3.6% in speaking. Comparable figures for age-matched peers were 2.9% (written) and 1.2% (spoken), and for language-matched peers were 4.4% and 1.6%, respectively. The structure with the highest error rate for children with LLD, who were between the ages of 10 and 13, was regular past tense, which they omitted in one-fourth of all obligatory contexts.

In my own clinical work, I have seen many examples of children and adolescents with language impairments who have made considerable progress in general language comprehension and expression and in reading, who can plan a good piece of writing and express well orally what they intend to write, but who nevertheless are terribly nonfluent and agrammatic in generating written sentences. In a sense, the core representational feature of SLI, difficulty with grammar, appears to "lurk" beneath the surface, rising to the top in writing, one of the premiere examples of a behavior that requires simultaneous attention to several different domains of functioning (for a discussion of this phenomenon, see Scott, 2004).

DISCOURSE-LEVEL MEASURES

Words and sentences sum to the overall text product. It is relatively easy to verbalize in general terms what makes a text a good one—it contains the right amount of content for the purpose, and it communicates that content effectively to readers. Bringing the reader into the equation is a reminder that the accomplished writer always has the reader in mind. It is more difficult to define in operational terms what constitutes the right amount of content or what makes a text effective from the reader's perspective.

The options for assessing writing at the discourse level depend entirely on the task. Most writing assessments could be considered open-ended in the sense that the student generates the content in response to some type of prompt, for example, a story starter, a topic (e.g., pros and cons of wearing school uniforms), a picture, or a series of pictures. Tasks differ in terms of exactly how much content is under the writer's control, depending on the actual prompt or the number of pictures (one versus an entire wordless picture book). Even so, these types of tasks are very different from others in which the writer is presented with information to summarize or, in which, given a smaller amount of input, he or she may be asked to recall "as much as possible." One measure used often in the recall task is the total number of information units or propositions from the input text that appear in the student's writing.

Assessments of self-generated (open-ended) writing lend themselves to both quantitative and qualitative measures. On the quantitative side, productivity in terms of total words and/or T-units is a straightforward measure. Many other discourse-level structures and devices can be quantified, such as the number of cohesion devices or the number and variety of intersentential connectives (e.g., *however, moreover, in other words*). What the assessor chooses to quantify is frequently genre-specific. In an analysis of students' expository (descriptive) writing, Scott and Jennings (2004) counted the number of generalizations and thus captured a higher level of content in a hierarchically structured text (examples include T-units 4, 5, and 26 in sample 5). Reporting on persuasive writing, Nippold et al. (2005) counted the number of reasons provided about a controversial topic. For text genres that have clear organizational templates, as when the task calls for a narrative with a classic story grammar structure, one quantifiable measure might be the number and variety of story components.

A common way of assessing writing at the discourse level is to assign points or a rating based on a rubric that has been developed specifically for a particular task. Rubrics vary (1) in the number and type of discourse domains evaluated and how extensively these domains (e.g., focus, organization, integration) are broken down into smaller traits and (2) whether the rubric applies to writing generally or is genre-specific (e.g., applies to narrative writing only). Researchers often devise a rating system unique to their own purposes. For example, Fey et al. (2004) assigned a subjective quality score to spoken and written narratives produced by second- and fourth-grade children with and without SLI; children earned points on a scale of 0–3 for how well they handled story characters, physical setting, story ending, and language sophistication and on a scale of 0–6 for overall plot complexity. The assessment of a text against a rubric is the most common method of examining writing competence for an entire system (a district or state-wide assessment), but rubrics can also be useful for purposes of planning the best instruction or intervention with individual students. Not surprisingly, rubric-based ratings of writing and quantitative measures of productivity are often highly correlated. This is obvious in a comparison of the least productive and most productive samples in Figure 14.1. The video that was summarized for these samples started with information about how deserts are formed, then turned attention to desert plants, next to desert animals and plant–animal interdependence, then to water conditions, and finally to a summary. Sample 1 is the shortest sample (140 words, 13 T-units) and starts with a generalization about the desert, skips to water conditions, then describes how deserts were formed. The text skips information about plants entirely and ends abruptly on the topic of animals. In contrast, sample 5 (335 words, 27 T-units) follows the major topics of the original video and includes several generalization statements that are located strategically at the beginning (T-units 1, 4), the middle (T-units 13, 22) and at the end (T-unit 26) of the summary.

Discourse-level measures show effects of age and language ability more consistently than some of the word- and sentence-level measures discussed earlier.[4] Regarding productivity, older writers produce more words than younger writers given the same writing assignment. The effect holds for comparisons at narrow age ranges, as well as for those across wider ranges that include young adults. To illustrate, 9-year-olds wrote only 60% as many words as 11-year-olds on both narrative and expository writing tasks in the Scott and Windsor (2000) study; as shown by Nippold et al. (2005), 11-year olds wrote 77% as many words as 17-year-olds, who wrote 70% as many words as 24-year-olds for persuasive essays. Asked to write an original story, fifth-grade children wrote five times as many words as first-grade children, with linear increases in the intervening grades (Nelson & Van Meter, 2007). Similar to findings for age effects, research has consistently shown that special education students and/or those with documented oral-language difficulties are less productive writers than typically developing age-matched children (Mackie & Dockrell, 2004; Nelson & Van Meter, 2007; Scott & Windsor, 2000). Likewise, on rubrics designed to measure discourse quality specific to the writing task, children and adolescents with lower language ability are poor performers compared with age peers (Cragg & Nation, 2006; Fey et al., 2004; Nelson & Van Meter, 2007; Nippold et al., 2005).

Two discourse-level measures have been reported recently that take advantage of the power of the computer. In spoken language, a permanent record of discourse fluency is easily captured by the tape recorder. Silent and filled pauses can be measured; word repetitions and reformulations involving word choice and/or grammar can be transcribed verbatim. Comparable formulation phenomena and timing factors in writing are lost to the delete key or the eraser, and therefore it is easy to forget that writing can be painfully nonfluent. In order to more fully compare spoken and written language generation processes, Strömqvist et al. (2004) developed ScriptLog, a program that tracks all text editing (and associated timing features) of writers at the computer keyboard. Not surprisingly, older writers made proportionally more content (as opposed to spelling) edits in stories, and their editing was more evenly distributed across the text. Younger writers (age 9), by comparison, were more active editors at the beginning of the story, with fewer edits as the story unfolded. The interpretation offered by the authors is that composition has more of a cumulative toll on the younger writers, and they cannot sustain the effort that editing requires. Having this type of processing information, coupled with a record of the final linguistic product, may allow us to marry processing and linguistic product information in a different, more productive way in the future.

A second promising analysis protocol uses the power of the computer to capture linguistic co-occurrences (both lexical and grammatical) and to build factors from these associations in a multidimensional manner. This corpus-based analytic procedure often has been used to study differences in various written and spoken registers (e.g., Biber, 1992). Gregg, Coleman, Stennett, and Davis (2002), by way of contrast, used this technique in the study of one register (expository essays) across four groups of college writers to explore differences in writers with and without disabilities (LD, attention-deficit/hyperactivity disorder [ADHD], LD/ADHD, and TD). They tagged every word in each essay for grammatical function, and computer modeling yielded five factors (time, reference elaboration, reduction, framing elaboration, and verbosity). Although the four groups of writers used the same factors, indicating similarities in basic use of linguistic features, distinctive factor loadings appeared for specific structures and features that were worthy of further exploration. An analysis scheme that capitalizes on statistical co-occurrences of linguistic features of written language stands in contrast to isolated counts of linguistic features and is worthy of continued study. The advantage in this procedure is that form–function interactions can be better captured.

A LOOK AT THE FUTURE

This chapter has approached the topic of language-based assessment of written expression from a framework of progressively larger linguistic levels—words, sentences, and discourse. This framework is a common heuristic for controlling the myriad of topics and tremendous complexity of language. But with gains in manageability come multiple caveats, including oversimplifying and obscuring interrelationships between various measures, both within and between levels. I have discussed and demonstrated several of these directly; for example, the dependence of lexical diversity, a word-level measure, on overall text length. I alluded to several others, such as the fact that a writer's broader intent, chosen topic and organization scheme, and ability to keep the reader in mind undoubtedly have an impact on sentence-level syntax and complexity. It follows that if a writer is not particularly good at these higher level skills, then sentence- and word-level proficiencies would suffer as well. This line of reasoning would seem to imply that poor writers would be expected to struggle "across the board" at all three levels. However, there are reports to the contrary that suggest that students' writing problems are more specific to a level (Juel, 1988; Whittaker, Berninger, Johnston, & Swanson, 1994). The presence of these disassociations rings true with my own clinical experience, particularly with students who struggle excessively to generate fluent, grammatical sentences but seem to have better control at higher levels. How can language-based writing assessments help to unravel these associations or disassociations? Most important is a clear understanding of what a measure really reflects. As shown with the comparisons among the five written texts analyzed in this chapter, it is possible to arrive at the same quantitative value in a variety of ways, some of which are developmentally more advanced than others. There is also a need for research designed to establish the nature of relationships between and among writing measures, for example, factor analytic techniques that reduce a large number of variables to a smaller number of dimensions (see, e.g., Gregg et al., 2002, who studied the writing of college students with LD and ADHD, and Justice, Bowles, Kaderauek, Ukrainetz, Eisenberg, & Gillam, 2006, who studied children's spoken narratives). To date, many studies of developmental and/or ability differences in writing do not discuss the rationale, other than precedent, for choosing certain measures, nor is there an attempt to examine relationships between measures.

A second issue that affects language-based writing assessment is the lack of detailed information about other language abilities of participant groups. In the typical research paradigm, children or adolescents with language and/or learning impairments are described only in the broadest terms (e.g., LD as determined by district criteria). Yet it is well known that individuals within these groups are heterogeneous with regard to patterns of linguistic and cognitive strengths and weaknesses. Most, but not every, student with LD has a reading disorder. Among those with reading disorders, the difficulty could be one of poor word recognition, poor general language comprehension, or both (Catts, Adlof, & Ellis Weismer, 2006). The dearth of this type of information about participants in writing research affects our ability to interpret findings. An example of the potential benefits of connecting writing measures with underlying language impairment in a more direct way is the finding that morphosyntactic error rates in writing are greatly exacerbated compared with those in speaking in children with SLI. As a language clinician, then, I am aware that this aspect of writing is unlikely to improve on its own or as a by-product of working on other areas of need. Several studies cited in this chapter have provided a more detailed profile of participants (Fey et al., 2004) and/or have been specifically designed to study writing in a narrowly defined group (Bishop & Clarkson, 2003; Cragg & Nation, 2006). A research protocol that provides more detailed accounts of writing *and* other language strengths and weaknesses in spoken language and reading would be welcomed (Scott, 2002a).

Language-based assessments would ideally be tied in a substantive way to instruction and the measurement of outcomes. By concentrating on actual language units (words, sentences, discourse) rather than general traits, these types of assessments are well suited to writing instruction and intervention within a contextualized skill framework in which language patterns needed for improved writing are taught explicitly and facilitated in purposeful writing activities (Ukrainetz, 2006). However, in a meta-analysis of 13 studies of the effects of teaching expressive writing to students with LD, the most common outcome measures were holistic quality scores or rubric-based mean scores (Gersten & Baker, 2001). In several studies that included instruction on text structure, the number of text components (a discourse-level measure) was measured, but sentence- and word-level changes were not examined. Few training studies to date have used the types of language measures discussed in this chapter as dependent variables. One exception is the work of Nelson and Van Meter (2006), who reported promising results for several word-, sentence-, and discourse-level measures using a classroom-based writing lab approach with typically developing and atypical elementary school children (although their work lacks experimental control, e.g., an untreated comparison group). For purposes of informing intervention and measuring outcomes, further research on language-based writing assessment is needed. Research designs that shed light on relationships between language measures and those that describe broader language abilities of writers should make important contributions.

NOTES

1. Note that total words rather than number of sentences should be used for standardizing sample size because average sentence length (in words) varies across children of different ages and language abilities. Thus two samples of the same length in number of sentences may vary in terms of total words.
2. I eliminated all animal and insect words, as well as the words *cactus* and *desert*, regardless of their word frequency, from analysis because of their high frequency in the video. All writers used these words frequently when summarizing the video.
3. T-units, or terminable units, after Hunt (1965), is the commonly used sentence-like unit in writing research with school-age children and adolescents. The T-unit is defined as a main clause and any attached dependent clauses. Sentences with several clauses conjoined with coordinating conjunctions (*and*, *or*, *but*, *so*) are divided into two or more T-units, and thus the transcriber has a structural criterion to follow rather than depending on semantic notions about whether clauses are related or not (e.g., as in compound sentences). Likewise, the writer's punctuation (sometimes inaccurate) is overridden by the structural criterion.
4. The statement of consistent findings of age and language ability effects on productivity measures (number of words, number of T-units) is tempered somewhat in studies of expository writing completed before 1990 and reviewed by Newcomer and Barenbaum (1991). These authors report consistent effects in narrative writing but less consistent findings for expository writing. In studies since 1990, productivity is often cited as a significant differentiator of age- and ability-based groups.

REFERENCES

Barenbaum, E., Newcomer, P., & Nodine, B. (1987). Children's ability to write stories as a function of variation in task, age, and developmental level. *Learning Disability Quarterly, 10*, 175–188.

Biber, D. (1988). *Variation across speech and writing*. Cambridge, UK: Cambridge University Press.

Biber, D. (1992). On the complexity of discourse complexity: A multidimensional analysis. *Discourse Processes, 15*, 133–163.

Bishop, D. V. M., & Clarkson, B. (2003). Written language as a window into residual language deficits: A study of children with persistent and residual speech and language impairments. *Cortex, 39,* 215–237.

Carlisle, J. (1996). An exploratory study of morphological errors in children's written stories. *Reading and Writing, 8,* 61–72.

Catts, H., Adlof, S., & Ellis Weismer, S. (2006). Language deficits in poor comprehenders: A case for the simple view of reading. *Journal of Speech, Language, and Hearing Research, 49,* 278–293.

Chafe, W., & Danielewicz, J. (1987). Properties of spoken and written language. In R. Horowitz & S. J. Samuels (Eds.), *Comprehending oral and written language* (pp. 83–113). New York: Academic Press.

Cragg, L., & Nation, K. (2006). Exploring written narrative in children with poor reading comprehension. *Educational Psychology, 26*(1), 55–72.

Fey, M., Catts, H., Proctor-Williams, K., Tomblin, J. B., & Zhang, X. (2004). Oral and written story composition skills of children with language impairment. *Journal of Speech, Language, and Hearing Research, 47,* 1301–1318.

Francis, W. N., & Kucera, H. (1982). *Frequency analysis of English usage.* New York: Houghton Mifflin.

Gersten, R., & Baker, S. (2001). Teaching expressive writing to students with learning disabilities. *Elementary School Journal, 101,* 251–272.

Gillam, R., & Johnston, J. (1992). Spoken and written language relationships in language/learning-impaired and normally achieving school-age children. *Journal of Speech and Hearing Research, 35,* 1303–1315.

Graham, S., & Harris, K. R. (2000). The role of self-regulation and transcription skills in writing and writing development. *Educational Psychologist, 35*(1), 3–12.

Gregg, N., Coleman, C., Stennett, R., & Davis, M. (2002). Discourse complexity of college writers with and without disabilities. *Journal of Learning Disabilities, 35,* 23–38.

Halliday, M. A. K. (1985). *Spoken and written language.* Oxford, UK: Oxford University Press.

Halliday, M. A. K. (1987). Spoken and written modes of meaning. In R. Horowitz & S. J. Samuels (Eds.), *Comprehending oral and written language* (pp. 55–82). New York: Academic Press.

Houck, C., & Billingsley, B. (1989). Written expression of students with and without learning disabilities: Differences across the grades. *Journal of Learning Disabilities, 22,* 252–565.

Hunt, K. (1965). *Grammatical structures written at three grade levels* (Research Rep. No. 3). Champaign, IL: National Council of Teachers of English.

Juel, C. (1988). Learning to read and write: A longitudinal study of 54 children from first through fourth grades. *Journal of Educational Psychology, 80,* 437–447.

Justice, L., Bowles, R., Kaderavek, J., Ukrainetz, T., Eisenberg, S., & Gillam, R. (2006). The index of narrative micro-structure (INIMIS): A clinical tool for analyzing school-aged children's narrative performances. *American Journal of Speech–Language Pathology, 15,* 177–191.

Juzwik, M., Curcic, S., Wolbers, K., Moxley, K., Dimling, L., & Shankland, R.

(2006). Writing into the 21st century: An overview of research on writing, 1999 to 2004. *Written Communication, 23*, 451–476.

Kroll, B. (1981). Developmental relationships between speaking and writing. In B. Kroll & R. Vann (Eds.), *Exploring speaking–writing relationships: Connections and contrasts* (pp. 32–54). Urbana, IL: National Council of Teachers of English.

Loban, W. (1976). *Language development: Kindergarten through grade twelve* (Research Rep. No. 18). Urbana, IL: National Council of Teachers of English.

Mackie, C., & Dockrell, J. (2004). The nature of written language deficits in children with SLI. *Journal of Speech, Language, and Hearing Research, 47*, 1469–1483.

McKee, G., Malvern, D., & Richards, B. (2000). Measuring vocabulary diversity using dedicated software. *Literacy and Linguistic Computing, 15*, 323–337.

Miller, J., & Chapman, R. (2000). *Systematic analysis of language transcripts* (SALT) [computer program]. Madison: University of Wisconsin, Waisman Center.

Morris, N., & Crump, D. (1982). Syntactic and vocabulary development in the written language of learning disabled and non-learning disabled students at four age levels. *Learning Disability Quarterly, 5*, 163–172.

National Commission on Writing. (2003). *The neglected "R": The need for a writing revolution.* New York: College Entrance Examination Board.

Nelson, N., & Van Meter, A. (2003, June). *Measuring written language abilities and change through the elementary years.* Poster presented at the annual Symposium for Research in Child Language Disorders, Madison, WI.

Nelson, N., & Van Meter, A. (2006). The writing lab approach for building language, literacy, and communication abilities. In R. McCauley & M. Fey (Eds.), *Treatment of language disorders in children* (pp. 383–422), Baltimore: Brookes.

Nelson, N., & Van Meter, A. (2007). Measuring written language ability in original story probes. *Reading and Writing Quarterly, 23*(3), 287–309.

Newcomer, P., & Barenbaum, E. (1991). The written composing ability of children with learning disabilities: A review of the literature from 1980 to 1990. *Journal of Learning Disabilities, 24*, 578–593.

Nippold, M. (1998). *Later language development* (2nd ed.). Austin, TX; PRO-ED.

Nippold, M., Ward-Lonergan, J., & Fanning, J. (2005). Persuasive writing in children, adolescents and adults: A study of syntactic, semantic, and pragmatic development. *Language, Speech, and Hearing Services in Schools, 36*, 125–138.

Owen, A., & Leonard, L. (2002). Lexical diversity in the spontaneous speech of children with specific language impairment: Application of D. *Journal of Speech, Language, and Hearing Research, 45*, 927–937.

Perera, K. (1984). *Children's writing and reading.* London: Blackwell.

Perera, K. (1986). Grammatical differentiation between speech and writing in children aged 8 to 12. In A. Wilkinson (Ed.), *The writing of writing* (pp. 90–108). London: Falmer Press.

Ravid, D., & Tolchinksy, L. (2002). Developing linguistic literacy: A comprehensive model. *Journal of Child Language, 29,* 417–447.

Scott, C. (1988). Spoken and written syntax. In M. Nippold (Ed.), *Later language development: Ages 9 through 19* (pp. 45–95). San Diego, CA: College Hill Press.

Scott, C. (2002a). A fork in the road less traveled: Writing intervention based on language profile. In E. Silliman & K. Butler (Eds.), *Speaking, reading, and writing in children with language learning disabilities: New paradigms in research and practice* (pp. 219–238). Mahwah, NJ: Erlbaum.

Scott, C. (2002b, June). *Speaking and writing the same texts: Comparisons of school children with and without language learning disabilities.* Paper presented at the annual meeting of the Society for Text and Discourse, Chicago.

Scott, C. (2003, June). *Literacy as variety: An analysis of clausal connectivity in spoken and written language of children with language learning disabilities.* Paper presented at the annual Symposium on Research in Child Language Disorders, Madison, WI.

Scott, C. (2004). Syntactic ability in children and adolescents with language and learning disabilities. In R. Berman (Ed.), *Language development across childhood and adolescence* (pp. 111–134). Philadelphia: Benjamins.

Scott, C. (2005). Learning to write. In H. Catts & A. Kamhi (Eds.), *Language and reading disabilities* (2nd ed., pp. 233–273). Boston: Pearson.

Scott, C., & Jennings, M. (2004, November). *Expository discourse in children with LLD: Text level analysis.* Paper presented at the annual meeting of the American Speech–Language–Hearing Association, Philadelphia.

Scott, C., & Nelson, N. (2006, June). *Capturing children's sentence complexity in writing: Promising new tasks and measures.* Paper presented at the annual meeting of the Society for Research in Child Language Disorders, Madison, WI.

Scott, C., & Stokes, S. E. (1995). An analysis of syntax norms for school-age children and adolescents. *Language, Speech, and Hearing Services in Schools, 25,* 309–319.

Scott, C., & Windsor, J. (2000). General language performance measures in spoken and written narrative and expository discourse in school-age children with language learning disabilities. *Journal of Speech, Language, and Hearing Research, 43,* 324–339.

Scott, C., Windsor, J., & Gray, T. (1998, November). *A typology of grammatical error in older children with language learning disorders.* Paper presented at the annual meeting of the American Speech–Language–Hearing Association, San Antonio, TX.

Strömqvist, S., Johansson, V., Kriz, S., Ragnarsdottir, H., Aisenman, R., & Ravid, D. (2002). Toward a cross-linguistic comparison of lexical quanta in speech and writing. *Written Language and Literacy, 5*(1), 45–68.

Strömqvist, S., Nordqvist, A., & Wengelin, A. (2004). Writing the frog story.

In S. Strömqvist & L. Verhoeven (Eds.), *Relating events in narrative* (pp. 359–394). Mahwah, NJ: Erlbaum.

Ukrainetz, T. (Ed.). (2006). *Contextualized language intervention.* Eau Claire, WI: Thinking Publications.

Whittaker, D., Berninger, V., Johnston, J., & Swanson, H. (1994). Intra-individual differences in levels of language in intermediate grade writers: Implications for the translating process. *Learning and Individual Differences, 6,* 107–130.

Windsor, J., Scott, C., & Street, C. (2000). Verb and noun morphology in the spoken and written language of children with language learning disabilities. *Journal of Speech, Language, and Hearing Research, 43,* 1322–1336.

Zipf, G. (1932). *Selected studies of the principle of relative frequency in language.* Cambridge, MA: Harvard University Press.

Index

f indicates a figure; *t* indicates a table

Academic language, English learners, 215
Academic self-efficacy
  in learning disabled, 57–58
  metacognitive skills link, 57
Accelerating Expository Literacy. *See*
  Project ACCEL
Adverbial clause instruction, 176
Age factors. *See also* Developmental
  factors
  assessment implications, 315–316
  and curriculum-based measurement,
    344–347
    validity coefficients, 346–347
Alphabetic principle
  cross-linguistic transfer study, 290–305
  definition, 292
  and English language learners, 290–305
  in language impairment instruction, 205
Alphabetics, in reading and writing,
  121–122
Amalgamation theory, 19–20
Analytical trait rubrics, 321
Anglo-Saxon word origin, orthography,
  283*t*
Apprenticeship instructional model
  expository text, 139
  in Project ACCEL, 143
Assessment. *See* Writing assessment
"Assessment conversations," 313–314
Assessment portfolios, 319–320
  English language learners, 327–328
  functions, 319
  learner-centered portfolios tension,
    329–330
  and learning disabilities, 325–326
  in progress monitoring, 319–
    320

  scoring procedures, 321–322
  standardization difficulties, 329
Assimilated prefixes, and spelling, 281–282
Attention, writing process effects, 33
Attention-deficit/hyperactivity disorder, 270
Attitudes
  and self-efficacy, 85, 91*t*, 94
  writing workshop effect, 91*t*, 92
Audience–author relationship, 139–140
Authentic assessment
  portfolios in, 314, 329
  strategy overview, 314
Authentic Literacy Assessment, 328
Author awareness factor
  in history study, 125
  reading and writing impact, 125–126
Authority-based evidence
  limitations, 166–167
  and writing instruction design, 166–167
Automated essay scoring, 255–256
Automatic processing
  versus controlled processing, 33–34
  in written language production, 33–34

Biology texts, classification schemes in,
  134

Categorical diagnosis
  language impairment, 189–190
  research evidence, 189–190
Cause–effect structure, instruction, 136
Chat rooms, 25
Chinese English language learners,
  293–302
  phonological processing study, 294,
    298–302
  pseudoword spelling, 301, 302*f*

Chinese English language learners
(*continued*)
and script-dependent hypothesis,
293–294, 296–302
spelling performance study, 296–302
spelling strategies, 300–301
Chronological sequence, discourse marker,
134
Classification, in expository texts, 134
Closed syllable, 281*t*
Cognitive flow, in writing process, 34
Cognitive processes
English learner instruction, 219–222
in reading and writing, 124
spelling role, 294–296
in writing instruction paradigms, 17–18,
20
writing link, 34
Cognitive strategy instruction
English language learners, 219–222
individual focus of, 219–222
steps in, 221
Cognitive Strategy Instruction in Writing,
138
Collaboration
apprenticeship instructional model,
139
and internet communication, 258–259
in language impairment instruction,
192–193
Commas, in reading versus writing, 122
Community culture, English learners, 219,
230–234
Community of writers
building of, 229–230
English language learners, 229–230
Compare–contrast device
as discourse marker, 134
explicit instruction, 136
in expository texts, 134
Composing hypermedia. *See* Hypertext
Composition
evidence-based instruction, 165–184
design of, 167–170
hypertext/hypermedia, 257–258
and language impairment, 187–208
discourse-level instruction, 194–199
instruction design, 191–194
sentence-level instruction, 200–
204
word-level instruction, 204–208
and learning disabilities, 165–184
in portfolio assessment, 315
strategy instruction, 137–138

Tier I instruction, 168, 170–173, 171*t*,
172*t*
Tier II instruction, 173–183
Computer keyboards
handwriting alternative, 20
neuropsychological processes in, 24–25
typing skill effects, 246–247
Computer technology, 243–261
current trends, 20
and learning disabilities, 242–262
speech recognition, 250–252
speech synthesis, 248–249
word prediction, 249–250
word processing, 245–248
Concept mapping, electronic versions,
254–255
Concept-Oriented Reading Instruction
(CORI)
results, 151
in science curriculum, 150–151
Conferencing techniques, and portfolios,
327
Confidence, self-efficacy differences, 52
Connectives, 202
Consonant graphemes, 276
Consonant-*le* syllable, 281*t*
Consonants, sound variations, 292
Content area writing. *See also* Expository
writing
curricular integration, 140–146
science studies, 150–153
social studies, 146–150
writing-to-learn strategies, 140–146
Controlled processing
versus automatic processing, 33–34
strategies in, 33
in written language production, 33–
34
Cooperative study
English language learners, 227–229
evidence-based recommendations,
176–177
Tier II students, 176–177
Correct minus incorrect word sequences
(CIWS), 342–343, 347–348
Correct word sequences (CWS), 342–345,
348, 354
Correlational studies
limitations, 115–116
in reading and writing connection,
115–116, 121
Creative writing, 21
Critical literacy, Project ACCEL studies,
145–146

Cross-word-form mapping, 35
Cultural factors. *See also* Sociocultural
    perspective
  and language impairment instruction,
    193
  non-native speakers of English,
    216
Culturally and linguistically diverse
    students
  cognitive strategy instruction, 219–222
  community/home values influence, 219,
    230–234
  dialogue journal use, 230
  family engagement, 231–232
  funds of knowledge value, 225–226
  grouping practices, 227–229
  individual level factors, 218–227
  institutional factors, 230–234
  language considerations, 215–216
  motivation, 226–227
  multiple levels conceptual model,
    217–234
  Optimal Learning Environment
    program, 223–224
  parent participation, 231–232
  process writing approaches, 222–224,
    223*f*
  social setting influence, 219
  socioeconomic factors, 216–217
  special needs, 214–217
  survey data, 213
  teacher considerations, 229–230
  writing instruction time, 233
Cumulative portfolios, 320
Curriculum-based measurement (CBM),
    337–357
  administration, 341
  age factors, 344–348
  case illustration, 340, 341*f*
  correct minus incorrect word sequences
    (CIWS), 342–343, 347–348
  correct word sequences (CWS),
    342–345, 348, 354
  incorrect word sequences (IWS),
    342–343, 354–356
  limitations, 348–349
  overview, 340–343
  and portfolio assessment, 326
  progress monitoring, 340, 341*f*
  studies, 347–349
  reliability, 344–346
  research, 344–348
  responsiveness to intervention measure,
    340
  scoring, 341–343, 354–357
  validity, 344–348
  words spelled correctly (WSC),
    342–345, 347
  words written (WW), 342–345, 347
  writing prompt effects, 346, 349
  writing time, 345–346
Curriculum-based writing. *See* Expository
    writing

Daily living, writing function, 26
DARE strategy
  historical writing, 147–148
  results, 148
Declarative knowledge cues, 33
Decoding skills
  in reading development, 117
  reading–writing relationship, 122–123
  writing positive impact on, 117
Deep orthographies, 292
Derivational morphology, 282–283
Describe-It study, 174–175
Developmental disorders, and writing
    process, 37–39
Developmental factors
  assessment implications, 315–316
  in curriculum-based measurement,
    344–348
    and validity, 346–347
  expository text structure acquisition,
    135–136
  instruction implications overview, 26–34
  reading development link, 117
  reading–writing relationship, 122–123
  triple-word-form theory, spelling, 34–37
  word prediction, 206
Dialogue, as plot element, 84, 110
Dialogue journals, English learners, 230
"Dictating" skill, 203
Dictation to a scribe, 252
Dictionary size issue, 250
Differentiated writing instruction, 34
Digraphs, 276, 278
Dimensional diagnosis
  language impairment, 189–190
  research evidence, 189–190
Diphthong vowel phonemes, 276, 281*t*
Direct assessment methods, 339
Direct instruction. *See* Explicit instruction
Discourse level
  balanced instruction research, 28
  language impairment instruction,
    194–200
  narrative context, 194–199

Discourse level (*continued*)
  story grammar analysis, 195, 196*t*,
    197*t*, 197–198
  in whole language instruction, 28
Discourse markers
  compare–contrast structure, 134
  problem–solution structure, 134
  strategy instruction, 138
Distancing, in writing revision, 126
Double consonant rules, 278, 282–283
Dysgraphia
  amelioration, 275
  differentiating deficits, 38
  overview, 37–38
  and spelling problems, 271
Dyslexia
  core deficits, 37
  current definition, 270
  developmental aspects, spelling, 273
  differentiating deficits, 38
  spelling difficulty component, 270

e letter, in orthography, 278–279
Early Literacy Project (ELP), 222–223
Editing. *See also* Revising
  evidence-based practices, 173–178
  strategy instruction, 137–138
  Tier II instruction, 173–178
  writing workshop effects, 91*t*, 93
Effect sizes
  interpretation guideline, 170, 173
  reading–writing combined instruction,
    179–180
  Tier I writing instructions, 170, 171*t*, 172*t*
  Tier II writing instructions, 173–174,
    177, 180
  word processing meta-analysis, 245
Egocentric writing, genre, 21–23
Electronic concept mapping
  advantages, 254–255
  research findings, 255
Electronic outlining, 254–255
  advantages, 254–255
  research findings, 255
Electronic text. *See also* Hypertext
  limited research on impact of, 257
  written text differences, 256–257
Elementary grades
  writing instruction paradigm shift, 16–17
  writing workshop instruction, 77–100
English language learners, 213–234,
  290–305
  analytic trait rubrics, 321
  cognitive strategy instruction, 219–222

community/home values influence,
  230–234
developmental aspects, 215
dialogue journals use, 230
family engagement, 231–232
fund of knowledge value, 225–226
grouping practices, 227–228
individual level factors, 218–227
institutional factors, 230–234
interpersonal level factors, 218–219,
  227–230
motivation, 226–227
native language considerations, 215–216
Optimal Learning Environment
  program, 223–224
parent participation, 231–232
portfolio assessment, 326–328
process writing approaches, 222–224,
  223*f*
social setting, 218–219, 227–230
sociocultural perspective, 213–234
socioeconomic considerations, 216–
  217
special needs, 214–217
spelling, 290–305
  cross-linguistic transfer, 293–305
  orthography role, 290–305
  recommendations, 302–304
survey data, 213
teacher considerations, 229–230
vocabulary development, 303–304
writing instruction time, 233
Ethnic minorities. *See* Culturally and
  linguistically diverse students
Evaluation portfolios. *See* Assessment
  portfolios
Evidence-based instruction
  versus authority/experience evidence,
    166–167
  implementation factors, 183–184
  and learning disabilities, composition,
    167–170
  teacher acceptance of, 183
  Tier I recommendations, 168–173
    effect sizes, 171*t*, 172*t*
  Tier II recommendations, 169–170,
    173–183
Exceptional teachers, qualitative study,
  172*t*
Executive functions
  increasing importance of, 40
  in keyboarding, 25
  writing integration, 24
  writing process effects, 33

Experience-based evidence
   limitations, 166–167
   and writing instruction designs,
      166–167
Experimental designs
   meta-analysis, 168–169
   quasi-experimental studies comparison,
      183
   Tier I recommendations, 170–173
   Tier II recommendations, 173–181
   word processing benefits, 180
   writing instruction effectiveness,
      167–168
Explanation, in expository text, 134
Explicit writing instruction
   English learners, 220
   expository texts, 136–140, 153–154
   learning disabilities, 316
   paradigm shift, 17–18
   spelling, 274
   Tier I students, 171*t*
   Tier II students, 173–175, 177
Expository writing, 132–155*f*
   ACCEL program, 141, 142*f*, 143–146
   developmental factors, 135–136
   discipline-based strategies, 146–153
   graphic organizers in, 137
   history studies, 147–150
   and language and learning disabilities, 136
   and language impairment, 199
   multicomponent instructional model,
      140–146
   proficiency statistics, 133
   science studies, 150–153
   self- and other-directed aspects, 22–23
   strategy instruction, 137–140
   text structure knowledge in, 134–140
      explicit instruction, 136–140
   writing-to-learn strategies, 140–146

Families
   English learners, 219, 231–232
   school participation, 231–232
   teacher engagement, 231
Feedback
   automated essay scoring, 255–256
   in spelling instruction, 285
Flow, in writing process, 34
Fluency. *See* Writing fluency
Formative assessment, 318
Functional writing systems, 27*f*, 29*f*, 40
Funds of knowledge
   cultural perspective, 216
   English learners, 225

Goal-line, curriculum-based assessment,
   343
Goal setting
   in curriculum-based measurement, 343
   evidence-based recommendations, 171*t*,
      178–179
   learner-centered portfolios, 323–324
   prompting programs, 254
   Tier I studies, 171*t*
   Tier II studies, 178–179
   writing workshops instruction need, 99
Grade level. *See also* Developmental
      factors
   assessment implications, 315–316
   and curriculum-based measurement,
      344–347
Grammar instruction
   English learners, and spelling, 295
   evidence-based impact, 175–176
   language impairment targets, 200, 202
   sentence level, 200–204, 201*t*, 202*t*
   in stories, 195, 196*t*, 197*t*
   Tier II level, 175–176
Grapheme–phoneme correspondences
   and alphabetic principle, 292
   language impairment instruction, 205
   orthographic depth hypothesis, 292
Grapheme–phoneme mappings
   alphabetic language spelling influence,
      301
   developmental factors, 35–36
   orthographic depth hypothesis
      framework, 292
Graphemes, in orthography, 272
Graphic organizers
   planning function, technology, 254
   and Project ACCEL, 145
   in storytelling, language impaired, 195,
      197
   in text structure instruction, 137
Graphomotor processes
   and spelling, 271
   in writing, 31, 271
Greek word origin, orthography, 283*t*
Grouping practices
   English language learners, 227–229
   evidence-based recommendations,
      176–177
   in Tier II, 176–177
Growth studies. *See* Progress monitoring
Guided Inquiry Supporting Multiple
      Literacies
   results, 152
   in science program, 151–152

Handwriting
    composition quality predictor, 204
    in language impaired, 204
    and letter formation instruction, 275
    Tier II instruction, 180–181
    writing quality correlates, 246
    writing workshop neglect, 99
Help-seeking, and procrastination, 66–67
Highlighting strategy
    Project ACCEL, 143–144
    summarization function, 143–144
Hispanics. *See* Culturally and linguistically
    diverse students
History studies
    literacy skill developmental function,
        149–150
    literacy skill learning opportunities, 150
    multimedia presentations function, 149
    primary source interpretation, 147
    research programs, 148–149
    text expository structure in, 134–135
Home setting, English learners, 219,
    230–231
Homework
    English learners, 233
    time management instruction, 30
Hypertext
    collaborative opportunities, 258
    creation of, 257–258
    and learning disabilities, 258
    qualitative case study, 257–258
    written text differences, 256–257

Ideas/content quality
    components, 84, 105
    writing workshop effects, 91*t*
Incorrect word sequences (IWS), 342–343,
    354–356
Indirect writing assessment, 338–339
Individualized education programs
    monitoring measures, 312
    portfolio assessment role, 323–326
Individualized instruction, 193–194
Inflectional morphemes, spelling, 282
Informational writing, 132–155
    ACCEL program, 141, 142*t*, 143–146
    curriculum integration, 140–146
    explicit instruction, 136–140, 153–
        154
    disciplinary-based strategies, 146–153
    history studies, 147–150
    proficiency statistics, 133
    science studies, 150–153
    strategy instruction, 137–140

text structure knowledge in, 134–140
    explicit instruction, 136–140
    writing-to-learn strategies in, 140–146
Inquiry skills, 171*t*
Institutional factors, English learners,
    230–234
Instructional portfolios, 317–319
Internet, 258–259
    authoring use, overview, 25–26
    collaborative writing opportunities,
        258–259
    hypermedia impact, 257
    intercultural use, 258–259
Interpersonal settings
    English learners, 218–219, 227–230
    and grouping practices, 227–229
Intervention techniques
    instruction nexus, 191–194
    in language impairment, 187–208
    narrative level, 194–199
    scaffolding role, 192–208
    sentence level, 200–204
    word level, 204–208
Irregular words, spelling, 279–280, 280*t*

Journal writing
    English learners, 226–227, 230
    function of, 22
    motivational level, 226–227

Keyboarding
    typing skill effects, 246–247
    writing process differences, 24–25
Knowledge telling strategy, 136

Language acquisition. *See* English language
    learners
Language and learning disabilities
    diagnostic aspects, 37–38, 190
    expository text writing, 136
    knowledge telling strategy, 136
Language instruction. *See* Writing
    instruction
Language impairment
    composition instruction, 187–208
    definitional issues, 199–191
    discourse-level instruction, 194–200
    expository contexts,199
    grammatical errors, 200, 201*t*, 202*t*
    intervention, 187–208
        instruction nexus, 191–194
    language-levels instruction model, 191
    learning disabilities overlap, 190
    narrative contexts, 194–199

scaffolding intervention, 192
sentence level instruction, 200–204, 201t, 202t
story grammar intervention, 195, 196t, 197t, 197–198
subtypes, 189–190
    dimensional differences, 189–190
word level instruction, 204–208
Language levels model, 28, 191
Latin word origin, orthography, 283t
Lax vowel phonemes, 276
Learner-centered portfolios, 317–319
    assessment for learning emphasis, 317–318
    assessment portfolios tension, 329–330
    conferences function, 327
    English language learners, 327
    genre-specific assessment criteria, 321
    instructional function, 317
    learning disabilities, 323–324
    purposes, 317–319
Learning disabilities
    assessment portfolios, 325–326
    computer technology, 243–261
    definitional issues, 52, 70n1
    evidence-based instruction, 165–183
    language impairment overlap, 190–191
    learner-centered portfolios, 323–324
    portfolio assessment, 315–316, 323–326
    and procrastination, 63–68
    self-efficacy beliefs, 51–74
        overestimation, 55–67
        recent research, 58–67
    spelling instruction, 269–285
        helpful strategies, 284–285
    Tier I instruction, 168–173, 171t, 172t
    Tier II instruction, 169–170, 173–182
    word processing applications, 245–248, 259–260
        effect sizes, 245
        planning and revision support, 252–256
Learning strategy instruction. See Strategy instruction
Length of writing, and word processors, 245
Letter e, orthography, 278–279
Letter formation, and spelling, 275
Letter naming, developmental variation, 123
Lexical processes, 31–32. See also Spelling
Linguistic-interdependence hypothesis. See Universalist hypothesis
Listening, writing integration, 24

Long vowel phonemes, 276
Long vowel rules, 278

Magic e, 281t, 283t
Making meaning, 144
Map-It method
    graphic organizer use, 145
    in Project ACCEL, 142, 145
Mark-It strategy
    making meaning function, 144
    in Project ACCEL, 144
Math disability. See Written math disability
Mean length of T-Units, 200, 202
Memorize-It strategy, 174–175
Mentor texts
    in reading–writing instruction, 120–121
    scaffolded analysis in, 120
Meta-analysis
    Tier I recommendations, 168–169
    Tier II recommendations, 169–170
    word processing effects, 245
    writing instruction studies, 168–169
Metacognitive awareness
    and academic self-efficacy beliefs, 57–59, 62
    explicit instruction role, 70
    and learning disabilities, 57–59, 62
    qualitative study, 62
Model-It strategy, 174–175
Model teachers, qualitative studies of, 172t
Models for composition, 172t
Morphemes
    in orthography, 273, 281–283
    and phonemes, spelling, 281–283
    spelling interventions, 205
    and word origin, 283t
Morphological deficits
    intervention, 205
    language impairment subtype, 189
Morphology
    and orthography, 281–283
    in spelling development, 34–37, 36t
    spelling mediation, 32
    triple-word-form theory, 34–37
Motivation
    English learners, 226–227
    internet communication, 259
    measures, 85–86
    science literacy program, 150–151
    writing workshop effect, 92, 97
Motivational beliefs
    developmental changes, 54
    future research suggestions, 69–70
    instructional suggestions, 68–69

Motivational beliefs (*continued*)
  and learning disabilities, 56–58
    recent research, 58–67
    self-efficacy overestimation, 55–58
    writing performance link, 51–67
Motor processes. *See* Graphomotor
  processes
Multimedia. *See also* Hypertext
  creation of, 257–258
  historical presentations, 149
  and learning disabilities, 258
  software, 244
Multiple-choice format
  strengths and weaknesses, 338–339
  in writing assessment, 338
Multisensory techniques
  in letter sequences practice, 274–275
  in spelling instruction, 274–275

Narratives
  analytic rubric, 321
  in language impairment instruction,
    194–199, 196t, 197t
  scaffolding, 195, 196t, 197t, 197–198
  self- and other-directed genre, 21
  writing workshop outcome, 91t, 92, 94
    measures, 84–85
National Assessment of Educational
  Progress (NAEP)
  English learners assessment, 213–
    214
  process writing instruction data, 78
  reading skill statistics, 133
  writing skill statistics, 133
National Writing Project, 234
Native language instruction, 215–216
Nonspecific language impairment (NLI)
  definition, 189
  dimensional diagnosis, 189–190
Notebook texts, science writing, 152
Note-taking, listening integration, 24
Notes-It method
  components, 144
  Project ACCEL phase, 142, 144
Number of different words measure
  confounding variables, 206
  language abilities sensitivity, 206

Online writing. *See* Internet
Open syllable, 281t
Opinion essays
  components, 85, 110–112
  text structure instruction, 136
  writing workshop effect, 91t, 92, 95f

Optimal Learning Environment (OLE)
  program
  activities in, 224
  English learners, 223–224
  qualitative studies, 224
  quasi-experimental study, 224
Oral and writer language disability (OWL
  LD), 37–38
Organizational patterns/quality
  components, 84, 105–106
  expository text, 134–140
  strategy instruction, 137–138
  writing workshop effect, 91t, 92
Orthographic depth hypothesis, 292
Orthographic loop impairment, 37
Orthography
  English language learners, 290–305
    cross-linguistic theories, 293–294
    spelling strategy influence, 296–302
  instruction relevance, 30–31
  language impairment intervention,
    205–207
  and learning disabilities, 273
  major principles, 272–273
  and morphology, 281–283
  scaffolding, 207
  spelling achievement link, 272–273
  in spelling development, 34–37, 36t
  in spelling processes, 296
  spelling rules, 274–278
  syllable types, 280–281, 281t
  triple-word-form theory, 34–37, 36t
  and word origin, 283–284, 283t
  written spelling mediator, 32
Other-directed writing, 21–23
Outlining, electronic versions, 254–255

Paradigm shifts
  in writing assessment, 19
  in writing instruction, 16–21
Paraphrasing, and language impairment,
  203–204
Parent–teacher conferences, 327
Parents
  English learners, 231–232
  school involvement, 231–232
  self-efficacy beliefs influence, 55
Partner work, English learners, 227–
  228
Past tense forms, spelling, 282
Peer cooperation. *See also* Cooperative
  study/work
  English learners, 227–228
  Tier II students, 176–177

Percentage of non-overlapping data
  interpretative guidelines, 173
  Tier II instruction effect, 175, 179, 181
Persian English language learners
  English-language spelling, 296–302
  grapheme–phoneme correspondence, 297
  spelling performance study, 298–302
  spelling strategies, 300–301
Persuasive writing
  components, 84–85, 110–112
  in expository text, 134
  self- and other-directed aspects, 23
  text structure instruction, 136
  writing workshop effects, 92–94
Phoneme awareness, and spelling, 272–273
Phoneme–grapheme correspondences, 276, 277f, 278
  and alphabetic principle, 292
  conditionality, 278
  English language learner spelling, 298–30
    nonalphabetic languages, 301–302
    orthographic influences, 298–302
  orthographic depth hypothesis, 298–302
  in spelling instruction, 276, 277f, 278
Phoneme–grapheme mapping
  development, 35–36
  orthographic depth hypothesis framework, 292
  in spelling instruction, 276
    recommendations, 303
Phonemes
  grapheme correspondences, 276, 277t, 278
  identification in spelling instruction, 275–276
  language impairment instruction, 205
  and morphology, spelling, 281–283
  in orthography, 272, 281–282
  in spelling instruction, 275–278, 281–283
  spelling mediator, 272–273
Phonological coding, 294
Phonology/phonological awareness
  English language learners, 294–295
  instruction relevance, 30–31
  and language impairment, 189
  spelling achievement link, 272–273
  in spelling development, 34–37, 36t
  in spelling instruction, 275–276
  spelling mediation process, 31–32
  in triple-word-form theory, 34–37
Picture prompts, 346

PLAN strategy, 137–138
Planning process
  cognitive factors, 124
  computer technology, 252–256
  explicit teaching, 171, 173–174
  peer group cooperative work, 176–177
  prompting programs, 253–254
  reading–writing support in, 124–125
  strategy instruction, 137–138
  Tier I evidence-based practices, 171
  Tier II evidence-based practices, 173–178
PLANS-It
  components, 141, 142f, 143
  Project ACCESS phase, 141, 142f, 143
PLANS strategy
  reading–writing combination study, 179–180
  in Tier II setting, 179–180
Poetry, self-directed genre, 22
Portfolio assessment, 311–331 See also Assessment portfolios
  advantages and disadvantages, 328–331
  authentic assessment link, 314
  and composition, 315
  conceptual overview, 313–316
  and curriculum-based measurement, 326
  definition, 313
  English language learners, 326–328
  feasibility issues, 330–331
  historical overview, 313–316
  implementation difficulties, 329
  and individual education program, 323–326
  learner-centered portfolios, 317–319
  learning disabilities, 323–326
  models, 316–320
  purposes, 317–320
  rubrics, 320–322
  scoring, 321–322, 330
  showcase portfolios, 318–319
  standardization problems, 329
  struggling writers, 322–331
  whole language movement influence, 313–314
  writing assessment criteria, 320–322
  writing development research influence, 315–316
  writing workshop effects, 95–96, 96f, 98
    method, 86
Possessives, explicit instruction, 176
Poverty, non-native speakers of English, 216–217

POWER writing process, 138
Pragmatic functions, writing, 26
Pragmatic language impairment
    definition, 189
    research evidence for, 189
Primary instruction. *See* Tier I
Primary sources, in expository writing,
    147–149
Problem–solution structure
    discourse markers, 134
    explicit instruction, 136
    in expository texts, 134
    history texts use of, 134
Process approach. *See* Writing process
Process portfolios, function, 320
Procrastination, 51–74
    definition, 64–65
    and help-seeking, 66–67
    in learning disabled, 63–68
        versus non-learning disabled, 63–68
    recent study, 63–67
    self-efficacy relationship, 53, 65–67
    writing proneness to, 63–64
Professional development, 233–234
Proficient writing. *See* Writing proficiency
Progress monitoring
    assessment portfolio function, 319–
        320
    curriculum-based measurement,
        347–349
        case illustration, 340, 341*f*
        procedure, 342–343
        research evidence, 347–348
    and learning-centered portfolios,
        324
    writing workshops need, 99
Project ACCEL
    phases in, 141–146
    results, 146
    strategies and text structure, 141, 142*f*,
        143–146
Prompting programs, 253–254
    and learning disabilities, 253–254
    in planning and revision, 253–254
    rationale, 254
    research findings, 253–254
Prompts
    in curriculum-based measurement,
        340–341, 341*f*, 346, 349
        adequacy evidence, 346
    in writing assessment, 339
Pronunciation, in spelling instruction,
    275–276
Proofreading, and spelling, 285

Pseudoword spelling
    Chinese English language learners,
        298–302
        scores, 298*t*, 302*f*
    English language learners, 298, 298*t*
Punctuation
    curriculum-based measurement scoring,
        355
    peer group cooperation impact, 177
    reading and writing differences,
        121–122
    workshop instruction effect, 91*t*, 93

Qualitative studies, Tier I instruction, 172*t*
Quality of writing, and work processing,
    245
Quality Traits Scale, 84, 105–107
Quasi-experimental designs
    experimental design studies comparison,
        183
    meta-analysis, 168–169
    Tier I recommendations, 170–173, 171*t*,
        172*t*
    Tier II recommendations, 173–181
    word processing study, 180
    in writing instruction, 167–168
    r-controlled vowel combinations, 278,
        281*t*

Rapid automatic naming, 38–39
Rapid automatic switching, 39
Reading ability
    achievement link, 113
    writing workshop outcome, 92
        measures, 82
Reading-centric literacy, current paradigm,
    18
Reading development, writing impact,
    117–118
Reading First program, 118
Reading instruction
    writing development link, 113–127
    writing instruction connection, 118–121
Reading–spelling connection
    common variance studies, 271
    in dyslexia, 270
Reading–writing connection, 113–127
    best practices in teaching, 118–126
    and cognitive processes, 124
    correlational studies, 115–116, 121
    developmental effects, 117–118,
        122–123
    evidence-based studies, 179–180
    function of, 23, 114

instruction implications, 23, 113–127
combined teaching, 118–121
language impairment intervention, 207
paradigm shifts, 18
positive impact of, 179–180
process similarity, 123–126
research on, 127
struggling learners, 113–127
effect sizes, 179–180
in writing planning process, 124–125
Reads-It method
Project ACCEL phase, 142f, 143–145
subcomponents, 142f, 143–145
Reinforcement, evidence-based impact, 182
Reliability
curriculum-based measurement,
344–346
direct and indirect assessment, 338–339
portfolio scoring, 330
Report-It strategy, Project ACCEL, 142f,
146
Respond-to-It strategy
critical literacy format, 142, 145–146
in Project ACCEL, 142f, 145–146
text structure format, 142f, 145
Responsiveness to intervention
curriculum-based measurement, 340
identification of learning disabilities,
340
Revision
computer technology, 252–256
distancing in, 126
evidence-based recommendations, 171t,
173–177
explicit teaching recommendations, 171t
peer group cooperation impact,
176–177
prompting programs, 253–254
reading–writing relationship, 126
speech synthesis effects, 248
strategy instruction, 137–139
Tier I recommendations, 171t
Tier II recommendations, 173–178
word processing effects, 246
Romance language word origin,
orthography, 283t
Rubrics
portfolio assessment, 320–321
scales and levels in, 321
Run-on sentences
curriculum-based measurement,
356
intervention targets, 202–203
special needs students, 202–203

Scaffolding
definition, 192
expository contexts, 199
in instruction paradigm shift, 17
language impairment intervention,
192–193, 199
in sentence combining, 203–204
in sentence-level intervention, 200–204,
201t, 202t
in spelling instruction, 284–285
in storytelling, 194–199, 196t, 197t
word knowledge level, 207
Science writing, 150–153
motivational support, 150–151
notebook texts in, 152
school-based programs, 150–153
Scoring
assessment portfolios, 320–322, 330
curriculum-based measurement,
341–343, 354–357
procedures, 354–357
Script-dependent hypothesis
English learner spelling, 293–305
orthography influence, 296–304
research support for, 293–294, 296–304
Second-language acquisition. *See* English
language learners
Secondary interventions. *See* Tier II writing
instruction
Seeds of Science/Roots of Reading project
in reading–writing curriculum, 152–153
results, 153
Self-concept beliefs
and learning disabilities, 56
self-efficacy beliefs differences, 52–53
Self-directed writing, 21–23
Self-efficacy beliefs, 51–74
confidence differences, 52
developmental changes, 54
future research suggestions, 69–70
instructional suggestions, 68–69
in learning disabilities, 51–74
overoptimistic estimates, 55–58
qualitative study, 60–63
recent research, 58–67
metacognitive skills link, 57–59
procrastination relationship, 53, 65–68
college student study, 65–67
self-concept beliefs differences, 52–53
sources of, 52
teachers and parents role, 55
teachers' perspective, 60–63
writing performance influence, 53–56
writing workshop effect, 91t, 92

Self-evaluation, in writing workshops, 99
Self-monitoring strategy, 181–182
Self-Regulated Strategy Development
    (SRSD)
    effect size, 174
    English learners, 221
    steps in, 138, 174
    in Tier II instruction, 174–175, 178
Self-regulation beliefs
    and academic self-efficacy beliefs, 58–59
    adolescent learning disabled, 58–59
    procrastination relationship, 65–68
    suggestions for teachers, 68–69
    writing workshop instruction need, 99
Self-regulation strategies, English learners,
    221
Semantic deficits, and language
    impairment, 189
Sentence combining
    and language impairment, 203–204
    method, 120
    reading and writing improvement, 120
    scaffolding, 203–204
Sentence fluency
    components, 84, 106
    writing workshop effect, 91t, 92–93,
        94f, 100
Sentence-level instruction
    balanced approach, 28
    evidence-based recommendations, 171t
    grammatical error targets, 200
    language impaired, 200–204, 201t, 202t
        intervention targets, 200, 202, 201t,
        202t
    and mean length of T-units, 200
    scaffolding, 200–204, 201t, 202t
Sequence markers, expository texts, 134
Setting elements
    components, 84–85, 108–109
    writing workshop study, 84–85
Shallow orthographics
    grapheme–phoneme mappings, 292
    script-dependent hypothesis, 293
Short vowel phonemes, 276
Short vowel rules, 278
Showcase portfolios
    and learning disabilities, 324
    research supported benefits, 318–319
    summative assessment function, 318
    in teacher–student conferences, 319
Single-subject designs
    meta-analysis, 168–169
    Tier I recommendations, 178t
    Tier II recommendations, 173–182

word processing benefits, 180
    in writing instruction effectiveness,
        167–168
Slider vowel phonemes, 276
Small group instruction
    continuous regrouping strategy in, 229
    English learners, 228–229
Social reinforcement, impact of, 182
Social setting, English learners, 218–219
Social studies writing
    literacy skill learning opportunities, 147
    multimedia presentation function, 149
    primary source interpretation, 147
    research programs, 148–149
    texts expository structure, 134
    writing-to-learn in, 146–150
Sociocentric writing genre, 21–23
Sociocultural perspective
    non-native speakers of English, 213–214
    process writing influence, 20
Socioeconomic conditions, English
    learners, 216–217
Specific language impairment (SLI)
    definition, 189
    diagnostic aspects, 37–38, 189–190
    dimensional differences, 189–190
Speech recognition, 250–252
    and learning disabilities, 250–252
    limitations, 251
    practical issues, 252
    research findings, 251–252
    tape recorder dictation comparison, 251
Speech sound identification, 275–276
Speech synthesis
    effects of, 180, 248
    revision use, 248
    struggling spellers, 285
    and word processors, 247–248
Spell Doctor, 285
SPELL-2, 285
Spelling
    adolescent learning disabled, 58–60
        self-efficacy overestimations, 58–60
    cognitive processes, 294–296
    composition quality predictor, 204
    curriculum-based measurement,
        341–347, 355
    development, 19, 34–37, 271
    English language learners, 290–305
        cross-linguistic transfer theory,
        293–305
        orthography influence, 296–304
    error analysis, 303
    irregular words, 279–280

language impairment instruction, 204–207
language structures in, 270–273
mediating lexical processes, 31–32, 270–273
multisyllable words, 280–281, 281*t*
orthographic rules, 274–278
peer group cooperation impact, 177
proofreading, 285
reading development effect, 117
in reading–writing relationship, 121–122
developmental changes, 122–123
research needs, 19–20, 41
script-dependent hypothesis, 293–305
Tier II evidence-based instruction, 180–181
triple-word-form developmental theory, 34–37
universalist hypothesis, 293–305
and word origin, 283–284, 283*t*
writing workshops neglect, 99
writing workshop study outcome, 91*t*, 93, 100
Spelling checkers
effectiveness, 247
limitations, 247, 285
Spelling instruction, 274–285
English language learners, 302–304
handwriting fluency, 275
helpful strategies, 284–285
irregular words, 279–280
mnemonic cues, 280*t*
letter formation, 275
mediating processes, 31–32
morphemes and phonemes in, 281–283
multisyllabic words, 280–281, 281*t*
phoneme–grapheme correspondence, 276, 277*f*, 278
pronunciation, 275–276
principles, 274
speech sounds identification, 275–276
and word origin, 283–284, 283*t*
Spelling Performance Evaluation for Language and Literacy (SPELL-2), 285
STOP strategy
in expository writing, 147
results, 148
Stories
frame technique, 198–199
grammar analysis, 195, 196*t*, 197*t*, 197–198
prompts, 346, 349
schema, 195, 196*t*, 197*t*, 197–198

writing workshop effect, 84–85, 91*t*, 105–110
Storytelling, process, 21
Strategy instruction
English language learners, 219–222
expository writing, 137–140
versus writing workshop approach, 17–18
Summarization instruction
automated method, 256
evidence-based recommendations, 171*t*, 177
explicit teaching effect size, 177
method, 120
reading and writing enhancement, 120
Tier I instruction effect, 171*t*
Tier II instruction effect, 177
Summary Street, 256
Super-Spell Assessment Disk, 285
Support-It strategy, 174–175
Syllable patterns, and word origin, 283*t*
Syllable spelling types, 280–281, 281*t*
Syntax
English language learners, 295
language impairment, 189, 193, 203
errors, 200, 201*t*, 202*t*
spelling link, 32, 295

Teachers
assessment bias, 339–340
critical areas of knowledge, 28–34
cross-cultural understanding role, 232–233
and English learners, 229–230
social acceptance promotion, 232–233
evidence-based practices implementation, 183
and learner-centered portfolios, 327
portfolio use in conferencing, 327
process instruction variability, 78–80
professional development, 233–234
qualitative studies, 172*t*
self-efficacy beliefs influence, 55, 60–63, 68–69
in writing workshop outcome, 97–98
Technology. *See* Computer technology
Tense vowel phonemes, 276
Testimonial-based evidence, 166
Text transcription skills, 180–181
Textbooks. *See* Expository writing
Think-aloud technique, 26
Thinking process. *See* Cognitive processes
Tier I writing instruction
effect sizes, 171*t*, 172*t*
recommendations, 168–173

Tier II writing instruction
  cooperative peer study benefits, 176–177
  evidence-based studies, 169, 173–183
  goal setting effect size, 178–179
  grammar skill studies, 175–176
  planning, revision and editing studies,
      173–175
  process approach evidence, 177–178
      strategy approach combination, 178
  reading–writing combination, 179–180
  recommendation, 169–170, 173–183
  reinforcement effect, 182
  summarization impact, 177
  transcription skills, 180–181
  and word processing, 180
Time factors
  English learner instruction, 233
  explicit instruction in, 30
  and homework assignments, 30, 233
  in writing instruction, 28–30, 233
Topic sentences, expository texts, 135
Transcription skills. See also specific skills
  assistive technology, 247–252
  evidence-based instruction, 180–181
  speech recognition technology, 250–252
  speech synthesis, 247–248
  Tier II recommendations, 180–181
  word prediction software, 249–250
  writing workshop neglect, 99
Transitional terms, instruction, 203
Triple-word-form theory
  versus sequential stage theory, 34–35
  spelling development, 34–37
TWA strategy, 179
Typing skills
  Tier II evidence-based instruction,
      180–181
  word processor effects correlation, 246–247

Unconscious thought processes, 20
Universalist hypothesis
  and English language learners, 293–305
  research support for, 293, 296–304

Validity
  curriculum-based measurement,
      344–348
  portfolio scoring, 330
V-C-e syllable, 281t
Vocabulary
  developmental variation, 123
  number of different words measure,
      205–206
  English learner instruction, 303–304

Vowel spellings, 276, 277f
Vowels
  phoneme types, 276
  sound variations, 292
  in spelling instruction, 276–279

Web authoring, 25–26. See also Internet
Whole language
  and portfolios, 314
  writing assessment influence, 313–314
Woodcock–Johnson–III Tests of
    Achievement
  writing workshop effects, 82–83, 89–95,
      90t, 91t
  spelling subtest study, 298–302
Word choice
  in Quality Traits Scale, 106
  writing workshop effect, 91t, 92–93, 94f
Word-level problems
  balanced instruction, 28
  content and form aspects, 205–207
  developmental aspects, 206
  language impairment instruction, 193,
      204–208
  number of different words measure,
      205–206
Word-pattern sorting, 278
Word prediction
  dictionary size issue, 250
  and learning disabilities, 180, 249–250
  single-subject design studies, 180,
      249–250
  struggling spellers, 285
Word processing, 245–248
  access issue, 247–248, 260
  advantages, 245, 259–260
  evidence-based recommendations, 171t,
      180
  and learning disabilities, 245–248
  meta-analysis effect sizes, 245
  revision effects, 246
  spelling checkers, 247
  Tier II impact, 180
  writing link overview, 25
Word sequences, scoring, 342–343, 355
Words spelled correctly (WSC), 342–345,
    347
Words written (WW), 342, 344–345, 347
Working memory
  components, 296
  in functional writing system, 29, 29f, 40
  increasing importance of, 40
  and spelling, 296
  writing process effects, 33

Working portfolio, function, 318
Workshops. *See* Writing workshop
    instruction
WRITE strategy, 137–138
Writing assessment
    component decisions, 339
    current trend, 19
    curriculum-based measurement
        approach, 337–357
    developmental research implications,
        315–316
    direct methods, 339
    indirect methods, 338–339
    portfolios in, 311–331
        criteria, 320–322
    process approach benefits, 19
    whole language influence, 313–314
Writing development. *See* Developmental
    factors
Writing fluency
    automatic and controlled processes,
        33–34
    workshop instruction effects, 91t, 92–
        93
Writing Goals Scale (WGS), 85, 91t, 94
Writing instruction. *See also* Writing
    workshop instruction
    developmental factors, 26–34
    expository texts, 136–140
    language impairment, 187–208
        discourse level, 194–199
        intervention nexus, 191–194
        sentence level, 200–204, 201t, 202t
        word level, 204–208
    and learning disabilities, 165–184
        evidence-based approach, 167–170
        Tier I recommendations, 168–173
        Tier II recommendations, 169–170,
          173–183
    levels of language in, 28
    mediating processes, 30–34
    organization in time, 28–30
    paradigm shifts, 16–21
    process approach, 26–34
        variability in, 78–79
    reading connection, 118–121
    theoretical perspectives, 15–41
    time management, 28–30
Writing Next (Graham & Perin), 168–169
Writing Partner program, 253–254
Writing process
    developmental disorders, 37–39
    English language learners, 222–224, 223f

evidence-based recommendations, 171t,
    177–178
    instruction, 26–34, 78–79
        implementation questions, 78
        variability, 78–79
    mosaic of, 21–26
    paradigm shift, 16–21
    process portfolio assessment, 320
    reading process similarity, 123–126
    Tier I recommendations, 171t
    Tier II recommendations, 177–178
    in writing development, 26–34
    workshop approach, 17–18, 77–100
Writing proficiency
    core components, 338
    curriculum-based measurement,
        340–347
Writing prompts. *See* Prompts
Writing–reading connection. *See* Reading–
    writing connection
Writing time
    age differences, 345–346
    curriculum-based measurement,
        345–346
Writing-to-learn, 132–155
    in content-area curricula, 140–146
    disciplinary-based strategies, 146–153
    Project ACCEL strategies, 141, 142f,
        143–146
    text structure knowledge in, 134–140
Writing workshop instruction, 77–100
    adaptations for struggling writers, 100
    cognitive process integration, 17–18
    elementary school study, 77–100
        empirical findings, 89–96
        important findings, 96–97
        instruction methods, 87–89
        interpretation issues, 97–98
    goal setting as essential aspect, 99
    good and poor writers, 77–100
    implementation variability, 97–98
    key elements, 77–78
    multidimensional product measures,
        83–85, 105–112
    progress monitoring, 99
    self-regulation need, 99
    versus strategy instruction approach,
        17–18
    teacher experience/attitudes, 97–98
    transcription skills neglect, 99
Written math disability, 38–39
Written text summarization. *See*
    Summarization